THE CONSTITUTIONAL CONVENTION
AND THE FORMATION OF THE UNION

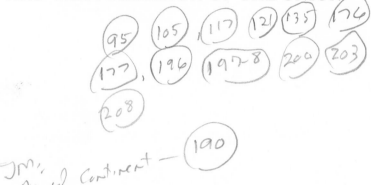

JM:
Armed Continent — 190

THE
CONSTITUTIONAL
CONVENTION
AND THE
FORMATION
OF THE UNION

SECOND EDITION

Edited, with an Introduction, by
WINTON U. SOLBERG

UNIVERSITY OF ILLINOIS PRESS
Urbana and Chicago

TO MY MOTHER

Originally published as *The Federal Convention and the Formation
of the Union of the American States* in the American Heritage Series
© 1958 by The Bobbs-Merrill Company, Inc.

This book is printed on acid-free paper.

Library of Congress Cataloging-in-Publication Data

The Constitutional convention and the formation of the union / edited,
  with an introduction, by Winton U. Solberg. — 2nd ed.
    p. cm.
    Rev. ed. of: The federal convention and the formation of the Union
  of the American States. 1958.
    Includes bibliographical references.
    ISBN 0-252-01727-7 (alk. paper). — ISBN 0-252-06124-1 (pbk. :
  alk. paper)
    1. United States—Constitutional history—Sources. 2. United
  States. Constitutional Convention (1787) I. Solberg, Winton U.,
  1922-   . II. Solberg, Winton U., 1922-   Federal convention and
  the formation of the Union of the American States.
  KF4510.C66 1990
  342.73′029—dc20
  [347.30229]   89-29686
                                                               CIP

PREFACE TO THE FIRST EDITION

My primary purpose in these pages is to illustrate the role of the Federal Convention in the formation of the American Constitution. Central to this endeavor are Madison's Notes of Debate, by far the most valuable single account of the complicated and lengthy 1787 meeting. My aim here is to make available the heart of this bulky eyewitness record, allowing it to relate the general principles which concerned delegates and to tell as much as it can of the complete story of shaping the Constitution. To Madison's description of Convention proceedings I have added various materials designed to facilitate understanding of the work of the Framers.

In addition, I have put the entire Philadelphia deliberations into a broader perspective. In my introductory remarks and through representative documents I relate the Federal Convention to constitutional development and the formation of the union in America during the Revolutionary era, especially from the Stamp Act Congress in 1765 through ratification of the Constitution and adoption of the first ten amendments in 1791. And in my opening comments I discuss the effect of the growth of constitutionalism in the Western world and in the American colonies before 1763 on the deliberations in Philadelphia.

With my task fulfilled I am particularly pleased to thank those who had a hand in bringing it to completion. Professor Thomas C. Mendenhall of Yale University was decisive in getting the project under way, for it was he who, at precisely the right moment, urged me to go through with it. And having reserved for myself any defects the work may possess, I gratefully acknowledge that whatever virtue it does have is largely owing to Professor Charles W. Hendel of Yale University and Mr. Oskar Piest, Editor of The Liberal Arts Press. My introduction benefited from Professor Hendel's reading of it, and I found his quiet enthusiasm for early American political thought as contagious as it was discerning. I have counted it a privilege as well as a pleasure to work with such a serious student of American Constitutionalism as Mr. Piest. I refrain here from further thanking Constance Walton for such help as only a wife can give.

W.U.S.

PREFACE TO THE SECOND EDITION

Today, as in the past, vital issues in American public life tend to become legal problems which the courts are called upon to adjudicate. In the American legal system the final arbiter on such controversial matters is the United States Supreme Court, and the fixed point of reference for the justices is the Constitution. To understand the Constitution it is essential to know what the Framers had in mind as they drafted the nation's fundamental law.

This book was originally designed to make the core of the debates in the Philadelphia convention of 1787 readily available and to place those deliberations in broad historical perspective. The first edition enjoyed a long and useful life, going through several printings. A second edition is now desirable. The title of the original edition, *The Federal Convention and the Formation of the Union of the American States*, has been altered to *The Constitutional Convention and the Formation of the Union*. The list of constitutional amendments has been updated; the Selected Bibliography has been enlarged to incorporate the results of recent scholarship; a few typographical errors have been corrected; and one footnote cites a book which was originally announced as forthcoming. But otherwise the text has not been changed.

W.U.S.

CONTENTS

THE CONSTITUTIONAL CONVENTION
AND THE FORMATION OF THE UNION

THE GENESIS OF AMERICAN
CONSTITUTIONALISM

For Americans the early months of 1787 were a winter of discontent. In the dawn of independence following the rupture with England, former colonial subjects had envisioned their infant republic inaugurating a new era in human affairs. However, this initial confidence soon yielded to disillusion as the young state faltered after winning its freedom. And by the autumn of 1786, when Shays' Rebellion commenced in Massachusetts, disintegration seemingly threatened an already tenuous national existence. Extending through the following winter, that disorder was a solemn warning which to many betokened ultimate disaster.

But as the sun came to renew the earth, hope rekindled in patriot breasts. In mid-May a convention, which became known as the Federal or Constitutional Convention, was to assemble in Philadelphia to devise means of rendering the government under the Articles of Confederation adequate to the needs of the union. Therefore this spring of 1787 was no mere harbinger of nature's recurring cycle. For young America it brought the seedtime of national destiny and of a new era for mankind—the moment when "the heritage of a culture became the promise of American life." [1]

The constitution-makers keenly appreciated the dramatic circumstances of their assembly. As the initial optimism in the Georgian State House faded, a deep sense of anxiety overcame the Philadelphia gathering. Succeed now, or perish forever! warned delegates—the flame of America's world mission, whose candle was no longer the religion of left-wing Protestantism but rather mundane perfectibility, was burning low.

[1] Walton Hamilton, "1937 to 1787, Dr.," in Conyers Read, ed., *The Constitution Reconsidered* (New York, 1938), p. ix. The signing of the completed document is the moment referred to by this author.

Hoping to redeem for the future the promise of their past, delegates announced that their meeting was not the affair of a moment or of America only. No, they wished to enlarge their ideas to the true interest of mankind, and to frame a system of representative government which would endure not only for ages but indeed forever.[2]

I. INTERPRETING THE FEDERAL CONVENTION

The document produced in Philadelphia marks a decisive point in the development of Western constitutionalism. It represents the flowering of long centuries of both European and American growth and in turn has scattered seeds which have since borne a ripe world harvest. During the nineteenth and twentieth centuries this instrument has exerted a decisive influence not only in the United States but also on political thought and institutions in Europe, Canada, South America, Africa, and Asia.[1]

The present volume is designed to afford understanding of how the Federal Constitution, foundation stone of the Union, came into being. The focus is on the proceedings of the Convention, one of the places, as James Madison once said, "where alone the true key to the sense of the Constitution" is to be found.[2] Other materials in this book help illuminate that unique and significant event in American and world history.

This introduction emphasizes three crucial problems related to the Constitution signed on September 17, 1787, and the ten amendments known as the Bill of Rights added soon after.

2 Madison, June 26, 29; King, June 30; Morris, July 5. See pp. 175-7, 188-90; 195-6; 203-4.

1 See the articles by various authors in Part Three, "Repercussions of the Constitution Outside the United States," in Read, *Constitution Reconsidered*, pp. 261-384.

2 Max Farrand, ed., *The Records of the Federal Convention of 1787* (Rev. ed., 4 vols., New Haven, 1937), III, 474. Madison names two others: "the contemporary expositions, and above all in the ratifying Conventions of the States." In the material quoted above I have combined two of Madison's phrases in reverse sequence.

First, what is the nature of the fundamental law in America? In what form is this expressed, and what institutional devices serve to implement it? More important, what basic postulates underlie it? For example, what does the statement of it imply concerning such issues as the quest for freedom within order and the capacity of human nature for self-government? And how does it reflect the "spirit" of our unwritten laws—the way of life and particular genius of the American people? In a word, on what principles—political, ethical, philosophical, and social—does American fundamental law rest?

Secondly, why do we have precisely the written Constitution which we do? The answer to this involves considering how political institutions come into being. It has been maintained that forms of government are either "an affair of invention and contrivance" or "a sort of spontaneous product" resulting from natural historical growth.[3] Of the various theories attempting to account for the American instrument, one subscribes to the "invention" school in holding that the Framers' accomplishment was unprecedented. Gladstone popularized this view with his declaration (in an essay on Tocqueville's *Democracy in America*) that the Constitution was "the most wonderful work ever struck off at a given time by the brain and purpose of man."[4] And John Stuart Mill, who befriended the notion of rational contrivance, saw the whole edifice as constructed "upon abstract principles."[5] Such statements make the work of 1787 a singularly notable accomplishment indeed!

On the other hand, the view that history controlled the Framers' pen shrinks the role of the assembled authors to relative insignificance. But if the past did predetermine the year 1787, then we want to know, *what* past? Were the chief features of the Constitution, as some scholars have contended,

[3] John Stuart Mill, *Considerations on Representative Government*, "Library of Liberal Arts" ed. (New York, 1958), p. 3. This work was written in 1861.

[4] As quoted in Archibald Cary Coolidge, *Theoretical and Foreign Elements in the Formation of the American Constitution* (Freiburg, 1892), p. 6.

[5] As quoted *ibid.*

skillfully synthesized from existing American state charters of government? Or were they, as others have held, a faithful imitation of the contemporary British constitution? [6]

The real problem in analyzing the role of history in the Convention, as these opinions show, is to determine the strains of influence, trace their sources, and watch the patterns in which they converge. What institutional structures were available for delegates to choose from, and what ideas and interests motivated them to select as they did? This involves considering the interrelationship between dominant presuppositions—conscious and unconscious—and the economic and sectional forces at work, as well as the psychological attitudes resulting from hard work throughout a long, hot summer. This search puts us on a historical trail leading back through the Revolutionary ferment which the Convention climaxes to the earliest beginnings of constitutionalism.

A third consideration is the Constitution as an expression of the American past (and thus a compass to the nation's future, a separate topic not discussed here). Perhaps the basic question is the relationship of the Constitution of 1787 to the American Revolution. Historians have sharply differed as to whether the Framers in constructing a basic charter fulfilled or denied the promise implicit in this movement. Some portray the Convention as a reactionary coup, a successful conspiracy on the part of wealthy Conservatives to overthrow radical gains dating from 1776. Others depict it as the logical unfolding of former developments—the culmination in the search for ultimate principles initiated by the break from Britain. [7]

[6] *Ibid.*, pp. 5-7; Edward S. Corwin, "The Progress of Constitutional Theory between the Declaration of Independence and the Meeting of the Philadelphia Convention," *American Historical Review,* XXX (April, 1925), 511-12; William C. Morey, "The First State Constitutions," *Annals of the American Academy of Political and Social Science,* IV (September, 1893), 201-2; Paul Merrill Spurlin, *Montesquieu in America, 1760-1801* (University, Louisiana, 1940), pp. 1-45; William Seal Carpenter, *The Development of American Political Thought* (Princeton, 1930), pp. 74-79.

[7] Edmund S. Morgan, *The Birth of the Republic, 1763-1789* (Chicago, 1956), p. 3.

The complexity of the controversy and its significance for the Convention are briefly shown by unraveling a few skeins. Certainly the Revolution was a War for Independence during which colonials formulated rights against Britain and then established a government to replace the one overthrown. This was the question of home rule. But was there intermixed with this an internal American Revolution to determine who should rule at home? Proponents of the dual-revolution thesis hold that the hitherto underprivileged element in the colonies first emerged by appropriating in its own behalf the statement of rights made against England. This argument rests on the long-maintained belief that American society before 1787 was undemocratic, which thus serves to explain that the upheaval unleashed a bid for power by the unfranchised and underrepresented which threatened the dominant colonial aristocracy. According to this view, the class struggle necessitated control of the government as a means of obtaining political and economic supremacy.

This, of course, raises the question of the locus of authority after the rupture from Britain. Was it in the thirteen former provinces or in one central government? Those who have said the former argue that Radicals garnered the fruits of the Revolution until 1789 by enfeebling the central government and dominating the new states. They say that the newly franchised were able to monopolize power with little restraint by dominating the lawmaking function, since, as they contend, there was no real separation of powers in the state governments and the Articles established only a legislative branch. In their view the Convention represents a reaction in which Conservatives finally succeeded in checking democratic license by writing a Constitution which centralized control, safeguarded property, curbed freedom and equality, and, in providing for the first time a genuine separation of powers, worked a major political revolution.[8]

[8] Some, but by no means all, of those who have expounded these views in a significant way are Claude H. Van Tyne, "Sovereignty in the American Revolution: An Historical Study," *American Historical Review*, XII

Other and more recent authorities insist that the society which produced the American Revolution and the Federal Constitution was far more democratic than has generally been realized. They maintain that the dispute was primarily about the security of private property, that much of the dual-revolution thesis has been exaggerated, and the class-struggle concept an erroneous reading back of later preconceptions into earlier times. These writers find a consciousness in 1776 that the United States was one nation. They depict the Constitution of 1787, which safeguarded property, not as a reversal but rather a fulfillment of earlier gains.[9] Awareness of these conflicting interpretations helps illuminate the complex drama which unfolded within the State House in Philadelphia.

(April, 1907), 529-45; Carl L. Becker, *The History of Political Parties in the Province of New York, 1760-1776* (University of Wisconsin Bulletin, No. 286, History Series, Madison, 1909); Charles A. Beard, *An Economic Interpretation of the Constitution of the United States* (New York, 1913); Merrill Jensen, *The Articles of Confederation: An Interpretation of the Social-Constitutional History of the American Revolution, 1774-1781* (University of Wisconsin Press, 1940); Merrill Jensen, *The New Nation: A History of the United States During the Confederation, 1781-1789* (New York, 1950); Max Savelle, "Review of Morgan, *Birth of the Republic,*" *William and Mary Quarterly,* 3 ser. XIV (October, 1957), 608-18. Needless to say, however, these authors do not share one common position on the events of the Revolution.

[9] For exponents of these views see Morgan, *Birth of the Republic,* and the bibliography he cites; Robert E. Brown, *Middle-Class Democracy and the Revolution in Massachusetts, 1691-1780* (Ithaca, 1955); Robert E. Brown, *Charles Beard and the Constitution: A Critical Analysis of "An Economic Interpretation of the Constitution"* (Princeton, 1956); Robert E. Brown, "Reinterpretation of the Revolution and Constitution," *Social Education,* XXI (March, 1957), 102-5, 114; Irving Brant, "Letter to the Editor," *William and Mary Quarterly,* 3 ser. XV (January, 1958), 137-39. Nor do these authors entirely agree among themselves.

II. THE WESTERN CONSTITUTIONAL INHERITANCE

Although definitions of the word "constitution" have constantly changed, this protean term has usually involved means of limiting government other than by dependence of government on the people themselves. For this purpose, on the one hand, are institutional devices like checks and balances, bicameralism and judicial review, which aim at protecting such substantial interests in society as property, status, and individual rights. On the other, closely allied, are jurisprudential considerations. First, two inferences from the proposition that law is a rule of conduct—namely, that law should be both general and prospective—further this end and lead to the doctrine of separated powers: legislatures are not to punish past offenses or consider particular cases, but to formulate general rules for the future; since executives are to apply general rules to individuals, they should therefore not share lawmaking power, which could bring unlimited and tyrannical government. The doctrine of judicial review traces its ancestry to this separation of functions. Secondly, and intimately related, is the notion of fundamental law, called variously the law of nature, the higher law, or the law of God. The essential concept is that of universal, eternal, and immutable postulates containing certain safeguards binding on all mankind and designed to assure man's dignity. As these remarks suggest, constitutionalism is to be understood by looking beyond definitions to the broad ends which it seeks to fulfill.

CLASSICAL ANTIQUITY

Greece

The tradition of constitutionalism became well-rooted in classical antiquity.[1] To the early Greeks, a constitution was

[1] This section draws on the following works: Francis D. Wormuth, *The Origins of Modern Constitutionalism* (New York, 1949), pp. 3-40; Charles

not written fundamental law but rather the total structure of
the state, or the prevailing ethos of their whole society. For
reasons sufficient to them they often accepted as binding laws
which they knew to be bad.[2] Since the only remedy for unconstitutional laws was revolution which overturned society
completely, the prospect of such an upheaval with its attend-
ant disequilibrium invited horror.

But contrasting with these grim realities was a standard
of right introduced by Greek thinkers, and especially Plato
and Aristotle, to challenge mere power or the *status quo*.
Both philosophers envisioned a state embodying perfect justice—where the general good of the whole was reciprocal with
the good of each individual member. Not only the ideas but
even the very word "republic" used by Plato to describe this
commonwealth constituted the image of perfection which
subsequently spurred men to seek its earthly realization.

Despite absence of a controlling fundamental law, belief in
a law of nature existed among the Greeks. Plato emphasized
the concept of a universal justice, itself justified in nature and
reason. Aristotle built on the prevalent notion of the law of
nature as customary law which was of divine origin. He distinguished between the fundamental or higher law which was
rooted in nature and the ordinary law or particular conventions of a local community. If the latter was positive law capable of injustice, his conception of the former led to a belief

---

Howard McIlwain, *Constitutionalism Ancient and Modern* (Ithaca, 1940),
pp. 3-68; Charles Grove Haines, *The Revival of Natural Law Concepts*
(Cambridge, 1930), pp. 3-12, 24-27; Benjamin Fletcher Wright, Jr., *American Interpretations of Natural Law* (Cambridge, 1931), pp. 3-12; Charles
F. Mullett, *Fundamental Law and the American Revolution* (New York,
1933), pp. 13-18; C. H. McIlwain, "The Fundamental Law Behind the
Constitution of the United States," in Read, *Constitution Reconsidered*,
pp. 3-14; Charles Howard McIlwain, *The Growth of Political Thought in
the West from the Greeks to the End of the Middle Ages* (New York, 1932),
pp. 23-101; Edward S. Corwin, "The 'Higher Law' Background of American Constitutional Law," *Harvard Law Review*, XLII (1928-29), 153-64.

2 McIlwain, *Constitutionalism*, 40-41.

in a natural justice within the reach of all men. Aristotle's definition of law as "Reason free from all passion," [3] after reformulation by Bracton in the thirteenth and Harrington in the seventeenth centuries, became a basic principle of American constitutional theory.[4]

The Federal Convention drew heavily on Greece in discussing property as a right which government was instituted to protect. What was property? This query extended back to Plato and Aristotle, who initiated a controversy which determined the nature of the subsequent dialectic. Plato made property consist of such things as knowledge, justice, virtue, and happiness as well as wealth and goods. Likening political to paternal control, he made property central in politics. Aristotle viewed property as merely instruments or possessions for living which were part of a household, and since he denied that the government of a household and of a small state were the same science, he assigned property a more restricted role.[5] As definitions varied in Philadelphia centuries later, so, too, would conceptions of the proper end which government existed to fulfill.

---

3 *The Politics of Aristotle,* Ernest Barker, ed. (Oxford, 1946), p. 146. (Book III, Ch. 16.)

4 In separating governmental powers, the Massachusetts Constitution adopted in 1780 offered as a rationale (in Part I, Article III), the phrase "to the end it may be a government of laws and not of men." Cf. Francis Newton Thorpe, ed., *The Federal and State Constitutions, Colonial Charters, and Other Organic Laws* (7 vols., Washington, 1909), III, 1893. John Adams wrote in his *Novanglus* papers during the winter following adjournment of the First Continental Congress in October, 1774: "If Aristotle, Livy, and Harrington knew what a republic was, the British Constitution is much more like a republic than an empire. They define a republic to be a *government of laws, and not of men.*" (Italics his.) Adams was the chief author of Part I (A Declaration of Rights) of the 1780 Massachusetts Constitution. Charles Francis Adams, ed., *The Works of John Adams* (10 vols., Boston, 1850-56) IV, 106.

5 Richard McKeon, "The Development of the Concept of Property in Political Philosophy: A Study of the Background of the Constitution," *Ethics,* XLVIII (1937-38), 297-366.

Rome

Despite the contribution of Greece, Roman influence in America was more important. This came in a variety of ways: through the Stoics, who built on Aristotle, the jurisconsults, and especially through Cicero (106-43 B.C.). In Rome, public law (*sponsio*) was regarded as a common engagement of the community, and the constitution was the public law of the realm. Cicero brought into touch with these legal and political ideas the conception of an older and higher norm—the natural law of Aristotle raised to a new level. He taught that nature implanted in man reason which enabled him to penetrate the universal rules which governed the cosmos. This cosmic reason was binding on everyone; no enacted law in derogation of it was binding. Professor McIlwain considers Cicero's achievement the beginning of the modern concept of constitutionalism and declares that probably no change in the history of political theory is more revolutionary.[6] Thus Roman constitutional doctrine made the ultimate source of political authority the people. In *theory* the prince possessed power conferred on him by the people, but the demise of the Republic brought the *practice* of exalting his might.

Mixed Government

Also dating from classical antiquity is the notion of mixed government. In classifying governments both Plato and Aristotle noted a form called polity, which had the advantage of balancing property and numbers (monarchy and democracy, rich and poor). Thereupon the idea lost popularity until revived by the historian Polybius (c. 203 - c. 120 B.C.), who found in his theory of revolution justification for pitting the organs of government representing monarchy, aristocracy and democracy against each other to achieve balance and thus stability. Cicero popularized these views. The practice of mixed government collapsed along with the Roman Republic, after which

6 McIlwain, *Constitutionalism*, pp. 39-40.

the prince alone ruled. But the doctrine retained vitality until it began a new life in seventeenth-century England, from which it passed to the New World.[7]

THE MIDDLE AGES

The concept of fundamental law assumed new importance in the Middle Ages as Christian thought and culture identified the rule of nature with God's eternal decree. The cosmic light found in human reason was ascribed now to the steady and brilliant illumination of God revealed in Holy Writ, pronouncements of the Church Fathers, and rulings of the Church. People soon found good use for these ideas, which permitted defense of human rights based on kinship with God as well as possession of reason.

During these years the doctrine of double majesty of law and king replaced that of the mixed state. Balancing monarchical control with the rule of law, this afforded limitations upon government which were essential to constitutionalism. And despite weaknesses in practice the theory of constitutionalism persisted. Though the situation became tenuous when power-hungry rulers arose and scored triumphs and as the papacy struggled with secular rulers for mastery, two restraints always helped to sustain the rule of law. One was the continuing influence of the Roman idea that law was a common engagement resting on popular will. In the late Middle Ages government was justified on grounds that the community ruled submitted voluntarily. Another was acceptance of natural law—whether universal reason or will of God—as not only fundamental but also "higher," a standard enabling the people to judge power by right. This belief sanctioned appeal from bad custom and wrong positive law, thus limiting monarchs, and on occasion even popes, and defending rights. Out

[7] See especially Wormuth, *Origins of Constitutionalism*, pp. 18-25; and Stanley Pargellis, "The Theory of Balanced Government," in Read, *Constitution Reconsidered*, pp. 37-49.

of such soil sprang the belief, later prominent in America, that man was pitted against the state.[8]

The key to English medieval constitutionalism lies in understanding Bracton (d. 1268), who introduced the doctrine of double majesty into English law in the thirteenth century. Henry of Bratton [9] was a justice and author of *De legibus et consuetudinibus Angliae,* the most thorough treatment of English law down to the time of Blackstone. Distinguishing between government (*gubernaculum*) and law (*jurisdictio*), he contended that the king was absolute in, but also limited to, the former sphere. In the latter both the constitution and his oath bound the king. When Roman legal ideas became influential throughout Europe, Bracton drew on the popular while the Continent bowed under the weight of the authoritarian strain in the legal dictum, "The will of the Prince has the force of law, since the people have transferred to him all their right and power." [10] He identified with custom the English common law, which was already tough and wellrooted before then, thus contributing to the notion that common law was closely related to the law of nature and of reason. By supporting English common law with conceptions of higher law, he invested the former with attributes which entitled it to limit authority legally. Thus the sanctity of private right always balanced the supreme authority of the monarch. "The king should be under no man," said Bracton, reformulating Aristotle's rule of law, "but under God and the law, for the

[8] The title of a work published in New York in 1884 by Herbert Spencer, the English social philosopher who enjoyed great popularity in the United States in the late nineteenth century, was *The Man versus the State.*

[9] Also known as Henry de Bracton.

[10] Ulpian was the source, and another statement of the principle was: "Whatever has pleased the prince has the force of law, since the Roman people by the *lex regia* enacted concerning his *imperium,* have yielded up to him all their power and authority." Justinian's *Institutes* embodied the precepts. Corwin, " 'Higher Law' Doctrine," *op. cit.,* p. 151; C. E. Merriam, Jr., *History of the Theory of Sovereignty Since Rousseau* (New York, 1900), p. 11.

law makes him king"—a thought later embedded in the American mind as well as on the façade of the Harvard Law School (*Non sub homine sed sub Deo et lege*). Although not without change, this theory of constitutionalism endured until the early seventeenth century, when opposing interpretations of *gubernaculum* and *jurisdictio* led to revolution.[11]

THE MODERN ERA

Some Basic Problems

For over three centuries prior to 1787, many deeply rooted and interrelated forces were working a reconstruction of Europe which entailed profound consequences for constitutionalism. In these years arose political theories and philosophical systems—not to mention the expansion of Europe, religious upheaval, economic and social change, and the birth of the modern state—which exerted a most decisive influence on the people then settling North America. From this complicated tapestry we must select for consideration here those strands which the Framers chose from in Philadelphia.

The medieval doctrine of double majesty succumbed under pressure from developments which converged to produce the modern nation-state. The rise of towns and expansion of trade accelerated the decay of feudalism, and national consolidation triumphed, vanquishing local particularism on the one hand, and, on the other, subduing both *imperium* and *sacerdotium,* as the antagonistic secular rulers and Church were called. The public bond between king and subject

[11] Wormuth, *Origins of Constitutionalism*, pp. 30-40; McIlwain, *Constitutionalism*, pp. 69-125; Corwin, " 'Higher Law' Background," *op. cit.*, pp. 164-85; Haines, *Revival of Natural Law*, pp. 12-17, 24-48; Mullett, *Fundamental Law*, pp. 18-21; Theodore F. T. Plucknett, "Henry de Bratton," *Encyclopedia of the Social Sciences*, Edwin R. A. Seligman and Alvin Johnson, eds. (15 vols., New York, 1930-35), II, 671; Wright, *American Interpretations*, pp. 5-6. I have quoted Bracton's formulation from Wormuth, p. 207.

now replaced the quasi-private feudal relation between lord and vassal, and the burgeoning sentiment of nationality invigorated these new unitary political forms. National rivalries and balance-of-power politics required both concentration of power in and frequent legislation by the state. No longer was this lawmaking the *finding* of precepts which depended for sanction on immemorial custom, universal reason, or the command of God, but rather the *making* of positive law by an organ of the state. The result was a contest between monarch and assembly to control the legislative function, and success by either meant a new conception of constitutionalism. This struggle over power within the state (paralleled at another level by the battle between nation-states for hegemony of Europe) evoked the modern question of sovereignty, or authority.

The historical analysis of sovereignty was inseparably linked with a modernized natural law theory, since the triumph of absolutists who found sanction in divine right was countered by defenders of popular control. A central issue in the ensuing struggle was the justification for rights, the attempt to solve which gave rise to the social compact theory. To support this, seventeenth-century thinkers reinterpreted a doctrine in which three separate conceptions of natural law—as custom, reason, and word of God—had converged.

Renaissance-awakened interest in classical antiquity led to reviving the pre-Christian, Ciceronian identification of natural law with universal reason. (Reacquaintance with the classics exerted a powerful democratic influence throughout the seventeenth and eighteenth centuries.) Then science, which made such remarkable progress in the years from Galileo to Newton, brought to the support of this changed outlook apparently irrefutable sanctions which sharply challenged theological sanctions. For the discovery that natural laws governed the universe was assumed to warrant the conclusion that similar rules applied to the study of man and society. Moreover, political and social thinkers also borrowed from physical scientists the technique for apprehending these truths. This was the geometrical procedure made famous by Descartes in his *Discourse on Method* (1637). One started with fixed premises assumed to be true (because they were self-evident) and advanced by careful deductive reasoning to conclusions. "A priori" and "reason" were the key terms, and until well into the eighteenth century Cartesian rationalism justified an assault on the authority of tradition and the tradition of authority. That the rational truths thus logically reached might differ from the factual truths apprehended by experience was an ambiguity which lurked in the doctrine until the empiricism of Newton and Locke dating from the late seventeenth century won out, and Hume was necessary to make the point clear. Nevertheless, significant political thinking, relying upon analogy from physical science and the method of scientific rationalism, made natural law central.

The theory that society is based on consent arose concomitantly because of common agreement that, to be binding, political obligations must be freely assumed. Thus the two essential elements of the political theory of natural law were the social contract, which concerned the means by which a society or a government or both came into existence, and the state of nature which existed apart from the contract. If the use of secular premises to support the consensual theory of society depended on scientific advances, theology nevertheless was closely allied. In the interval from Calvin to the early seventeenth century, Protestant divines delineated a covenant theology. The substance of this was voluntary agreement between two parties—agreement which governed relations between man and God as well as in and between both church and society. Although the exact tie between secular social contract and religious covenant theories is difficult to determine, probably the former gave impetus to the latter. Significantly, the two later united. The religious notion of covenant was influential throughout the seventeenth-century English revolutionary movement and through Puritanism in

American development. Religion aided also in the full emergence of a theory of natural rights. Anticipated by earlier exponents of natural law, adumbrated by medieval Christian spokesmen, and furthered by Luther's teaching, the quest for rights gained immeasurably from the zeal for religion in the early seventeenth century.[12]

Opposing Schools

By the eve of the Federal Convention two schools of political thought had arisen in response to the issues described above. The more important of these centered around John Locke (1632-1704), who may be said to symbolize the dominant political tradition in America down to and in the Convention of 1787. Chronologically he comes about midway in a stream of influence which includes Sir Edward Coke, English republicans such as Milton, Sidney, and Harrington, the Revolution of 1688, and exponents of English constitutionalism—Montesquieu, Hume, Blackstone, and Delolme.

The second school of thought represents opposing viewpoints which by contrast help to illuminate the significance of the former. This includes Bodin, Hobbes, and later Rousseau, and to some extent Englishmen such as Joseph Priestley and Richard Price. Rousseau, symbolizing this group less neatly than Locke does the other, was for a quarter of a century preceding 1787 enormously significant. If the contribution of the former school tends to the popular and natural rights side, that of the latter tends to either absolutism or anti-natural rights or both.[13] But it is essential to note that these categories simplify and stress internal similarities at the expense of noting differences.

12 McIlwain, *Growth of Political Thought,* pp. 364-94; George H. Sabine, *A History of Political Theory* (London, 1937), pp. 354-69; Perry Miller, *The New England Mind: The Seventeenth Century* (New York, 1939), pp. 365-462.

13 Coolidge, *Theoretical and Foreign Influences,* p. 18.

Continental Theorists

On the Continent, the theory of natural law was always more important than in England, where customary right was embodied in common law. Yet radically divergent interpretations arose here under pressure from historical forces earlier set in motion. In response to the chaos created in France by religious wars and disunity appeared Jean Bodin (1530-1596), the first philosopher of modern sovereignty. To him the division of authority within a state, such as afforded by mixed government or double majesty, was the door to anarchy. Searching, as had others, for a community in which power accompanied right, he announced in his *Six livres de la république* (1576) how this could be done. The distinguishing feature of the state, according to Bodin, is sovereignty, which he called the "supreme power over citizens and subjects unrestrained by law." [14] For him, sovereignty was perpetual, inalienable, and indivisible—the latter alone a rock on which the Framers in building a new American union might have foundered. But if inconsistent, Bodin nevertheless testified to an older legacy in limiting his sovereign by the laws of nature, God, and the French constitution, and especially by the individual right to property.[15]

The German Johannes Althusius (1557-1638) in the early seventeenth century answered Bodin while adjusting political theory to Calvinist theology. His works marked the beginning of popular interpretation of the contract theory. He agreed that sovereignty was by nature indivisible. But, arguing that the state was only the most complex of the groups which come into existence by association, he asserted that the people were formed into a corporate body by one contract, and conferred power on government in a second. Sovereignty, an essential condition of the existence of the political community,

14 As quoted in Sabine, *Political Theory,* p. 345.
15 *Ibid.,* pp. 340-52; Merriam, *Theory of Sovereignty Since Rousseau,* pp. 13-17.

resided in the people and could not be surrendered by them. As with Locke, the contract he described limited government.[16]

Writers like Hugo Grotius (1583-1645) and Samuel Pufendorf (1632-1694), on whom Americans early drew for natural law theories, took a middle position. They accepted the doctrine of two contracts, the *pactum unionis*, which formed a people, and the *pactum subjectionis*, by which people put themselves under government. But while stressing moral restraints on rulers, they failed to emphasize the people's right of resistance.[17]

British Influences

In England, historical developments produced opposing interpretations of *gubernaculum* and *jurisdictio* which became the crux of conflict. Inflated with divine right theories, the first two Stuarts exalted the monarch's absolute over his ordinary powers. Court decisions in a series of famous controversies made the supremacy of government over law depend on the king's discretion, which entailed virtual abandonment of an older constitutional conception of power as the possession of king and the courts, of which Parliament was the highest. That agency, in rejecting the idea of royal prerogative without originally holding any countertheory of its own supremacy, initiated a Revolution which concluded with the determination, in 1688, that Parliament should be supreme.

Sir Edward Coke

Early in that conflict Sir Edward Coke (1552-1634), lawyer, chief justice, and Parliamentarian, gained fame leading to

16 *Ibid.*, pp. 17-21; Sabine, *Political Theory*, pp. 355-58; Carl J. Friedrich, "Johannes Althusius," *Encyclopedia of the Social Sciences*, II, 13-14.

17 Sabine, *Political Theory*, pp. 358-62; Merriam, *Theory of Sovereignty Since Rousseau*, pp. 21-24, 28-30; Coolidge, *Theoretical and Foreign Elements*, pp. 24-25; Wright, *American Interpretations*, p. 7. Continental authors such as Jean Jacques Burlamaqui (1694-1748) and Emmerich de Vattel (1714-1767) tended to the popular interpretation of the natural law theory.

influence in America which was not eclipsed until Locke's ideas became dominant.[18] Before liberty came to be regarded as a political value, he stressed the existence of a fundamental law of the realm which neither Crown nor Parliament could alter. After Bracton's day, the common law, regarded as comparable to the law of nature and of reason and objectively valid, was deemed to possess a superiority which made it capable of limiting the power of the king. Although Magna Carta, after having been absorbed in the common law, fell into disuse after the fourteenth century, Coke revived it as a weapon against James I, to whom he quoted Bracton's dictum: "Quod rex non debet esse sub homine, sed sub Deo et lege." [19] And in Dr. Bonham's case he declared, in an opinion which suggests the roots of judicial review, that "when an act of parliament is against common right and reason, or repugnant, or impossible to be performed, the common law will control it and adjudge such act to be void." [20] Neither king nor Parliament was sovereign, but rather English law, which for Coke was a constitution protecting the liberty of the subject. In this he found a guarantee similar to natural rights.[21]

Balanced Government

After Charles I overstepped bounds considered proper, a variety of ideas designed to restore stability arose during the

[18] In preparing the draft of a legal code, the Massachusetts General Court on November 11, 1647, testified to Coke's early influence when it chose for reference books to afford "better light for making and proceeding about laws" three out of a total of six titles from Coke. They were Coke upon Littleton and upon Magna Carta, and Coke's Reports. Nathaniel B. Shurtleff, ed., *Records of the Governor and Company of the Massachusetts Bay in New England* (5 vols., Boston, 1853-54), II, 212.

[19] Corwin, " 'Higher Law' Background," *op. cit.*, p. 183. See also pp. xxiv-xxv.

[20] *Ibid.*, p. 368; but see also S. E. Thorne, "The Constitution and the Courts: a Re-examination of the Famous Case of Dr. Bonham," Read, *Constitution Reconsidered*, pp. 15-24.

[21] Corwin, " 'Higher Law' Background," *op. cit.*, pp. 365-80; Wormuth, *Origins of Constitutionalism*, pp. 163, 207-10.

Civil War and Commonwealth (1640-1660). Englishmen independently discovered many basic principles of balanced government, including mixed monarchy, separation of powers, and checks and balances, despite classical origins of these ideas. The notion of mixed monarchy became prominent in the 1640's as a means of promoting order by giving such substantial interests as King, Lords, and Commons (not quite the same as the three medieval estates) joint possession of the supreme function of sovereignty—legislative power. But a growing concern for liberty during the English upheaval, teaching anew that laws should be general and prospective, demonstrated the need for separating the powers of government, each of which should originate in a different source and be held to its own sphere by checks. Emphasis was on dividing legislative and executive functions, lest tyranny ensue. In somewhat different form Montesquieu later made famous this doctrine widely held during the Commonwealth.[22]

Hobbes

Meanwhile, before these doctrines bore fruit, Thomas Hobbes (1588-1679) had constructed a rigid absolutistic system. Seeking peace amidst civil war, Hobbes, who said that he was born a twin with fear (it was the year of the Armada), described the state of nature as a war of each against all. Therefore, his *Leviathan* (1651) argued, individuals mutually and voluntarily consented to bind themselves to a sovereign in return for security. People alienated their rights, worthless in a state of nature anyway, and in an irrevocable contract subordinated themselves to a sovereign who thereby gave the people a moral being by making them one and allowing privileges. To resist sovereignty, which was the sole and indivisible power to command and to dispense justice, was to invite a relapse to the state of nature. No Hobbesian ghost stalked the Federal Convention chamber.

[22] *Ibid.*, pp. 50-72; Pargellis, "Balanced Government," in Read, *Constitution Reconsidered*, pp. 37-49.

Republicans: Harrington

Although their ideas were never a practicable alternative in seventeenth-century England, republican spokesmen constitute an important link on the road to realization of a republic in the United States. John Milton (1608-1674), whose literary accomplishments and Puritanism assured him of notice in the colonies, was also significant for the views expressed in his political writings: [23] supporting the sovereign power of the people, he argued for freedom of publication and justified the death penalty for tyrants. Algernon Sidney (1622-1682), an advocate of balanced government whose motto was "Manus haec inimica tyrannis," became increasingly a favorite of Americans as the Revolutionary conflict deepened. A prolix and unoriginal work written in the 1680's but not published until 1698, his *Discourses Concerning Government* found readers made receptive by Locke.[24]

Of greater significance were the ideas James Harrington (1611-1677) embodied in *Oceana* (1656), a republican constitution for England in the guise of a utopia. The author's method was inductive: going to history for facts he arrived at the crucial point in his thought. He concluded that since power *does* (not merely *should*) follow property, especially

[23] Milton's most important political essays are the following: "Of Reformation Touching Church Discipline in England"; "Areopagitica"; "The Tenure of Kings and Magistrates"; "The First Defence" and "The Second Defence." The two latter essays were an answer to Salmasius and to Peter du Moulin (and Alexander More) respectively.

[24] Sabine, *Political Theory*, pp. 421-22; 431-37; C. H. Firth, "Algernon Sidney," *Dictionary of National Biography*, Leslie Stephen and Sydney Lee, eds. (New York and London, rev. ed. since 1917), XVIII, 202-10. Other Englishmen who exerted an important influence in the colonies and are not mentioned above include Bolingbroke, John Somers, Benjamin Hoadly, Addison, Pope, Thomas Gordon, and John Trenchard. The ideas of the hugely influential Sidney were available in Cato's *Letters*, which were apparently the work of Gordon and Trenchard. Liberty was the main theme of these *Letters*, which were especially popular with American subjects. Cf. Clinton Rossiter, *Seedtime of the Republic* (New York, 1953), p. 141.

landed property, the stability of society depends on political representation reflecting the actual ownership of the state. Destruction of the nobility traced back to the Wars of the Roses [25] resulted in commoners owning most of the land, which for Harrington explained the Civil War and dictated republicanism for England. The distinguishing feature of the commonwealth Harrington envisioned was, as he expressed it, "an empire of laws and not of men." For him, government required the coincidence of power and authority (which included the idea of justice), and he sought in his republic the reconciliation of public and private interest.

To further these ends Harrington proposed several contrivances in addition to his agrarian law, all of which were important for America. These included the elective ballot, rotation in office, indirect election, and a two-chamber legislature. Indirect election was a complex scheme for insuring government by consent by dividing the country into tribes, which were in turn divided into hundreds and again into parishes. The former and latter were new divisions to be used instead of counties and boroughs in parliamentary elections. For the Convention in Philadelphia the significance of this seemingly antiquarian fact soon becomes apparent. In dealing with the problem of obviating faction in a large republic, David Hume admittedly drew on Harrington for the device of fragmenting election districts. And James Madison, faced with the same problem in preparation for the Federal Convention, found the clue to the idea of an extended republic in Hume's solution.[26] Harrington proposed legislative bicameralism as a precaution against the dangers of extreme democracy, even for a com-

[25] The lengthy conflict (1455-1485) between the Houses of Lancaster and York for supremacy in England. In 1485 Henry VII of the House of Tudor became king.

[26] Douglass Adair," 'That Politics May Be Reduced to a Science': David Hume, James Madison and the Tenth *Federalist,*" *The Huntington Library Quarterly,* XX (August, 1957), 343-60. H. F. Russell Smith, *Harrington and His Oceana: A Study of a 17th Century Utopia and Its Influence in America* (Cambridge, [England], 1914), pp. 129-51.

monwealth in which property ownership was widespread. He argued that a small (and conservative) senate should be able to initiate and discuss but not decide measures, whereas a large (and popular) house should resolve for or against these without discussion.

Then novel, these significant ideas became influential in America, as their subsequent familiarity might suggest. They helped shape colonies planted during the Restoration, especially Pennsylvania, and admirably suited American institutional development. After 1776, *Oceana* became a guide in constitution-making, and the activities and writings of John Adams, Harrington's most ardent American disciple, testify to the use he gave his two copies of this volume.[27]

The Revolution of 1688

The Revolution of 1688 decided once for all that supreme authority was to be in the hands of Parliament rather than of monarchs. Popular right triumphed over divine right. Power rested with the people, who periodically elected representatives responsible to themselves. These they vested with the lawmaking function and control of the purse—money bills were confided solely to Commons. Moreover, liberty was to accompany authority. Government in England was under the fundamental law of the constitution, which was still capable of controlling acts against right and reason. For at least a generation after 1688 power was roughly balanced between the executive and legislative branches. And various settlement measures affecting habeas corpus, religious liberty, freedom of speech and petition, trial by jury, and other provisions (such as those in the Bill of Rights) gave added legal protection to Englishmen. Many of these passed over almost unchanged through the American state instruments into the Federal Constitution.

27 *Ibid., passim,* esp. pp. 13-74, 122-200; Sabine, *Political Theory,* pp. 421-30.

Locke

Closely associated with the revolutionary settlement and a new mental outlook was John Locke (1632-1704), who published two significant works in 1690. His *Second Treatise Concerning Civil Government*, a justification for the English Revolution, at once summed up the historical forces which converged in 1688 and continued to shape European and American political thought long thereafter. During the conflict with Britain this essay made Locke America's foremost philosopher, a position he retained through much of the nineteenth century. His *Essay Concerning Human Understanding*, which substituted for the older notion that truth is reached by reasoning deductively from self-evident propositions the doctrine that the mind is furnished through sense impressions formed by experience, led to a way of thinking which featured an empirical, experimental approach and inductive reasoning. Thereafter historical studies received new prominence, especially for scholars seeking valid data concerning man and society. Besides his direct influence, Locke contributed indirectly to America by helping to shape the thought of Montesquieu, Hume, Rousseau, and Blackstone, who through their own works exerted a strong influence on jurisprudence and political thinking in America. In the infant republic Locke's political views remained ascendant, despite reformulation of them by Rousseau and Hume, and despite the latter's critique of Locke's theory of knowledge.

Locke's main political achievement was to defend philosophically the individual rights which were the central ethical idea of the English Revolution. This he did by employing the natural law and consensual theories. He started by refuting the Hobbesian state of nature. Rather than the war of each versus all, Locke depicted free and equal rational men existing in a condition of relative peace. To enhance his welfare, man invests his labor with the earth and the fruits thereof, thus earning private title to possessions previously deemed to be held in common. Property, which Locke equated with "life, liberty, and estate," is thus the crucial right on which man's development depends.[28] Nature, therefore, creates right: society and government are only auxiliaries which arise, when men consent to create them, in order to preserve property in the larger sense and rights.

Locke specifies that a community calls government into being to secure additional protection for existing rights. Thus government has a fiduciary character. As representative of the people, the legislature is supreme. But nevertheless all government is limited, primarily by the moral law, which is that of nature. According to Locke, the legislative power does not establish but is itself controlled by the fundamental law, which suggests the distinction between constitutional higher law and statutory law found in America. The legislative function is specifically limited in other ways: for example, it can neither delegate its lawmaking duties nor impose taxes without the people's consent. Moreover, Locke limits government by separating the legislative and administrative functions of government to the end that power may not be monopolized. But separation of powers is subordinate in his thought and differs from that later described by Montesquieu. Finally, the people forever possess the ultimate right of resisting a government which abuses its delegated powers.[29] Such a violation of the contract justifies the community in resuming authority.

English Constitutionalists

In the century which divides the Revolution of 1688 from the Federal Convention, the doctrine of balance through separation of powers received new sanction while declining in practice. Montesquieu was the foremost of observers (later known as English Constitutionalists) who praised this principle, as in varying ways did Blackstone and Delolme (1740-1806).

[28] *Second Treatise on Government*, ch. 7, sect. 87; ch. 9, sect. 123.
[29] Corwin, " 'Higher Law' Background," *op. cit.*, pp. 380-409; Merriam, *Theory of Sovereignty since Rousseau*, pp. 30-33; Sabine, *Political Theory*, pp. 438-39, 442-57.

Meanwhile Hume and Rousseau, often following on lines originally indicated by Locke, struck out in new directions significant for the Framers.

Montesquieu

Extravagant but conflicting claims are made for the influence of Charles Secondat, Baron de Montesquieu (1689-1755), on American constitutional development. Usually, however, his significance is equated with separation of powers, which was neither the central theme in his political philosophy nor his primary contribution in Philadelphia. Though the Framers would presumably have balanced powers had Montesquieu never lived, they did resort to him—his name is the most frequently cited authority in Philadelphia—in establishing three branches of government. But Convention delegates undoubtedly drew more deeply on this author (although without specific attribution) in insisting that their constitution accommodate what they called the genius of the American people and what Montesquieu would have called the "spirit of the nation."

A Frenchman who lived under the despotic *ancien régime* where nobility vied with royalty for monopolization of control, Montesquieu had a passion for liberty. As a political philosopher he sought the underlying principles of a form of government which would achieve this by reconciling authority with right. Although a Cartesian who acknowledged that natural law created universal standards of justice, Montesquieu was an empiricist who collected evidence concerning the principles of liberty by studying history and traveling—on the Continent and in England. For over twenty years he worked on his *Spirit of the Laws* (1748), which was enormously influential even if not, as has been asserted, the greatest book in the eighteenth century. Montesquieu concluded that societies (nations) differed in interpreting natural law because such factors as climate, soil, and historical legacies conditioned them differently. The result was that each people had a unique constitutive principle, and it was this—the spirit of the laws—which determined their form of government and operated as a limit on power. Thus the ultimate check on government was deeply rooted in historical development. The author viewed the constitutive principle of democratic republics as virtue, or public spirit, of monarchies as honor, and of despotisms as fear. He threw the weight of his authority behind the former. These were vital ideas for a country about to experiment with republicanism.

As the first real and most important theorist of the separation of powers, Montesquieu advocated this principle as a device for fostering liberty by securing the rule of law rather than the rule of despotism. He drew on observations made in England from 1729-31, where he thought he saw that separation furthered liberty. But his observation was faulty. Parliamentary ascendancy and the cabinet system were already well entrenched under Sir Robert Walpole, prime minister from 1721 to 1742. The author's "description" of a system whose continued existence seemed indicated by the structure if not by the operation of the government provided Americans with "evidence" as to how the British constitution worked. In the *Spirit of the Laws,* Montesquieu treats together both the theory of separated powers and the notion of mixed government, two distinct ideas often regarded as one. He favored the former as a constitutional principle which would enable power to check power to the end that concentration of authority would not yield tyranny. He favored the latter as a means of obtaining balance by drawing the three branches of government from various social and economic interests: the legislature from the many (with the lower house more democratic than the upper); the executive from the few, the judiciary representing the whole people. With Montesquieu, although not always with his American disciples, the theory of separation was not primarily a negative restraint on government but a subordinate element in a scheme for creating liberty.

Montesquieu was primarily responsible for the deliberators in Philadelphia being haunted by the fixed belief that America's immense size threatened its national future. His statement that foreign force could easily destroy small republics—which the Revolutionary generation knew from experience—was granted, but his contention that internal imperfections ruined large republics caused deep concern. To insure republican government over a vast expanse required force and energy which were, as history amply taught, concomitants of tyranny. How avoid that dilemma in 1787? Montesquieu recommended several small states establishing a large one, as in the Lycian Confederacy—what he called a confederate republic. His remarks were not lost on Convention delegates.[30]

David Hume

When Montesquieu's *Esprit des Lois* first appeared in 1748, David Hume (1711-1776) was just gaining the threshold of fame. During the eighteenth century this rested primarily on his political and historical writing. To his keen disappointment, Hume's first literary venture, the *Treatise of Human Nature,* had fallen *"dead-born from the press"* in 1739.[31] But the praise which greeted his *Essays Moral and Political* (1742), an experiment in recasting the philosophy of his earlier work in different literary form, assuaged his previous sorrow. Thereafter this most prominent of the moral philosophers of the Scottish Renaissance allowed the reputation gained from his essays and *History of England* (1754-62) to promote the philosophical views for which later generations have acclaimed him.

A gentle but controversial figure, Hume attacked many of the most cherished eighteenth-century notions: the pretensions

[30] Franz Neuman, "Introduction" to Baron de Montesquieu, *The Spirit of the Laws* (Hafner Library of Classics, No. 9 [New York, 1949]), pp. ix-lxiv; Coolidge, *Theoretical and Foreign Elements,* pp. 30-38; Sabine, *Political Theory,* pp. 465-73; Spurlin, *Montesquieu, passim.*

[31] Hume's phrase and italics. This is from his brief autobiographical account entitled *My Own Life.* David Hume, *Essays Moral, Political, and Literary.* T. H. Green and T. H. Grose, eds. (2 vols., London, 1875), I, 2.

of natural law to scientific validity, natural religion, rational ethics, and the contract theory. Thus he was to a large extent anathema in an America which was wedded to Christian orthodoxy and the social contract. Yet he made other contributions which were significant in the founding of the Republic and the formation of the Constitution of 1787, and for these he deserves more credit than he has hitherto been granted.

Hume attempted simultaneously to apply the empiricism of Newton and Locke to the theory of knowledge and lay the basis for a new mental outlook. This involved erecting a body of principles concerning man and society which would permit increased mastery over human affairs. Desiring especially to reduce the study of politics to a science, Hume enlisted history and the empirical method to discover the "constant and universal principles of human nature." [32] Experience and observation would furnish the materials for a scientific study of the rules governing behavior, knowledge of which was prerequisite to intelligent social thought.

In addition to his methodology, the political views expounded by Hume in his *Essays* and *History* proved important for the Framers. The Scottish philosopher shared with Montesquieu both devotion to liberty and the conviction that laws must be understood in their total cultural and social context. Moreover, he stressed the need to limit power by exalting law over government and by balancing and separating authority. In lauding constitutionalism and especially the British constitution, he showed how English traditions limited the abuse of power. In the first volumes of his *History*, Hume analyzed the dialectic between freedom and authority under the Stuarts in England during the seventeenth-century crisis. These con-

---

Also see Charles W. Hendel, ed., *David Hume: An Inquiry Concerning Human Understanding* (The Library of Liberal Arts, No. 49 [New York, 1955]) pp. 3-11.

[32] Hume, *Essays Moral, Political, and Literary*. Green and Grose, eds., II, 68. (From the Section "Of Liberty and Necessity" in *Concerning Human Understanding*.)

cerns struck home to Americans after the Stamp Act, and colonials undoubtedly drew something of value from Hume
during their own revolution. But delegates who gathered in
1787 in the old State House—or Independence Hall—were
especially indebted to Hume.[33] Besides political views which
spoke directly to their own situation, this author afforded
them a technique for constitution-making. He not only
praised constructive statesmanship, but offered a guide thereto

[33] Most of Hume's literary efforts, and all of those most relevant to the
science of politics and the formation of the Constitution of 1787, were
published before 1765. They were available in the colonies, as a variety
of evidence attests, but it is difficult to say with finality at this time how
much they were read and with what effect. The problem is illustrated by
Jefferson, who had the first volume (edition unknown) of Hume's *Essays*
and thought several of the political ones good. But along with many English contemporaries he disliked the *History*, which he read when young. A
copy purchased from the bookshop of the *Virginia Gazette* on March 7,
1764, was in the Shadwell library. Jefferson often commented on the
work, on one occasion (in 1810) praising the charms of its style and re-
membering well "the enthusiasm with which I devoured it when young,
and the length of time, and the research & reflection which were necessary to eradicate the poison it had instilled into my mind." He thought
that Hume, who admitted having presumed to shed a "generous tear" for
Charles I and Strafford, was an apologist for the Stuarts, and that the
Scot's later volume dealing with earlier periods of English history proceeded from the same "perverted" view. "[A]ltho' all this is known," said
Jefferson, "he still continues to be put into the hands of all our young
people, and to infect them with the poison of his own principles of government . . . and . . . spread toryism over the land. [A]nd the book will
still continue to be read here as well as there." E. Millicent Sowerby,
Catalogue of the Library of Thomas Jefferson, (4 vols., Washington, 1952-
1955), I, 157; II, 14. Hume's influence in America is a hitherto largely
neglected story which deserves far more scholarly study. I am indebted to
Professor Charles W. Hendel of Yale University and Mr. Oskar Piest,
Editor of The Liberal Arts Press, for arousing my interest in this topic.
    The available records reveal that Hume was mentioned but once by
name in the Federal Convention (by Hamilton, who cited him on the subject of corruption when legislators held other civil offices), although his
ideas were used much without attribution, as noted below, pp. cix ff. John
Adams was familiar with Hume's writings, and of the Convention delegates, at least Hamilton, Franklin, and Madison knew them well. Franklin
had been personally acquainted with the Scottish philosopher.

in his essay entitled "Idea of a Perfect Commonwealth." [34] Here alone, and through Madison especially, Hume made a lasting contribution to the Constitution of 1787 and the American Union.[35]

Jean-Jacques Rousseau

Hume's quondam friend Jean-Jacques Rousseau (1712-1778) exerted tremendous influence on European thought in the generation before the Constitutional Convention and the French Revolution. He performed a task similar to that of his Scottish contemporary, David Hume: by logically unraveling some of Locke's ideas, he arrived at conclusions opposite to those of the Whig philosopher. The individualism exalted by Lockean teachings posed a question for Rousseau, who sought to balance the general welfare with the good of each, or reconcile the establishment of political authority with preservation of the free individual. Rousseau found release from his dilemma in Plato, and in the *Social Contract* (1762) announced a form of association which made the political subjection of the individual to the community an ethical act. Like Hobbes, Rousseau denied the existence of natural rights. It was the community which made a moral person of the individual, and it was from here, where the welfare of each coincided with the welfare of all, that the individual received those capacities which were his. Differentiating society from state, Rousseau insisted on the virtue of a small state in which the people ruled directly, with the government as its executive agency only.

Rousseau's influence on early American development has

[34] Hume, *Essays*, Green and Grose, eds., 1, 480-93. This essay is also in Charles W. Hendel, ed., *David Hume's Political Essays* (The Library of Liberal Arts, No. 34 [New York, 1953]), pp. 145-58.

[35] *Ibid.*, pp. vii-lx; Ernest Campbell Mossner, *The Life of David Hume* (Austin, Texas, 1954), p. 139; Sabine, *Political Theory*, pp. 503-11; Gladys Bryson, *Man and Society: The Scottish Inquiry of the Eighteenth Century* (Princeton, 1945), pp. 1-29; Daniel J. Boorstin, *The Mysterious Science of the Law* (Cambridge, 1941), pp. 31-61; Adair, "Hume, Madison, and Tenth *Federalist*," *op. cit.*

been much controverted. Colonials had a fair acquaintance
with his ideas. His *Social Contract* was advertised in Boston as
early as 1764, the year in which James Otis cited it in a
pamphlet against Britain. Other authors—like the Swiss
Delolme—spread Rousseau's name and theories in the colonies.
as did French officers during the Revolution. Among those
familiar with Rousseau, or who owned his books, were John
Adams, Jefferson, Madison, Franklin, Washington, and Wilson.

Nevertheless, Americans largely opposed his ideas. If many
sympathized with his passion for equality, most found mean-
ingless his call to a people in chains for a social as well as
political revolution. And his denial of natural rights struck
an unresponsive chord. Rousseau's ideas are not those employed in the Federal Convention, and there is no record that
his name was ever mentioned there. But even so, he probably
influenced the Philadelphia deliberations. Even if the Framers
knew his ideas only to reject them, it is likely that Rousseau
thereby contributed to sharpening their awareness of the
philosophical presuppositions on which their labor rested.[36]

William Blackstone

In Sir William Blackstone (1732-1780) many of the ideas
and tendencies previously mentioned converged and took on
renewed authority before passing on to the colonies. In Oxford law lectures and in his writing, Blackstone sought to reduce to a systematic statement based on scientific principles
the confused array of laws which had accumulated since Bracton's time. In doing so he proved sensitive to the prevalent
outlook of his own day but not an original thinker. While he
employed the new empirical method to discover the natural
principles underlying English common law, he had no intention of following logic so far as to undermine cherished val-

---

[36] Sabine, *Political Theory*, pp. 485-502; Charles W. Hendel, *Jean-
Jacques Rousseau, Moralist* (2 vols., London and New York, 1934), I, 1-19;
Paul M. Spurlin, "Rousseau in America," *The French American Review*,
I (January-March, 1948), 8-15; Coolidge, *Theoretical and Foreign Ele-
ments*, pp. 42-51.

ues. For him as for Locke, life, liberty, and property were the proper ends of government. And with Montesquieu, he lauded the English system for separating powers.

Yet, if Blackstone borrowed copiously in defending the eighteenth-century British constitution, it was not always done consistently. In praising natural law as a controlling standard of justice, he paid lip service to earlier ideals. Paralleling developments since the Revolution of 1688, his real view was that Parliament was supreme in the British system. For him the locus of sovereignty was in the lawmaking agency, since law was the will of a superior and government possessed not power derived from the people or God, but intrinsic power as embodied in the constitution. He used the language of Coke and Locke to pave the way to the opposite position of Hobbes. His absolute doctrine was summed up in the aphorism that "Parliament can do anything except make a man a woman or a woman a man." [37]

Blackstone's four-volume *Commentaries on the Laws of England* (1765-69) became enormously influential in the colonies. In meeting immediate needs, its subject matter, comprehensiveness—it was the most complete survey of the English legal system ever composed by a single hand—and style won the treatise instant popularity. Publication of the first American edition in 1771-72 aimed at making the work more easily available. Gaining recognition as the core of a lawyer's professional education, the *Commentaries* seized a crucial role in legal education which they maintained for over a century. Hence Blackstone's ideas were uppermost in the years from 1776 to 1787, with vital significance for constitutional development both in the states and in Philadelphia. Delegates in the State House acknowledged Blackstone as the authority on English law, yet from other views of his they succeeded in emancipating themselves.[38]

[37] This is Delolme's statement, as quoted in Corwin, " 'Higher Law' Background," *op. cit.*, p. 407.

[38] *Ibid.*, pp. 405-9; Lewis C. Warden, *The Life of Blackstone* (Charlottesville, 1938), pp. 313-48; Boorstin, *Mysterious Science, passim;* Charles

By the eve of the Federal Convention, Blackstone was but the most recent manifestation of a constitutional tradition stretching back to classical Greece. For two thousand years men had struggled not only to realize the republican ideal enunciated by Plato, but also to find satisfactory solutions to the problems raised in the attempt. Could power be reconciled with right? Could a vigorous government be established on the foundation of fundamental law? What was the nature of authority and right, and where in the political community was the seat of this authority, or sovereignty? What institutional devices and jurisprudential considerations would limit the abuse of power? What in the civil order was the "sure and legitimate rule of administration" [39] which promoted at one and the same time the public welfare and the individual good? In short, could Western man create the institutions of freedom within order?

To Americans in 1765 the answer seemed to be one of cautious optimism: freedom had not yet found a large or permanent home, although the achievement of England and her provinces contained promise. Thereafter the entire problem became one of primary concern for colonials, who were familiar with its lineaments by virtue of long acquaintance with the constitutional legacy described above. However, the contribution of these doctrines in the establishment of republicanism in 1787 is only part of the story.

Warren, *A History of the American Bar* (Boston, 1911), pp. 157-87; Randolph Greenfield Adams, *Political Ideas of the American Revolution: Britannic-American Contribution to the Problem of Imperial Reorganization, 1765-1775* (Durham, 1922), ch. 6-8; H. D. Hazeltine, "William Blackstone," *Encyclopedia of the Social Sciences*, II, 580-81; Spurlin, *Montesquieu*, pp. 99-137.

[39] Jean-Jacques Rousseau, *The Social Contract and Discourses*, G. D. H. Cole, Translator, (New York, 1950), p. 3.

III. FROM JAMESTOWN TO THE REVOLUTION:
THE COLONIAL AMERICAN TRADITION

Formation of the Federal Constitution must also be traced on native grounds. A product of the upheaval which made for constitutional remolding in Europe, settlement of the New World began just as the Puritan Revolution commenced in England. In the long period from the planting of Jamestown and Plymouth to the Philadelphia Convention the seeds of American culture germinated slowly. Then in the forcing bed of conflict with the mother country they quickly flowered. A "resistless wave of seeking men" [1] had gone out Englishmen and become Americans. Distinguishing features of this century and a half of development are, on one hand, the rise of colonial autonomy and the political institutions which contained it, and, on the other, the growth of individual liberty and popular authority.

COLONIAL AUTONOMY AND POLITICAL STRUCTURE

In spite of the tensions which later made for open revolt, Americans enjoyed a not unfavorable position with respect to Britain by the eve of the Revolution. Materially well off, the provinces generally prospered under mercantilistic regulations which benefited them as long as they lacked capacity for economic independence. The political situation was even more favorable. Theoretically Britain controlled; actually colonists governed themselves. They did this under political organs which arose on American soil. The transition of trading companies into governments based upon written constitutions represents the first stage in the indigenous development of the

[1] Stephen Vincent Benet, *Western Star* (New York, 1943), p. 180.

institutional structure later embodied in the Constitution of 1787.[2]

On the eve of American settlement, some European nations fostered overseas expansion by granting to private companies of merchant adventurers written charters incorporating them and enabling formation of a government based on their patent. The typical and famous English East India Company charter of December 31, 1600, empowered a General Assembly consisting of a governor, council, and freemen (or members) meeting together to make laws, impose penalties, and otherwise direct affairs. Structurally this followed earlier guild and corporation models rather than the British government. Besides providing the basis for political authority and institutions, these charters as well as later proprietary patents for America contained assurance that migrating settlers and their children were to enjoy the rights of Englishmen, and that the laws made in the colonies were to conform to those of England as near as could be. Thus Magna Carta and in time the Petition of Right and the Bill of Rights became safeguards of provincial liberty.

Virginia

Against a background of domestic political strife, James I in 1606 issued the first Virginia charter for the settlement of the entire American coast to two related groups, with the London Company receiving the southern and the Plymouth Company the northern part. Significantly, this document omitted the usual democratic features. Government of the colony was in the hands of a local resident council which was under a council in London, and both were responsible to the king. But subsequent charters (in 1609 and 1612) awarded the Company political power and enabled increasing self-govern-

[2] William C. Morey, "The Genesis of a Written Constitution," *Annals of the American Academy of Political and Social Science*, I (April, 1891), 529-57.

ment. The chief executive officer along with a council of twenty-four received both administrative and judicial powers. The governor, council, and members of the Company were to meet together as a General Court four times yearly. Here they were to handle judicial tasks beyond the competence of lesser courts, choose the council and, as long as they did not violate the laws and statutes of England, legislate for the colony. The essential elements of a written constitution were present.

In 1619, after several years of autocratic control and other difficulties in Virginia, the London Company instituted representative government in America. (The system was sanctioned in writing by a London Company ordinance of 1621, "the first written constitution granted to an American colony." [3]) Henceforth the Company was to appoint a governor and a Council of Assistants, who were to share political authority with the residents. Freemen in each of the eleven plantations were to elect two burgesses as their deputies to Jamestown. Although the initial General Assembly met as one body in the church, the governor and council occupied the choir seats and the burgesses the body of the edifice. The chief executive and the council together formed a court of justice. The entire assembly was to make laws. But the governor possessed in the veto a means of defending the Company's interests, and no legislation was to bind unless both the General Assembly and the General Court of the Company in England assented. In 1624, Virginia became a royal colony, and the king now replaced the London Company in appointing the governor and assuming ultimate control.

Thus in response to concrete American situations arose a system whose outline included representative government, rudimentary bicameralism, and rudimentary separation of powers. Burgesses chosen by and responsible to local interests balanced a Crown-appointed governor and his Council of Assistants. Although the shape of these two branches (legislative and executive) was clearly discernible, their sharing of judicial functions made separation of powers and an independent judiciary slow in growing. With alterations this structure became the model for the government of other Southern provinces, and a similar organization came to prevail in all of the colonies. In each case statutory enactments rather than mere custom formed the foundation stone.[4]

Massachusetts

In 1629 the Massachusetts Bay Company, which was interested primarily in religious colonization rather than trade, received a charter vesting control of Company affairs—and hence authority over the New-World settlement—in the governor and assistants. But after a brief spell of oligarchic rule, political power came to reside in the General Court. This consisted of a body of deputies elected to represent the towns by freemen who were church members, as well as an elective governor and his Court of Assistants. These three organs met together four times yearly as a General Court, where they made the laws (as long as these were not repugnant to those of Britain), interpreted them, and also administered the colony. As early as 1636 the assistants won a negative voice, and after a long controversy between the council and deputies bicameralism came into being in 1644. The governor and his Court of Assistants retained judicial functions long after the Assembly lost them. The executive and legislative branches were not separated until the establishment of royal government which accompanied the loss of the first patent, so highly prized by Massachusetts Puritans. Under the new charter of 1691, the governor became a royal appointee and Plymouth Colony was united to that of the Massachusetts Bay.[5]

4 *Ibid.*, I, 535-48; Charles M. Andrews, *The Colonial Period of American History* (4 vols., New Haven, 1934-38), I, 98-126, 180-90; Benjamin F. Wright, Jr., "The Origins of the Separation of Power in America," *Economica*, XIII (1933), 171-72, 175.

5 *Ibid.*, XIII, 173-75; Morey, "Genesis of a Written Constitution," *op. cit.*, pp. 548-50.

Connecticut and Rhode Island

Government in Virginia and Massachusetts rested on power emanating from the English sovereign. Thus Connecticut and Rhode Island, after breaking off from the Bay Colony and creating institutions based on the authority of the people, applied for and received corporate charters from the Crown. A 1662 patent united New Haven with the Connecticut River settlements and embodied a form of government similar to that in Massachusetts and Virginia. Much the same process occurred in the Rhode Island charter of 1663. In these provinces governors and assistants chosen by and responsible to the Assembly were re-elected as often as they would serve because they co-operated with rather than antagonized the popular house. The result of this response to distinctly American conditions was creation of a unique type of executive office.[6]

Pennsylvania

In the Middle Colonies somewhat similar governmental structures arose by a different process, with proprietary grants preceding concessions of authority to the people. Pennsylvania may serve as an example. By a royal charter of 1681, William Penn became absolute proprietor and received power to legislate with the approval of freeholders. The frame of government which Penn devised for his "holy experiment" shows the influence of Harrington's *Oceana*. A governor and council (where the principle of elective rotation operated) were to propose all laws. Until 1696 the Assembly, elected by freemen, could merely resolve measures sent to it. In that year, however, this chamber gained the right to initiate acts, a victory consolidated by the Charter of 1701. This made the Council solely advisory to the proprietary-appointed governor, and Pennsylvania became a unicameral province in which the Assembly controlled the lawmaking function.[7]

[6] *Ibid.*, pp. 550-53.

[7] *Ibid.*, pp. 553-56; Andrews, *Colonial Period*, III, 268-328; Smith, *Harrington*, pp. 164-83.

The Legacy of the Formative Years: A Summary

Thus the process of founding American plantations resulted by mid-eighteenth century in governmental structures based on written constitutions or charters which looked back to the trading companies and forward to the Federal Convention. Everywhere except in Connecticut and Rhode Island legislative and executive branches drawn from different sources and exercising different functions arose. Governors represented the Crown or, in the case of Pennsylvania, Delaware, and Maryland, the English-resident proprietors who appointed them. Bicameral legislatures prevailed everywhere except in Pennsylvania and Georgia. In these the upper chamber was an evolution from the executive's advisory council. Although elected in three New England provinces, elsewhere members were usually appointed by the Crown or proprietor out of native aristocrats nominated by the governors. The lower house or Assembly was everywhere representative of the people. Property tests for the franchise prevailed, but property was widely held throughout most of the colonies, and probably most white adult males could meet property qualifications. Often, however, inequality of representation favored settled Eastern sections at the expense of the newer West. Subject to the executive veto, laws required the assent of the two separate and co-ordinate chambers. American colonial history is a long contest to determine the locus of authority, which for practical purposes meant control of lawmaking and the purse. Everywhere the victory went to the Assemblies.

After the first decades of settlement a judiciary branch usually consisting of local justices of the peace, county courts, a supreme or superior court, and a chancellor for equity gradually took shape. Long after General Courts as such or lower chambers lost their judicial powers, governors along with their councils—or upper houses—retained those functions. Often they were courts of appeal in civil or criminal cases and tried impeachments. But Assemblies frequently succeeded in depriving them of control over judicial appointments and tenure.

These essentials of subsequent American political structure which took firm root in native soil provided the framework for the great autonomy which colonials possessed. After slow growth three separate branches of government had emerged. The different sources on which these rested made for mixed government, and this together with separation of powers and bicameralism implemented the practice of checks and balances. Nevertheless, the Assemblies had gained the upper hand in the struggle with governors and councils which was part of the contest between the colonies and mother country. Broadly based representative government was the rule, and only the people, through their deputies, could impose taxes in America. Natural developments created a classic example of the situation for which Locke provided a rationalization, and therefore provincials compared their situation with England, where the Revolution of 1688 awarded Parliament control of the purse. Parliament could not tax the colonials but it could legislate for them. Americans cherished their status because they enjoyed practical independence, while Britain reserved to itself regulation of trade and the royal disallowance to protect other vital interests. Thus for decades Americans gained political experience and self-confidence in assuming responsibility for their own affairs.

INDIVIDUAL LIBERTY AND THE SOURCE OF AUTHORITY

Inhabitants of British North-America also enjoyed unparalleled individual liberty by mid-eighteenth century. Forces released by the unfolding of an Old-World inheritance in a New-World environment helped significantly in molding attitudes which underlay the Revolution and found expression in the new state constitutions. Besides the political institutions already noted, the abundance of land, the psychology of the frontier, religious diversity, and the plasticity of society in America were all part of the colonial matrix. But the role of English law and the philosophy of social contract deserve special stress.

English Law

In defense of their rights, early emigrants affirmed the safeguards found in their corporate or proprietary charters. They also found succor from Sir Edward Coke, who resurrected the tradition of Magna Carta and brandished it before King James I to protect the rights of Englishmen. Consequently, Americans gloried in Coke throughout most of the seventeenth century. But these sources, supplemented even by the Petition of Right and various statutes, were often deemed insufficient. And the common law proved a weak reed to lean on. It was neither popular nor a source of pride in England in the early seventeenth century. Although followed in the Middle and Southern colonies, the common law in New England was next to nothing—in force only so far as specific statutes were adopted. Yet before the eighteenth century opened, all colonies possessed written charter guarantees which protected religious and political rights especially. Subsequently the provincials claimed additional security from the trans-Atlantic application of English common and statute law and gains (such as the Bill of Rights and the Habeas Corpus Act of 1679 [8]) accruing from the constitutional settlement. Thus American subjects insisted on their rights and liberties as freeborn Englishmen.[9]

[8] There was a real problem as to whether such Acts of Parliament as the Habeas Corpus Act took automatic effect in the chartered colonies.

[9] Corwin, "'Higher Law' Background," *op. cit.*, pp. 365-80, 394-96; Zechariah Chafee, Jr., *How Human Rights Got Into the Constitution* (Boston, 1952), pp. 26-47, 51-57; Robert Allen Rutland, *The Birth of the Bill of Rights* (Chapel Hill, 1955), pp. 3-23; Warren, *American Bar*, pp. 10-11.

The Social Contract

Religion and the Puritan Covenant

Meanwhile, long experience with the social contract theory in the interval from the first colonial settlements to the Stamp Act Crisis produced firm convictions regarding the nature of individual rights and the source of authority. Despite much diversity of theological belief, Americans were in matters of dogma largely products of Calvinism. And at the outset religion was basic in shaping other views as well. This was especially true of New England Puritanism, America's first distinct intellectual tradition.

In seventeenth-century colonial thought divine law, a fusion of the law of nature and the Old and New Testaments, usually stood as fundamental law. (The Mayflower Compact exemplified both this and the doctrine of covenant or contract.) Puritanism, which particularly exalted the Biblical component, drew on certain Scriptural passages for a theological outlook which contained a basically pessimistic conception of human nature. Yet these ideas were nevertheless pregnant with possibilities for democracy. Called the covenant or federal theology, this was a theory of contract regarding man's relations with God and the nature of church and state. Man was deemed an impotent sinner until he received God's grace, and then he became the material out of which sacred and civil communities were built. Churches were "gathered" when "saints" covenanted among themselves and with God. Although members alone possessed full power to name their pastors, once called, ministers derived their authority immediately from God. Likewise magistrates, who were essential to curb evil in the civil state which arose as a result of the Fall, received election from the people (in Massachusetts only church members) but power from God. Thus the New England Way featured a speaking aristocracy and a silent democracy.

But just as God was limited by divine law, so too was authority in a Puritan society limited by fundamental law. For early New England colonies the Bible rather than English common or statute law—much to the annoyance of certain dissidents—was the written constitution on which they patterned their legal codes. These not only restrained the exercise of power by stating its limits, but provided an additional safeguard by embodying the individual rights which were deemed God-given. Moreover, acts contrary to the fundamental law were not deemed binding. The free individual, voluntary association, and consent were postulates of Puritanism. New England clergymen early discussed all of the rights later asserted in the Declaration of Independence, and these ministers form the one unbroken line of descent between the political philosophy of the seventeenth century and the constituent assembly of 1787.[10]

Enlightenment and the Secular Contract

Preoccupation with theology gave way to absorption in politics as the eighteenth century reformulated these principles. The European scientific and intellectual revolution noted earlier quickly reshaped American views. Pufendorf, relied on in a colonial religious controversy of the early eighteenth century, and Grotius were harbingers of the new era. But Newton and Locke became the authorities for the changed outlook. Nature replaced God, who now became for many the Supreme Workman who governed the universe not by remarkable providences but by laws as old as creation. The notion of rights was transformed by the doctrine that the law of

[10] Alice M. Baldwin, *The New England Clergy and the American Revolution* (Durham, 1928), pp. 170, 172. On the New England contribution to the formation of the Constitution, see also Andrew C. McLaughlin, *The Foundations of American Constitutionalism* (New York, 1932), esp. chs. 1, 3. Hume paid tribute to the role of the ministers in a letter written on October 26, 1775, to his publisher. Referring to some of the drastic measures which the British Government would have to take if it wished to conquer and rule the Americans, Hume stated that they would have to "hang three fourths of their clergy." Hendel, ed., *Hume's Political Essays*, p. lii.

nature was to be found in human experience and that the contract was a device for limiting authority and protecting inalienable rights. The switch from religious to property qualifications for the franchise in different colonies paralleled the shift from supernatural to natural sanctions for authority.[11] And the process of transforming common law rights of Englishmen into natural law rights within the British constitution was complete and familiar to Americans long before they put it to use. Locke's influence quickly eclipsed that of Coke, and by the 1730's the new views were ascendant in the colonies. For over a generation before the Revolution these comfortable notions made their way via college classrooms, pamphlets, almanacs, newspapers, and from the pulpits (and printed sermons) of Puritan clergymen.

In summary, on the eve of the rupture with Britain the colonies dominated their own affairs. Never taxed except by themselves, they enjoyed greater freedom and liberty under law than any other people in the world. Yet they stressed the merits of positive statutes rather than the vague, unwritten assurances afforded by the law of nature. Proud Englishmen, they called the mother country home and swore allegiance to George III when he mounted the throne in 1760. Formally united only through the Crown, these transatlantic subjects possessed more in common than their lack of political unity revealed. A shrewd contemporary, John Adams, later noted that the "real American Revolution" was the radical transformation in "principles, opinions, sentiments, and affections" which overcame provincials—a change complete before the crisis with England commenced.[12]

[11] In Massachusetts, for example, the change came in 1691, when the new charter stipulated that the suffrage was to rest on property rather than religious qualifications.

[12] Adams, *Works*, X, 283.

IV. THE EXPERIMENT IN REPUBLICANISM

Although the American Revolution may be interpreted in a variety of ways, it cannot be understood except in terms of the constitutional issues which loomed so large to contemporaries. For them the upheaval centered around two problems long familiar but never before the source of controversy. One concerned the nature of colonial rights, or the role of fundamental law. Defense of a specific right—property—initiated the contest with Britain and underlay the entire struggle. This led to a second problem, that of federalism, or the source of authority as it related to the structure of the British empire. What rules governed relationships between mother country and colonies? Seeking an answer, Britons emphasized the authority of Parliament and the Crown resting on prescriptive law. The colonial argument with Britain proceeded in two stages. First, provincials attacked the alleged usurpations of Parliament on the grounds of charter rights, common law, and the English constitution. This proving insufficient, their search for an ultimate principle brought them to the law of nature, with which in the second stage they undercut the claims of the Crown. Before declaring independence Americans foreshadowed the later structure of the British empire and paved a way for the federal system which emerged at Philadelphia in 1787. In insisting on a particular version of the fundamental law, they deepened an existing channel in which the current of American life (and especially constitution-making) subsequently flowed. If the Revolution initiated an internal conflict, this was neither as profound nor as widespread as often depicted, nor did it outlast the early 1780's.[1] Certainly the domestic antagonisms of 1776 did not remain in force down to and in the Federal Convention.

[1] See, for example, Oscar and Mary F. Handlin, "Radicals and Conservatives in Massachusetts," *New England Quarterly*, XVII (1944), 343-55; Brown, *Democracy and Revolution in Massachusetts.*

The Stamp Act Congress

Throughout the first decade of the revolutionary debate Americans viewed Parliament as antagonistic and the king as their defender. The storm broke after preliminary rumbles with passage in March, 1765, of the Stamp Act,[2] which was part of a British plan to shift to the transatlantic subjects some of the domestic tax burden while at the same time attempting extensive imperial reorganization. Since this was the first attempt of Parliament to impose a tax on the colonies without the consent of local authorities, Americans became alarmed as never before. That autumn nine provinces met in New York City to define the colonial position. The Stamp Act Congress was the first example of united opposition to Britain and the earliest manifestation of a national "government" to which all Americans could appeal.

With the "Declaration of Rights" of this Congress the colonies overtly took a path which led to independence and the formation of the Constitution. The textual material of this volume, therefore, opens with that document, which stressed the idea that by a fundamental law of the English constitution subjects could not be taxed without their consent.[3] Not only did the colonists withhold this, but they also spurned the doctrine of virtual representation, which held that since members of Parliament spoke for the interests of the entire realm, all Britons were virtually if not actually represented. This Declaration is a precedent for all subsequent statements

---

[2] The Stamp Act was designed to raise £60,000 by imposing the first direct tax ever levied by Parliament on the colonies after November 1, 1765. This provided for stamp duties of varying amounts to be affixed to legal documents of all types (including wills, contracts, bonds, guardianships, etc.), educational degrees, appointments to various public offices, licenses, ship's papers, newspapers, pamphlets, broadsides, almanacs, and even playing cards and dice.

[3] See pp. 5-7.

of rights, although here the emphasis is on common law, statutory, and constitutional rights of Englishmen. At this time, however, some colonial spokesmen were making assertions of natural rights.

Moreover, the Congress asserted that Parliament had no power to lay taxes, which was reserved to the people in their provincial assemblies. Although Americans thus resisted external taxes, they did not prohibit Parliamentary regulation of trade. But it was dangerous if not supererogatory for the Stamp Act Congress openly to admit that Britain could so control imperial commerce, since some recent measures for this purpose had produced incidental revenue. Hence deputies defended the fundamental right of self-taxation and made no distinction between internal and external levies, rejecting both. But for several reasons which we need not discuss here, Englishmen concluded that the colonies permitted Parliament to impose the latter but not the former. Skillfully directed resistance by colonials prevented enforcement of the Stamp Act, and a year after its passage Parliament nullified the measure. But domestic reasons and not provincial opposition motivated this repeal, coupled with which was a Declaratory Act asserting Parliament's authority to bind the colonies "in all cases whatsoever." [4]

The Townshend Duties

Thereupon both sides assumed they possessed sole power over the colonial purse. When Chancellor of the Exchequer Charles Townshend at a time of turmoil in 1767 seized on the putative distinction to lay new duties on provincial imports in the form of trade regulations, a terrific outcry and eco-

[4] Edmund S. and Helen M. Morgan, *The Stamp Act Crisis: Prologue to Revolution* (Chapel Hill, 1953); Adams, *Political Ideas*, chs. 1-5; Edmund Cody Burnett, *The Continental Congress* (New York, 1941), pp. 3-22; Rutland, *Bill of Rights*, pp. 24-25; William Clarence Webster, "Comparative Study of the State Constitutions of the American Revolution," *Annals of the American Academy of Political and Social Science*, IX (1897), 384-89.

nomic boycott ensued. In several opposition addresses drafted for the Massachusetts legislature, Samuel Adams announced that since legislative supremacy was derived from a constitution rooted in the law of God and the law of nature, all lawmaking power was limited. Parliament therefore could not destroy the right to property, which the charters, the common law, and the law of nature combined to protect.[5] This statement was an important step in the growth of constitutional law in America.

The First Continental Congress

Repeal of the duties smoothed roiled waters for three years, but a new tempest broke in May, 1773, when Parliament aided the East India Company with a virtual monopoly over the colonial tea trade. That December Bostonians destroyed a valuable cargo of the leaf, and Parliament adopted three measures designed as punishment. The Administration of Justice Act provided that certain trials could be removed to England from the Bay port where justice was deemed likely to miscarry. The Massachusetts Government Act transferred several powers formerly possessed by the people and General Court to the king or governor. This arbitrarily violated the charter, palladium of everything considered most dear. What then remained of the doctrine of the consent of the governed, written fundamental law, or the concept of constitutionalism? Yet it was the Boston Port Act, cutting off trade until compensation for damages (and customs) was forthcoming, which electrified the colonies. News of this arrived in Boston on May 10 (before passage of the other two measures), and spread quickly along the seaboard, motivating other provinces to make the martyrs' cause their own. A combination of legal and extralegal bodies proposed common action.

Thus the First Continental Congress convened in Carpenter's Hall in Philadelphia on September 5, 1774. Fifty-six dele-

---

[5] See pp. 7-9.

gates representing every colony except Georgia marked the closest union yet achieved.[6] As a direct predecessor of the United States Congress under the Federal Constitution, this gathering was but preliminary to further common action. The diversity among delegates in manners, tastes, looks, spirit, laws, religion, and education testified to the dominant American particularism. This necessitated many social affairs to afford delegates opportunity for stocktaking.

Of the organizational questions, one involving the method of voting was recognized as especially important for the precedent it might set for future congresses. Should the vote be by colonies, numbers of people, or amount of wealth? To prevent equality of provinces and gain proportional weight in balloting for Virginia, Patrick Henry declared that by Parliamentary oppression government was dissolved. "We are in a state of nature, sir. . . . The distinctions between Virginians, Pennsylvanians, New Yorkers, and New Englanders, are no more. I am not a Virginian, but an American." [7] Perhaps these lofty sentiments accelerated American nationalism; certainly they were recalled in 1787 at a low point in the Philadelphia debates. But the actual decision favored voting by colonies, since the alternatives were even less satisfactory and a specific warning was included against creating a precedent. Naturally this became a precedent, thereby laying a powder charge which almost wrecked the Federal Convention.

Despite internal divisions, the work of the Continental Congress struck a balance between opposing views. It was the wish of those present, and perhaps of the country in even larger degree, to restore harmonious relations with England.

[6] Among delegates present were Samuel and John Adams of Massachusetts, Roger Sherman of Connecticut, James Duane of New York, William Livingston of New Jersey, Joseph Galloway and John Dickinson of Pennsylvania, Peyton Randolph, Richard Henry Lee, George Washington, and Patrick Henry of Virginia, and Christopher Gadsden and John and Edward Rutledge of South Carolina.

[7] Adams, *Works*, II, 366-67; Robert Douthat Meade, *Patrick Henry: Patriot in the Making* (Philadelphia and New York, 1957), pp. 314-39.

The attitude expressed in the "Declaration and Resolves" represented an advance over that of 1765, but the position taken was largely moderate if not conservative.[8] However, formation of the Association, a device to support the Declaration by imposing economic sanctions, was a victory for radicalism. This measure became a powerful instrument facilitating the growth of American union. And moderation triumphed in explanatory letters sent to the king and to other British subjects. Before adjourning, Congress vowed to reassemble on May 10 if colonial grievances remained unredressed.

The nature of Parliament's authority was the main question before the Continental Congress. Although a committee on colonial rights easily composed a statement of grievances, determination of the foundation of provincial rights provoked heated controversy. On the one hand were those Conservatives (like James Duane and Joseph Galloway) who, largely repeating the stand taken by the Stamp Act Congress, found ample security in the colonial charters and law codes, English common and statutory law, and the British constitution. On the other hand were those (like John and Samuel Adams) who drew a different lesson from the intervening decade. While they accepted the older guarantees, they insisted also on resort to the law of nature. Written into the Declaration, this provided a rationale for viewing men as possessing equal rights as well as a strategical position which could be defended against all attack. From here a straight line runs to the Declaration of Independence and the Bill of Rights in the federal Constitution.

The fourth resolution of the Declaration embraced much of the emerging doctrine of colonial autonomy which Franklin, James Wilson, John Adams, and Jefferson had each adumbrated before the Continental Congress met. Having already indicted Parliament for invading rights by regulating their commerce certain ways, colonists realized that to oppose all control was to lose the advantage of inclusion within the pat-

8 See pp. 10-14.

tern of imperial trade. Thus Congress escaped a dilemma by following the lead of James Duane, who argued that the provinces had always accepted supervision of their trade by Parliament and should continue to do so provided it was exercised for the common benefit.

After the First Continental Congress adjourned, John Adams helped push the doctrine of colonial autonomy to its logical conclusion in his *Novanglus* papers. As finally elaborated, this theory held that although the colonies permitted Parliament to control their trade, such regulatory measures were to be considered as treaties between independent states. The colonies were not subordinate to the British legislative body, but autonomous entities co-ordinate in authority with Parliament under the Crown. "We owe allegiance to the person of his majesty, King George III," wrote Adams, "whom God preserve." [9]

COLONIES VERSUS KING

Adjournment of the First Continental Congress initiated the second stage of the revolutionary debate. In turning from Parliament to George III, provincials were unaware that the king fully backed his lawmakers. Dawning realization of the monarch's alleged perfidy culminated at last in a disavowal of allegiance. Into the vacuum created by this rupture and the removal of royal authority rushed a myriad of problems, the attempted solutions to which illuminate the path to the Constitutional Convention. Certainly the rise of local and central

[9] The Adams quotation (from his *Works*, IV, 114) may be found in George A. Peek, ed., *The Political Writings of John Adams: Representative Selections* (The American Heritage Series, No. 8 [New York, 1954]), p. 46; Worthington C. Ford, *et al.*, eds., *Journals of the Continental Congress, 1774-1789* (34 vols., Washington, 1904-1937), I; Adams, *Works*, II, 340-402; Burnett, *Continental Congress*, pp. 23-59; Becker, *Political Parties in New York*, pp. 142-57; Adams, *Political Ideas*, ch. 3. However, Becker dismisses the contention that the First Continental Congress was moderate to argue, on the evidence of The Association, that it was radical.

governments in the wake of independence and the relationship between the two is one proper focus in describing the process of American constitutional growth. Was the union older than and superior to, or was it the creature of, the states?

The Second Continental Congress

Meeting as planned in Philadelphia, on May 10, 1775, the Second Continental Congress faced problems raised by armed conflict. This had begun at Lexington and Concord when Britain determined to enforce the Coercive Acts, which Massachusetts disobeyed. The Congress now assumed full responsibility for colonial military affairs. George Washington, dispatched to Boston as commander of the Continental Army, was given "A Declaration of the Causes and Necessity of Taking up Arms" to read to his troops.[10] This drew a careful line between defense of colonial rights, which it reaffirmed, and dissolution of ties with England, thus hinting at the contradictory views within the State House.

Hostilities also raised fundamental problems of government. In each province defense of lives and rights demanded united action. Temporary governments which made their appearance after the Intolerable Acts served this purpose. Most important were the provincial congresses (alternately conferences, conventions) which came into being when prorogued legislative assemblies met in new chambers or when special political bodies arose in opposition to the regular ones. Maryland set the pace in June, 1774, when a convention of county delegates met in Annapolis to assume control, following dissolution of the Assembly in April. By October the process was practically complete, although New York and Georgia delayed until early the next year. The old government held out longest in Pennsylvania, although a special convention met as early as July, 1774, and an extralegal body shared actual authority with the regularly constituted Assembly after January, 1775. Connecticut and Rhode Island merely continued to govern themselves

10 See pp. 16-23.

under their charters. These provincial congresses usually entrusted executive power to a committee (or council) of safety, and charged it with directing provincial military affairs and enforcing the Continental Association. County and local committees aided in the work of execution.[11]

A movement to replace these transient agencies began before the last ones appeared. Their many inadequacies demanded improvement, and worsening relations with Britain made permanence imperative. Whatever their merits, these governments were extralegal. And to argue that survival justified such illegality raised the specter of a Hobbesian state of nature. Why juggle dynamite when a less explosive alternative was nearby? Thus people took power into their own hands, thereby launching the social contract theory and natural rights philosophy on one of their greatest triumphs.

From Colonies to Commonwealths

For Americans the Revolution involved the novel problem of relations between their own central and local governments. For over a year after assembling in May, 1775, the Second Continental Congress remained divided on whether to break completely with Britain, and if it did, what priority to assign the three related tasks of declaring America free, seeking foreign alliances, and forming a confederation. The achievement of separation was actually the result of reciprocal action. Congress could declare no final rupture until the colonies authorized it, and that authorization was in turn essential to the independence of the individual provinces. Hence events

[11] Allan Nevins, *The American States during and after the Revolution, 1775-1789* (New York, 1924), pp. 26-60; Charles Albro Barker, *The Background of the Revolution in Maryland* (New Haven, 1940), p. 370; H. J. Eckenrode, *The Revolution in Virginia* (Boston, 1916), pp. 32-35; Charles H. Lincoln, *The Revolutionary Movement in Pennsylvania: 1760-1776* (Philadelphia, 1901), pp. 167-88; J. Paul Selsam, *The Pennsylvania Constitution of 1776: A Study in Revolutionary Democracy* (Philadelphia, 1936), pp. 49-93.

unfolding at the local level underlay the conflict which im-
mobilized Congress and dictated future lines of action.

A variety of factors, including the spread of war, shaped
the pace at which provincials clamored to snip the tie with
England. Nevertheless, the pattern of transforming colonies
into commonwealths was with local variations almost everywhere the same. First, provincial conventions applied to the
only agency of central political authority, the Continental
Congress, for permission to form a proper government.[12]
Having obtained this, they later devised written constitutions
which erected permanent institutions upon the base of popular sovereignty. This process represents an intermediate stage
in American constitutional development, the link between colonial governments which sprang out of trading company
charters and the federal instrument of 1787.[13] Discussion of
the constitutions themselves, which (except for one) came into
being in the sixteen months of 1776 and early 1777, is reserved
for later.

When the Second Continental Congress met, many delegates
from the North and South ardently desired action.[14] New
England, long familiar with republican institutions and already the scene of carnage, sent partisans of independence to
Philadelphia. Conflict raged in Massachusetts, whose charter
had earlier been abrogated. To conduct war necessitated civil
government, which the colony was reluctant to create on its
own responsibility. Consequently in mid-March Massachusetts
asked Congress for authority to settle its affairs on a more established basis. A June 9 resolution granted approval, and in
July the province resumed operations under its charter.

Some Southerners also hankered for immediate separation.
One manifestation of revolt appeared in piedmont North

---

[12] For one example of such an application see pp. 15-16.

[13] Nevins, *American States*, pp. 88-95; Morey, "First State Constitutions,"
op. cit., pp. 201-32.

[14] Among new delegates were John Hancock, Benjamin Franklin, James
Wilson, and Thomas Jefferson. Some Conservatives like Galloway were
missing.

Carolina, where a demand for at least temporary self-government arose in the Mecklenburg County Resolves (May, 1775).[15] Sent to Philadelphia, these were never introduced in Congress. In the Middle Colonies the pattern of trade, the social structure, and deep-seated political conflicts prevented precipitancy. Conservative Whigs might agree with Radical Whigs in desiring liberty under law, but they saw no reason (at least not yet) why this necessitated rebellion. Pennsylvania proved especially recalcitrant.

The Final Step

Meanwhile, the Second Continental Congress continued to conduct war until the sands of reconciliation ran out.[16] Allegiance to the king persisted unbelievably long. Although the Congress renounced disloyalty as late as December, sentiment soon shifted radically, as demonstrated by the popularity accorded Thomas Paine's *Common Sense* in mid-January, 1776. This popular pamphlet attacked the monarch and called for a new constitution. Exposing George III as the "Royal Brute" backing Parliament, Paine announced that it was time for colonies and mother country to part. Assemble a colonial delegation to frame a continental charter, Paine advised, and let this "be brought forth placed on the Divine Law, the Word of God; let a crown be placed thereon, by which the world may know, that so far as we approve of monarchy, that in America the law is king. For as in absolute governments the

15 See pp. 23-26.

16 In August, 1775, King George III proclaimed the colonies to be in open rebellion, and in November the House of Commons spurned the conciliatory Olive Branch Petition adopted by the Second Continental Congress on July 5 at the behest of those most reluctant to break with Britain. Thereupon, with armed conflict spreading throughout the North and South, the Congress on December 6 replied to the royal proclamation by disavowing subordination to Parliament while disclaiming any purpose of denying allegiance to the king. On December 23, however, the king declared all colonies closed to commerce as of the following March 1

King is law, so in free countries the law ought to be king; . . ." [17] George III is dead! Long live the fundamental law! This trumpet blast greatly swayed public opinion.

By the spring of 1776 the last bond uniting the colonies with Britain maintained a precarious hold. Yet its severing remained always difficult and at times seemingly impossible. While New England and the South demanded action, Middle-Colony delegates often lacked appropriate instructions or were bound, on grounds that their people were unready, not to sanction a decision for freedom. In April, as the struggle in Pennsylvania between the Assembly and the Provincial Convention took final shape, North Carolina specifically authorized its Congressional delegation to support independence.[18] Now from within the Continental Congress, John Adams and Richard Henry Lee, working with Radicals in Pennsylvania, determined to nudge those laggard colonies which waited on the people. Accordingly, they obtained from Congress on May 10 a resolution which recommended that any province lacking a proper government should form such. Five days later they secured adoption of a preamble in which the Continental Congress advised throwing off oaths of allegiance and suppressing the authority of the Crown, while resting colonial governments on the authority of the people.[19] John Adams, charged with fabricating a machine for independence, correctly answered that this was independence itself. That same day the Virginia Convention instructed its delegation in Philadelphia to propose a declaration of independence and formation of foreign alliances and a confederation.[20] At the same time Virginia went ahead to frame its own Declaration of Rights and

[17] Moncure D. Conway, ed., *The Writings of Thomas Paine* (4 vols., New York, 1894-96), I, 89, 97-99; also Nelson F. Adkins, ed., *Thomas Paine: Common Sense and Other Political Writings* ("American Heritage Series" No. 5, The Liberal Arts Press, New York, 1953), p. 32.

[18] See pp. 27-28.

[19] See pp. 28-29; also Burnett, *Continental Congress*, pp. 170-97; Selsam, *Pennsylvania Constitution*, pp. 94-135.

[20] See pp. 30-31.

plan of government without further reference to Philadelphia.[21]

Soon the yeast of the May 10-15 resolutions completed its
work. These measures provided the additional leaven needed
in Pennsylvania, where a profound social and political ferment
was approaching culmination, to raise partisans of independence to power. Completely replacing the Assembly, the Provincial Convention quickly swung this keystone in the colonial
arch to support separation and issued a call for a state constitutional convention. And other colonies dispatched to
Philadelphia fresh instructions authorizing the final step.
Without dissenting vote the Continental Congress accepted
the Declaration of Independence on July 2, although New
York (which did not sanction approval until July 9) refrained
from voting. On July 4 Congress ordered the document authenticated and printed.[22]

V. THE CONFEDERATION

THE ADOPTION OF THE ARTICLES

Simultaneously the Continental Congress began to put its
informal structure on a constitutional basis. Having rebuffed
proposals in 1775 to form a permanent union, delegates now
overwhelmingly supported the confederation proposed on
June 7 along with independence. The draft scheme submitted
to Congress owed most to John Dickinson and then Benjamin
Franklin. The Committee of the Whole discussed this for nearly
a month before agreeing on revisions. This deliberation foreshadowed that in the Federal Convention. In debate on the
main issues of representation, taxation, and disposition of
Western land, unequal states claimed equality. Compromise

21 See pp. 30-32.
22 See pp. 33-38.

was necessary on the subjects of voting and slave representation. Belief that it was "confederate or perish" held delegates to their arduous task. Underlying the formation of this confederation was an assumption that the Declaration of Independence had created not only the several states but also the United States, and that the Continental Congress was "as much a provisional government for the nation as the provincial congresses were for the states." [1] Certainly Dickinson's original draft scheme subordinated the individual states to the general government.[2]

But the Articles of Confederation met obstacles which delayed their adoption, and the rise of particularism after 1776 stimulated hostility to the idea of a unified central government which led to a revision featuring the principle of state sovereignty.[3] Inflation and monetary collapse brought diminished confidence in the government which normally sat in Philadelphia. Some states feared loss of their political power. Others without Western land (especially Maryland and New Jersey) hoped to retain parity with more fortunate neighbors (Massachusetts, Connecticut, New York, Virginia, North and South Carolina, and Georgia) by refusing to accept the Articles until Congress was made beneficiary of this rich resource for the common good. After 1779, Maryland alone held out, and neighboring Virginia, as the last to surrender its territory, proved her most formidable antagonist. However, early in 1781, motivated partly by the prevalent belief that large republics could not successfully endure, Virginia sought to

[1] Morgan, *Birth of the Republic*, p. 103.

[2] Burnett, *Continental Congress*, pp. 213-29; *Journals of the Continental Congress* (Ford, ed.), V, 546-54, 674-89.

[3] Thomas Burke of North Carolina led this movement for state sovereignty. His comments as quoted by Irving Brant, as well as Brant's entire "Letter to the Editor" in the *William and Mary Quarterly*, 3 ser. XV (January, 1958), 137-39 are vital to the subject of American nationhood at the time of the Revolution. Brant maintains there is a mountain of evidence to dispose of the contention that thirteen separate independent states were envisioned. On the James Rankin Brant mentions, see also Selsam, *Pennsylvania Constitution*, p. 125.

enhance its future by ceding its large Western domain to Congress. Maryland then capitulated, with assistance of pressure to do so from land speculators and Edmond Charles Genêt, the French Minister to the United States, who both desired, though for different reasons, adoption of the Articles of Confederation.[4] Thus on March 1, nearly five years after initially being proposed, the new government went into effect.[5]

As the direct precursor of the Constitution of 1787, the earlier frame provided much timber used in the edifice fashioned by the Framers. Yet the governmental structure of this document differed radically both from that of the state constitutions which were emerging simultaneously, and the later federal instrument. The Articles mirrored the fact that they were proposed for a Continental Congress which had started as a league of separate colonies or states. This first federal charter conferred much power on the central government, most of which the Constitution of 1787 incorporated intact. Yet the Confederation lacked the vital powers of taxation and control of commerce, and enforcement of others was left to the states, which often proved unwilling. Moreover, power was not separated among various branches of government. There was neither an executive possessing authority nor a judiciary department, which threw everything into the hands of Congress, a unicameral legislative assembly. Need for nine states to approve important measures impeded action, especially when centrifugal tendencies reduced attendance in the Continental Congress. And change was impossible, because amendment required unanimity.

If symbolically anticipated by the Stamp Act Congress, government under the Articles grew directly out of the First and Second Continental Congresses. The latter accomplished much in the interval from 1775 until replaced in 1781. For a year it conducted war before finally declaring independence, after which, while still conducting hostilities, it secured for-

4 See pp. 41-53.

5 Burnett, *Continental Congress*, pp. 248-58, 472-501; Morgan, *Birth of the Republic*, pp. 101-12.

eign alliances and adoption of the constitution which now provided a supposedly permanent foundation. Most Americans agreed with Locke that dissolution of government (ties with Britain) had not thrown people back into a state of nature. The transition from colonies into independent states had been under the aegis of the Continental Congress, and despite particularism and assertions of state primacy, the central government was widely recognized as the controlling political body in America. Such an agency was essential to pursuance of common concerns, and it had successfully brought the war nearly to an end.

THE CENTRAL GOVERNMENT UNDER THE ARTICLES

Government under the Articles of Confederation of 1781 forms the immediate background to the Federal Convention and the foundation of the union until 1789. Long known as the "critical period," these years remain the subject of lively controversy. Historians have offered a variety of reasons to explain just what was critical. Often their interpretations have been conditioned by attitudes toward the Constitution of 1787. These conflicting outlooks cannot now be rehearsed. The viewpoint taken here is that despite the achievements of the Confederation Congress under the Articles, the American constitutional system broke down in the years from 1781 to 1787 at both the national and the local level, thus making constitutional reform desirable if not mandatory.

The Articles must be assessed as a stage in the evolution from localism to nationalism. The closest confederation yet known in history, provision was made for tightening political and social bonds. The Congress was conspicuously successful in its Western land policy. In the Northwest Ordinance of 1787, the text of which is not included here, delegates emphasized equality of persons and states, thus keeping faith with Revolutionary principles and encouraging liberality in the Convention debate then under way in Philadelphia. In foreign relations as well as in economic and commercial affairs, developments over which the central organ had little or no control enormously aggravated genuine weaknesses under the Articles. Thus a sharp economic slump which set in after the war (by 1784) brought considerable distress, and during the depth of the despair—the summer of 1786—a wave of complaint began to inundate both the Articles and the Confederation Congress. This setback further complicated an already difficult situation. Driven in upon themselves, states erected trade barriers which only accentuated their problems. And Congress, lacking both funds and power to tax, pleaded for money as it suffered progressive anemia resulting from the inability or unwillingness of states to remit assigned quotas. By 1786, after repeated attempts to obtain a five per cent impost, all states had finally approved except New York. This selfish dissident, profiting from tribute levied on Connecticut and New Jersey, prevented united action. The Continental Congress was powerless to correct the situation. Thus despite the credits attributable to the government after 1781 the debits were real and large. These created a steady, concerted clamor to replace the Articles of 1781, whose defects seemed all the greater because of the situation within the states.

PROBLEMS OF THE STATES

The main troubles in the new nation in the years immediately preceding 1787 arose within the states. This created a demand for reform at the local level as well as aggravating the desire for reconstruction of the Confederation government. Although the task of revision involved fourteen separate political units, keen minds realized that the American political system was ultimately one and that a lasting solution to the vexatious problems would have to treat it accordingly. To understand the state abuses and the growth of the idea of unity it is essential to start by looking at the first frames of state government.

The State Constitutions

The most eventful constitution-making epoch in American history occurred at the time of separation from Great Britain. In the crucial half year of 1776 before America declared independence, four colonies adopted new basic codes.[6] New Hampshire and South Carolina, both of whom intended theirs to last only until reconciliation, led the procession, followed by Virginia—which adopted the first permanent state constitution on June 29, 1776—and New Jersey. By the end of the year, Pennsylvania, Maryland, Delaware, and North Carolina followed suit. Georgia and New York joined step in February and April of 1777 respectively. Connecticut and Rhode Island merely employed their cherished patents as "new" fundamental laws. Apart from Massachusetts, which retained its charter until 1780, the whole cycle was completed in sixteen months.

As mentioned above, this transition from temporary to permanent governments based on written documents represents a decisive step in American constitutional development. The new instruments link the structural outline of the colonial institutions with that of the central government under the Constitution of 1787. Yet this relationship is not always simple and direct. The state constitutions, each of which drew on the heritage of the particular colony involved, contain both details and general principles on which the Federal Convention delegates heavily relied. But often in the years after 1776 states gave only lip service to their expressed ideals, and even these often modified the older tradition in the light of the dispute with Britain. A decade of experience with defects and shortcomings of these American state constitutions proved a valuable school for those assembled in Philadelphia in 1787.

Growing naturally out of the colonial past, the new state charters emerged speedily, often in a matter of only weeks. Of

6 Morey, "First State Constitutions," *op. cit.;* Webster, "State Constitutions of the Revolution," *op. cit.,* pp. 380-420; Nevins, *American States,* pp. 117-70; Wright, "Origins of Separation," *op. cit.,* pp. 176-79.

course the machinery of construction was familiar. The colonies used their regular legislative assemblies, since the device of the constitutional convention was not devised until 1778 by New Hampshire (in replacing its temporary 1776 constitution) and given more prominence by Massachusetts in 1779. The choice of lawmakers fell to the electorate, and the fact that most white American males undoubtedly possessed the right to vote shows that the people possessed all power in the new order. They selected many able delegates whose duties included all the tasks of a legislative body during wartime plus the extraordinary job of constitution-making. Hence committees, often one for the frame of government and another for the bill of rights, received instructions to submit draft proposals. As a result a few or even one man—as with Mason in Virginia—sometimes largely authored these. After adoption by the representatives, the new documents were not referred to the people for ratification. Thus the first constitutions ranked with ordinary legislative enactments and could therefore be easily superseded by subsequent statutes. They lacked the character of fundamental law. This violation of the social contract theory, arising primarily from ignorance of its proper principles, initiated controversies which the Framers determined to avoid.

Moreover, other inheritances from the past facilitated the work of devising new codes for the states. No one needed to invent a philosophical justification for the instruments being devised, since the theory of social compact and of natural right was already an integral part of American thought. And the tripartite separation of governmental powers which had grown up in the colonies and found defenders in Locke, Blackstone, and especially Montesquieu, provided at least a base from which to start in elaborating the structure of new governments.

But there was no slavish imitation of the past. Confronting experience directly, incipient states often undermined such theories as balanced government and the separation of powers. Colonial political arrangements, paralleling the mixed-monarchy of seventeenth-century England, specifically provided for representation of various classes in society as a means of achieving stability. But the constitutions of 1776-77, despite attempting to institutionalize some balance by means of suffrage and office-holding requirements, shifted the bulk of power to the people as a whole.

Nor did events surrounding the assertion of independence facilitate a real separation of powers. Based on their previous acquaintance with the practice as well as the classical defense of Montesquieu, which became widely known in the colonies between 1748 and 1776,[7] several states, but not all, specifically endorsed the principle in their new constitutions. Writings by John Adams did much to facilitate adoption of these ideas.[8] Later, Massachusetts rejected a proposed constitution in 1778 partly because it provided no adequate separation of powers. Nevertheless, the decade following 1776 witnessed only superficial employment of the doctrine of checks and balances. King George III and his provincial governors had destroyed beyond immediate repair any possibility of achieving balance through a strong executive. And legislatures brooked little restraint. It took a decade of experience before the teaching of Montesquieu could be exalted in the Federal Convention.

As worked out, attachment to the principles of balanced government and separated powers resulted in establishing in almost all states single executive officers with property qualifications higher than for any other post. South Carolina imposed a £10,000 requirement. And even so, gubernatorial chairs were weak. The executive (called "president" in four states) was elected in eight instances by the legislature, and in

---

[7] Spurlin, *Montesquieu*, pp. 46-98. Emphasis should be laid on the fact that although Montesquieu was the most popular and important theorist of the separation of powers for America, other writers widely read in the colonies—such as Harrington, Locke, and Blackstone—also defended the doctrine.

[8] Especially Adams' *Thoughts on Government*, which is found in his *Works*, IV, 193-200, or in Peek, ed., *Political Writings*, pp. 84-92; and see Nevins, *American States*, pp. 121-126; Adams, *Works*, I, 208-10; IV, 185-87.

six the governor shared appointive power with that body. Usually executives served only a one-year term and possessed no veto power. In North Carolina the chief magistrate exercised almost his complete authority in signing a receipt for his salary.

Nor were judges a check on the legislature. The judiciary branch, despite its growth since early colonial days into a separate department of importance, was no match for the lawmakers. During the Revolutionary decade the regular court system, lawyers, and law codes were often nonexistent or inadequate, and usually judges appointed by the legislature or the governor held office during good behavior. Since the practice of judicial review made no appearance until 1780 and then only rarely before 1787, the fundamental law could not be invoked by judges to curb legislative excesses.

Moving into the void left by royal authority, legislatures seized power under the sanction of the social contract theory. For the time being people who viewed fundamental law as the positive enactment of human will as inscribed in a constitution saw no reason to limit themselves when they spoke through a representative body based on a written frame of government. The need to possess property in order to share the loaves and fishes of power excluded few, and thus the newly exalted people became heady with their authority. When lawmaking bodies absorbed executive and judicial functions as well as their own, and in addition proved careless of popular rights, a demand arose for reaffirmation of constitutionalism. This led to reform of the state constitutions and the meeting in Philadelphia.

Among institutional checks designed to restrain the representative will, bicameralism was most important. This arrangement was already familiar in the colonies, as we have noted earlier. The continuity of the historical legacy is demonstrated by the fact that all states retained bicameralism except Pennsylvania and Georgia, which perpetuated the unicameral legislatures they had long enjoyed. The substitution of elective senates for the old appointive governors' councils required constitutional innovation, including creation of bodies to advise the chief executives. John Adams, a Harringtonian and strong advocate of checks and balances, urged erection of strong upper houses. In conferring power on these organs, the constitutions demonstrated an ambivalent attitude toward the whole concept of balanced government. If second chambers were to represent property rights, as higher qualifications for senate than for house membership indicated, the requirements for electors of the two bodies were nevertheless the same or almost the same. Moreover, popular assemblies representing the whole people possessed power to tax, thus vindicating a principle of the Revolution, and in nine instances the sole authority to initiate money bills. Thus within the legislature the lower house dominated. However, rotation limited possible abuses by making legislators stand for election annually in every state except three—two of which had semiannual elections.[9] But above all, there was a more basic safeguard—the bill of rights.

Believing that the guarantees contained in colonial charters, law codes, and common law inadequately protected rights, lawmakers desired to provide safeguards. It has been suggested that eagerness to preserve religious liberty from legislative interference actuated Americans to insist on defining their rights.[10] While this was undoubtedly important, certainly the rights asserted in the documents produced by colonials in the clash with Parliament and king in the years from 1765 to 1776 also were significant. Then too, and perhaps above all else, statesmen wished to transmute natural into civil rights and enshrine these in their fundamental law—the written constitution. George Mason authored the first state bill of rights, which Virginia adopted on June 12, 1776, before accepting the constitution whose original draft Mason also wrote. For

[9] Morey, "First State Constitutions," *op. cit.;* Webster, "State Constitutions of the Revolution," *op. cit.,* pp. 380-420; Nevins, *American States,* pp. 117-70; Wright, "Origins of Separation," *op. cit., passim.*

[10] Georg Jellinek, *The Declaration of the Rights of Man and of Citizens* (New York, 1901), pp. 59-77.

both, this apostle of Enlightenment drew deeply on English and American experience. Seven states followed Virginia in prefacing their constitutions with explicit statements of rights, while others incorporated similar guarantees within the text of the document itself. The people of Massachusetts, after rejecting one proposed document lacking such a bill, adopted another containing this feature. By 1784, when New Hampshire fell in line, all states possessed such bastions of liberty. When the Constitution of 1787 went to the states for ratification, agitation for amendments to it revived the concern for rights at the national level.[11]

In addition to these broad outlines, the state constitutions incorporated other institutional devices which afforded precedents for the deliberations in 1787. The Pennsylvania instrument provided a plural executive and unsalaried public service. And also, for seven years the basic law was not to be altered, after which a Council of Censors was to inquire whether the governmental frame had been violated. Somewhat similarly, New York empowered a Council of Revision to alter, on grounds of unconstitutionality or inexpediency, all bills about to become law. In reflecting the belief that a legislature could judge the constitutionality of its acts, these organs perpetuated the confusion between statutory and fundamental law. In New York also a Council of Appointment was able to hamstring the governor's selection of subordinates. Maryland created an electoral college to select its senate. Massachusetts first inaugurated the practice of referring its constitution to the people for ratification, unsuccessfully in 1778 and successfully in 1780.

Government in the States

Experience soon demonstrated serious flaws both of structure and underlying philosophy in these first documents. The

11 Hugh Blair Grigsby, *The Virginia Convention of 1776* (Richmond, 1855), pp. 161-67; Chafee, *Human Rights*, pp. 18-25; Rutland, *Bill of Rights*, pp. 24-40; Webster, "Comparative Study," *op. cit.*, pp. 384-89.

gravest defect arose from the unrestrained acts of legislatures. On the one hand organs for checking them were lacking: the executive branch was a frail reed and judges possessed no authority to speak with finality on questions of law. On the other was the doctrine of legislative supremacy. Although anticipated when colonial assemblies triumphed over royal governors, this manifested itself especially after power shifted from the British Crown to the American people, who delegated it to elected representatives. By this time the ascendant practice had been popularized and justified by Sir William Blackstone, nearly two and a half thousand copies of whose *Commentaries* arrived in America before 1776. Throughout the eighteenth century Parliament gradually consolidated the victory it achieved in the Revolution of 1688, and at Oxford in the middle of that century Blackstone taught that the law-making power was uncontrollable. His praise of the natural law as a fixed standard which could limit all power was largely supererogatory, a concession to the past. His emphasis was not on the objective content but rather on the source of legislation: viewing law as the positive expression of human desire, he made the representatives of the people supreme.[12]

In America results were for a decade often unfortunate, but of greatest value in shaping the Constitution of 1787. In relations between the two levels of government, the Blackstonian doctrine undoubtedly inspired the dogma of state particularism which undercut the unity noted at the time of separation from Britain. And along with the absence of other organs to check the assemblies, Blackstone helped enthrone the legislatures, which then played tyrant. Jefferson, observing as early as 1781 the concentration of all power in the same hands, equated this with despotism and warned that not even *elective* despotism had been the aim of the Revolution. He wanted power distributed among three governmental branches so that they could balance each other. The Pennsylvania

[12] Corwin, " 'Higher Law' Doctrine," *op. cit.*, pp. 405-09; Adams, *Political Ideas*, chs. 7-8; Warren, *American Bar*, pp. 177-80; Corwin, "Progress of Constitutional Theory," *op. cit.*, pp. 517-27.

Council of Censors in 1784 reported that lawmakers there had violated both the constitution and the bill of rights. In New Hampshire separated powers had been intermixed.[13] From Europe John Adams noted these failings. In his *Defence of the Constitutions of Government of the United States of America,* a reply to Turgot's criticism of the state constitutions for attempting to divide rather than concentrate power, Adams reasserted his belief in checks and balances. (His ideas arrived just in time to make an impression on delegates in the Federal Convention.)[14] In short, as Madison and others insisted in the Constitutional debate, the decade demonstrated all the evils resulting from a "tendency in the Legislature to absorb all power into its vortex."[15]

The most flagrant abuses were connected with social and economic problems arising when the hard times of 1784 to 1786 exacerbated creditor-debtor relations. Every state witnessed struggles for legislative relief in the form of reduced

[13] Thomas Jefferson, *Notes on the State of Virginia,* William Peden, ed. (Chapel Hill, 1955), p. 120. Jefferson began writing this work in October, 1780, and his manuscript was virtually complete by the following August. Peden, pp. xii-xiv. Nevins, *American States,* pp. 164-70. Corwin, "Progress of Constitutional Theory," *op. cit.,* pp. 514-15, 519-20.

[14] In a letter to Richard Price written on March 22, 1778, the Frenchman Turgot blamed the American states for imitating English usages in devising their new constitutions. He argued for unitary control of the state rather than the separation of power. Price published the letter in London in 1784, and in September, 1786, Adams began collecting materials to answer Turgot and defend the state constitutions. Although proceeding rapidly, he felt that Shays' Rebellion necessitated that he publish at once. Hence the first volume of his prolix rebuttal appeared early in 1787, in time to circulate among those in the Constitutional Convention. Madison referred unkindly to the work but admitted that it would become a powerful engine in forming public opinion. Adams, *Works,* I, 426-35; IV, 269-VI, 220; Alfred Iacuzzi, *John Adams, Scholar* (New York, 1952), pp. 60-61, 94, 188; Charles Warren, *The Making of the Constitution* (Cambridge, 1947), pp. 155-57, 815-18; Corwin, "Progress of Constitutional Theory," *op. cit.,* 520-21.

[15] Madison on July 21. See p. 236. See also discussion on pp. 225-26.

tax burdens, the staying of foreclosures, issuance of paper money and legal tender acts. "Rag-money" parties, as the adherents of paper money were called, won out in seven states by 1786. In Rhode Island creditors fled debtors when the legislature decreed its own worthless currency legal tender. Then lawmakers defied the state supreme court which declared this act unconstitutional. Discontent in Massachusetts swelled after the General Court adjourned in July, 1786, without affording desired relief. Insurgents combined to denounce artificers of their plight and sought relief by preventing courts from sitting. Daniel Shays, a veteran and ex-captain of the Revolution, found himself the leader of an armed host. The state mobilized militia, and civil war wracked Massachusetts during the autumn and winter of 1786-87. Symbolizing and climaxing excesses in other states, this rebellion sent a shiver of terror through the nation. Social disorder imperiled property and other rights alike, thus jeopardizing the fruits of independence.

The Road to Reform

Hence a difficult situation confronted the young republic both on the national and local scene. Remedy was sought by amending the state constitutions and new-modeling the Articles of Confederation. But were these two separate tasks, or merely different sides of the same coin? Could one political organ protect the federal and state governments and the people as well from disruptive factions such as Shays's rebels? By Convention eve a fertile mind like Madison's concluded that safeguarding private rights and invigorating the central government were essentially one problem.[16]

[16] Nevins, *American States*, pp. 171-96; Corwin, "Progress of Constitutional Theory," *op. cit.*, 532-36. On the eve of the meeting in Philadelphia, Madison wrote a paper on existing evils which he entitled "Vices of the Political System of the United States," significantly referring to *one* system. James Madison, *Writings*, Gaillard Hunt, ed. (9 vols., New York,

Reforms occurring within the states before 1787 laid important foundations on which the Framers built. These helped restore balance in line with the older practice as well as the theory of separated powers.[17] One achievement, which contributed to creation of the presidential system in the Federal Convention, was to shore up the executive office through amendments granting veto power. A second was judicial review, which grew, in the years from 1780 to 1786, both as a doctrine and as a practice, although by constitutional interpretation rather than amendment.

Concerning the *doctrine*, the central question was how both legislature and judiciary were limited in determining whose interpretation of law embodied in a supreme constitution is final. Gradually the view emerged which formed a starting point for the delegates in 1787: the judiciary possesses exclusive power to interpret with finality standing law, but the latter must meet the tests imposed by "higher" law— i.e., it must be intrinsically just. Legislatures erred when (as in Rhode Island) they interfered with the dispensation of justice through the courts. This confuted Blackstone, who exalted legal over moral obligation.

Moreover, the *practice* of judicial review buttressed the authority of the central government. Faced with state actions which undermined treaties made by the Confederation government with foreign powers, state judges (and other public spokesmen) announced that the national government possessed a perfect though limited power for purposes beyond

---

1900-10), II, 361-69; Irving Brant, *James Madison, The Nationalist, 1780-1787* (Indianapolis, 1948), pp. 411-14.

17 The separation now instituted actually exceeded that existing just before the Revolution, when the assemblies were dominant. Nevertheless, there was an older tradition to resume. This was compounded in part of the theoretical power to restrain the lower house which governors and councils along with the Privy Council and Crown had always possessed, and in part of the fact that until the assemblies became dominant a real separation was in effect.

the competence of any one state. Therefore a treaty bound the entire country without the consent of the individual legislatures, and state judiciaries were obligated to uphold it. Improved upon, this doctrine emerged as part of the "supreme law of the land" in Article VI of the Constitution of 1787.[18]

For a decade following Paine's call in 1776 for a "Continental Conference," the movement for national constitutional reform waxed and waned. Hamilton in 1780 seized a commanding position in the struggle for a strong union which he never relinquished despite adoption of the Articles of Confederation. But there was always much resistance to such schemes. Even as late as the dark days of August, 1786, Congress accepted with modification Charles Pinckney's resolutions to reorganize the government, but did not submit them to the states because amendment was impossible.[19] Jericho-like, the citadel of opposition withstood much marching and trumpet blowing.

Confronted with these seemingly impregnable walls, leaders of the movement for reform—whose chiefs included Washington, Hamilton, and Madison—turned to commercial problems. Always they hoped to generate a current of improvement whose vibrations would help clear the way to political betterment. Madison, tracing political and ultimately moral evils to distress arising from stagnant trade and economic depression, induced Virginia to treat with Maryland concerning jurisdiction and navigation of the Potomac. He also obtained a Virginia resolution inviting other states to attend a convention which met in Annapolis to restore commercial health.[20] When paucity of response to this bid indicated that such was impossible, Hamilton along with Madison converted the occasion into a vehicle of success by issuing a call which led to the Federal Convention some eight months later.[21] But despite

---

[18] Corwin, "Progress of Constitutional Theory," *op. cit.,* 527-32.

[19] Burnett, *Continental Congress,* pp. 663-65.

[20] See p. 54.

[21] See p. 57.

prolonged dissatisfaction which deepened in 1786, only three states responded by year's end in appointing delegates to assemble and devise provisions necessary "to render the constitution of the Federal Government adequate to the exigencies of the Union; . . ." [22] Thereupon the eruption of Shays' Rebellion applied a final smarting whip which soon hastened the naming of deputies. In February Congress itself recommended such a meeting.[23] And throughout the summer of 1787 the specter of the Massachusetts uprising haunted the State House chamber in Philadelphia.

Thus after a long period during which safeguards for rights and the institutions of self-government grew in the New World, two decades of crisis produced a rapid maturation in American political thought. At the outset of the conflict, colonials appealed to the fundamental law of the *status quo*. This meant enlisting their charters, common and statute law, and the English constitution to protect their rights, and particularly that of property. Then as the controversy deepened they shifted their argument so that it rested on the law of nature, expanding their conception of rights to include the rights of man, and thus emphasizing equality. Moreover, final separation from the mother country fostered nationalism, and with thirteen colonies seeking direction from one central government, a union older than the states was born. But then many difficulties subsequently beset the young republic. The Confederation Congress lacked vital powers and was weak, and the situation in the states bred trouble. Disruptive factions imperiled all rights. To many the new nation seemed on the verge of dissolution, and the quest for union arrested in its development.

Yet delegates who met to deal with this situation in the spring of 1787 could draw much on their heritage. In protecting and providing a new basis for the freedom which had already developed in the New World, the American Revolution

---

22 See pp. 59-62.
23 See pp. 63-64.

conserved the liberal tendencies in the national past. Now the Framers could enjoy the unique luxury of being conservative and liberal at the same time.[24]

VI. THE FEDERAL CONVENTION

THE MEN AND THEIR MEETING

On the appointed second Monday in May, too few delegates gathered in the State House in Philadelphia to commence deliberations. Hence the Constitutional Convention opened eleven days later, when representatives from a majority of states were on hand. Both contemporaries and posterity have agreed that the fifty-five men who attended the sessions (whose biographical sketches appear in Appendix I), included the most respectable characters in the United States. Even then, certain eminent Revolutionary figures were not there: Jefferson and Adams were in Europe on government missions; Richard Henry Lee, Patrick Henry, and Samuel Adams remained away.

Leading the distinguished group present was a creative, hard-working minority, the ablest of whom supported strong national and usually also popular government. These included Washington and Franklin, who loaned their prestige and made other important contributions as well, Madison and Wilson, the two most constructive members, and (Gouverneur) Morris, King, Randolph, and Mason. Hamilton co-

[24] Hence, for example, popular devotion to the state constitutions, whose earliest imperfections were removed by a wave of reform preceding the Federal Convention, facilitated and conditioned the work in Philadelphia. For detailed treatment of this subject, see Warren, *Making of the Constitution, passim.* On the relationship between conservatism and liberalism, see Louis Hartz, *The Liberal Tradition in America: An Interpretation of American Political Thought Since the Revolution* (New York, 1955).

operated in producing a system which he thought unsatisfactory but better than none.[1] Perhaps somewhat less talented than the best of the former men were prominent "small state" representatives, such as Paterson, Sherman, Ellsworth, and Dickinson. Certainly in helping transform a plan for national government into a federal system they were scarcely less important. Apparently some deputies made no or at best a slight mark on the proceedings, although they may have proved worthy in ways the available records do not reveal. A brief glance at the entire pattern of the proceedings should help illuminate the remainder of these introductory remarks.

The Convention met from May 25 through September 17, except for Sundays, one two-day adjournment over July 4 and another of eight working days between July 26 and August 6. Those present realized that the meeting was critical for America and republicanism. Valuing the role of intellect in human affairs, they desired rational discussion free from extraneous influences. Hence, to stifle distracting noise, delegates ordered the streets outside their chamber covered with earth. A resolution for secrecy—which meant neither impropriety nor cabal, though it resulted in sentry-guarded doors and closed windows —encouraged flexibility and frankness within and liberated participants from external pressures.[2] The average size of the working body was from thirty to forty (although not always the same men), and despite late arrivals, early departures, and absences, an inner core of regulars was in constant attendance.[3] Usually delegates met for a relatively brief but concentrated session from eleven to three o'clock. This kept evenings and mornings for other essentials—correspondence, re-

[1] The assertion of a recent biographer, Broadus Mitchell, that the psychological value of Hamilton's June 18 speech for consolidated national government was superior to substantive virtue, in that without his projection of dominant national authority the final instrument would have been more equivocal, seems to hit over the mark. Broadus Mitchell, *Alexander Hamilton, Youth to Maturity, 1755-1788* (New York, 1957), p. 392.

[2] Warren, *Making of the Constitution,* p. 627.

[3] Farrand says "forty or less" (*Records,* IJI, 586 f.n.), while Warren makes it "little more than thirty" (*Making of the Constitution,* p. 124).

laxation and society, and particularly the out-of-chamber politicking vital to the task at hand.

For the first two months delegates debated general principles of the new government, focusing on the Virginia resolutions and paying some attention to alternative plans offered by Paterson and Hamilton. Initial confidence in the Convention's ability to quickly produce effective government soon evaporated. Within a month came a call for prayer, and dissensions which threatened to wreck the proceedings produced deep despair. With the crisis passed, members charged the Committee of Detail with producing a draft constitution and in late July adjourned—it was their only real break from steady application—to await a report. This draft, which combined other materials, especially from the Articles and the state constitutions, with Convention recommendations, then received detailed examination for over a month after being submitted to the reassembled gathering on August 6.

During these hot days delegates complained of the length and tedium of proceedings and extended daily sessions an hour at each end to expedite things. Close confinement and constant association made members irritable, and they grew vexatious and skeptical of the outcome. However, a revised draft finally went to the Committee of Style and Arrangement, which reported on September 12. After additional inspection and last-minute correction, the Constitution was engrossed and on September 17 approved and referred to the Confederation Congress to be submitted for ratification. At the very end Franklin with characteristic felicity epitomized the work of the Convention with a symbol found within the chamber.[4]

THE TASK AND POWER OF THE FRAMERS

A weak Confederation and excesses in the states presented delegates with the age-old problem of reconciling liberty and authority. The need was to strengthen the central government

4 See p. 344.

and secure private rights against any temporary majority, which raised the problems of federalism and democracy. To rejuvenate the central government and use it in controlling popular disorders meant meshing that organ with thirteen independent political entities called states, since every delegate except two meant to preserve local self-government. And yet, though there was opposition to "the turbulence and follies of democracy," [5] which recent events—e.g., Shays's Rebellion—accentuated, Convention members had neither the desire nor the capacity to abolish so pervasive an institution. Possession of the franchise was widespread, extending in some states beyond property holders, and the Framers acknowledged that any reactionary innovation or disfranchisement would make the people unhappy. To create a federal system and restrain but not eliminate democracy was the task, and it assumed immense proportions.

While delegates knew that they must accommodate their results to the people, they wished also to erect the best government possible. Within the State House a difference of opinions as to what power the Convention possessed for this work raised fundamental issues. One faction insisted that deputies representing the states were authorized only to propose revision of the Articles and refer such to the state legislatures for consideration. This narrow though tenable viewpoint would make the union a league based on treaty, and thus revocable at will by participants. A second faction contended that members representing the whole people were at liberty to propose anything but conclude nothing. This outlook, necessitating ratification of the constitution by special conventions representing the people in the states, involved a permanent union resting on popular will. In following the latter method the Convention staged no revolutionary coup against the Confederation Congress, as has been asserted, but chose to form a social contract according to the accepted canon of eighteenth-century political philosophy.

[5] Randolph, May 31. See p. 87.

Although the tone of the Convention was pragmatic rather than abstract, representatives ransacked the ages for abstruse theories and ideas with which to illuminate their immediate problems. Inextricably entwined with practical concerns were basic premises drawn from the rich legacy of constitutionalism and other fields of thought bearing on man as a political animal. These facilitated discussion by giving participants a central pool of basic ideas and even a common vocabulary. Hence deliberations were often molded by material and ideological influences so fundamental that contemporaries did not make them explicit. Knowledge of these assumptions permits deeper penetration into the work of the constitution makers.

Material Interests

Naturally material interests were at work in Philadelphia. Considering property vital, the Framers agreed that government existed to secure such rights. But differences in types of property led to dispute. This was related to the vital clash arising out of sectional rather than large-small state differences. Human and natural resources, geography, climate, and the legacy of the past had all combined to produce different regions with special attachments. Thus carrying states opposed producing areas; upper and lower South pursued conflicting objectives concerning slavery, which the South as a whole defended; and some Easterners who feared depopulation and ultimate domination by new states tried to impede Western development. Numerous other interests exerted pressure. Inevitably selfish desire appeared in disguise before the Convention. Hence all of the debate must not be taken at face value. If the words are those of "sovereignty" and "liberty," the intent may be that of state rights or slave breeding.

Yet lofty expressions did not always mask baser motives. On the whole, the deliberators were a remarkably disinterested group.

View of Human Nature

In defining man's nature, delegates were heirs of the traditions of Protestant Christianity and the Enlightenment. A deeply ingrained pessimism rooted in the conception of man as sinner, especially as expounded by Calvin and Puritanism, was in the warp and woof of the religion that had dominated colonial America. Belief that the "carnal mind is at enmity with God" colors debate and illuminates the emphasis on checks and balances.[6] But it explains only part of the Framers' outlook. The conditions of life in the New World had constantly attenuated Calvinism, and the rise of rationalism, empiricism, and the Scottish common-sense philosophy in eighteenth-century America undermined older Christian orthodoxy. Reason, both as man's distinguishing faculty and as a quality of the universe, became pre-eminent. Yet since pure reason might mislead man (as both preacher and *philosophe* agreed), experience was its handmaid. Thus Dickinson's remark—"Experience must be our only guide. Reason may mislead us."[7]—does not, as often asserted, represent reaction

[6] Horace White (in the *Fortnightly Review*, October, 1879) as quoted by Coolidge, *Theoretical and Foreign Elements,* p. 54. White also said that the Constitution is based on the philosophy of Hobbes. While this is not true in any real sense, the delegates' profound desire to check the free play of passion may easily lead one to this conclusion.

[7] Dickinson made this remark on August 13 in connection with debate on money bills (Art. IV, Sec. 5 of the August 6 Report). He was contending that reason was limited, and had discovered neither such a mechanism as the English constitution nor trial by jury. He applied this to the point at issue by announcing that "experience verified the utility of restraining money bills to the immediate representatives of the people." The parallel between his thought and language and that of Hume in the latter's essay "Of the Rise and Progress of the Arts and Sciences" is worth noting:

To balance a large state or society, [said Hume] whether monarchical or republican, on general laws, is a work of so great difficulty, that no

against revolutionary liberalism. Delegates believed that man's capacity for reason made self-government possible, while his incapacity made it both a risk and, since no one man, or for that matter even any few men, could be entrusted with all power, also a necessity. This ambivalence permitted them to vary the emphasis as circumstances dictated.

View of Society

The Framers' attitude toward human nature and their belief that immutable laws governed relations between individuals and between man and the state also shaped their conceptions of society and government. Since by the law of nature man possessed reason and inalienable rights, the state—or society—was deemed separate from and anterior to government. Political authority belonged to the people, who formed society and then erected government, delegating power to the latter as a means of further protecting their rights. Although largely accepting Locke's interpretation of the social contract, delegates faced vexing problems in trying to apply the notion of compact to specific American conditions.

The Idea of a Constitution

To erect a government of laws rather than of men, the Convention embodied fundamental law in a written constitution. American history afforded ample precedent for this de-

---

human genius, however comprehensive, is able, by the mere dint of reason and reflection to effect it. The judgments of many must unite in this work: Experience must guide their labour: Time must bring it to perfection: And the feeling of inconveniencies must correct the mistakes, which they inevitably fall into, in their first trials and experiments.

This statement, which bears so directly on the problems of constitution-making, must have indelibly impressed many Framers besides Dickinson. Hamilton, for example, cites it in entirety in *The Federalist*, No. 85, where he italicized "inevitably." For the passage quoted see Hume, *Essays*, Green and Grose, eds., I, 185, or Hendel, ed., *Hume's Political Essays*, p. 117.

vice which permitted important principles to be made explicit. The law of the constitution was general and prospective. Containing only certain delegated powers (further distributed among separate branches to insure restraint), the written charter thus limited all government implicitly, and certain rights were further safeguarded by explicit guarantees. Hence the Constitution of 1787 prevented the national legislature from the supremacy which Parliament attained in England and which in the states had led to such evils. Two ideas concerning the nature of fundamental law converged in the Federal Constitution to establish this. One, in the tradition of Cicero, Coke, and Puritanism, held that it was not only basic but also "higher," and deserved to control because it embodied intrinsic justice. The other, deriving from conceptions of popular rule as stressed by Locke especially and also Blackstone, imputed supremacy to it because it emanated from the people's will.[8] The confluence of these streams in a written fundamental law marks a significant point in the history of constitutionalism.

The Ends of Constitutional Government

The men in Philadelphia believed that government under such an instrument existed to serve certain ends, the most inclusive and important of which was the dispensation of justice. However, discussion of this was usually couched in other terms—such as property and democracy. Wilson exalted the cultivation of the human mind over property as the primary object of government, while Madison was the most systematic and penetrating in considering property in material possessions.[9] Anticipating the tenth *Federalist* paper, he argued that

[8] Corwin, " 'Higher Law' Background," *op. cit., passim.*

[9] Wilson, July 13. The difference perpetuates the distinction initiated by Plato and Aristotle. See above, p. 217. There is also fleeting reference in the debates to happiness as an end of government. But the Constitution of 1787 does not institutionalize this part of the famous trinity stated by Jefferson in the Declaration of Independence. On the influence of

the greatest struggles in society would arise over property, since natural differences in men would inevitably lead them to accumulate unequal amounts. In insisting that government protect the natural right to property by preserving a free field for the inequality implanted in man by his Maker, Madison exalted liberty over equality. And delegates rendered unconstitutional future assaults on property, especially those coming from paper money and legal tender acts in the states. Moreover, they protected property in slaves. Government existed to protect rights also, but, as already noted, these were not then thought to need additional protection.

The Structure of Republican Government

The question of property touched on that of democracy, and both related to governmental structure. This involved not only such technical features as balanced and separated powers, but also elements in the pervasive spirit—republicanism, liberty, and virtue. For both, but especially the latter, Montesquieu's influence was of supreme importance. Although delegates often admired foreign laws and manners (especially the British constitution), an insistent Convention theme was that such were not applicable in America, where the people, as a result of their unique development, differed from any other people known in history. The fixed genius of the young nation was for liberty and a democratic republic in which the people ruled through representatives rather than directly, and to the spirit of these unwritten laws delegates were determined to accommodate their written constitution. Perhaps they would have come to this same conclusion had Montesquieu never lived, but the fact is that without mentioning his name in this respect they paid him repeated tribute by using his ideas and terminology.

Burlamaqui's idea of human happiness as an end of government, see Ray Forrest Harvey, *Jean Jacques Burlamaqui: A Liberal Tradition in American Constitutionalism* (Chapel Hill, 1937), pp. 14, 17 ff. See also Howard Mumford Jones, *The Pursuit of Happiness* (Cambridge, 1953).

Even so, commitment to a democratic republic was cautious. Certainly no one wanted another national government in which a unicameral legislature was practically the sole organ, nor state lawmaking bodies which tended to absorb and abuse all authority. Hence there was insistence on such institutional safeguards as balanced government and separation of powers, while an additional restraint arose from the necessities which dictated two levels of government in a federal system. The theory of balance exerted a potent and partially unwarranted influence in Philadelphia. The notion of government as a mechanical equipoise of powers which grew out of Newtonian thought captivated delegates (although but few employed metaphors comparing the national to the solar system). This is paradoxical: in England, the curve of acceptance of balanced government corresponds to the curve of acceptance of classical, system-building thought associated with mathematics and physics, while Convention members were empirical and historical in their outlook.[10] (The paradox is, of course, resolvable). Moreover, the essential purpose of mixed government had always been to draw the various organs from different sources, such as orders and estates. Madison contended in 1787 that the people were not yet homogeneous. But if Americans were all in or becoming part of the middle class, as Franklin and Charles Pinckney insisted, it would be difficult to give different orders power to defend their individual interests and restrain that of others.

Refusing to abandon completely this ancient notion, however, delegates integrated vestigial remnants of the theory of balanced government with the doctrine of separated powers. For the latter they resorted to their own colonial experience, agreeing on separation where this was clear, and compromising elsewhere. To secure guidance they resorted to theorists who, while recognizing the existence of independent judicial departments but not judicial review, emphasized the need to

[10] Pargellis, "Theory of Balanced Government," in Read, *Constitution Reconsidered*, p. 46.

keep legislative and executive powers distinct. Foremost among these was Montesquieu. Despite drawing heavily on the *Spirit of the Laws* (although the author's name was invoked only once for this purpose), the Framers were so eager to restrain the lawmaking branch that they were willing to violate the theory of separation by joining together executive and judiciary officials in a revisionary council.

The deputies brought to Philadelphia few clear ideas concerning the executive office, establishment of which proved to be the second most difficult problem in the Convention. The presidential system, rising slowly and laboriously, took final shape late in the proceedings. As for judicial review, the Framers referred only in general terms to state court decisions which illustrated the practice before 1787, and they did not specifically establish this novel doctrine in the Constitution. Yet comments of several delegates indicate comprehension of judicial review, and the Convention laid the essential basis for this cardinal bulwark against legislative supremacy. Finally, members combined in the first three articles of the fundamental charter a thorough system of checks and balances with some blending of the three separate governmental departments, but made no explicit reference to the theory involved.

Further to curb the legislature itself, the Convention overwhelmingly favored bicameralism (Franklin, Sherman, and perhaps Martin disagreed). This perpetuated the dominant earlier practice. With the first volume of John Adams' *Defence* to freshen their attachment to balanced government, many Framers envisioned creating a wealthy and aristocratic upper house capable of checking the leveling spirit of the popular chamber. And although they did establish a Senate which was more stable, more conservative and often more powerful than the House, the tide of life in America was running against these Old World notions. Try as it might, for example, the Convention proved unable to differentiate much between qualifications for Senators and Representatives.

Obstacles to Republican Government

Also influencing deliberations was the belief that construction of successful republican government faced nearly insurmountable difficulties. This rested on two facts: knowledge of the republican manners and amazing extent of the country, and the assumption that only small states could be republican (and thus well governed and the home of a happy people). Undoubtedly delegates drew the latter idea largely (and perhaps erroneously) from the *Spirit of the Laws,* although Rousseau was more clear in stressing the same point. Faction riddled states which were too small (Rhode Island, for example, was too small); the need for strength in large states, where governmental powers could not easily pervade the whole, led to tyranny (as history proved, witness George III). Wilson explicitly announced the dilemma on June 1, after which a shadow disturbed the Convention until solution came in the "confederated Republic" for which the Pennsylvanian called. Montesquieu had made this notion familiar in discussing the Lycian Confederacy, and division of America into local governmental units presented a sound basis for such federalism. But it was Madison who led the way to the solution, the key to which—enlarging the sphere of government—he found on the eve of the Convention in reading Hume.[11] Now, could history reverse its pattern and produce an executive of "con-

---

11 See above, p. xxxiv. Also see p. xl; Adair, "Hume, Madison, and Tenth *Federalist," op. cit.*

The essay which stimulated Madison was "Idea of a Perfect Commonwealth," in which Hume declared:

> We shall conclude this subject with observing the falsehood of the common opinion that no large state . . . could ever be modeled into a commonwealth, but that such a form of government can only take place in a city or small territory. The contrary seems probable. Though it is more difficult to form a republican government in an extensive country than in a city, there is more facility, when once it is formed, of preserving it steady and uniform without tumult and faction.

See Hume, *Essays,* Green and Grose, eds., I, 492, or Hendel, ed., *Hume's Political Essays,* p. 157.

tinental reputation" who would not be a tyrant? As presiding officer of the deliberations, Washington had ample opportunity to ponder that crucial question.

The Science of Man and Society

One further set of assumptions underlay all others, imparting a mood of confidence to the proceedings which offset anxiety or despair. This was the prevalent belief that the recent emergence of an empirical science concerning man and society gave delegates a new tool with which to shape their own destiny. In general this sprang from achievements of the scientific revolution and the Age of Enlightenment. But a closely knit group of moral philosophers of the Scottish Renaissance was particularly important in shaping these ideas in America. Among these were Frances Hutcheson, Adam Smith, Thomas Reid, Adam Ferguson, and Dugald Stewart. An independent although closely related figure was David Hume. The influence of the former centered in Princeton, which was then more of a national institution than Harvard, Yale, King's, or William and Mary. To the New Jersey institution the Scot John Witherspoon came as president in 1768, and there, besides the emphasis on Montesquieu introduced by the *émigré* teacher, the common-sense school of Scottish thought was featured. The significance of this is attested by the fact that Princeton sent nine of the twenty-five college graduates who attended the Convention, and Witherspoon signed diplomas for six of these. Other colleges also used the works of the Scottish moral philosophers, although Hume was anathema in educational centers. However, his *History* and *Essays* were presumably widely read in the colonies, and his ideas appear with and without attribution in Philadelphia.[12]

12 Bryson, *Man and Society*, pp. 1-29; W. S. Carpenter, "Political Education in the Time of John Witherspoon," *Princeton Alumni Weekly*, XXVIII (February 10, 1928), 487-90; Hendel, ed., *Hume's Political Essays*, pp. vii-lx; Adair, "Hume, Madison and Tenth *Federalist*," *op. cit.*; Varnum

The related elements in this outlook inspired confidence because they held out promise of rational control over human affairs. Exponents of this view started with the premise of a static society. They maintained that the nature of man, who was the foundation for all social relations and customs, was constant. Perhaps inconsistently, this conclusion was thought to afford a basis for the growth of a set of principles that could be applied to the solution of concrete situations, as Hume suggested in his essay, "That Politics May Be Reduced to a Science." Historical method was the clue to the enterprise, as Locke, Montesquieu, and Hume helped demonstrate. History afforded the rational investigator a body of experience which he could ransack for materials with which to form universally valid generalizations concerning human nature, political behavior, and the equilibrium of states. 'Thus it has been all the world over," said Morris, one of the many Framers who drew on the ages to illuminate the work of 1787. "So it will be among us." [13] Though young, this body of knowledge was expanding ("the *then* infancy of the science, of constitutions, and of confederacies," said Randolph of 1776),[14] and it contained hope for the future. In constructing a republic delegates avoided the "benighted" Middle Ages to draw guidance primarily from the ancients and moderns. Their knowledge was impressive in its breadth and accuracy, and moreover they *acted* on lessons from the past. For example, constitutional provisions pertaining to money bills, appropriations for the army, the president's oath, and office holding for legislators all sought to avoid specific evils observed in English development. These conceptions of the science of man and society underlay the conviction that Americans met as representatives of the whole human race to frame a system for the ages. Humanity's fate seemed to rest on their deliberations. Yet on the crucial problem—creation of a successful federation—history offered no precedent. Despite

Lansing Collins, *President Witherspoon: A Biography* (2 vols., Princeton, 1925), I, *passim;* Boorstin, *Mysterious Science,* pp. 31-61.

[13] Morris, July 2.

[14] Randolph, May 29. Italics mine.

their deep indebtedness to the past, they would therefore turn toward the present and the future. This "reversal of the time sense" [15] helps to charge the Federal Convention with drama and permanent significance.

THE WORK AND ACHIEVEMENT OF THE FRAMERS

The most difficult problem to confront the Framers merits a word of explanation. This, the battle for control of the central government, arose out of the attempt to establish national government and the need to determine its source of authority. The latter involved defining in its American setting the age-old problem of the locus of sovereignty. While there was never any serious question that the Virginia Plan introduced at the opening would be adopted, its resolutions concerning the rule of suffrage in the national legislature and making that body supreme over the states quickly aroused ˙ɔitter opposition. Although the word "national" was soon replaced, the real contest over the resolutions submitted by Randolph was never over how strong a government to create, but rather who should control the new establishment.

The immediate background to this contest for power, which involved important material interests and opposing interpretations of political philosophy, was the predominant Lockean theory and the legacy of the Revolution. The first attributed authority to the whole community; the second was responsible for different views as to just where this power had reverted when America declared independence: the whole people, the people of the states, or the states themselves, six of which avowed the doctrine of state sovereignty in their state constitutions. The political structure of the United States largely ruled out the former alternative, so that two conflicting schools dominated Convention thought. One favored

[15] Arthur M. Wilson attributes this phrase to Dean Christian Gauss of Princeton University in a review in *William and Mary Quarterly*, 3 ser. XIV (January, 1957), 93.

strong and popularly based government. Significantly, this contained the leaders and undoubtedly the best minds in Philadelphia, which of course does not validate the "rightness" of their views nor establish the "intention" of the Framers as a whole. The other threatened to wreck the proceedings unless it obtained a measure of equality for each state under the proposed constitution. With this assured by early July, the gravest crisis passed. Thus when members turned to consider how much power to grant the federal government, both groups, having received the means of self-defense, were able to face that problem without fear.

The strife over the basis of representation in the national legislature raised many important and lasting issues. The argument that authority lay with the people rather than the states emphasized popular sovereignty. And in the Convention suffrage based on wealth rather than numbers lost out repeatedly. Defense of proportional representation inevitably advanced the concept of democracy by furthering the principle of the equality of persons. Yet in the final result the states rather than the people were to be represented in one chamber. However, proponents of this dearly bought victory subsequently lost its advantage when the Convention made voting in the Senate per capita rather than by states. A government approaching the democratic and majoritarian principle was nevertheless limited, both by the "higher" law and the fact that all its powers were derived from the people, who did not delegate all their authority. The people conferred on the government certain powers but not sovereignty, although representatives in Philadelphia were confused or lacked understanding on this point. Even so, too great stress cannot be laid on the fact that, although the combined national-federal features of the Constitution prevented the government from being as high-mounted as many Framers wished, in 1787 Convention leaders insisted that the states were political societies entitled to rights, but not separate entities possessing sovereignty. These spokesmen, who met opposition from some colleagues, wished definitely to subordinate the states, but they did not, with two exceptions, desire to destroy the states. The result was to incorporate separate subordinate political units within the federal system. Failure to announce explicitly in the Constitution where sovereignty lay gave rise subsequently to prolonged and bitter controversy. This helped bring on the War for Southern Independence and continues to trouble relations between the federal and state governments until today.

The achievement of the constitution-makers was to blend old and new features in the fundamental law which they proposed for ratification. Members reached far back through time to bring lessons of the past to bear upon pressing contemporary problems. Although extremely practical in their approach, they nevertheless constantly invoked both European history and European theorists to illuminate their way. While the document produced in Philadelphia owes a heavy debt to the rich constitutional inheritance antedating New World beginnings, it is primarily a product of American growth—a skillful synthesis of mainly indigenous elements, drawn mostly from existing state constitutions, but also from the Articles of Confederation and other native sources as well as experience.

Not only was it an act of creative statesmanship to combine these materials into fresh combinations, but the Framers also, in devising original solutions to unique problems, transcended the point to which history and experience had brought them. Perhaps the most important of these innovations was the federal union. For this history knew no precedent, although previous structures had borne similar names and certain resemblances. Rather than a loose federation depending on force to coerce member states, the new federal-national system was to operate directly on individuals. This, plus the judicial power of the central government, made the proposed unit the first federation ever to find a peaceful means of securing the obedience of states. Could this confederated republic, unlike all predecessors, prove successful?

Moreover, other novel features characterized the Constitution as the basis of a federation. Among these were provisions assuring the federal government an independent and adequate revenue and control of all external and interstate commerce, a refusal to allow individual states to make treaties with foreign powers or each other, a willingness by the supreme government to dispossess itself of territory under its exclusive control, and readiness to leave the separate states unreserved power over internal police. Likewise, proportional representation in the lower house was original as applied to a federation. In effect, the American federal union was a new form of government.

The presidential system established in Philadelphia was also new. Creation of a separate executive branch, which other federations had lacked, followed the practice in the American states and in various monarchies. Yet the chief magistracy as established in the Constitution was unique: the office was more powerful than that of the state governors and yet denied the special claims to authority possessed by royal rulers. Delegates who feared both impotence and tyranny rejected both the idea of a plural executive and of a king. Yet they provided for a powerful president whom they denied support by an executive council or council of revision, and this isolated official they subjected to checks by two other branches of government.

In one of these the Convention made still further innovations. Having denied Congress power to negative state laws, the Framers made the Constitution along with federal enactments and treaties the supreme law of the land and gave the judicial branch coextensive authority to hear cases which arose. Hence the written charter enabled the federal courts to become the guardian of public welfare by preserving the constitutionality of fundamental and statutory law and protecting the rights of the people.

Finally, the guiding principles of the federal union were new as applied to such a political organization, or such fresh statements of older themes as to appear novel. For in spirit the proposed American government was republican and even democratic, and the implicit corollary was the need for virtue in the people who would attempt to make it work. It was in these people and the fundamental or "higher" law, and not in priests or kings or legislative assembles, that absolute power was to rest.[16]

VII. THE RATIFICATION STRUGGLE

The Problem of Ratification

When the Framers decided in effect that they were empowered to propose everything but conclude nothing, they raised two related questions. Who was to pass on their recommendations? How was the new government to be put into operation? The former was a substantive issue which merited a separate article in the final Constitution.[1] Some delegates, ostensibly on grounds that the Articles of Confederation declared the union to be perpetual and changeable only upon unanimous consent, insisted that the completed document be referred to the rapidly expiring Congress for approval. Since this promised certain defeat, others demanded that it be sent to the old government merely for submission to the states. Here specially called conventions, a device recently popularized in Massachusetts, were to act. Acceptance by the people in nine of these was to be sufficient for establishing the Constitution between those ratifying, a provision which avoided the old unanimity rule and allowed jealous state officials to be neutralized. But more fundamental principles were involved, as Madison especially insisted. Since the new govern-

16 Albert Bushnell Hart, *Introduction to the Study of Federal Government*, Harvard Historical Monographs No. 2 (Boston, 1891), 50; James Harvey Robinson, "The Original and Derived Features of the Constitution," *Annals of the American Academy of Political and Social Science*, I (1890-1891), 203-43.

1 The last three articles of the August 6 Report of the Committee of Detail indicate solutions then proposed to the problems of ratification and establishing government under the Constitution. See p. 269.

ment drew its authority from the people and was to operate on individuals, the Constitution must meet their approval. Moreover, a league was a structure made by treaty, and what participant states could create by ratification they could destroy by withdrawal; a constitution, however, was a compact made by the people, and once made was irrevocable (except by the process provided, or in defense of inalienable rights). The latter views triumphed, as the seventh article of the complete instrument testifies.[2]

Chairman Washington dispatched this to Congress with a covering letter dated September 17.[3] This illuminating document, which Madison may well have authored,[4] succinctly summarized the tone and results of the Convention. It underscored the role of compromise and implicitly announced the social contract and natural rights philosophies. Its pervading spirit breathed nationalism, and its emphasis on the attempt of delegates to reconcile the welfare of each (both individuals and states) with that of all is a link between the Greek origins of Western political thought and the realization of justice in organized political society.

The Contest over the Constitution

The struggle over adoption began when Congress forwarded the Constitution for ratification in late September.[5] Then began the real attack on the work of the Framers, an assault which by comparison dwarfs the opposition voiced in Philadelphia. Because the forces which produced them long antedated adjournment of the Convention, two factions quickly emerged to contest the Constitution. Antifederalists tended to be older in age than their foes, which perhaps helps to ex-

---

[2] On September 13 the Convention cast into the form of resolutions the instructions for putting the new government into effect. These were in essence the last three articles of the August 6 Report, minus what became Article VII.

[3] See pp. 363-4.

[4] Brant, *Madison, Father of the Constitution*, p. 147.

[5] See pp. 366-74.

plain their more inflexible commitment to the republicanism of 1776. Although the Federalists later gained prestige from attachment to a winning cause, they did not always have the better arguments. And yet we need not believe that only high and correct principles motivated opponents of the proposed government. It is possible to argue that both sides were "right" and neither "wrong," but then it is also inescapable that the Constitution's foes looked to the past and its supporters to the future. At any rate, the battle between these contending forces is, as Madison suggested, one of the places where a key to the true sense of the Philadelphia document is to be found.[6] Unfortunately, neither this dispute nor the Antifederalists themselves have received from scholars the attention they merit. History tends to ignore and even scorn losers.[7]

The conflict over ratification lasted some ten months.[8] The initial attempt to win seats in the conventions prompted only about one sixth of the adult white males, most of whom were undoubtedly eligible, to vote for delegates. But for the most part people watched the progress of the Constitution carefully, and often close competition led to heated debate and bitter campaigns. Of the first five states to act, four returned easy victories for establishing the republic on a new foundation. But a sharp clash in Pennsylvania, where Antifederalists proposed fifteen amendments and adjournment to allow time for popular consideration, set the tone for what was to come. Obviously such a course might imperil everything gained.

The Antifederalists, who drew strength from many geographical areas and socioeconomic levels, offered diverse reasons for their opposition. The most important of these were fear of the strength of Congress, which they expressed primarily in terms of the taxing power, absence of provisions to safeguard individual rights, and doubts about the success of

[6] See above, p. xiv.

[7] On this subject see Cecilia M. Kenyon, ed., *The Antifederalists* (New York, 1966) and additional works listed in the Selected Bibliography of the present book.

[8] See p. 375.

republican government in such a large country. Underlying and imparting vigor to their entire case was the dread of consolidated government. Since citizens found it hard to understand the new system proposed, men like Patrick Henry could effectively play on their bewilderment and suspicion. Against such simple and convincing interpretations, Madison's more accurate and complex argument that the government was neither merely national nor merely federal but both—a representative federal republic—made slow headway. Although only fourteen years earlier members of the First Continental Congress had treated each other almost as delegates of different countries, the swift pace of events had outrun those who now insisted that the proffered replacement for the Confederation would be unable to legislate wisely for a nation of such diverse sections. And however brilliant or effective the opposition case, the Federalists possessed precisely what the men of lesser faith lacked—a completed instrument with which to launch a new union.

Early in 1788 the clashing forces experienced their most crucial struggle to date in Massachusetts. There a widely circulated letter written by George Mason, which warned against the document he had refused to sign, indicated the national scope of the contest. As that state pondered whether to refuse ratification or ratify conditionally, Washington's proposal—which was also Jefferson's—that the states adopt first and seek amendments later provided a solution. Each of the seven subsequent ratifying states except Maryland followed suit, with five of them stressing the need for immediate amendments. Thus Federalist leaders, who had hitherto faced the alternative of risking outright defeat or the calling of a second constitutional convention, were now in effect committed to work for such additions. These could be far reaching, as Massachusetts revealed. That state called for limitation of Congressional power by an explicit avowal that all powers not expressly delegated by the Constitution were to be reserved to the several states. This later became the Tenth Amendment.

Although New Hampshire's June 21 action enabled the

President of the Confederation Congress to announce (on July 2) that nine states had accepted the Constitution, no successful trial of the new government was assured until the vital states of Virginia and New York fell into line by close margins shortly after New Hampshire ratified. Along with John Jay, Hamilton and Madison defended the Constitution in a series of newspaper articles designed to influence the decision in New York. This practical effort resulted in a genuine classic of political thought in America—*The Federalist* papers. Despite ratification, New York adopted a circular letter recommending to the states a second constitutional convention. The favorable reception of this helps demonstrate the intensity of the opposition to the Constitution.

By midsummer of 1788 a successful trial of the Constitution was thus a certainty. Soon thereafter, to anticipate somewhat, the 1787 charter was amplified by ten amendments. Leaders in the First Congress who had been in the Philadelphia Convention and ratification assemblies moved quickly to redeem their pledge. On September 25 the Congress recommended to the states twelve amendments, of which ten went into effect on December 15, 1791. The first eight alone, which guaranteed individual rights, are properly the Bill of Rights. Despite the logical validity of the Federalists' contention that natural rights could not be alienated and that the individual was amply protected by safeguards existing in 1787, these eight articles did give the Courts something specific to rely upon in defending popular rights. Certainly history has vindicated the demand of Antifederalists. And although the word "national" had been dropped from the Virginia resolutions early in the Convention proceedings, the ninth and tenth amendments did much to revolutionize the government envisioned by the Framers by making it even more of a federal system.

The Congress of the Articles quietly passed into oblivion as the year 1788 waned. Congress transacted its last official business on October 10, after having arranged for inauguration of the new government. Elections for the forthcoming administration were held early in 1789, and the First Congress under the Constitution met on March 4 without a quorum. Yet the presence of fifty-four members who had served in the Federal Convention or the ratification meetings—all but seven of whom had favored the new instrument—was auspicious. After organization of the House and Senate in April, the latter counted the ballots for president and informed Washington of his unanimous choice. That heroic figure, after having had to borrow money to leave Mount Vernon, proceeded to New York City along a route garlanded and made noisy by enthusiastic crowds.

The chancellor of the state of New York administered the oath of inauguration on April 30, 1789. It was the eve of the French Revolution, which was to embroil not only Europe but also the United States, and Washington's administration would be especially momentous for the future of America. The government was fluid and plastic in his hands, since a Constitution silent or vague on many points meant that his decisions and actions would constitute precedents. His task was to preside over the destiny of the new nation and reap the harvest of the American Revolution, of which the supreme law embodied in the written Constitution was the choicest fruit.

Thus did the quarter century following the Stamp Act close. After declaring independence and establishing thirteen republican state governments, the new nation successfully fought a war to maintain its existence. In Philadelphia the Framers solved the problem of imperial organization by devising an enlightened colonial system, and they attempted to reconcile the interests of the many with those of the few—the rights of local communities with the claims of the central government and individual interests with those of the general welfare. The formation of the Constitution and inauguration of the government under this supreme law were an attempt to supplant the Articles of Confederation and provide a new and more effective basis of union.

Yet the Constitution was frankly an experiment. Although its authors largely avoided the hoary question of sovereignty to speak of authority, they carefully refrained from explicitly defining the relationship between the state and central governments. Whether the distribution of authority between the nation and states would prove satisfactory was unknown in 1789. But if the Constitution was an experiment, there is absolutely no evidence, as Professor McLaughlin wrote more than a half century ago, to support the notion that the Framers "believed they were simply entering into a new order of things in which the states would have the right, as before, to refuse obedience and to disregard obligations, or from which they could at any time quietly retire when they believed the Union did not suit their purposes." [9] A real and permanent union was intended and in time both were achieved. However, this should not blind one to the fact that twentieth-century Americans do not live under the Constitution as it was understood in 1787, 1789, or 1791. Not only have subsequent amendments been added, but even more important, the Constitution has been modified by the process of judicial interpretation which Chief Justice John Marshall first made so significant. And beyond this is the understanding of the Constitution as it exists in the minds and hearts of the people who live under it.

WINTON U. SOLBERG

[9] Andrew Cunningham McLaughlin, *The Confederation and the Constitution, 1783-1789* (New York, 1905), p. 314.

CONTENTS AND SOURCES OF DOCUMENTS
AND OTHER MATERIAL INCLUDED
IN THIS VOLUME

SELECTED BIBLIOGRAPHY

I. PRIMARY SOURCES

Cooke, Jacob E., ed. *The Federalist.* Middletown, Conn., 1961.

Farrand, Max, ed. *The Records of the Federal Convention of 1787.* Rev. ed., 4 vols. New Haven, 1937.

Ford, Worthington, C., et al., eds. *Journals of the Continental Congress, 1774–1789.* 34 vols. Washington, 1904–37.

Hunt, Gaillard, and James Brown Scott, eds. *The Debates in the Federal Convention of 1787.* New York, 1920.

Jensen, Merrill, John P. Kaminski, and Gaspare J. Saladino, eds. *The Documentary History of the Ratification of the Constitution.* 15 vols. Madison, 1976–.

Kenyon, Cecilia M., ed. *The Antifederalists.* Indianapolis, 1966.

Strayer, Joseph R., ed. *The Delegate from New York; or, Proceedings of the Federal Convention of 1787 from the Notes of John Lansing, Jr.* Princeton, 1939.

U.S. Congress. *Documents Illustrative of the Formation of the Union of the American States.* 69th Congress, 1st session, house document no. 398. Selected, arranged, and indexed by Charles C. Tansill. Washington, 1927.

II. SECONDARY SOURCES

Adair, Douglass. *Fame and the Founding Fathers: Essays by Douglass Adair.* Edited by Trevor Colbourn. New York, 1974.

Adams, Randolph G. *Political Ideas of the American Revolution: Britannic-American Contribution to the Problem of Imperial Organization, 1765–1775.* Durham, 1922.

Adams, Willi P. *The First American Constitutions: Republican Ideology and the Making of the State Constitutions in the Revolutionary Era.* Chapel Hill, 1980.

Bailyn, Bernard. *The Ideological Origins of the American Revolution.* Cambridge, Mass., 1967.

Baldwin, Alice M. *The New England Clergy and the American Revolution.* Durham, 1928.

Beard, Charles A. *The Supreme Court and the Constitution.* New York, 1912.

————. *An Economic Interpretation of the Constitution of the United States.* New York, 1913.

Becker, Carl. *The Declaration of Independence: A Study in the History of Political Ideas.* New York, 1922.

Brant, Irving. *James Madison, Father of the Constitution, 1787–1800.* Indianapolis, 1950.

Brown, Robert E. *Middle-Class Democracy and the Revolution in Massachusetts, 1691–1780.* Ithaca, 1955.

————. *Charles Beard and the Constitution: A Critical Analysis of "An Economic Interpretation of the Constitution."* Princeton, 1956.

Burnett, Edmund C. *The Continental Congress.* New York, 1941.

Burns, Edward McN. *James Madison, Philosopher of the Constitution.* New Burnswick, 1938.

Carpenter, William S. *The Development of American Political Thought.* Princeton, 1930.

Chafee, Zechariah, Jr. *How Human Rights Got into the Constitution.* Boston, 1952.

Conkin, Paul K. *Self-Evident Truths: Being a Discourse on the Origins and Development of the First Principles of American Government—Popular Sovereignty, Natural Rights, and Balance and Separation of Powers.* Bloomington, 1974.

Coolidge, Archibald C. *Theoretical and Foreign Elements in the Formation of the American Constitution.* Freiburg, 1892.

Corwin, Edward S. *Court over Constitution: A Study of Judicial Review as an Instrument of Popular Government.* Princeton, 1938.

————. "The 'Higher Law' Background of American Constitutional Law." *Harvard Law Review* 42 (1928–29): 149–85, 365–409.

————. *The President: Office and Powers, 1787–1957.* 4th rev. ed. New York, 1957.

————. "The Progress of Constitutional Theory between the Declaration of Independence and the Meeting of the Philadelphia Convention." *American Historical Review* 30 (1924–25): 511–36.

Dargo, George. *Roots of the Republic: A New Perspective on Early American Constitutionalism.* New York, 1974.

Douglass, Elisha P. *Rebels and Democrats: The Struggle for Equal Political Rights and Majority Rule during the American Revolution.* Chapel Hill, 1955.

Eidelberg, Paul. *The Philosophy of the American Constitution: A Reinterpretation of the Intentions of the Founding Fathers.* New York, 1968.

Epstein, David F. *The Political Theory of the Federalist.* Chicago, 1984.

Gwyn, W. B. *The Meaning of the Separation of Powers: An Analysis of the Doctrine from Its Origin to the Adoption of the United States Constitution.* Tulane Studies in Political Science, vol. 9. New Orleans, 1965.

Haines, Charles G. *The Revival of Natural Law Concepts.* Cambridge, Mass., 1930.

Harvey, Ray F. *Jean Jacques Burlamqui: A Liberal Tradition in American Constitutionalism.* Chapel Hill, 1937.

Holcombe, Arthur N. "The Role of Washington in the Framing of the Constitution." *The Huntington Library Quarterly* 19 (August 1956): 317–34.

Jensen, Merrill. *The Articles of Confederation: An Interpretation of the Social-Constitutional History of the American Revolution, 1774–1781.* Madison, 1940.

———. *The New Nation: A History of the United States during the Confederation, 1781–1789.* New York, 1950.

Ketcham, Ralph. *James Madison: A Biography.* New York, 1971.

Lutz, Donald S. *Popular Consent and Popular Control: Whig Political Theory in the Early State Constitutions.* Baton Rouge, 1980.

———, and Jack D. Warren, *A Covenanted People: The Religious Tradition and the Origins of American Constitutionalism.* Providence, 1987.

McDonald, Forrest. *E Pluribus Unum: The Formation of the American Republic, 1776–1790.* Indianapolis, 1979.

———, *Novus Ordo Seclorum: The Intellectual Origins of the Constitution.* Lawrence, Kansas, 1985.

McIlwain, Charles H. *Constitutionalism Ancient and Modern.* Ithaca, 1940.

McKeon, Richard. "The Development of the Concept of Property in Political Philosophy: A Study of the Background of the Constitution." *Ethics* 48 (April 1938): 297–366.

McLaughlin, Andrew C. *The Foundations of American Constitutionalism.* New York, 1932.

Meyers, Marvin. *The Mind of the Founder: Sources of the Political Thought of James Madison.* Indianapolis, 1973.

Morgan, Edmund S. *The Birth of the Republic, 1763–1789.* Chicago, 1956.

———, and Helen M. Morgan, *The Stamp Act Crisis: Prologue to the Revolution.* Chapel Hill, 1953.

Mullett, Charles F. *Fundamental Law and the American Revolution, 1760–1776.* New York, 1933.

Nevins, Allan. *The American States during and after the Revolution, 1775–1789.* New York, 1924.

Read, Conyers, ed. *The Constitution Reconsidered.* New York, 1938.

Rossiter, Clinton. *Seedtime of the Republic: The Origin of the American Tradition of Political Liberty.* New York, 1953.

Rossum, Ralph A., and Gary L. McDowell, eds. *The American Founding: Politics, Statesmanship, and the Constitution.* Port Washington, N.Y., 1981.

Rutland, Robert A. *The Birth of the Bill of Rights, 1776–1791.* Chapel Hill, 1955.

———. *The Ordeal of the Constitution: The Antifederalists and the Ratification Struggle of 1787–1788.* Norman, Okla., 1965.

Smith, Charles P. *James Wilson, Founding Father, 1742–1798.* Chapel Hill, 1956.

Smith, H. F. Russell. *Harrington and His Oceana: A Study of a 17th-Century Utopia and Its Influence in America.* Cambridge, 1914.

Spurlin, Paul M. *Montesquieu in America, 1760–1801.* University, La., 1940.

Storing, Herbert. *What the Anti-Federalists Were For.* Chicago, 1981.

Thach, Charles C., Jr. *The Creation of the Presidency, 1775–1789: A Study in Constitutional History.* Baltimore, 1922.

Vile, M. J. C. *Constitutionalism and the Separation of Powers.* Oxford, 1967.

Warren, Charles. *The Making of the Constitution.* Cambridge, Mass., 1948.

White, Morton. *Philosophy,* The Federalist, *and the Constitution.* New York, 1987.

————. *The Philosophy of the American Revolution.* New York, 1978.

Wills, Garry. *Explaining America:* The Federalist. Garden City, N.Y., 1981.

————. *Inventing America: Jefferson's Declaration of Independence.* Garden City, N.Y., 1978.

Wood, Gordon. *The Creation of the American Republic, 1776–1787.* Chapel Hill, 1969.

Wormuth, Francis D. *The Origins of Modern Constitutionalism.* New York, 1949.

Wright, Benjamin F. *American Interpretations of Natural Law.* Cambridge, Mass., 1931.

————. "The Origins of the Separation of Power in America." *Economica* 13 (1933): 169–85.

THE CONSTITUTIONAL CONVENTION
AND THE FORMATION OF THE UNION

*Of all men, that distinguish themselves by memorable achieve-
ments, the first place of honour seems due to Legislators and
founders of states, who transmit a system of laws and institutions
to secure the peace, happiness, and liberty of future generations.*

DAVID HUME

NOTE ON THE TEXT

The sources of the documents included in this volume are given in detail on pages cxii and cxiii. Every effort has been made to reprint the documents as accurately as the sources cited present them. In a few instances the editor found it necessary, however, to revise capitalization, punctuation, and spelling.

For a more detailed statement on Madison's Notes of Debates the reader is referred to the Editor's Foreword to the "Notes" on page 67.

The unmarked footnotes in Part Three are those of James Madison. The footnotes in parentheses have been reprinted from Hunt and Scott (eds.), *The Debates in the Federal Convention of 1787*. Folio references in these notes refer to pages in that edition.

The editor has contributed a number of headnotes, interpolated text notes, and footnotes. The text notes are set off from the text and thus clearly marked. All other notes of the editor, either footnotes or occasional explanatory notes in Madison's text, have been bracketed.

W.U.S.

I

TOWARD INDEPENDENCE

THE STAMP ACT CONGRESS

In October, 1765, twenty-eight delegates from nine colonies met in New York City for the Stamp Act Congress in response to a call for common action issued by the Massachusetts House of Representatives. Previously the perfervid Patrick Henry had introduced in the Virginia House of Burgesses seven resolutions opposing the Stamp Act, in the debate on which he warned that "Caesar had his Brutus." The two most radical of Henry's proposals, which failed of adoption, appeared along with the other five in newspapers, where they emboldened Bay Colony leaders to rally the host. Four colonies—New Hampshire, Virginia, North Carolina, and Georgia—sent no spokesmen, and some organ other than the provincial assembly appointed delegates in New York, New Jersey, and Delaware. An accurate barometer of colonial opinion, the Congress was dominated by moderates, who drew on many sources in reaching their conclusions. Among the most influential of these was a pamphlet by Maryland lawyer Daniel Dulany entitled *Considerations on the Propriety of Imposing Taxes in the British Colonies, for the Purpose of Raising a Revenue, by Act of Parliament.* On October 19 the Stamp Act Congress issued a "Declaration of Rights" setting forth the colonial position—or as much of it as was desirable to state explicitly. John Dickinson prepared the original resolutions on which the final draft was based. Before adjournment the Congress summarized these views in a separate petition to the king, memorial to the Lords, and address to the Commons.

DECLARATION OF RIGHTS

October 19, 1765

The members of this congress sincerely devoted, with the warmest sentiments of affection and duty to his majesty's person and government, inviolably attached to the present happy establishment of the protestant succession, and with minds deeply impressed by a sense of the present and impending misfortunes of the British colonies on this continent; having considered as maturely as time would permit, the circumstances of said colonies, esteem it our indispensable duty to make the following declarations, of our humble opinions, respecting the most essential rights and liberties of the colonists, and of the grievances under which they labor, by reason of several late acts of parliament.

1st. That his majesty's subjects in these colonies, owe the same allegiance to the crown of Great Britain, that is owing from his subjects born within the realm, and all due subordination to that august body, the parliament of Great Britain.

2d. That his majesty's liege subjects in these colonies are entitled to all the inherent rights and privileges of his natural born subjects within the kingdom of Great Britain.

3d. That it is inseparably essential to the freedom of a people, and the undoubted rights of Englishmen, that no taxes should be imposed on them, but with their own consent, given personally, or by their representatives.

4th. That the people of these colonies are not, and from their local circumstances, cannot be represented in the house of commons in Great Britain.

5th. That the only representatives of the people of these colonies, are persons chosen therein, by themselves; and that no taxes ever have been, or can be constitutionally imposed on them, but by their respective legislatures.

6th. That all supplies to the crown, being free gifts of the people, it is unreasonable and inconsistent with the principles and spirit of the British constitution, for the people of Great Britain to grant to his majesty the property of the colonists.

7th. That trial by jury is the inherent and invaluable right of every British subject in these colonies.

8th. That the late act of parliament entitled, an act for granting and applying certain stamp duties, and other duties in the British colonies and plantations in America, etc., by imposing taxes on the inhabitants of these colonies, and the said act, and several other acts, by extending the jurisdiction of the courts of admiralty beyond its ancient limits, have a manifest tendency to subvert the rights and liberties of the colonists.

9th. That the duties imposed by several late acts of parliament, from the peculiar circumstances of these colonies, will be extremely buthensome and grievous, and from the scarcity of specie, the payment of them absolutely impracticable.

10th. That as the profits of the trade of these colonies ultimately centre in Great Britain, to pay for the manufactures which they are obliged to take from thence, they eventually contribute very largely to all supplies granted there to the crown.

11th. That the restrictions imposed by several late acts of parliament, on the trade of these colonies, will render them unable to purchase the manufactures of Great Britain.

12th. That the increase, prosperity, and happiness of these colonies, depend on the full and free enjoyment of their rights and liberties, and an intercourse, with Great Britain, mutually affectionate and advantageous.

13th. That it is the right of the British subjects in these colonies, to petition the king or either house of parliament.

Lastly, That it is the indispensable duty of these colonies to the best of sovereigns, to the mother country, and to themselves, to endeavor, by a loyal and dutiful address to his majesty, and humble application to both houses of parliament, to procure the repeal of the act for granting and applying certain stamp duties, of all clauses of any other acts of parliament, whereby the jurisdiction of the admiralty is extended as aforesaid, and of the other late acts for the restriction of the American commerce.

FUNDAMENTAL LAW AND THE TOWNSHEND ACTS

In 1768 the Massachusetts House of Representatives adopted several statements drafted by Samuel Adams in protest against the Townshend Acts. These included a letter to Dennis De Bredt, agent of the province in England, a circular letter to the other colonies, addresses to leading English officials, and a petition to the king. The core of these statements, one of the earliest formulations of the idea of fundamental law in the colonies, is well represented in the selections which follow. Several of Adams' theories became important in American constitutional development.

LETTER OF THE MASSACHUSETTS HOUSE TO THE AGENT OF THE PROVINCE IN ENGLAND

January 12, 1768

The fundamental rules of the constitution are the grand security of all British subjects; and it is a security which they are all *equally* entitled to, in all parts of his Majesty's extended dominions. The supreme legislative, in every free state, derives its power from the constitution by the fundamental rules of which it is bounded and circumscribed. As a legislative power is essentially requisite, where any powers of government are exercised, it is conceived, the several legislative bodies in America were erected, because their existence, and the free exercise of their power, within their several limits, are essentially important and necessary, to preserve to His Majesty's subjects in America the advantages of the fundamental laws of the constitution. . . .

It is the glory of the British constitution, that it hath its foundation in the law of God and nature. It is an essential, natural right, that a man shall quietly enjoy, and have the sole disposal of his own property. This right is adopted into the constitution. . . . The security of right and property, is the great end of government. Surely, then, such measures as tend to render right and property precarious, tend to destroy both property and government; for these must stand and fall together. . . .

The original contract between the King and the first planters here, was a royal promise in behalf of the nation . . . that if the adventurers would . . . enlarge the King's dominions, they and their posterity should enjoy such rights and privileges as in their charters are expressed; which are, in general, all the rights, liberties and privileges of His Majesty's natural born subjects within the realm. ... By the common law, the colonists are adjudged to be natural born subjects. So they are declared by royal charter; and they are so, by the spirit of the law of nature and nations.

LETTER OF THE MASSACHUSETTS HOUSE TO THE EARL OF SHELBURNE

January 15, 1768

There are, my Lord, fundamental rules of the constitution, which it is humbly presumed, neither the supreme legislative nor the supreme executive can alter. In all free states, the constitution is fixed; it is from thence, that the legislative derives its authority; therefore it cannot change the constitution without destroying its own foundation. If, then, the constitution of Great Britain is the common right of all British subjects, it is humbly referred to your Lordship's judgment, whether the supreme legislative of the empire may rightly leap the bounds of it, in the exercise of power over the subjects in America, any more than over those in Britain.

THE FIRST CONTINENTAL CONGRESS

Fifty-six delegates representing twelve colonies met in Philadelphia during September and October, 1774, in the First Continental Congress. Although conservatives and radicals differed on the central question of what authority could properly be allowed Parliament, as a group the Congress was moderate and interested primarily in restoring harmony with Britain. A keen debate raised many of the issues relating to the source of rights and the structure of government which were to dominate the period through the Constitutional Convention. The major achievements of the Congress were formation of The Association, an instrument for economic coercion, and adoption of the "Declaration and Resolves." This statement contains both a defense of colonial rights and a specification of their violations. The former, which includes one profoundly significant point not asserted by the Stamp Act Congress, marks a well-advanced stage in the transition from contesting Parliament's authority to rejecting it completely. The "Declaration" is the product of several pens.

DECLARATION AND RESOLVES

October 14, 1774

Whereas, since the close of the last war, the British parliament, claiming a power of right to bind the people of America by statute in all cases whatsoever, hath, in some acts, expressly imposed taxes on them, and in others, under various pretences, but in fact for the purpose of raising a revenue, hath imposed rates and duties payable in these colonies, established a board of commissioners, with unconstitutional powers, and extended the jurisdiction of courts of admiralty, not only for collecting the said duties, but for the trial of causes merely arising within the body of a county:

And whereas, in consequence of other statutes, judges, who before held only estates at will in their offices, have been made dependant on the crown alone for their salaries, and standing armies kept in times of peace: And it has lately been resolved in parliament, that by force of a statute, made in the thirty-fifth year of the reign of king Henry the eighth, colonists may be transported to England, and tried there upon accusations for treasons and misprisions, or concealments of treasons committed in the colonies, and by a late statute, such trials have been directed in cases therein mentioned:

And whereas, in the last session of parliament, three statutes were made [the Boston Port Act, the Massachusetts Government Act, and the Administration of Justice Act], and another statute was then made [the Quebec Act], All which statutes are impolitic, unjust, and cruel, as well as unconstitutional, and most dangerous and destructive of American rights:

And whereas, assemblies have been frequently dissolved, contrary to the rights of the people, when they attempted to deliberate on grievances; and their dutiful, humble, loyal, and reasonable petitions to the crown for redress, have been repeatedly treated with contempt, by his majesty's ministers of state:

The good people of the several colonies of New-Hampshire, Massachusetts-Bay, Rhode-Island and Providence plantations, Connecticut, New-York, New-Jersey, Pennsylvania, Newcastle, Kent, and Sussex on Delaware, Maryland, Virginia, North-Carolina, and South-Carolina, justly alarmed at these arbitrary proceedings of parliament and administration, have severally elected, constituted, and appointed deputies to meet and sit in general congress, in the city of Philadelphia, in order to obtain such establishment, as that their religion, laws, and liberties, may not be subverted: Whereupon the deputies so appointed being now assembled, in a full and free representation of these colonies, taking into their most serious consideration, the best means of attaining the ends aforesaid, do, in the first place, as Englishmen, their ancestors in like cases have usually done, for asserting and vindicating their rights and liberties, declare,

That the inhabitants of the English colonies in North-America, by the immutable laws of nature, the principles of the English constitution, and the several charters or compacts, have the following RIGHTS:

Resolved, N. C. D.[1] 1. That they are entitled to life, liberty and property: and they have never ceded to any sovereign power whatever, a right to dispose of either without their consent.

Resolved, N. C. D. 2. That our ancestors, who first settled these colonies, were at the time of their emigration from the mother country, entitled to all the rights, liberties, and immunities of free and natural-born subjects, within the realm of England.

Resolved, N. C. D. 3. That by such emigration they by no means forfeited, surrendered, or lost any of those rights, but that they were, and their descendants now are, entitled to the exercise and enjoyment of all such of them, as their local and other circumstances enable them to exercise and enjoy.

Resolved, 4. That the foundation of English liberty, and of

1 [*Nemine contradicente,* without dissenting vote, or unanimously.]

all free government, is a right in the people to participate in their legislative council: and as the English colonists are not represented, and from their local and other circumstances, cannot properly be represented in the British parliament, they are entitled to a free and exclusive power of legislation in their several provincial legislatures, where their right of representation can alone be preserved, in all cases of taxation and internal polity, subject only to the negative of their sovereign, in such manner as has been heretofore used and accustomed: But, from the necessity of the case, and a regard to the mutual interest of both countries, we cheerfully consent to the operation of such acts of the British parliament, as are bona fide, restrained to the regulation of our external commerce, for the purpose of securing the commercial advantages of the whole empire to the mother country, and the commercial benefits of its respective members; excluding every idea of taxation internal or external, for raising a revenue on the subjects in America, without their consent.

Resolved, N. C. D. 5. That the respective colonies are entitled to the common law of England, and more especially to the great and inestimable privilege of being tried by their peers of the vicinage, according to the course of that law.

Resolved, 6. That they are entitled to the benefit of such of the English statutes as existed at the time of their colonization; and which they have, by experience, respectively found to be applicable to their several local and other circumstances.

Resolved, N. C. D. 7. That these, his majesty's colonies, are likewise entitled to all the immunities and privileges granted and confirmed to them by royal charters, or secured by their several codes of provincial laws.

Resolved, N. C. D. 8. That they have a right peaceably to assemble, consider of their grievances, and petition the king; and that all prosecutions, prohibitory proclamations, and commitments for the same, are illegal.

Resolved, N. C. D. 9. That the keeping a standing army in these colonies, in times of peace, without the consent of the legislature of that colony, in which such army is kept, is against law.

Resolved, N. C. D. 10. It is indispensably necessary to good government, and rendered essential by the English constitution, that the constituent branches of the legislature be independent of each other; that, therefore, the exercise of legislative power in several colonies, by a council appointed, during pleasure, by the crown, is unconstitutional, dangerous, and destructive to the freedom of American legislation.

All and each of which the aforesaid deputies, in behalf of themselves and their constituents, do claim, demand, and insist on, as their indubitable rights and liberties; which cannot be legally taken from them, altered or abridged by any power whatever, without their own consent, by their representatives in their several provincial legislatures.

In the course of our inquiry, we find many infringements and violations of the foregoing rights, which, from an ardent desire, that harmony and mutual intercourse of affection and interest may be restored, we pass over for the present, and proceed to state such acts and measures as have been adopted since the last war which demonstrate a system formed to enslave America.

Resolved, N. C. D. That the following acts of Parliament are infringements and violations of the rights of the colonists; and that the repeal of them is essentially necessary, in order to restore harmony between Great-Britain and the American colonies, viz:

The several acts of 4 Geo. III. ch. 15, and ch. 34.—5 Geo. III ch. 25.—6 Geo. III. ch. 52.—7 Geo. III. ch. 41, and ch. 46.—8 Geo. III. ch. 22, which impose duties for the purpose of raising a revenue in America, extend the power of the admiralty courts beyond their ancient limits, deprive the American subject of trial by jury, authorize the judges' certificate to indemnify the prosecutor from damages, that he might otherwise be liable to, requiring oppressive security from a claimant of ships and goods seized, before he shall be allowed to defend his property, and are subversive of American rights.

Also 12 Geo. III. ch. 24. entituled, "An act for the better securing his majesty's dockyards, magazines, ships, ammunition, and stores," which declares a new offence in America, and deprives the American subject of a constitutional trial by jury of the vicinage, by authorizing the trial of any person, charged with the committing any offence described in the said act, out of the realm, to be indicted and tried for the same in any shire or county within the realm.

Also the three acts passed in the last session of parliament, for stopping the port and blocking up the harbour of Boston, for altering the charter and government of Massachusetts-Bay, and that which is entituled, "An act for the better administration of justice, etc."

Also the act passed in the same session for establishing the Roman Catholick religion, in the province of Quebec, abolishing the equitable system of English laws, and erecting a tyranny there, to the great danger (from so total a dissimilarity of religion, law, and government) of the neighbouring British colonies, by the assistance of whose blood and treasure the said country was conquered from France.

Also the act passed in the same session for the better providing suitable quarters for officers and soldiers in his majesty's service, in North-America.

Also, that the keeping a standing army in several of these colonies, in time of peace, without the consent of the legislature of that colony, in which such army is kept, is against law.

To these grievous acts and measures, Americans cannot submit, but in hopes their fellow subjects in Great-Britain will, on a revision of them, restore us to that state, in which both countries found happiness and prosperity, we have for the present only resolved to pursue the following peaceable measures: 1st. To enter into a non-importation, non-consumption, and non-exportation agreement or association. 2. To prepare an address to the people of Great-Britain, and a memorial to the inhabitants of British America: and 3. To prepare a loyal address to his majesty, agreeable to resolutions already entered into.

THE SECOND CONTINENTAL CONGRESS

Following the battles of Lexington and Concord the Second Continental Congress was organized and met in May, 1775. It immediately became the recognized revolutionary government, with its main task to conduct the war and lead the colonies ultimately to independence. The "Resolution of Congress" of June 9, 1775, advising Massachusetts on government, is indicative of its authority and the direction of its policy.

RESOLUTION OF CONGRESS

June 9, 1775

From Watertown, on May 16, 1775, the Provincial Congress of Massachusetts dispatched to the Second Continental Congress a letter seeking advice. This said that the colony labored under a double handicap: the battle of Lexington inaugurated a conflict which necessitated military operations, but abrogation of the charter left the province without proper authority. The sword should be subservient to the civil power, but since the question affected others the colony declined to grasp the reins of government without the "advice and consent" of the Congress. At the same time Massachusetts asked the Congress to assume regulation of the army collecting around Boston. Congress adopted the recommendation of a committee assigned to consider the letter.

RESOLVED, That no obedience being due to the Act of parliament for altering the charter of the Colony of Massachusetts bay, nor to a Governor, or a lieutenant-Governor, who will not observe the directions of, but endeavour to subvert that charter, the govr. and lieutenant-govr. of that Colony are to be considered as absent, and these offices vacant; and as there is no council there, and the inconveniences, arising from the suspension of the powers of Government, are intollerable, especially at a time when Genl. Gage hath actually levied war, and is carrying on hostilities, against his Majesty's peaceable and loyal subjects of that Colony: that, in order to conform, as near as may be, to the spirit and substance of the charter, it be recommended to the provincial Convention, to write letters to the inhabitants of the several places, which are intituled to representation in Assembly, requesting them to chuse such representatives, and that the Assembly, when chosen, do elect counsellors; which assembly and council should exercise the powers of Government, until a Governor, of his Majesty's appointment, will consent to govern the colony according to its charter.

CONGRESS JUSTIFIES TAKING UP ARMS

Motivated by its continuing passion to explain and defend its actions to Americans and the world, Congress prepared a statement offering reasons for taking up arms. A first draft said to have been prepared by John Rutledge caused fervent debate and was recommitted. Jefferson then tried his hand, but his remarks were too strong for John Dickinson, who desired reconciliation, and William Livingston thought they contained "much fault-finding and declamation, with little sense or dignity." Then Dickinson took over, writing a "Declaration" which includes the last part of Jefferson's draft and is similar in other ways.

DECLARATION OF THE CAUSES AND NECESSITY OF TAKING UP ARMS

July 6, 1775

.   .   .   .

If it was possible for men, who exercise their reason to believe, that the divine Author of our existence intended a part of the human race to hold an absolute property in, and an unbounded power over others, marked out by his infinite goodness and wisdom, as the objects of a legal domination never rightfully resistible, however severe and oppressive, the inhabitants of these colonies might at least require from the parliament of Great Britain some evidence, that this dreadful authority over them, has been granted to that body. But a reverence for our great Creator, principles of humanity, and the dictates of common sense, must convince all those who reflect upon the subject, that government was instituted to promote the welfare of mankind, and ought to be administered for the attainment of that end. The legislature of Great Britain, however, stimulated by an inordinate passion for a power not only unjustifiable, but which they know to be peculiarly reprobated by the very constitution of that kingdom, and desparate of success in any mode of contest, where regard should be had to truth, law, or right, have at length, deserting those, attempted to effect their cruel and impolitic purpose of enslaving these colonies by violence, and have thereby rendered it necessary for us to close with their last appeal from reason to arms.—Yet, however blinded that assembly may be, by their intemperate rage for unlimited domination, so to slight justice and the opinion of mankind, we esteem ourselves bound by obligations of respect to the rest of the world to make known the justice of our cause.

Our forefathers, inhabitants of the island of Great Britain, left their native land, to seek on these shores a residence for civil and religious freedom. At the expense of their blood, at the hazard of their fortunes, without the least charge to the country from which they removed, by unceasing labor, and an unconquerable spirit, they effected settlements in the distant and inhospitable wilds of America, then filled with numerous and warlike nations of barbarians. Societies or governments, vested with perfect legislatures, were formed under charters from the crown, and an harmonious intercourse was established between the colonies and the kingdom from which they derived their origin. The mutual benefits of this union became in a short time so extraordinary, as to excite astonishment. It is universally confessed, that the amazing increase of the wealth, strength, and navigation of the realm, arose from this source; and the minister who so wisely and successfully directed the measures of Great Britain in the late war [1] publicly declared, that these colonies enabled her to triumph over her enemies.—Towards the conclusion of that war, it pleased our sovereign to make a change in his counsels.—From that fatal moment, the affairs of the British empire began to fall into confusion, and gradually sliding from the summit of glorious prosperity, to which they had been advanced by the virtues and abilities of one man, are at length distracted by the convulsions, that now shake it to its deepest foundations. The new ministry finding the brave foes of Britain, though frequently defeated, yet still contending, took up the unfortunate idea of granting them a hasty peace, and of then subduing her faithful friends.[2]

These devoted colonies were judged to be in such a state, as to present victories without bloodshed, and all the easy emoluments of statuteable plunder.—The uninterrupted tenor of their peaceable and respectful behaviour from the beginning of colonization, their dutiful, zealous, and useful services during the war, though so recently and amply acknowledged in the most honorable manner by his majesty, by the late king, and by parliament, could not save them from the meditated innovations.—Parliament was influenced to adopt the pernicious project, and assuming a new power over them, have in the course of eleven years, given such decisive specimens of the spirit and consequences attending this power, as to leave no doubt concerning the effects of acquiescence under it. They have undertaken to give and grant our money without our consent, though we have ever exercised an exclusive right to dispose of our own property; statutes have been passed for extending the jurisdiction of courts of admiralty and vice-

[1] [William Pitt, first Earl of Chatham (1708-78), was in effect prime minister of Great Britain from 1756 until George III mounted the throne in 1760. The brilliant director of the Seven Years' War, one of his chief goals was to humiliate France.]

[2] [John Stuart, third Earl of Bute (1713-92), was the intimate of George III who helped ease Pitt out of office during the Seven Years' war. He preferred immediate peace, and became extremely unpopular for the treaty ending the war with France and Spain in 1763.]

admiralty beyond their ancient limits; for depriving us of the accustomed and inestimable privilege of trial by jury, in cases affecting both life and property; for suspending the legislature of one of the colonies; for interdicting all commerce to the capital of another; and for altering fundamentally the form of government established by charter, and secured by acts of its own legislature solemnly confirmed by the crown; for exempting the "murderers" of colonists from legal trial, and in effect, from punishment; for erecting in a neighboring province, acquired by the joint arms of Great Britain and America, a despotism dangerous to our very existence; and for quartering soldiers upon the colonists in time of profound peace. It has also been resolved in parliament, that colonists charged with committing certain offences, shall be transported to England to be tried.

But why should we enumerate our injuries in detail? By one statute it is declared, that parliament can "of right make laws to bind us in all cases whatsoever." What is to defend us against so enormous, so unlimited a power? Not a single man of those who assume it, is chosen by us; or is subject to our control or influence; but, on the contrary, they are all of them exempt from the operation of such laws, and an American revenue, if not diverted from the ostensible purposes for which it is raised, would actually lighten their own burdens in proportion as they increase ours. We saw the misery to which such despotism would reduce us. We for ten years incessantly and ineffectually besieged the throne as supplicants; we reasoned, we remonstrated with parliament, in the most mild and decent language. But administration, sensible that we should regard these oppressive measures as freemen ought to do, sent over fleets and armies to enforce them. The indignation of the Americans was roused, it is true; but it was the indignation of a virtuous, loyal, and affectionate people. A Congress of delegates from the United Colonies was assembled at Philadelphia, on the fifth day of last September. We resolved again to offer an humble and dutiful petition to the King, and also addressed our fellow-subjects of Great Britain. We have pursued every temperate, every respectful measure; we have even proceeded to break off our commercial intercourse with our fellow-subjects, as the last peaceable admonition, that our attachment to no nation upon earth should supplant our attachment to liberty.—This, we flattered ourselves, was the ultimate step of the controversy; but subsequent events have shewn, how vain was this hope of finding moderation in our enemies.

Several threatening expressions against the colonies were inserted in his majesty's speech; our petition, though we were told it was a decent one, and that his majesty had been pleased to receive it graciously, and to promise laying it before his parliament, was huddled into both houses among a bundle of American papers, and there neglected. The lords and commons in their address, in the month of February, said, that "a rebellion at that time actually existed within the province of Massachusetts-Bay; and that those concerned in it, had been countenanced and encouraged by unlawful combinations and engagements, entered into by his majesty's subjects in several of the other colonies; and therefore they besought his majesty, that he would take the most effectual measures to enforce due obedience to the laws and authority of the supreme legislature."—Soon after, the commercial intercourse of whole colonies, with foreign countries, and with each other, was cut off by an act of parliament; by another, several of them were entirely prohibited from the fisheries in the seas near their coasts, on which they always depended for their sustenance; and large reinforcements of ships and troops were immediately sent over to General Gage.

Fruitless were all the entreaties, arguments, and eloquence of an illustrious band of the most distinguished peers and commoners, who nobly and strenuously asserted the justice of our cause, to stay, or even to mitigate the heedless fury with which these accumulated and unexampled outrages were hurried on. . . .

. . . [G]eneral Gage, who in the course of the last year had taken possession of the town of Boston, in the province of Massachusetts Bay, and still occupied it as a garrison, on the 19th day of April, sent out from that place a large detachment of his army, who made an unprovoked assault on the inhabitants of the said province, at the town of Lexington, as appears by the affidavits of a great number of persons, some of whom were officers and soldiers of that detachment, murdered eight of the inhabitants, and wounded many others. From thence the troops proceeded in warlike array to the town of Concord, where they set upon another party of the inhabitants of the same province, killing several and wounding more, until compelled to retreat by the country people suddenly assembled to repel this cruel aggression. Hostilities, thus commenced by the British troops, have been since prosecuted by them without regard to faith or reputation.—The inhabitants of Boston being confined within that town by the general their governor, and having, in order to procure their dismission, entered into a treaty with him, it was stipulated that the said inhabitants having deposited their arms with their own magistrates, should have liberty to depart, taking with them their other effects. They accordingly delivered up their arms, but in open violation of honor, in defiance of the obligation of treaties, which even savage nations esteemed sacred, the governor ordered the arms deposited as aforesaid, that they might be preserved for their owners, to be seized by a body of soldiers, detained the greatest part of the inhabitants in the town, and compelled the few who were permitted to retire to leave their most valuable effects behind.

. . . .

The general, further emulating his ministerial masters, by a proclamation bearing date on the 12th day of June, after venting the grossest falsehoods and calumnies against the good people of these colonies, proceeds to "declare them all, either by name or description, to be rebels and traitors, to supersede the course of the common law, and instead thereof to publish and order the use and exercise of the law martial."—His troops have butchered our countrymen, have wantonly burnt Charlestown, besides a considerable number of houses in other places; our ships and vessels are seized; the necessary supplies of provisions are intercepted; and he is exerting his utmost power to spread destruction and devastation around him.

We have received certain intelligence, that General Carleton, the governor of Canada, is instigating the people of that province and the Indians to fall upon us; and we have but too much reason to apprehend, that schemes have been formed to excite domestic enemies against us. In brief, a part of these colonies now feels, and all of them are sure of feeling, as far as the vengeance of administration can inflict them, the complicated calamities of fire, sword, and famine. We [3] are reduced to the alternative of chusing an unconditional submission to the tyranny of irritated ministers, or resistance by force.—The latter is our choice.—We have counted the cost of this contest, and find nothing so dreadful as voluntary slavery.—Honor, justice, and humanity, forbid us tamely to surrender that freedom which we received from our gallant ancestors, and which our innocent posterity have a right to receive from us. We cannot endure the infamy and guilt of resigning succeeding generations to that wretchedness which inevitably awaits them, if we basely entail hereditary bondage upon them.

Our cause is just. Our union is perfect. Our internal resources are great, and, if necessary, foreign assistance is undoubtedly attainable.—We gratefully acknowledge, as signal instances of the Divine favour towards us, that his Providence would not permit us to be called into this severe controversy, until we were grown up to our present strength, had been previously exercised in warlike operation, and possessed of the means of defending ourselves. With hearts fortified with these animating reflections, we most solemnly, before God and the world, *declare*, that, exerting the utmost energy of those powers, which our beneficent Creator hath graciously bestowed upon us, the arms we have been compelled by our enemies to assume, we will, in defiance of every hazard, with unabating firmness and perseverance, employ for the preservation of our liberties; being with one mind resolved to die freemen rather than to live slaves.

[3] [From this point the declaration follows Jefferson's draft.]

Lest this declaration should disquiet the minds of our friends and fellow-subjects in any part of the empire, we assure them that we mean not to dissolve that union which has so long and so happily subsisted between us, and which we sincerely wish to see restored.—Necessity has not yet driven us into that desperate measure, or induced us to excite any other nation to war against them.—We have not raised armies with ambitious designs of separating from Great Britain, and establishing independent states. We fight not for glory or for conquest. We exhibit to mankind the remarkable spectacle of a people attacked by unprovoked enemies, without any imputation or even suspicion of offence. They boast of their privileges and civilization, and yet proffer no milder conditions than servitude or death.

In our own native land, in defence of the freedom that is our birth-right, and which we ever enjoyed till the late violation of it—for the protection of our property, acquired solely by the honest industry of our fore-fathers and ourselves; against violence actually offered, we have taken up arms. We shall lay them down when hostilities shall cease on the part of the aggressors, and all danger of their being renewed shall be removed, and not before.

With an humble confidence in the mercies of the supreme and impartial Judge and Ruler of the universe, we most devoutly implore his divine goodness to protect us happily through this great conflict, to dispose our adversaries to reconciliation on reasonable terms, and thereby to relieve the empire from the calamities of civil war.

THE MECKLENBURG COUNTY RESOLVES

Believing that the Parliamentary proclamation declaring Massachusetts to be in rebellion affected all the American colonies, radical frontiersmen in the piedmont section of North Carolina made provision in late May, 1775, for the preservation of local order and for harmonizing county and provincial affairs with those of the central government. Al-

though the adopted proposals were sent to the North Carolina delegation in Philadelphia, they were never brought
before the Second Continental Congress. Later a myth holding that these resolutions were the first declaration of independence found many believers.

RESOLVES ADOPTED IN CHARLOTTE TOWN, MECKLENBURG COUNTY, NORTH CAROLINA

May 31, 1775

.   .   .   .

Whereas by an Address presented to his Majesty by both
Houses of Parliament in *February* last, the *American* Colonies
are declared to be in a State of actual Rebellion, we conceive
that all Laws and Commissions confirmed by, or derived from
the Authority of the King or Parliament, are annulled and
vacated, and the former civil Constitution of these Colonies for
the present wholly suspended. To provide in some Degree for
the Exigencies of the County in the present alarming Period, we
deem it proper and necessary to pass the following Resolves,
viz.

1. That all Commissions, civil and military, heretofore
granted by the Crown, to be exercised in these Colonies, are null
and void, and the Constitution of each particular Colony
wholly suspended.

2. That the Provincial Congress of each Province, under the
Direction of the Great Continental Congress, is invested with
all legislative and executive Powers within their respective
Provinces; and that no other Legislative or Executive does or
can exist, at this Time, in any of these Colonies.

3. As all former Laws are now suspended in this Province,
and the Congress have not yet provided others, we judge it
necessary, for the better Preservation of good Order, to form
certain Rules and Regulations for the internal Government of
this County, until Laws shall be provided for us by the Congress.

4. That the Inhabitants of this County do meet on a certain
Day appointed by this Committee, and having formed them-

selves into nine Companies, to *wit,* eight for the County, and one for the Town of *Charlotte,* do choose a Colonel and other military Officers, who shall hold and exercise their several Powers by Virtue of this Choice, and independent of *Great-Britain,* and former Constitution of this Province.

5. That for the better Preservation of the Peace, and Administration of Justice, each of these Companies do choose from their own Body two discreet Freeholders, who shall be impowered each by himself, and singly, to decide and determine all Matters of Controversy arising within the said Company under the Sum of Twenty Shillings, and jointly and together all Controversies under the Sum of Forty Shillings, yet so as their Decisions may admit of Appeals to the Convention of the Select Men of the whole County; and also, that any one of these shall have Power to examine, and commit to Confinement, Persons accused of Petit Larceny.

6. That those two Select Men, thus chosen, do, jointly and together, choose from the Body of their particular Company two Persons, properly qualified to serve as Constables, who may assist them in the Execution of their Office.

7. That upon the Complaint of any Person to either of these Select Men, he do issue his Warrant, directed to the Constable, commanding him to bring the Aggressor before him or them to answer the said Complaint.

8. That these eighteen Select Men, thus appointed, do meet every third *Tuesday* in *January, April, July,* and *October,* at the Court-House, in *Charlotte,* to hear and determine all Matters of Controversy for Sums exceeding Forty Shillings; also Appeals; And in Cases of Felony, to commit the Person or Persons convicted thereof to close Confinement, until the Provincial Congress shall provide and establish Laws and Modes of Proceeding in all such Cases. . . .

.   .   .   .

12. That all Receivers and Collectors of Quitrents, Public and County Taxes, do pay the same into the Hands of the Chairman of this Committee, to be by them disbursed as the public Exigencies may require. And that such Receivers and Collectors

proceed no farther in their Office until they be approved of by, and have given to this Committee good and sufficient Security for a faithful Return of such Monies when collected.

13. That the Committee be accountable to the County for the Application of all Monies received from such public Officers.

14. That all these Officers hold their Commissions during the Pleasure of their respective Constituents.

15. That this Committee will sustain all Damages that may ever hereafter accrue to all or any of these Officers thus appointed, and thus acting, on Account of their Obedience and Conformity to these Resolves.

16. That whatever Person shall hereafter receive a Commission from the Crown, or attempt to exercise any such Commission heretofore received, shall be deemed an Enemy to his Country; and upon Information being made to the Captain of the Company where he resides, the said Captain shall cause him to be apprehended, and conveyed before the two Select Men of the said Company, who, upon Proof of the Fact, shall commit him the said Offender, into safe Custody, until the next setting of the Convention, who shall deal with him as Prudence may direct.

17. That any Person refusing to yield Obedience to the above Resolves shall be deemed equally criminal, and liable to the same Punishments as the Offenders above last mentioned.

18. That these Resolves be in full Force and Virtue, until Instructions from the General Congress of this Province, regulating the Jurisprudence of this Province, shall provide otherwise, or the legislative Body of *Great-Britain* resign its unjust and arbitrary Pretentions with Respect to *America*.

19. That the several Militia Companies in this county do provide themselves with proper Arms and Accoutrements, and hold themselves in Readiness to execute the commands and Directions of the Provincial Congress, and of this committee. . . .

NORTH CAROLINA FURTHERS INDEPENDENCE

On April 8, 1776, the Provincial Congress of North Carolina appointed a select committee of seven to consider the "usurpations and violences attempted and committed by the King and Parliament of Britain against America," and the measures to be taken for frustrating them. The report submitted four days later was unanimously adopted, making North Carolina the first colony specifically to empower its delegation in Congress to support independence. Thomas Burke, a member of this committee, later successfully led the movement in the Continental Congress to incorporate the reservation in the last paragraph of this document into the Articles of Confederation.

REPORT AND RESOLUTION OF THE PROVINCIAL CONGRESS OF NORTH CAROLINA

April 12, 1776

It appears to your committee, that pursuant to the plan concerted by the British Ministry for subjugating America, the King and Parliament of Great Britain have usurped a power over the persons and properties of the people unlimited and uncontrouled; and disregarding their humble petitions for peace, liberty, and safety have made divers legislative acts, denouncing war, famine, and every species of calamity, against the Continent in general. The British fleets and armies have been, and still are daily employed in destroying the people, and committing the most horrid devastations on the country. That Governors in different Colonies have declared protection to slaves, who should imbrue their hands in the blood of their masters. That the ships belonging to America are declared prizes of war, and many of them have been violently seized and confiscated. In consequence of all which multitudes of the people have been destroyed, or from easy circumstances reduced to the most lamentable distress.

And whereas the moderation hitherto manifested by the United Colonies and their sincere desire to be reconciled to the mother country on constitutional principles, have procured no mitigation of the aforesaid wrongs and usurpations, and no hopes remain of obtaining redress by those means alone which have been hitherto tried, your committee are of opinion that the House should enter into the following resolve, to wit:

Resolved, That the delegates for this Colony in the Continental Congress be impowered to concur with the delegates of the other Colonies in declaring Independency, and forming foreign alliances, reserving to this Colony the sole and exclusive right of forming a Constitution and laws for this Colony, and of appointing delegates from time to time (under the direction of a general representation thereof), to meet the delegates of the other Colonies for such purposes as shall be hereafter pointed out.

CONGRESS URGES SELF-GOVERNMENT ON THE COLONIES

Throughout the spring of 1776 some colonies—especially middle ones—remained relatively immune to the contagion which prompted others to move toward independence. This prevented the Continental Congress from breaking with Britain. To spread the virus John Adams and Richard Henry Lee induced the Committee of the Whole to report the resolution (only the last paragraph below) which Congress unanimously adopted on May 10. Then Edward Rutledge joined these two on a committee to prepare a preamble, of which Adams claimed authorship. The third "whereas" of this contained an explosive charge which aimed at dissolving old authority in reluctant colonies and thereby stimulating creation of new governments prepared to help Congress on the highway to independence. Despite objections that these provinces could manage their own affairs and that only royal colonies needed congressional permission to resort to the sovereignty of the people, the preamble was adopted five days after the resolution.

RESOLUTION OF CONGRESS

May 10-15, 1776

Whereas, His Britannic Majesty, in conjunction with the Lords and Commons of Great Britain, has, by a late act of Parliament, excluded the inhabitants of these United Colonies from the protection of his crown; and whereas, no answer, whatever, to the humble petitions of the colonies for redress of grievances and reconciliation with Great Britain has been or is likely to be given; but the whole force of that kingdom, aided by foreign mercenaries, is to be exerted for the destruction of the good people of these colonies; and whereas, it appears absolutely irreconcileable to reason and good conscience for the people of these colonies now to take the oaths and affirmations necessary for the support of any government under the crown of Great Britain, and it is necessary that the exercise of every kind of authority under the said crown should be totally suppressed, and all the powers of government exerted, under the authority of the people of the colonies, for the preservation of internal peace, virtue, and good order, as well as for the defence of their lives, liberties, and properties, against the hostile invasions and cruel depradations of their enemies; therefore,

Resolved, That it be recommended to the respective assemblies and conventions of the United Colonies, where no government sufficient to the exigencies of their affairs have been hitherto established, to adopt such government as shall, in the opinion of the representatives of the people, best conduce to the happiness and safety of their constituents in particular, and America in general.

VIRGINIA INSTRUCTS FOR
INDEPENDENCE

On May 15, 1776, the Virginia Convention, composed of
members of the House of Burgesses who had assembled in
Williamsburg nine days earlier, passed resolutions instructing
the Virginia delegation in Philadelphia and recommending
action at home. The former resolution was laid before Congress on May 27 along with the North Carolina instrument
of April 12, but it was not until June 7 that Richard Henry
Lee complied by introducing there a resolution which linked
three objects needed to achieve independence and established a priority among them. Meanwhile, emboldened by
the congressional recommendations of May 10-15, Virginia
pursued its own path toward independence. On June 12 the
Convention adopted a bill of rights prepared under its
auspices, and on June 29 a constitution which, in a preamble
by Jefferson, declared the colony independent.

PREAMBLE AND RESOLUTION

May 15, 1776

Forasmuch as all the endeavours of the United Colonies, by
the most decent representations and petitions to the King and
Parliament of *Great Britain,* to restore peace and security to
America under the *British* Government, and a reunion with
that people upon just and liberal terms, instead of a redress of
grievances, have produced, from an imperious and vindictive
Administration, increased insult, oppression, and a vigorous
attempt to effect our total destruction:—By a late act all these
Colonies are declared to be in rebellion, and out of the protection of the *British* Crown, our properties subjected to confisca-
tion, our people, when captivated, compelled to join in the
murder and plunder of their relations and countrymen, and all
former rapine and oppression of *Americans* declared legal and
just; fleets and armies are raised, and the aid of foreign troops
engaged to assist these destructive purposes; the King's representative in this Colony hath not only withheld all the powers

of Government from operating for our safety, but, having retired on board an armed ship, is carrying on a piratical and
savage war against us, tempting our slaves by every artifice to
resort to him, and training and employing them against their
masters. In this state of extreme danger, we have no alternative
left but an abject submission to the will of those overbearing
tyrants, or a total separation from the Crown and Government
of *Great Britain,* uniting and exerting the strength of all
America for defence, and forming alliances with foreign Powers
for commerce and aid in war:—Wherefore, appealing to the
Searcher of hearts for the sincerity of former declarations expressing our desire to preserve the connection with that nation,
and that we are driven from that inclination by their wicked
councils, and the eternal law of self-preservation:

Resolved, unanimously, That the Delegates appointed to
represent this Colony in General Congress be instructed to propose to that respectable body to declare the United Colonies
free and independent States, absolved from all allegiance to, or
dependance upon, the Crown or Parliament of *Great Britain;*
and that they give the assent of this Colony to such declaration,
and to whatever measures may be thought proper and necessary
by the Congress for forming foreign alliances, and a Confederation of the Colonies, at such time and in the manner as to them
shall seem best: *Provided,* That the power of forming Government for, and the regulations of the internal concerns of each
Colony, be left to the respective Colonial Legislatures.

Resolved, unanimously, That a Committee be appointed to
prepare a Declaration of Rights, and such a plan of Government as will be most likely to maintain peace and order in this
Colony, and secure substantial and equal liberty to the
people. . . .

RESOLUTION INTRODUCED IN THE CONTINENTAL CONGRESS BY RICHARD HENRY LEE

June 7, 1776

Resolved, That these United Colonies are, and of right ought to be, free and independent States, that they are absolved from all allegiance to the British Crown, and that all political connection between them and the State of Great Britain is, and ought to be, totally dissolved.

That it is expedient forthwith to take the most effectual measures for forming foreign Alliances.

That a plan of confederation be prepared and transmitted to the respective Colonies for their consideration and approbation.

CONGRESS DECLARES INDEPENDENCE

Following introduction of Lee's resolution, conservatives secured postponement of the question of independence until July 1. Nevertheless on June 11 Congress appointed a committee (Jefferson, John Adams, Franklin, Roger Sherman, R. R. Livingston) to prepare a declaration. The ferment in the middle colonies initiated by the May 15 preamble proved auspicious for their labors. They reported on June 28, and at last, on July 2, Congress decided for independence without dissenting vote. To accomplish this, however, the New York delegates, prevented by instructions from assenting, refrained from balloting, and the Pennsylvania, South Carolina, and Delaware delegates had to change their decisions of the previous day. This crucial hurdle passed, the delegates considered the text of the Declaration for two days, adopting changes on July 4 and ordering the document authenticated and printed. News that New York had approved on July 9 reached Philadelphia on July 15, and four days later Congress ordered the statement engrossed. On August 2 signatures were affixed, although all "signers" were not then present. Since the Declaration was an act of treason, the names subscribed were initially kept secret by Congress. The text itself was widely publicized.

The product of Jefferson's pen, the instrument briefly enunciates a philosophy of government and then catalogues grievances which compel abandonment of allegiance to a perfidious king, exposed now as accomplice of Parliament ("He has combined with others [i.e., Parliament], . . . giving his assent to their acts of pretended legislation . . ."). In the eighteenth century this list of violations of the social compact overshadowed the philosophy, which was tacitly accepted. The later flow of events relegated the litany of oppressions to the historical scrap heap, while the philosophy disembodied itself to begin a career of its own. The language of the document sheds light on the multifaceted problem of nationhood in 1776.

IN CONGRESS, *July 4, 1776*

THE UNANIMOUS DECLARATION OF THE THIRTEEN UNITED STATES
OF AMERICA

WHEN in the Course of human events, it becomes necessary for one people to dissolve the political bands which have connected them with another, and to assume among the powers of the earth, the separate and equal station to which the Laws of Nature and of Nature's God entitle them, a decent respect to the opinions of mankind requires that they should declare the causes which impel them to the separation.—We hold these truths to be self-evident, that all men are created equal, that they are endowed by their Creator with certain unalienable Rights, that among these are Life, Liberty and the pursuit of Happiness.—That to secure these rights, Governments are instituted among Men, deriving their just powers from the consent of the governed,—That whenever any Form of Government becomes destructive of these ends, it is the Right of the People to alter or to abolish it, and to institute new Government, laying its foundation on such principles and organizing its powers in such form, as to them shall seem most likely to effect their Safety and Happiness. Prudence, indeed, will dictate that Governments long established should not be changed for light and transient causes; and accordingly all experience hath shown, that mankind are more disposed to suffer, while evils are sufferable, than to right themselves by abolishing the forms to which they are accustomed. But when a long train of abuses and usurpations, pursuing invariably the same Object evinces a design to reduce them under absolute Despotism, it is their right, it is their duty, to throw off such Government, and to provide new Guards for their future security.—Such has been the patient sufferance of these Colonies; and such is now the necessity which constrains them to alter their former Systems of Government. The history of the present King of Great Britain is a history of repeated injuries and usurpations, all having in direct object the establishment of an absolute Tyranny over these States. To prove this, let Facts be submitted to a candid world.—He has refused his Assent to Laws, the most wholesome and necessary for the public good.—He has forbidden his Governors to pass Laws of immediate and pressing importance, unless suspended in their operation till his Assent should be obtained; and when so suspended, he has utterly neglected to attend to them.—He has refused to pass other Laws for the accommodation of large districts of people, unless those people would relinquish the right of Representation in the Legislature, a right inestimable to them and formidable to tyrants only.—He has called together legislative bodies at places unusual, uncomfortable, and distant from the depository of their public Records, for the sole purpose of fatiguing them into compliance with his measures.—He has dissolved Representative Houses repeatedly, for opposing with manly firmness his invasions on the rights of the people.—He has refused for a long time, after such dissolutions, to cause others to be elected; whereby the Legislative powers, incapable of Annihilation, have returned to the People at large for their exercise; the State remaining in the mean time exposed to all the dangers of invasion from without, and convulsions within.—He has endeavoured to prevent the population of these States; for that purpose obstructing the Laws for Naturalization of Foreigners; refusing to pass others to encourage their migration hither, and raising the conditions of new Appropriations of Lands.—He has obstructed the Administration of Justice, by refusing his Assent to Laws for establishing Judiciary powers.—He has made Judges dependent on his Will alone, for the tenure of their offices, and the amount and payment of their salaries.—He has erected a multitude of New Offices, and sent hither swarms of Officers to harrass our people, and eat out their substance.—He has kept among us, in times of peace, Standing Armies, without the Consent of our legislatures.—He has affected to render the Military independent of and superior to the Civil power.—He has combined with others to subject us to a jurisdiction foreign to our constitution, and unacknowledged by our laws; giving his Assent to their Acts of pretended Legislation:—For quartering large bodies of armed troops among us:—For protecting them, by a mock Trial, from punishment for any Murders which they should commit on the Inhabitants of these States:—For cutting off our Trade with all parts of the world:—For imposing Taxes on us without our Consent:—For depriving us in many cases, of the benefits of Trial by Jury:—For transporting us beyond Seas to be tried for pretended offences:—For abolishing the free System of English Laws in a neighbouring Province, establishing therein an Arbitrary government, and enlarging its Boundaries so as to render it at once an example and fit instrument for introducing the same absolute rule into these Colonies: —For taking away our Charters, abolishing our most valuable Laws, and altering fundamentally the Forms of our Governments:—For suspending our own Legislatures, and declaring themselves invested with power to legislate for us in all cases whatsoever.—He has abdicated Government here, by declaring us out of his Protection and waging War against us.—He has plundered our seas, ravaged our Coasts, burnt our towns, and destroyed the lives of our people.—He is at this time transporting large Armies of foreign Mercenaries to compleat the works of death, desolation and tyranny, already begun with circumstances of Cruelty & perfidy scarcely paralleled in the most barbarous ages, and totally unworthy the Head of a civilized nation.—He has constrained our fellow Citizens taken Captive on the high Seas to bear Arms against their Country, to become the executioners of their friends and Brethren, or to fall themselves by their Hands.—He has excited domestic insurrections amongst us, and has endeavoured to bring on the inhabitants of our frontiers, the merciless Indian Savages, whose known rule of warfare, is an undistinguished destruction of all ages, sexes and conditions. In every stage of these Oppressions We have Petitioned for Redress in the most humble terms: Our repeated Petitions have been answered only by repeated injury. A Prince, whose character is thus marked by every act which may define a Tyrant, is unfit to be the ruler of a free people. Nor have We been wanting in attentions to our Brittish brethren. We have warned them from time to time of attempts by their legislature to extend an unwarrantable jurisdiction over us. We have reminded them of the circumstances of our emigration and settlement here. We have appealed to their native justice and magnanimity, and we have conjured them by the ties of our common kindred to disavow these usurpations, which, would inevitably interrupt our connections and correspondence. They, too, have been deaf to the voice of justice and of consanguinity. We must, therefore, acquiesce in the necessity, which denounces our Separation, and hold them, as we hold the rest of mankind, Enemies in War, in Peace Friends.—

WE, THEREFORE, the REPRESENTATIVES of the UNITED STATES OF AMERICA, in General Congress, Assembled, appealing to the Supreme Judge of the world for the rectitude of our intentions, do, in the Name, and by Authority of the good People of these Colonies, solemnly publish and declare, That these United Colonies are, and of Right ought to be FREE AND INDEPENDENT STATES; that they are Absolved from all Allegiance to the British Crown, and that all political connection between them and the State of Great Britain, is and ought to be totally dissolved; and that as Free and Independent States, they have full Power to levy War, conclude Peace, contract Alliances, establish Commerce, and to do all other Acts and Things which Independent States may of right do.—And for the support of this Declaration, with a firm reliance on the protection of Divine Providence, we mutually pledge to each other our Lives, our Fortunes and our sacred Honor.

JOHN HANCOCK

New Hampshire

JOSIAH BARTLETT,
WM. WHIPPLE,
MATTHEW THORNTON.

Massachusetts Bay

SAML. ADAMS,
JOHN ADAMS,

Delaware

CAESAR RODNEY,
GEO. READ,
THO. M'KEAN.

Maryland

SAMUEL CHASE,
WM. PACA,

ROBT. TREAT PAINE,
ELBRIDGE GERRY.

Rhode Island

STEP. HOPKINS,
WILLIAM ELLERY.

Connecticut

ROGER SHERMAN,
SAM'EL HUNTINGTON,
WM. WILLIAMS,
OLIVER WOLCOTT.

New York

WM. FLOYD,
PHIL. LIVINGSTON,
FRANS. LEWIS,
LEWIS MORRIS.

New Jersey

RICHD. STOCKTON,
JNO. WITHERSPOON,
FRAS. HOPKINSON,
JOHN HART,
ABRA. CLARK.

Pennsylvania

ROBT. MORRIS,
BENJAMIN RUSH,
BENJA. FRANKLIN,
JOHN MORTON,
GEO. CLYMER,
JAS. SMITH,
GEO. TAYLOR,
JAMES WILSON,
GEO. ROSS.

THOS. STONE,
CHARLES CARROLL of Car-
rollton.

Virginia

GEORGE WYTHE,
RICHARD HENRY LEE,
TH. JEFFERSON,
BENJA. HARRISON,
THS. NELSON, JR.,
FRANCIS LIGHTFOOT LEE,
CARTER BRAXTON.

North Carolina

WM. HOOPER,
JOSEPH HEWES,
JOHN PENN.

South Carolina

EDWARD RUTLEDGE,
THOS. HEYWOOD, JUNR.,
THOMAS LYNCH, JUNR.,
ARTHUR MIDDLETON.

Georgia

BUTTON GWINNETT,
LYMAN HALL,
GEO. WALTON.

II

THE CONFEDERATION

CONGRESS ADOPTS THE ARTICLES
OF CONFEDERATION

On June 12, 1776, Congress appointed a committee of twelve to prepare a form of confederation. Their draft plan, reported on July 12, was written by John Dickinson. He drew much on a plan submitted by Franklin (not a member of the committee), although rejecting some of Franklin's crucial proposals. These included proportional representation, taxation based on all male polls (between sixteen and sixty), amendment of the constitution by majority of the legislature, and enumeration only in general terms of powers to be granted Congress. Dickinson both particularized and included negative restrictions on the power of Congress, thereby establishing a precedent of great influence. Thus when the Federal Convention finally decided on an enumerated rather than a general grant, the Framers borrowed directly from the Articles. After debate in the Committee of the Whole (which centered on the problems of taxation, representation, and the control of Western lands), the document was reported to Congress on August 20. A series of obstacles delayed consideration until the following year. Dickinson's original draft severely subordinated local governments to the central, which reflected prevailing sentiment at the time. Thereafter occurred a shift in outlook which Thomas Burke of North Carolina did most to encourage. This culminated with acceptance of the first three articles in April, 1777, which reversed the whole tenor of the original document. Approval of the remainder then waited primarily upon states which lacked Western territory, and after the last of these (Maryland) capitulated in February, 1781, Congress adopted the Articles, having meanwhile somewhat altered other parts.

ARTICLES OF CONFEDERATION

March 1, 1781

Royal formula

*To all to whom these Presents shall come, we the under signed
Delegates of the States affixed to our Names, send greeting.*

Whereas the Delegates of the United States of America, in
Congress assembled, did, on the 15th day of November, in the
Year of Our Lord One thousand Seven Hundred and Seventy-
seven, and in the Second Year of the Independence of America,
agree to certain articles of Confederation and perpetual Union
between the States of Newhampshire, Massachusetts-bay,
Rhodeisland and Providence Plantations, Connecticut, New
York, New Jersey, Pennsylvania, Delaware, Maryland, Virginia,
North-Carolina, South-Carolina, and Georgia in the words fol-
lowing, viz. "Articles of Confederation and perpetual Union
between the states of Newhampshire, Massachusetts-bay, Rhode-
island and Providence Plantations, Connecticut, New-York,
New-Jersey, Pennsylvania, Delaware, Maryland, Virginia,
North-Carolina, South-Carolina and Georgia."

Article I. The Stile of this confederacy shall be "The United
States of America."

Article II. Each state retains its sovereignty, freedom, and
independence, and every Power, Jurisdiction and right, which
is not by this confederation expressly delegated to the United
States, in Congress assembled.

Article III. The said states hereby severally enter into a firm
league of friendship with each other, for their common defence,
the security of their Liberties, and their mutual and general
welfare, binding themselves to assist each other, against all force
offered to, or attacks made upon them, or any of them, on account of religion, sovereignty, trade, or any other pretence
whatever.

Article IV. The better to secure and perpetuate mutual friendship and intercourse among the people of the different states in this union, the free inhabitants of each of these states, paupers, vagabonds and fugitives from justice excepted, shall be entitled to all privileges and immunities of free citizens in the several states; and the people of each state shall have free ingress and regress to and from any other state, and shall enjoy therein all the privileges of trade and commerce, subject to the same duties, impositions, and restrictions as the inhabitants thereof respectively, provided that such restriction shall not extend so far as to prevent the removal of property imported into any state, to any other state, of which the Owner is an inhabitant; provided also that no imposition, duties or restriction shall be laid by any state, on the property of the united states, or either of them.

If any Person guilty of, or charged with, treason, felony, or other high misdemeanor in any state, shall flee from Justice, and be found in any of the united states, he shall, upon demand of the Governor or executive power, of the state from which he fled, be delivered up and removed to the state having jurisdiction of his offence.

Full faith and credit shall be given in each of these states to the records, acts and judicial proceedings of the courts and magistrates of every other state.

Article V. For the more convenient management of the general interests of the united states, delegates shall be annually appointed, in such manner as the legislature of each state shall direct, to meet in Congress on the first Monday in November, in every year, with a power reserved to each state, to recal its delegates, or any of them, at any time within the year, and to send others in their stead, for the remainder of the Year.

No state shall be represented in Congress by less than two, nor by more than seven Members; and no person shall be capable of being a delegate for more than three years in any term of six years; nor shall any person, being a delegate, be capable of holding any office under the united states, for which he, or another for his benefit, receives any salary, fees or emolument of any kind.

Each state shall maintain its own delegates in a meeting of the states, and while they act as members of the committee of the states.

In determining questions in the united states in Congress assembled, each state shall have one vote.

Freedom of speech and debate in Congress shall not be impeached or questioned in any Court, or place out of Congress, and the members of congress shall be protected in their persons from arrests and imprisonments, during the time of their going to and from, and attendance on congress, except for treason, felony, or breach of the peace.

Article VI. No state, without the Consent of the united states in congress assembled, shall send any embassy to, or receive any embassy from, or enter into any conference, agreement, alliance or treaty with any King, prince, or state; nor shall any person holding any office of profit or trust under the united states, or any of them, accept of any present, emolument, office or title of any kind whatever from any king, prince or foreign state; nor shall the united states in congress assembled, or any of them, grant any title of nobility.

No two or more states shall enter into any treaty, confederation, or alliance whatever between them, without the consent of the united states in congress assembled, specifying accurately the purposes for which the same is to be entered into, and how long it shall continue.

No state shall lay any imposts or duties, which may interfere with any stipulations in treaties, entered into by the united states in congress assembled, with any king, prince or state, in pursuance of any treaties already proposed by congress, to the courts of France and Spain.

No vessels of war shall be kept up in time of peace by any state, except such number only, as shall be deemed necessary by the united states in congress assembled, for the defence of such state, or its trade; nor shall any body of forces be kept up by any state, in time of peace, except such number only, as in the judgment of the united states, in congress assembled, shall be deemed requisite to garrison the forts necessary for the defence of such state; but every state shall always keep up a well regulated and disciplined militia, sufficiently armed and accoutred, and shall provide and constantly have ready for use, in public stores, a due number of field pieces and tents, and a proper quantity of arms, ammunition and camp equipage.

No state shall engage in any war without the consent of the united states in congress assembled, unless such state be actually invaded by enemies, or shall have received certain advice of a resolution being formed by some nation of Indians to invade such state, and the danger is so imminent as not to admit of a delay till the united states in congress assembled can be consulted: nor shall any state grant commissions to any ships or vessels of war, nor letters of marque or reprisal, except it be after a declaration of war by the united states in congress assembled, and then only against the kingdom or state and the subjects thereof, against which war has been so declared, and under such regulations as shall be established by the united states in congress assembled, unless such state be infested by pirates, in which case vessels of war may be fitted out for that occasion, and kept so long as the danger shall continue, or until the united states in congress assembled, shall determine otherwise.

Article VII. When land-forces are raised by any state for the common defence, all officers of or under the rank of colonel, shall be appointed by the legislature of each state respectively, by whom such forces shall be raised, or in such manner as such state shall direct, and all vacancies shall be filled up by the State which first made the appointment.

Article VIII. All charges of war, and all other expences that shall be incurred for the common defence or general welfare, and allowed by the united states in congress assembled, shall be defrayed out of a common treasury, which shall be supplied by the several states in proportion to the value of all land within each state, granted to or surveyed for any Person, as such land

and the buildings and improvements thereon shall be estimated according to such mode as the united states in congress assembled, shall from time to time direct and appoint. The taxes for paying that proportion shall be laid and levied by the authority and direction of the legislatures of the several states within the time agreed upon by the united states in congress assembled.

Article IX. The united states in congress assembled, shall have the sole and exclusive right and power of determining on peace and war, except in the cases mentioned in the sixth article —of sending and receiving ambassadors—entering into treaties and alliances, provided that no treaty of commerce shall be made whereby the legislative power of the respective states shall be restrained from imposing such imposts and duties on foreigners as their own people are subjected to, or from prohibiting the exportation or importation of any species of goods or commodities whatsoever—of establishing rules for deciding in all cases, what captures on land or water shall be legal, and in what manner prizes taken by land or naval forces in the service of the united states shall be divided or appropriated—of granting letters of marque and reprisal in times of peace—appointing courts for the trial of piracies and felonies committed on the high seas and establishing courts for receiving and determining finally appeals in all cases of captures, provided that no member of congress shall be appointed a judge of any of the said courts.

The united states in congress assembled shall also be the last resort on appeal in all disputes and differences now subsisting or that hereafter may arise between two or more states concerning boundary, jurisdiction or any other cause whatever; which authority shall always be exercised in the manner following. Whenever the legislative or executive authority or lawful agent of any state in controversy with another shall present a petition to congress stating the matter in question and praying for a hearing, notice thereof shall be given by order of congress to the legislative or executive authority of the other state in con-

troversy, and a day assigned for the appearance of the parties
by their lawful agents, who shall then be directed to appoint by
joint consent, commissioners or judges to constitute a court for
hearing and determining the matter in question; but if they
cannot agree, congress shall name three persons out of each of
the united states, and from the list of such persons each party
shall alternately strike out one, the petitioners beginning. until
the number shall be reduced to thirteen; and from that number
not less than seven, nor more than nine names as congress shall
direct, shall in the presence of congress be drawn out by lot, and
the persons whose names shall be so drawn or any five of them,
shall be commissioners or judges, to hear and finally determine
the controversy, so always as a major part of the judges who
shall hear the cause shall agree in the determination: and if
either party shall neglect to attend at the day appointed, without showing reasons, which congress shall judge sufficient, or
being present shall refuse to strike, the congress shall proceed
to nominate three persons out of each state, and the secretary of
congress shall strike in behalf of such party absent or refusing;
and the judgment and sentence of the court to be appointed, in
the manner before prescribed, shall be final and conclusive;
and if any of the parties shall refuse to submit to the authority
of such court, or to appear or defend their claim or cause, the
court shall nevertheless proceed to pronounce sentence, or
judgment, which shall in like manner be final and decisive, the
judgment or sentence and other proceedings being in either
case transmitted to congress, and lodged among the acts of
congress for the security of the parties concerned: provided that
every commissioner, before he sits in judgment, shall take an
oath to be administered by one of the judges of the supreme or
superior court of the state, where the cause shall be tried, "well
and truly to hear and determine the matter in question, according to the best of his judgment, without favour, affection or
hope of reward:" provided also, that no state shall be deprived
of territory for the benefit of the united states.

All controversies concerning the private right of soil claimed
under different grants of two or more states, whose jurisdictions

as they may respect such lands, and the states which passed such grants are adjusted, the said grants or either of them being at the same time claimed to have originated antecedent to such settlement of jurisdiction, shall on the petition of either party to the congress of the united states, be finally determined as near as may be in the same manner as is before prescribed for deciding disputes respecting territorial jurisdiction between different states.

The united states in congress assembled shall also have the sole and exclusive right and power of regulating the alloy and value of coin struck by their own authority, or by that of the respective states—fixing the standard of weights and measures throughout the united states—regulating the trade and managing all affairs with the Indians, not members of any of the states, provided that the legislative right of any state within its own limits be not infringed or violated—establishing or regulating post-offices from one state to another, throughout all the united states, and exacting such postage on the papers passing thro' the same as may be requisite to defray the expences of the said office—appointing all officers of the land forces, in the service of the united states, excepting regimental officers—appointing all the officers of the naval forces, and commissioning all officers whatever in the service of the united states—making rules for the government and regulation of the said land and naval forces, and directing their operations.

The united states in congress assembled shall have authority to appoint a committee, to sit in the recess of congress, to be denominated "A Committee of the States," and to consist of one delegate from each state; and to appoint such other committees and civil officers as may be necessary for managing the general affairs of the united states under their direction—to appoint one of their number to preside, provided that no person be allowed to serve in the office of president more than one year in any term of three years; to ascertain the necessary sums of money to be raised for the service of the united states, and to appropriate and apply the same for defraying the public expences—to borrow money, or emit bills on the credit of the united states, transmitting every half year to the respective states on account of the sums of money so borrowed or emitted,—to build and equip a navy—to agree upon the number of land forces, and to make requisitions from each state for its quota, in proportion to the number of white inhabitants in such state; which requisition shall be binding, and thereupon the legislature of each state shall appoint the regimental officers, raise the men and cloath, arm and equip them in a soldier-like manner, at the expence of the united states; and the officers and men so cloathed, armed and equipped shall march to the place appointed, and within the time agreed on by the united states in congress assembled: But if the united states in congress assembled shall, on consideration of circumstances, judge proper that any state should not raise men, or should raise a smaller number than its quota, and that any other state should raise a greater number of men than the quota thereof, such extra number shall be raised, officered, cloathed, armed and equipped in the same manner as the quota of such state, unless the legislature of such state shall judge that such extra number cannot be safely spared out of the same, in which case they shall raise officer, cloath, arm and equip as many of such extra number as they judge can be safely spared. And the officers and men so cloathed, armed and equipped, shall march to the place appointed, and within the time agreed on by the united states in congress assembled.

The united states in congress assembled shall never engage in a war, nor grant letters of marque and reprisal in time of peace, nor enter into any treaties or alliances, nor coin money, nor regulate the value thereof, nor ascertain the sums and expences necessary for the defence and welfare of the united states, or any of them, nor emit bills, nor borrow money on the credit of the united states, nor appropriate money, nor agree upon the number of vessels of war, to be built or purchased, or the number of land or sea forces to be raised, nor appoint a commander in chief of the army or navy, **unless nine states** assent to the same: nor shall a question on any other point, except for adjourning from day to day be determined, unless by the votes of a majority of the united states in congress assembled.

The congress of the united states shall have power to adjourn to any time within the year, and to any place within the united states, so that no period of adjournment be for a longer duration than the space of six Months, and shall publish the Journal of their proceedings monthly, except such parts thereof relating to treaties, alliances or military operations, as in their judgment require secrecy; and the yeas and nays of the delegates of each state on any question shall be entered on the Journal, when it is desired by any delegate; and the delegates of a state, or any of them, at his or their request shall be furnished with a transcript of the said Journal, except such parts as are above excepted, to lay before the legislatures of the several states.

Article X. The committee of the states, or any nine of them, shall be authorized to execute, in the recess of congress, such of the powers of congress as the united states in congress assembled, by the consent of nine states, shall from time to time think expedient to vest them with; provided that no power be delegated to the said committee, for the exercise of which, by the articles of confederation, the voice of nine states in the congress of the united states assembled is requisite.

Article XI. Canada acceding to this confederation, and joining in the measures of the united states, shall be admitted into, and entitled to all the advantages of this union: but no other colony shall be admitted into the same, unless such admission be agreed to by nine states.

Article XII. All bills of credit emitted, monies borrowed and debts contracted by, or under the authority of congress, before the assembling of the united states, in pursuance of the present confederation, shall be deemed and considered as a charge against the united states, for payment and satisfaction whereof the said united states, and the public faith are hereby solemnly pledged.

Article XIII. Every state shall abide by the determinations of the united states in congress assembled, on all questions which by this confederation are submitted to them. And the Articles of this confederation shall be inviolably observed by every state, and the union shall be perpetual; nor shall any alteration at any time hereafter be made in any of them; unless such alteration be agreed to in a congress of the united states, and be afterwards confirmed by the legislatures of every state.

And Whereas it hath pleased the Great Governor of the World to incline the hearts of the legislatures we respectively represent in congress, to approve of, and to authorize us to ratify the said articles of confederation and perpetual union. Know Ye that we the undersigned delegates, by virtue of the power and authority to us given for that purpose, do by these presents, in the name and in behalf of our respective constituents, fully and entirely ratify and confirm each and every of the said articles of confederation and perpetual union, and all and singular the matters and things therein contained: And we do further solemnly plight and engage the faith of our respective constituents, that they shall abide by the determinations of the united states in congress assembled, on all questions, which by the said confederation are submitted to them. And that the articles thereof shall be inviolably observed by the states we respectively represent, and that the union shall be perpetual.

In Witness whereof we have hereunto set our hands in Congress. Done at Philadelphia in the state of Pennsylvania the ninth day of July, in the Year of our Lord one Thousand seven Hundred and Seventy-eight, and in the third year of the independence of America.

On the part & behalf of the State of New Hampshire
JOSIAH BARTLETT JOHN WENTWORTH, Junr
August 8th, 1778

On the part and behalf of the State of Massachusetts Bay

JOHN HANCOCK

SAMUEL ADAMS

ELBRIDGE GERRY

FRANCIS DANA

JAMES LOVELL

SAMUEL HOLTEN

On the part and behalf of the State of Rhode Island and Providence Plantations

WILLIAM ELLERY

HENRY MARCHANT

JOHN COLLINS

On the part and behalf of the State of Connecticut

ROGER SHERMAN

SAMUEL HUNTINGTON

OLIVER WOLCOTT

TITUS HOSMER

ANDREW ADAMS

On the part and behalf of the State of New York

JAS. DUANE

FRA. LEWIS

GOUV. MORRIS

WM. DUER

On the part and in behalf of the State of New Jersey Novr. 26, 1778

JNO. WITHERSPOON

NATHL. SCUDDER

On the part and behalf of the State of Pennsylvania

ROBT. MORRIS

DANIEL ROBERDEAU

JNO. BAYARD SMITH

WILLIAM CLINGAN

JOSEPH REED, 22d July, 1778

On the part & behalf of the State of Delaware

THOS. M'KEAN, Feby. 12, 1779

NICHOLAS VAN DYKE

JOHN DICKINSON, May 5th, 1779

On the part and behalf of the State of Maryland

JOHN HANSON, March 1, 1781

DANIEL CARROLL, Mar. 1, 1781

On the part and behalf of the State of Virginia

RICHARD HENRY LEE

JOHN BANISTER

THOMAS ADAMS

JNO. HARVIE

FRANCIS LIGHTFOOT LEE

On the part and behalf of the State of No. Carolina

JOHN PENN, July 21, 1778   JNO. WILLIAMS
CORNS. HARNETT

On the part & behalf of the State of South Carolina

HENRY LAURENS   RICHD. HUTSON
WILLIAM HENRY DRAYTON   THOS. HEYWARD, Junr
JNO. MATTHEWS

On the part & behalf of the State of Georgia

EDWD. TELFAIR   EDWD. LANGWORTHY
JNO. WALTON, 24 July,
   1778

THE ANNAPOLIS CONVENTION

Among men who discerned a close connection between commercial and political distress was Madison, who encountered much opposition in Virginia in his attempt to improve the government under the Articles of Confederation. Unable to approach his goal directly, he emphasized the importance of commercial improvement. After inducing Virginia to meet with Maryland in 1785, he secured—it was the most he could obtain—a resolution from the General Assembly in 1786 to promote this end. Though the commercial convention at Annapolis failed, commissioners snatched victory from their seeming defeat. Hamilton undoubtedly pointed the way. He drafted for the committee a report calling for a constitutional convention which boldly asserted that grave conditions necessitated a powerful government. Madison urged caution lest Edmund Randolph and thus Virginia be lost. Then, in a statement which President Dickinson transmitted to the Continental Congress, Hamilton with superb literary craftsmanship almost imperceptibly and irrevocably transmuted a call for a general commercial convention into a call for a genuine constitutional convention.

RESOLUTION OF THE GENERAL ASSEMBLY OF VIRGINIA

January 21, 1786

Resolved, That Edmund Randolph, James Madison, jun. Walter Jones, Saint George Tucker, and Meriwether Smith, Esquires, be appointed commissioners, who, or any three of whom, shall meet such commissioners as may be appointed by the other States in the Union, at a time and place to be agreed on, to take into consideration the trade of the United States; to examine the relative situations and trade of the said States; to consider how far a uniform system in their commercial regulations may be necessary to their common interest and their permanent harmony; and to report to the several States, such an act relative to this great object, as, when unanimously ratified by them, will enable the United States in Congress, effectually to provide for the same.

PROCEEDINGS OF COMMISSIONERS TO REMEDY
DEFECTS OF THE FEDERAL GOVERNMENT
ANNAPOLIS IN THE STATE OF MARYLAND

September 11, 1786

At a meeting of Commissioners, from the States of New York, New Jersey, Pennsylvania, Delaware and Virginia—

Present

ALEXANDER HAMILTON EGBERT BENSON	*New York*
ABRAHAM CLARKE WILLIAM C. HOUSTON JAMES SCHUARMAN	*New Jersey*
TENCH COXE	*Pennsylvania*
GEORGE READ JOHN DICKINSON RICHARD BASSETT	*Delaware*
EDMUND RANDOLPH JAMES MADISON, Junior SAINT GEORGE TUCKER	*Virginia*

Mr Dickinson was unanimously elected Chairman.

The Commissioners produced their Credentials from their respective States; which were read.

After a full communication of Sentiments, and deliberate consideration of what would be proper to be done by the Commissioners now assembled, it was unanimously agreed: that a Committee be appointed to prepare a draft of a Report to be made to the States having Commissioners attending at this meeting . . . .

September 14, 1786

. . . the Report . . . was unanimously agreed to, and is as follows, to wit.

To the Honorable, the Legislatures of Virginia, Delaware, Pennsylvania, New Jersey, and New York—
The Commissioners from the said States, respectively assembled at Annapolis, humbly beg leave to report.

That, pursuant to their several appointments, they met, at Annapolis in the State of Maryland, on the eleventh day of September Instant, and having proceeded to a Communication of their powers; they found that the States of New York, Pennsylvania, and Virginia, had, in substance, and nearly in the same terms, authorised their respective Commissioners "to meet such Commissioners as were, or might be, appointed by the other States in the Union, at such time and place, as should be agreed upon by the said Commissioners to take into consideration the trade and Commerce of the United States, to consider how far an uniform system in their commercial intercourse and regulations might be necessary to their common interest and permanent harmony, and to report to the several States such an Act, relative to this great object, as when unanimously ratified by them would enable the United States in Congress assembled effectually to provide for the same."

That the State of Delaware, had given similar powers to their Commissioners, with this difference only, that the Act to be framed in virtue of those powers, is required to be reported "to the United States in Congress assembled, to be agreed to by them, and confirmed by the Legislatures of every State."

That the State of New Jersey had enlarged the object of their appointment, empowering their Commissioners, "to consider how far an uniform system in their commercial regulations and *other important matters,* might be necessary to the common interest and permanent harmony of the several States," and to report such an Act on the subject, as when ratified by them "would enable the United States in Congress assembled, effectually to provide for the exigencies of the Union."

That appointments of Commissioners have also been made by the States of New Hampshire, Massachusetts, Rhode Island, and North Carolina, none of whom however have attended; but that no information has been received by your Commissioners, of any appointment having been made by the States of Connecticut, Maryland, South Carolina or Georgia.

That the express terms of the powers to your Commissioners supposing a deputation from all the States, and having for object the Trade and Commerce of the United States, Your Commissioners did not conceive it advisable to proceed on the business of their mission, under the Circumstance of so partial and defective a representation.

Deeply impressed however with the magnitude and importance of the object confided to them on this occasion, your Commissioners cannot forbear to indulge an expression of their earnest and unanimous wish, that speedy measures may be taken, to effect a general meeting, of the States, in a future Convention, for the same, and such other purposes, as the situation of public affairs, may be found to require.

If in expressing this wish, or in intimating any other sentiment, your Commissioners should seem to exceed the strict bounds of their appointment, they entertain a full confidence, that a conduct, dictated by an anxiety for the welfare, of the United States, will not fail to receive an indulgent construction.

In this persuasion, your Commissioners submit an opinion, that the Idea of extending the powers of their Deputies, to other objects, than those of Commerce, which has been adopted by the State of New Jersey, was an improvement on the original plan, and will deserve to be incorporated into that of a future Convention; they are the more naturally led to this conclusion, as in the course of their reflections on the subject, they have been induced to think, that the power of regulating trade is of such comprehensive extent, and will enter so far into the general System of the fœderal government, that to give it efficacy, and to obviate questions and doubts concerning its precise nature and limits, may require a correspondent adjustment of other parts of the Fœderal System.

That there are important defects in the system of the Fœderal Government is acknowledged by the Acts of all those States, which have concurred in the present Meeting; That the defects, upon a closer examination, may be found greater and more numerous, than even these acts imply, is at least so far probable, from the embarrassments which characterise the present State of our national affairs, foreign and domestic, as may reasonably be supposed to merit a deliberate and candid discussion, in some mode, which will unite the Sentiments and Councils of all the States. In the choice of the mode, your Commissioners are of opinion, that a Convention of Deputies from the different States, for the special and sole purpose of entering into this investigation, and digesting a plan for supplying such defects as may be discovered to exist, will be entitled to a preference from considerations, which will occur, without being particularised.

Your Commissioners decline an enumeration of those national circumstances on which their opinion respecting the propriety of a future Convention, with more enlarged powers, is founded; as it would be an useless intrusion of facts and observations, most of which have been frequently the subject of public discussion, and none of which can have escaped the penetration of those to whom they would in this instance be addressed. They are however of a nature so serious, as, in the view of your Commissioners to render the situation of the United States delicate and critical, calling for an exertion of the united virtue and wisdom of all the members of the Confederacy.

Under this impression, Your Commissioners, with the most respectful deference, beg leave to suggest their unanimous conviction, that it may essentially tend to advance the interests of the union, if the States, by whom they have been respectively delegated, would themselves concur, and use their endeavours to procure the concurrence of the other States, in the appointment of Commissioners, to meet at Philadelphia on the second Monday in May next, to take into consideration the situation of the United States, to devise such further provisions as shall appear to them necessary to render the constitution of the Fœderal Government adequate to the exigencies of the Union; and to report such an Act for that purpose to the United States in Congress assembled, as when agreed to, by them, and afterwards confirmed by the Legislatures of every State, will effectually provide for the same.

Though your Commissioners could not with propriety address these observations and sentiments to any but the States they have the honor to Represent, they have nevertheless concluded from motives of respect, to transmit Copies of this Report to the United States in Congress assembled, and to the executives of the other States.

APPOINTING DELEGATES TO AND RECOMMENDING A FEDERAL CONVENTION

Madison returned from Annapolis to pen the resolution by which Virginia appointed deputies to the Federal Convention. Subsequently, and before Congress acted, six other states followed suit: New Jersey (November), Pennsylvania (December), North Carolina (January 6), New Hampshire (January 17; followed by a new act on June 27), Delaware (February 3), Georgia (February 10). Virginia granted generous power in a phrase including the words "all such alterations" and "adequate to the exigencies of the Union" (which Madison largely borrowed from Hamilton), and the Virginia instructions were copied or paraphrased by others. Delaware added the unique stipulation that her delegates could not accept any alteration of that clause of the Articles which guaranteed the equal representation of all states. But when Congress, which temporarily expired after receiving the report of the Annapolis Convention, finally did something, it restricted the role of the deputies. Even this resolution had first to contend with one (from New York) which aimed at issuing a new call under the auspices of Congress, which some in that body saw as a move to frustrate the whole enterprise or create two or more confederacies. Of the five states which subsequently commissioned delegates—New York (February 28), South Carolina (March 8), Massachusetts (March 10),

Connecticut (May 10), Maryland (May 26)—three incorporated the restrictive proviso from the February 21 resolution of Congress. (Cf. p. 63.)

THE VIRGINIA RESOLUTION

October 16, 1786

WHEREAS the Commissioners who assembled at Annapolis on the fourteenth day of September last for the purpose of devising and reporting the means of enabling Congress to provide effectually for the Commercial Interests of the United States have represented the necessity of extending the revision of the fœderal System to all it's defects and have recommended that Deputies for that purpose be appointed by the several Legislatures to meet in Convention in the City of Philadelphia on the second [Mon]day of May next, a provision which was preferable to a discussion of the subject in Congress where it might be too much interrupted by the ordinary business before them and where it would besides be deprived of the valuable Counsels of sundry Individuals who are disqualified by the Constitution or Laws of particular States or restrained by peculiar circumstances from a Seat in that Assembly: AND WHEREAS the General Assembly of this Commonwealth, taking into view the actual situation of the Confederacy as well as reflecting on the alarming representations made from time to time by the United States in Congress particularly in their Act of the fifteenth day of February last [1] can no longer doubt that the Crisis is arrived at which

[1] [This centered on the money question. Congress lacked funds and was unable to do much about it. A committee which reported on February 15 had considered the operation of the revenue system recommended to the states on April 18, 1785. (This stipulated the proportion of a total sum, then $1,500,000, which each state should contribute annually to Congress until a new rule regarding revenue could be carried into effect. On September 27, 1785, this total and the share of each state were doubled. See p. 74 and Appendix II.) As a result of the failure of states to comply with the system which successive congresses had approved over a period of three years, the committee stated, the public embarrassments over the shortage of money were so great that Congress should declare that a crisis had arrived when the people for whom the federal government was instituted must

the good People of America are to decide the solemn question whether they will by wise and magnanimous Efforts reap the just fruits of that Independence which they have so gloriously acquired and of that Union which they have cemented with so much of their common Blood, or whether by giving way to unmanly Jealousies and Prejudices or to partial and transitory Interests they will renounce the auspicious blessings prepared for them by the Revolution, and furnish to its Enemies an eventual Triumph over those by whose virtue and valor it has been accomplished: AND WHEREAS the same noble and extended policy and the same fraternal and affectionate Sentiments which originally determined the Citizens of this Commonwealth to unite with their Bretheren of the other States in establishing a Fœderal Government cannot but be Felt with equal force now as motives to lay aside every inferior consideration and to concur in such farther concessions and Provisions as may be necessary to secure the great Objects for which that Government was instituted and to render the *United States* as happy in peace as they have been glorious in War: BE IT THEREFORE ENACTED by the General Assembly of the Commonwealth of Virginia that seven Commissioners be appointed by joint Ballot of both Houses of Assembly who, or any three of them, are hereby authorized as Deputies from this Commonwealth to meet such Deputies as may be appointed and authorized by other States to assemble in Convention at Philadelphia as above recommended and to join with them in devising and discussing all such Alterations and farther Provisions as may be necessary to render the Fœderal Constitution adequate to the Exigencies of the Union and in reporting such an Act for that purpose to the United

decide whether they would support their rank as a nation. Thereupon Congress, announcing that the most fatal evils would flow from a breach of public faith, resolved that the 1783 recommendations again be presented to the states which had not fully complied, and earnestly urged upon those which had only partly done so, and those—Rhode Island, New York, Maryland, and Georgia—which had done neither. Worthington C. Ford, ed., *Journals of the Continental Congress*, XXX, 70-76. (Hereafter referred to as Ford, *Journals*.)]

States in Congress as when agreed to by them and duly confirmed by the several States will effectually provide for the same. ... AND the Governor is requested to transmit forthwith a Copy of this Act to the United States in Congress and to the Executives of each of the States in the Union.

THE DELAWARE RESOLUTION

February 3, 1787

... Whereas the General Assembly of this State are fully convinced of the Necessity of revising the Federal Constitution, and adding thereto such further Provisions, as may render the same more adequate to the Exigencies of the Union; And Whereas the Legislature of Virginia have already passed an Act of that Commonwealth, appointing and authorizing certain Commissioners to meet, at the City of Philadelphia, in May next, a Convention of Commissioners or Deputies from the different States: And this State being willing and desirous of co-operating with the Commonwealth of Virginia, and the other States in the Confederation, in so useful a design.

Be it therefore enacted by the General Assembly of Delaware, that . . . George Read, Gunning Bedford, John Dickinson, Richard Bassett and Jacob Broom, Esquires, or any three of them, are hereby constituted and appointed Deputies from this State, with Powers to meet such Deputies as may be appointed and authorized by the other States to assemble in the said Convention at the City aforesaid, and to join with them in devising, deliberating on, and discussing, such Alterations and further Provisions as may be necessary to render the Fœderal Constitution adequate to the Exigencies of the Union; and in reporting such Act or Acts for that purpose to the United States in Congress Assembled, as when agreed to by them, and duly confirmed by the several States, may effectually provide for the same: So always and Provided, that such Alterations or further Provisions, or any of them, do not extend to that part of the Fifth Article of the Confederation of the said States, finally ratified on the first day of March, in the Year One thousand seven hundred and eighty one, which declares that "in determining Questions in the United States in Congress Assembled each State shall have one Vote." . . .

PROCEEDINGS IN CONGRESS

February 21, 1787

The report of a grand com^ee^ . . . was called up and which is contained in the following resolution viz

"Congress having had under consideration the letter of John Dickinson esq^r^ chairman of the Commissioners who assembled at Annapolis during the last year also the proceedings of the said commissioners and entirely coinciding with them as to the inefficiency of the federal government and the necessity of devising such farther provisions as shall render the same adequate to the exigencies of the Union do strongly recommend to the different legislatures to send forward delegates to meet the proposed convention on the second Monday in May next at the city of Philadelphia."

The delegates for the state of New York thereupon laid before Congress Instructions which they had received from their constituents, and in pursuance of the said instructions moved to postpone the farther consideration of the report in order to take up the following proposition to wit:

"That it be recommended to the States composing the Union that a convention of representatives from the said States respectively be held at   on   for the purpose of revising the Articles of Confederation and perpetual Union between the United States of America and reporting to the United States in Congress assembled and to the States respectively such alterations and amendments of the said Articles of Confederation as the representatives met in such convention shall judge proper and necessary to render them adequate to the preservation and support of the Union."

On the question to postpone for the purpose above mentioned . . . the question was lost.

A motion was then made by the delegates for Massachusetts to postpone the farther consideration of the report in order to take into consideration a motion which they read in their place; this being agreed to, the motion of the delegates for Massachusetts was taken up and being amended was agreed to as follows

Whereas there is provision in the Articles of Confederation and perpetual Union for making alterations therein by the assent of a Congress of the United States and of the legislatures of the several States; And whereas experience hath evinced that there are defects in the present Confederation, as a mean to remedy which several of the States and particularly the State of New York by express instructions to their delegates in Congress have suggested a convention for the purposes expressed in the following resolution, and such convention appearing to be the most probable mean of establishing in these states a firm national government.

Resolved that in the opinion of Congress it is expedient that on the second Monday in May next a Convention of delegates who shall have been appointed by the several states be held at Philadelphia for the sole and express purpose of revising the Articles of Confederation and reporting to Congress and the several legislatures such alterations and provisions therein as shall, when agreed to in Congress and confirmed by the states render the federal constitution adequate to the exigencies of Government and the preservation of the Union.

III

THE FEDERAL CONVENTION:
MADISON'S NOTES OF DEBATES

IS IT NOT the glory of the people of America, that, whilst they have paid a decent regard to the opinions of former times and other nations, they have not suffered a blind veneration for antiquity, for custom, or for names, to overrule the suggestions of their own good sense, the knowledge of their own situation, and the lessons of their own experience? To this manly spirit, posterity will be indebted for the possession, and the world for the example, of the numerous innovations displayed on the American theatre, in favor of private rights and public happiness. Had no important step been taken by the leaders of the Revolution for which a precedent could not be discovered, no government established of which an exact model did not present itself, the people of the United States might, at this moment, have been numbered among the melancholy victims of misguided councils, must at best have been laboring under the weight of some of those forms which have crushed the liberties of the rest of mankind. Happily for America, happily, we trust, for the whole human race, they pursued a new and more noble course. They accomplished a Revolution which has no parallel in the annals of human society. They reared the fabrics of governments which have no model on the face of the globe. . . . If they erred most in the structure of the Union, this was the work most difficult to be executed; this is the work which has been new modelled by the act of your convention. . . .

JAMES MADISON

Federalist No. 14.

EDITOR'S FOREWORD

In his "Notes of Debates" Madison admirably fulfilled his pre-Convention resolve to keep a full account of the constitutional deliberations. However, the secrecy surrounding the conclave long kept his and other records from the public. During the time following the Convention, Madison came to be less in favor of a strong central government and joined Jefferson in placing stronger emphasis on state rights.

In preparing his report for posthumous publication, this change in his political outlook caused Madison some embarrassment, especially after the appearance in 1819 and 1821 of two fragmentary accounts of the Convention. Since Madison's "Notes of Debates," of which the following abbreviated version forms the core of this volume, are the major source of information of what transpired at the Convention, a review of these circumstances may be of interest.

Madison had learned from pre-Convention research that material on the formation of ancient confederacies was inadequate. Thus he went to Philadelphia determined to preserve as exact an account as possible of what went on there. This would be valuable, he thought, for the history of a constitution on which would be staked "the happiness of a people great even in its infancy, and possibly the cause of liberty throughout the world."[1] Absent neither a single day nor more than a casual fraction of an hour, Madison believed he missed no speech, unless a very short one. From the commanding position he chose in front of the presiding officer, he recorded in abbreviated form everything that occurred and wrote out his notes between sessions, finishing within a few days after adjournment. He recounted all speeches, even his own, in the third person. Added to the incredible industry of making such copious notes, which diminished in quantity after late August, was the leading role the Virginian took in the deliberations. He nearly broke under the total strain.

Madison's worthy account was first published in 1840, more than half a century after the delegates disbanded, and

[1] Gaillard Hunt, *The Writings of James Madison.* 9 vols. (New York, 1900-10), II, 410.

at a time when the growing sectional struggle charged every scrap of evidence bearing on the formation of the Constitution with great significance. Earlier, after retiring from the Presidency in 1817, Madison had begun to revise his notes, perfecting the style and polishing his handiwork. Shortly thereafter, two other eyewitness records were published. The official journal was a poorly kept set of dry bones which recounted motions and votes but no speeches. Delegates directed secretary William Jackson to turn this over to the presiding officer, which he did without ever putting it into final shape. In 1796 Washington had deposited these papers with the Department of State, which assembled and published them in 1819. This breach of the secrecy hitherto surrounding the Framers' work was widened by publication in 1821 of the notes of Robert Yates. These, though second in importance only to Madison's, had certain inadequacies and went no further than July 5, which was just before Yates quit the sessions for good. As these two versions appeared, Madison added to or corrected his chronicle in the light of them. From the former he obtained the wording of motions previously missed and actions previously unrecorded, and he changed some votes in his record to comply with the not always reliable journal. He drew on Yates to supplement his report of certain speeches.

After the Convention Madison abandoned the high nationalism he expounded there and became, along with Jefferson, a leading spokesman for the doctrine of state sovereignty. But since secrecy long shrouded the Philadelphia debates, his past never embarrassed him until publication of Yates's notes first disclosed Madison's true position of 1787. He then met these revelations with denials and countercharges. As sectionalism and state rights feelings deepened in the late twenties, he refused when urged to issue his own account. He was undoubtedly restrained by awareness that this would confirm Yates's version, although his announced reason was that two other Framers—Rufus King and William Few—were still living. Nevertheless, he highly valued his notes, and in his will (dated April 19, 1835) stated that "it is not an unreasonable inference that a careful and extended report of the proceedings and discussions of that body, which were within closed doors, by a member who was constant in his attendance, will be particularly gratifying to the people of the United States, and to all who take an interest in the progress of political science and the cause of true liberty. It is my desire," he added, "that the report as made by me should be published. . . ." [2] But in preparing his material for posthumous publication he had had to resolve a dilemma: should he let the record stand and undermine his later position, or alter his earlier to justify his subsequent views?

In working through his original manuscript he made many revisions, most of which were merely corrections and additions from the published journal and from Yates. He also personally supervised the copying of a transcript of this by his brother-in-law, John C. Payne. In perusing this Madison made a few final additions in his own hand. (Payne then made a few alterations and corrections in the original manuscript, at the end of which Madison wrote that all such changes not in his own hand were dictated by him and made by Payne in his presence.) Thus the original manuscript notes are free from possible errors of transcription, but the former needs to be compared with the transcript copy to determine Madison's final judgments.

Subsequent to 1840, when Madison's notes were first published (based on Payne's transcript), four different editions of Madison's original manuscript have been printed. Two of these indicate on the printed page the alterations Madison made in his original manuscript. The most recent of these is Max Farrand's edition of *The Records of the Federal Convention of 1787,* published in three volumes in 1911 and in a revised four-volume edition in 1937. *The Debates in the Federal Convention of 1787,* edited by Gaillard Hunt and James Brown Scott in 1920, prints Madison's original manuscript and the changes he made in it without distinguishing between the two. Either of these texts is, as Farrand maintains, sufficiently accurate to be followed without the slightest hesitation.[3] (Thus both read the same, the chief practical difference being that Farrand prints certain material in angular brackets to show changes, and in footnotes tells what Madison struck out.) However, the Hunt and Scott text includes in footnotes the additions Madison made in the transcript, the most important of which are given in footnotes to the text as printed here. As for the changes Madison effected in his origi-

2 *Ibid.,* IX, 549.

3 Max Farrand, *The Records of the Federal Convention of 1787* (New Haven, 1937), IV, xii.

nal notes, his latest biographer concludes that upon close inspection these "fade away as evidence of distortion or become the contrary." Madison struck out a few state names from harsh remarks and deleted a few words to tone down nationalism. "But the change is microscopic," says Irving Brant. "The notes stand as an impressive example of integrity and impartiality, in the face of powerful motives for suppression."[4] Around the turn of the century were published the more fragmentary records of King (1894), Pierce (1898), Paterson (1904), Hamilton (1905), and McHenry (1906), followed by those of Lansing (1939). Presumably few if any new accounts by participants will be discovered. The available evidence all testifies to Madison's authenticity.[5]

This abstract of Madison's record is based on the Hunt and Scott text as that is reproduced in *Documents Illustrative of the Formation of the Union of the American States*, a volume published by direction of the First Session of the Sixty-Ninth Congress as House Document No. 398 in Washington in 1927. (The materials in that work were selected, arranged, and indexed by Charles C. Tansill.) Thus the text here is based on the original manuscript as amended, and the important changes added to the transcript copy are indicated in footnotes. Although I have not compared the texts in Hunt and Scott and *Documents Illustrative* word for word, I have read the latter against the former and also Farrand on doubtful points, and in a few instances have changed the text—usually only a letter or a word—in the light of those readings. In no case would failure to do so have resulted in change of meaning. Hunt and Scott believed their text to be accurate in so far as a long text can be, and every effort has been made to insure that the text printed here is accurate in substance. For the editorial arrangement see also the Note on the Text, p. cxviii.

[4] Irving Brant, *James Madison: Father of the Constitution, 1787-1800* (Indianapolis, 1950), p. 22.

[5] All of these notes except those of Lansing are brought together along with the official journal and other materials bearing on the formation of the Constitution in both the three- and four-volume works edited by Max Farrand. Joseph Reese Strayer edited Lansing's notes under the title, *The Delegate from New York, or, Proceedings of the Federal Convention of 1787 from the Notes of John Lansing, Jr.*, Princeton, 1939.

MADISON'S NOTES OF DEBATES
IN THE FEDERAL CONVENTION

In studying the Philadelphia deliberations one should real-ize that a Convention rule permitting reconsideration of mat-ters once determined meant that issues which seemed settled frequently reappeared, often occasioning re-examination of other topics closely related. The resulting flux, along with the intrinsic complexity of the proceedings, created a situa-tion which requires close attention to be understood. Madi-son's notes as reprinted in this edition set forth the general principles with which delegates primarily concerned them-selves, but they omit much repetition, most minor detail, the seconding of many motions, and similar material. The chron-ological sequence of Madison's report is scrupulously fol-lowed here with one exception: after grouping together de-liberations concerning "Navigation Acts and Slavery" which ran from August 21 through August 29 (see pp. 278-87), I then retrace the period August 22 through August 31 in covering "Other Important Provisions" (see pp. 287-300).

PRELIMINARIES

Monday May 14th 1787 was the day fixed for the meeting of the deputies in Convention for revising the federal system of Government. On that day a small number only had assembled. Seven States were not convened till [Friday, May 25].

Friday, May 25

Twenty-nine delegates were present from nine states, only seven of which had quorums. Each state stipulated in its credentials how many deputies were necessary to represent the state. These figures and the names of those in attend-ance on May 25 follow: New Hampshire, 2; Massachusetts, 3 (King); Connecticut, 1; New York, 3 (Yates, Hamilton); New Jersey, 3 (Brearly, Houston, Paterson); Pennsylvania, 4 (R. Morris, Fitzsimons, Wilson, G. Morris); Delaware, 3 (Reed, Bassett, Broom); Virginia, 3 (Washington, Randolph, Blair, Madison, Mason, Wythe, McClurg); North Carolina,

3 (Martin, Davie, Spaight, Williamson); South Carolina, 2 (Rutledge, C. C. Pinckney, C. Pinckney, Butler); Georgia, 2 (Few).

Mr RORERT MORRIS informed the members assembled that . . . he proposed George Washington Esqr late Commander in chief for president of the Convention.[1] Mr J^{no} RUTLIDGE seconded the motion; expressing his confidence that the choice would be unanimous, and observing that the presence of Genl Washington forbade any observation on the occasion which might otherwise be proper.

General WASHINGTON was accordingly unanimously elected by ballot, and . . . in a very emphatic manner he thanked the Convention for the honor they had conferred on him, reminded them of the novelty of the scene of business in which he was to act, lamented his want of better qualifications, and claimed the indulgence of the House towards the involuntary errors which his inexperience might occasion.

. . . .

On reading the credentials of the deputies it was noticed that those from Delaware were prohibited from changing the article in the Confederation establishing an equality of votes among the States. . . .

Members appointed a committee to prepare rules, consideration and adoption of which consumed all of May 28 and part of the following day. The most important of these provided that seven states should form a quorum, and all decisions were to be made by the majority of states fully represented. This ended an attempt sponsored by Pennsylvania to unite the large states so as to refuse the small ones an equal vote, and set the stage for Convention battles. A rule providing that nothing spoken in the House was to be printed or communicated without permission insured secrecy for the deliberations.

1 [Washington's only conceivable competitor was Franklin, whom the state of the weather and of his health kept from making the nomination.]

Tuesday, May 29

The day before, new delegates had arrived as follows: from Massachusetts, Gorham and Strong; from Connecticut, Ellsworth; from Delaware, Bedford; from Maryland, McHenry; from Pennsylvania, Franklin, Clymer, Mifflin and Ingersoll. On May 29 Dickinson of Delaware and Gerry of Massachusetts took their seats.

THE VIRGINIA PLAN

Initial consideration of the Virginia Plan lasted from May 29 through June 13. Arriving early in Philadelphia, the Virginia delegation prepared this draft while awaiting a quorum. His latest biographer claims that the plan "undoubtedly was written by Madison," [1] and since it corresponds so closely with documents he wrote on the eve of the Convention this is quite likely. Washington, nevertheless, may have had great influence in shaping it.[2] As originally constructed, the plan presumably called for creation of a national government. The sixth resolution contains the heart: a grant of general power, legislative veto, and coercion by force. But as initially presented the plan called ostensibly for revision of the Articles. Presumably this change was in deference to Governor Randolph, who submitted it. On the following day, after amendment, national government again became the objective (making the "therefore" of the second resolution *now* consistent with what must have been the original first resolution).[3]

The Virginia Plan also provided for proportional representation. The second resolution made the rule of suffrage the number of free inhabitants or the quotas of contribution. This latter was according to the congressional rule of 1783 fathered by Madison. This new rule altered the provision

[1] [Irving Brant, *James Madison: Father of the Constitution, 1787-1800* (Indianapolis, 1950), p. 23. (Hereafter referred to as Brant, *Madison*.)]

[2] [Arthur N. Holcombe, "The Role of Washington in the Framing of the Constitution," *The Huntington Library Quarterly*, XIX (August, 1956), 317-34.]

[3] [Brant, *Madison*, pp. 29-30.]

dating from 1777 whereby general expenses were apportioned on the basis of land values with their improvements so as to make contributions in proportion to the number of whites (and other free citizens) and three fifths of the Negroes.

To effectuate the plan of his state, Madison as floor strategist needed to form a coalition of those favoring both national and broadly based government in support of it. For the latter he counted on the most populous states (which also sent the ardent nationalists) and those becoming populous. These latter included the Carolinas and Georgia, which, with the three former, virtually assured victory. The figures given in the Population Estimates in Appendix II reveal where the strength lay. Catching many delegates unprepared, the well-formulated Virginia Plan gave large states the initiative, and they dominated the Convention's early stages, as votes show. Proportional representation in the lower house, for example, was never seriously in question.

However, the first battles came not over what *powers* to confer on national government but rather over who was to *control* whatever type of government was created. Upon first consideration of the second resolution a small-state bloc appeared and became thereafter increasingly prominent. Which states would side with which bloc was the question that now emerged. States small in population saw that proportional representation in both branches would swallow them up. If Delaware possessed one vote and suffrage was tied to quotas of contribution, then, according to figures based on congressional recommendations (of 1785) of how much each state should give to yield Congress a total annual revenue of $3,000,000, Virginia would receive sixteen votes.[4] Combining with small states were others (often geographically large or of middling population rank) which had peculiar interests to guard. For example, New York wanted primarily to prevent creation of any strong government, while Connecticut demanded power which would enable her to defend her recently acquired Western Reserve. Hence states in this bloc insisted on gaining the means to defend themselves as political entities and safeguard their special interests, of which the Western land problem was uppermost. Without protection here they could be made to suffer end-

4 [Ford, *Journals*, XXIX, 767; Max Farrand, *The Records of the Federal Convention of 1787* (New Haven, 1937), I, 574. (Hereafter referred to as Farrand, *Records*.) See also Appendix II.]

lessly. No one was serious about throwing everything into "hotchpot," but such a proposal warned of serious intentions to obtain a measure of equality. Thus when Maryland fell to Madison's foes (after Luther Martin replaced McHenry, whom illness called home), and the balance became six large to five small, the tension mounted. What if one of the former yielded? For various reasons, including the increasing importance of sectional considerations, this possibility became increasingly likely.

Mʳ RANDOLPH then opened the main business.

. . . .

He expressed his regret, that it should fall to him, rather than those, who were of longer standing in life and political experience, to open the great subject of their mission. But, as the convention had originated from Virginia, and his colleagues supposed that some proposition was expected from them, they had imposed this task on him.

He then commented on the difficulty of the crisis, and the necessity of preventing the fulfilment of the prophecies of the American downfal.

He observed that in revising the fœderal system we ought to inquire 1. into the properties, which such a government ought to possess, 2. the defects of the confederations, 3. the danger of our situation & 4. the remedy.

1. The Character of such a government ought to secure 1. against foreign invasion: 2. against dissentions between members of the Union, or seditions in particular states: 3. to procure to the several States various blessings, of which an isolated situation was incapable: 4. to be able to defend itself against incroachment: & 5. to be paramount to the state constitutions.

2. In speaking of the defects of the confederation he professed a high respect for its authors, and considered them, as having done all that patriots could do, in the then infancy of the science, of constitutions, & of confederacies,—when the inefficiency of requisitions was unknown—no commercial discord had arisen among any states—no rebellion had appeared as in

Massts.—foreign debts had not become urgent—the havoc of paper money had not been foreseen—treaties had not been violated—and perhaps nothing better could be obtained from the jealousy of the states with regard to their sovereignty.

He then proceeded to enumerate the defects: 1. that the confederation produced no security against foreign invasion; congress not being permitted to prevent a war nor to support it by their own authority—Of this he cited many examples; most of which tended to shew, that they could not cause infractions of treaties or of the law of nations, to be punished: that particular states might by their conduct provoke war without controul; and that neither militia nor draughts being fit for defence on such occasions, inlistments only could be successful, and these could not be executed without money.

2. that the fœderal government could not check the quarrels between states, nor a rebellion in any, not having constitutional power nor means to interpose according to the exigency:

3. that there were many advantages, which the U. S. might acquire, which were not attainable under the confederation—such as a productive impost—counteraction of the commercial regulations of other nations—pushing of commerce ad libitum —&c &c.

4. that the fœderal government could not defend itself against the incroachments from the states.

5. that it was not even paramount to the state constitutions, ratified, as it was in ma[n]y of the states.

3. He next reviewed the danger of our situation, appealed to the sense of the best friends of the U. S.—the prospect of anarchy from the laxity of government every where; and to other considerations.

4. He then proceeded to the remedy; the basis of which he said must be the republican principle

He proposed as conformable to his ideas the following resolutions, which he explained one by one. . . .

1. Resolved that the Articles of Confederation ought to be so

corrected & enlarged as to accomplish the objects proposed by their institution; namely, "common defence, security of liberty, and general welfare."

2. Res^d therefore that the rights of suffrage in the National Legislature ought to be proportioned to the Quotas of contribution, or to the number of free inhabitants, as the one or the other rule may seem best in different cases.

3. Res^d that the National Legislature ought to consist of two branches.

4. Res^d that the members of the first branch of the National Legislature ought to be elected by the people of the several States every   for the term of   ; to be of the age of   years at least, to receive liberal stipends by which they may be compensated for the devotion of their time to public service; to be ineligible to any office established by a particular State, or under the authority of the United States, except those peculiarly belonging to the functions of the first branch, during the term of service, and for the space of   after its expiration; to be incapable of reelection for the space of   after the expiration of their term of service, and to be subject to recall.

5. Resol^d that the members of the second branch of the National Legislature ought to be elected by those of the first, out of a proper number of persons nominated by the individual Legislatures, to be of the age of   years at least; to hold their offices for a term sufficient to ensure their independency; to receive liberal stipends, by which they may be compensated for the devotion of their time to public service; and to be ineligible to any office established by a particular State, or under the authority of the United States, except those peculiarly belonging to the functions of the second branch, during the term of service, and for the space of   after the expiration thereof.

6. Resolved that each branch ought to possess the right of originating Acts; that the National Legislature ought to be impowered to enjoy the Legislative Rights vested in Congress by the Confederation & moreover to legislate in all cases to which

the separate States are incompetent, or in which the harmony of the United States may be interrupted by the exercise of individual Legislation; to negative all laws passed by the several States, contravening in the opinion of the National Legislature the articles of Union; [5] and to call forth the force of the Union ag[st] any member of the Union failing to fulfill its duty under the articles thereof.

7. Res[d] that a National Executive be instituted; to be chosen by the National Legislature for the term of   years, to receive punctually at stated times, a fixed compensation for the services rendered, in which no increase or diminution shall be made so as to affect the Magistracy, existing at the time of increase or diminution, and to be ineligible a second time; and that besides a general authority to execute the National laws, it ought to enjoy the Executive rights vested in Congress by the Confederation.

8. Res[d] that the Executive and a convenient number of the National Judiciary, ought to compose a Council of revision with authority to examine every act of the National Legislature before it shall operate, & every act of a particular Legislature before a Negative thereon shall be final; and that the dissent of the said Council shall amount to a rejection, unless the Act of the National Legislature be again passed, or that of a particular Legislature be again negatived by   of the members of each branch.

9. Res[d] that a National Judiciary be established to consist of one or more supreme tribunals, and of inferior tribunals to be chosen by the National Legislature, to hold their offices during good behaviour; and to receive punctually at stated times fixed compensation for their services, in which no increase or diminution shall be made so as to affect the persons actually in office at the time of such increase or diminution; that the jurisdiction of the inferior tribunals shall be to hear & determine in the first instance, and of the supreme tribunal to hear and determine in

[5] (The phrase "of any treaty subsisting under the authority of the Union" is here added in the transcript.)

the dernier resort, all piracies & felonies on the high seas, captures from an enemy, cases in which foreigners or citizens of other States applying to such jurisdictions may be interested, or which respect the collection of the National revenue; impeachments of any National officers, and questions which may involve the national peace and harmony.

10. Resolv⁴ that provision ought to be made for the admission of States lawfully arising within the limits of the United States, whether from a voluntary junction of Government & Territory or otherwise, with the consent of a number of voices in the National legislature less than the whole.

11. Res⁴ that a Republican Government & the territory of each State, except in the instance of a voluntary junction of Government & territory, ought to be guarantied by the United States to each State

12. Res⁴ that provision ought to be made for the continuance of Congress and their authorities and privileges, until a given day after the reform of the articles of Union shall be adopted, and for the completion of all their engagements.

13. Res⁴ that provision ought to be made for the amendment of the Articles of Union whensoever it shall seem necessary, and that the assent of the National Legislature ought not to be required thereto.

14. Res⁴ that the Legislative Executive & Judiciary powers within the several States ought to be bound by oath to support the articles of Union.

15. Res⁴ that the amendments which shall be offered to the Confederation, by the Convention ought at a proper time, or times, after the approbation of Congress to be submitted to an assembly or assemblies of Representatives, recommended by the several Legislatures to be expressly chosen by the people, to consider & decide thereon.

He concluded with an exhortation, not to suffer the present opportunity of establishing general peace, harmony, happiness and liberty in the U. S. to pass away unimproved.

It was then Resolved—That the House will tomorrow resolve

itself into a Committee of the Whole House to consider of the state of the American Union.—and that the propositions moved by Mr Randolph be referred to the said Committee. ...

Here Charles Pinckney offered the draft of a plan which was referred to the same Committee, no details of which were given. On July 24, without any intervening action recorded on his proposal, it was formally discharged from the Committee of the Whole and sent to the Committee of Detail. Pinckney subsequently laid the basis on several occasions for the belief that his plan was remarkably similar to the final Constitution. His actual motive in May was reform of the government along lines similar to those provided by amendments he had offered in Congress in 1786. Called by one historian a "sponger and a plagiarist," Pinckney had combined features from the Virginia Plan, the Articles of Confederation, his own 1786 amendments, and the New York State Constitution.[6]

Wednesday, May 30

Roger Sherman (from Connecticut) took his seat.

The House went into Committee of the Whole on the State of the Union. Mr Gorham was elected to the Chair by Ballot.

The propositions of Mr RANDOLPH which had been referred to the Committee being taken up. He moved on the suggestion of Mr G. Morris, that the first of his propositions to wit "Resolved that the articles of Confederation ought to be so corrected & enlarged, as to accomplish the objects proposed by their institution; namely, common defence, security of liberty & general welfare:—should be postponed, in order to consider the 3 following:

1. that a Union of the States merely federal will not accomplish the objects proposed by the articles of Confederation, namely common defence, security of liberty, & genl welfare.

---

[6] [Brant, *Madison,* pp. 27-29. The whole topic is treated in Farrand, *Records,* III, 595-609, where Pinckney's plan of May 29 (as reconstructed) is given.]

2. that no treaty or treaties among the whole or part of the States, as individual Sovereignties, would be sufficient.

3. that a *national* Government ought to be established consisting of a *supreme* Legislative, Executive & Judiciary.

The motion for postponing was seconded by Mr Govr MORRIS and unanimously agreed to.

Some verbal criticisms were raised agst the first proposition, and it was agreed on motion of Mr BUTLER, seconded by Mr RANDOLPH, to pass on to the third, which underwent a discussion, less however on its general merits than on the force and extent of the particular terms *national* & *supreme*.

Mr CHARLES PINKNEY wished to know of Mr Randolph whether he meant to abolish the State Governts altogether. Mr R. replied that he meant by these general propositions merely to introduce the particular ones which explained the outlines of the system he had in view.

Mr BUTLER said he had not made up his mind on the subject, and was open to the light which discussion might throw on it. After some general observations he concluded with saying that he had opposed the grant of powers to Congs heretofore, because the whole power was vested in one body. The proposed distribution of the powers into different bodies changed the case, and would induce him to go great lengths.

Genl PINKNEY expressed a doubt whether the act of Congs recommending the Convention, or the Commissions of the Deputies to it, could authorise a discussion of a System founded on different principles from the federal Constitution.

Mr GERRY seemed to entertain the same doubt.

Mr Govr MORRIS explained the distinction between a *federal* and *national, supreme,* Govt; the former being a mere compact resting on the good faith of the parties; the latter having a compleat and *compulsive* operation. He contended that in all Communities there must be one supreme power, and one only.

Mr MASON observed that the present confederation was not only deficient in not providing for coercion & punishment agst delinquent States; but argued very cogently that punishment could not in the nature of things be executed on the States collectively, and therefore that such a Gov^t was necessary as could directly operate on individuals, and would punish those only whose guilt required it.

Mr SHERMAN . . . admitted that the Confederation had not given sufficient power to Cong^s and that additional powers were necessary; particularly that of raising money, which he said would involve many other powers. He admitted also that the General & particular jurisdictions ought in no case to be concurrent. He seemed however not be disposed to make too great inroads on the existing system; intimating as one reason that it would be wrong to lose every amendment, by inserting such as would not be agreed to by the States. . . .

A motion to postpone consideration of a national government in order "to carry into execution the Design of the States in forming this Convention" received a tie vote: Massachusetts, Connecticut, Delaware, South Carolina, yea; New York, Pennsylvania, Virginia, North Carolina, nay.

On the question as moved by Mr Butler, on the third proposition it was resolved in Committee of the whole that a national govern^t ought to be established consisting of a supreme Legislative Executive & Judiciary. Mass^{ts} being ay—Connect.—no. N. York divided (Col. Hamilton, ay; Mr Yates, no) Pen^a ay. Delaware ay. Virg^a ay, N. C. ay. S. C. ay. [Ayes, 6; noes, 1; divided, 1.]

. . . .

The following Resolution being the 2^d of those proposed by Mr Randolph was taken up, viz—"that the rights of suffrage in the National Legislature ought to be proportioned to the quotas of contribution, or to the number of free inhabitants, as the one or the other rule may seem best in different cases."

. . . .

Mr MADISON, moved . . . the following resolution—"that the equality of suffrage established by the articles of Confederation ought not to prevail in the national Legislature, and that an equitable ratio of representation ought to be substituted." This was 2^{ded} by Mr Govr MORRIS, and being generally relished, would have been agreed to; when,

M͏ͬ REED moved that the whole clause relating to the point of Representation be postponed; reminding the Com͏ᵉ that the deputies from Delaware were restrained by their commission from assenting to any change of the rule of suffrage, and in case such a change should be fixed on, it might become their duty to retire from the Convention.

M͏ͬ Gov͏ͬ MORRIS observed that ... so early a proof of discord in the Convention as a secession of a State, would add much to the regret; that the change proposed was, however, so fundamental an article in a national Gov͏ᵗ that it could not be dispensed with.

M͏ͬ MADISON observed that whatever reason might have existed for the equality of suffrage when the Union was a federal one among sovereign States, it must cease when a national Goverm͏ᵗ should be put into the place. In the former case, the acts of Cong͏ˢ depended so much for their efficacy on the co-operation of the States, that these had a weight both within & without Congress, nearly in proportion to their extent and importance. In the latter case, as the acts of the Gen͏ˡ Gov͏ᵗ would take effect without the intervention of the State legislatures, a vote from a small State w͏ᵈ have the same efficacy & importance as a vote from a large one .... . He suggested as an expedient for at once taking the sense of the members on this point and saving the Delaware deputies from embarrassment, that the question should be taken in Committee, and the clause on report to the House be postponed without a question there. This however did not appear to satisfy M͏ͬ Read.

By several it was observed that no just construction of the Act of Delaware, could require or justify a secession of her deputies, even if the resolution were to be carried thro' the House as well as the Committee. It was finally agreed however that the clause should be postponed: it being understood that in the event the proposed change of representation would certainly be agreed to, no objection or difficulty being started from any other quarter than from Delaware.

The motion of M͏ͬ Read to postpone being agreed to,

The Committee then rose. The Chairman reported progress,

and the House, having resolved to resume the subject in Committee tomorrow,

Adjourned to 10 o'clock.

Thursday, May 31

William Pierce from Georgia took his seat.

In Committee of the whole on Mᵣ Randolph's propositions.

The 3ᵈ Resolution "that the national Legislature ought to consist of two branches" was agreed to without debate or dissent, except that of Pennsylvania, given probably from complaisance to Docᵣ Franklin who was understood to be partial to a single House of Legislation.

Resol: 4. first clause "that the members of the first branch of the National Legislature ought to be elected by the people of the several States" being taken up,

Mᵣ SHERMAN opposed the election by the people, insisting that it ought to be by the State Legislatures. The people he said, immediately should have as little to do as may be about the Government. They want information and are constantly liable to be misled.

Mᵣ GERRY. The evils we experience flow from the excess of democracy. The people do not want virtue, but are the dupes of pretended patriots. In Massᵗˢ it had been fully confirmed by experience that they are daily misled into the most baneful measures and opinions by the false reports circulated by designing men, and which no one on the spot can refute. One principal evil arises from the want of due provision for those employed in the administration of Governmᵗ It would seem to be a maxim of democracy to starve the public servants. He mentioned the popular clamour in Massᵗˢ for the reduction of salaries and the attack made on that of the Govᵣ though secured by the spirit of the Constitution itself. He had he said been too republican heretofore: he was still however republican, but had been taught by experience the danger of the levelling spirit.

Mᵣ MASON argued strongly for an election of the larger

branch by the people. It was to be the grand depository of the democratic principle of the Govtᵗ It was, so to speak, to be our House of Commons—It ought to know & sympathise with every part of the community; and ought therefore to be taken not only from different parts of the whole republic, but also from different districts of the larger members of it, which had in several instances particularly in Virgᵃ, different interests and views arising from difference of produce, of habits &c &c. He admitted that we had been too democratic, but was afraid we sᵈ incautiously run into the opposite extreme. We ought to attend to the rights of every class of the people. He had often wondered at the indifference of the superior classes of society to this dictate of humanity & policy; considering that however affluent their circumstances, or elevated their situations, might be, the course of a few years, not only might but certainly would, distribute their posterity throughout the lowest classes of Society. Every selfish motive therefore, every family attachment, ought to recommend such a system of policy as would provide no less carefully for the rights and happiness of the lowest than of the highest orders of Citizens.

Mᵣ WILSON contended strenuously for drawing the most numerous branch of the Legislature immediately from the people. He was for raising the federal pyramid to a considerable altitude, and for that reason wished to give it as broad a basis as possible. No government could long subsist without the confidence of the people. In a republican Government this confidence was peculiarly essential. He also thought it wrong to increase the weight of the State Legislatures by making them the electors of the national Legislature. All interference between the general and local Governmᵗˢ should be obviated as much as possible. On examination it would be found that the opposition of States to federal measures had proceded much more from the officers of the States, than from the people at large.

Mᵣ MADISON considered the popular election of one branch of the National Legislature as essential to every plan of free Government. He observed that in some of the States one branch of the Legislature was composed of men already removed from the people by an intervening body of electors. That if the first branch of the general legislature should be elected by the State Legislatures, the second branch elected by the first—the Executive by the second together with the first; and other appointments again made for subordinate purposes by the Executive, the people would be lost sight of altogether; and the necessary sympathy between them and their rulers and officers, too little felt. He was an advocate for the policy of refining the popular appointments by successive filtrations, but thought it might be pushed too far. He wished the expedient to be resorted to only in the appointment of the second branch of the Legislature, and in the Executive & judiciary branches of the Government. He thought too that the great fabric to be raised would be more stable and durable, if it should rest on the solid foundation of the people themselves, than if it should stand merely on the pillars of the Legislatures.

Mᵣ GERRY did not like the election by the people. The maxims taken from the British constitution were often fallacious when applied to our situation, which was extremely different. Experience he said had shewn that the State legislatures drawn immediately from the people did not always possess their confidence. He had no objection however to an election by the people if it were so qualified that men of honor & character might not be unwilling to be joined in the appointments. He seemed to think the people might nominate a certain number out of which the State legislatures should be bound to choose.

. . . .

On the question for an election of the first branch of the national Legislature by the people:

Massᵗˢ ay. Connecᵗ divᵈ N. York ay. N. Jersey no. Penᵃ ay. Delawᵉ divᵈ Vᵃ ay. N. C. ay. S. C. no. Georgᵃ ay. [Ayes, 6; noes, 2; divided, 2.]

. . . .

The Committee proceeded to Resolution 5. "that the second (or senatorial) branch of the National Legislature ought to be chosen by the first branch out of persons nominated by the State Legislatures."

Mr SPAIGHT contended that the 2^d branch ought to be chosen by the State Legislatures and moved an amendment to that effect.

Mr BUTLER apprehended that the taking so many powers out of the hands of the States as was proposed, tended to destroy all that balance and security of interests among the States which it was necessary to preserve; and called on Mr Randolph ... to explain the extent of his ideas, and particularly the number of members he meant to assign to this second branch.

Mr RAND[OLPH] observed that he had at the time of offering his propositions stated his ideas as far as the nature of general propositions required; that details made no part of the plan, and could not perhaps with propriety have been introduced. If he was to give an opinion as to the number of the second branch, he should say that it ought to be much smaller than that of the first; so small as to be exempt from the passionate proceedings to which numerous assemblies are liable. He observed that the general object was to provide a cure for the evils under which the U. S. laboured; that in tracing these evils to their origin every man had found it in the turbulence and follies of democracy: that some check therefore was to be sought for agst this tendency of our Governments: and that a good Senate seemed most likely to answer the purpose.

. . . .

Mr WILSON opposed both a nomination by the State Legislatures, and an election by the first branch of the national Legislature, because the second branch of the latter, ought to be independent of both. He thought both branches of the National Legislature ought to be chosen by the people, but was not prepared with a specific proposition. ...

On the whole question for electing by the first branch out of nominations by the State Legislatures, Mass. ay. Con^t. no. N. Y. no. N. Jersey. no. Pen^a no. Del. no. Virg^a ay. N. C. no. S. C. ay. G^a no. [Ayes, 3; noes, 7.]

. . . .

The sixth Resolution stating the cases in which the national Legislature ought to legislate was next taken into discussion:

On the question whether each branch sh^d originate laws, there was an unanimous affirmative without debate. On the question for transferring all the Legislative powers of the existing Cong^s to this Assembly, there was also a silent affirmative nem. con.

On the proposition for giving "Legislative power in all cases to which the State Legislatures were individually incompetent."

Mr PINKNEY & Mr RUTLEDGE objected to the vagueness of the term *incompetent,* and said they could not well decide how to vote until they should see an exact enumeration of the powers comprehended by this definition.

Mr BUTLER repeated his fears that we were running into an extreme in taking away the powers of the States, and called on Mr Randolp for the extent of his meaning.

Mr RANDOLPH disclaimed any intention to give indefinite powers to the national Legislature, declaring that he was entirely opposed to such an inroad on the State jurisdictions, and that he did not think any considerations whatever could ever change his determination. His opinion was fixed on this point.

Mr MADISON said that he had brought with him into the Convention a strong bias in favor of an enumeration and definition of the powers necessary to be exercised by the national Legislature; but had also brought doubts concerning its practicability. His wishes remained unaltered; but his doubts had become stronger. What his opinion might ultimately be he could not yet tell. But he should shrink from nothing which should be found essential to such a form of Gov^t as would provide for the safety, liberty, and happiness of the community. This being the end of all our deliberations, all the necessary means for attaining it must, however reluctantly, be submitted to.

On the question for giving powers, in cases to which the States are not competent, Mass^ts ay. Con^t div^d (Sharman no Elseworth ay) N. Y. ay. N. J. ay. P^a ay. Del. ay. V^a ay. N. C. ay. S. Carolina ay; Georg^a ay. [Ayes, 9; noes, 0; divided, 1.]

The other clauses giving powers necessary to preserve harmony among the States to negative all State laws contravening in the opinion of the Nat. Leg. the articles of union, down to the last clause, (the words "or any treaties subsisting under the authority of the Union," being added after the words "contra-vening &c. the articles of the Union," on motion of Dᴿ FRANKLIN) were agreed to with̲ᵗ̲ ̲d̲e̲b̲a̲t̲e̲ ̲o̲r̲ ̲d̲i̲s̲s̲e̲n̲t̲.

The last clause of Resolution 6. authorizing an exertion of the force of the whole agˢᵗ a delinquent State came next into consideration.

Mʳ MADISON observed that the more he reflected on the use of force, the m̲o̲r̲e̲ ̲h̲e̲ ̲d̲o̲u̲b̲t̲e̲d̲ ̲t̲h̲e̲ ̲p̲r̲a̲c̲t̲i̲c̲a̲b̲i̲l̲i̲t̲y̲, the justice, and the efficacy of it when applied to people collectively and not individually.—A union of the States containing such an in-gredient seemed to provide for its own destruction. The use of force agˢᵗ a State, would look more like a declaration of war, than an infliction of punishment, and would probably be con-sidered by the party attacked as a dissolution of all previous compacts by which it might be bound. He hoped that such a system would be framed as might render this recourse unneces-sary, and moved that t̲h̲e̲ ̲c̲l̲a̲u̲s̲e̲ ̲b̲e̲ ̲p̲o̲s̲t̲p̲o̲n̲e̲d̲. This motion was agreed to nem. con.

The Committee then rose & the House
Adjourned

Friday, June 1

William Houston from Georgia took his seat.

The Committee of the whole proceeded to Resolution 7. "that a national Executive be instituted, to be chosen by the national Legislature—for the term of   years &c to be in-eligible thereafter, to possess the executive powers of Congress &c."

Mʳ PINKNEY was for a vigorous Executive but was afraid the Executive powers of the existing Congress m̲i̲g̲h̲t̲ ̲e̲x̲t̲e̲n̲d̲ ̲t̲o̲ ̲p̲e̲a̲c̲e̲ ̲&̲ ̲w̲a̲r̲ &c., which would render the Executive a monarchy, of the worst kind, to wit an elective one.

Mʳ WILSON moved that the E̲x̲e̲c̲u̲t̲i̲v̲e̲ ̲c̲o̲n̲s̲i̲s̲t̲ ̲o̲f̲ ̲a̲ ̲s̲i̲n̲g̲l̲e̲ ̲p̲e̲r̲-̲son. Mʳ C. PINKNEY seconded the motion, so as to read "that a N̲ational Ex. to consist of a single person, be instituted.

Gorham

A considerable pause ensuing and the Chairman asking if he should put the question, Doc⸱ᵣ FRANKLIN observed that it was a point of great importance and wished that the gentlemen would deliver their sentiments on it before the question was put.

M⸱ᵣ RUTLIDGE animadverted on the shyness of gentlemen on this and other subjects. He said it looked as if they supposed themselves precluded by having frankly disclosed their opinions from afterwards changing them, which he did not take to be at all the case. He said he was for vesting the Executive power in a single person, tho' he was not for giving him the power of war and peace. A single man would feel the greatest responsibility and administer the public affairs best.

M⸱ᵣ SHERMAN said he considered the Executive magistracy as nothing more than an institution for carrying the will of the Legislature into effect, that the person or persons ought to be appointed by and accountable to the Legislature only, which was the depositary of the supreme will of the Society. As they were the best judges of the business which ought to be done by the Executive department, and consequently of the number necessary from time to time for doing it, he wished the number might not be fixed but that the legislature should be at liberty to appoint one or more as experience might dictate.

M⸱ᵣ WILSON preferred a single magistrate, as giving most energy dispatch and responsibility to the office. He did not consider the Prerogatives of the British Monarch as a proper guide in defining the Executive powers. Some of these prerogatives were of Legislative nature. Among others that of war & peace &c. The only powers he conceived strictly Executive were those of executing the laws, and appointing officers, not appertaining to and appointed by the Legislature.

. . . .

M⸱ᵣ RANDOLPH strenuously opposed a unity in the Executive magistracy. He regarded it as the fœtus of monarchy. We had, he said no motive to be governed by the British Governm⸱ᵗ as our prototype. He did not mean however to throw censure on that Excellent fabric. If we were in a situation to copy it he did

not know that he should be opposed to it; but the fixt genius of
the people of America required a different form of Government.
He could not see why the great requisites for the Executive department, vigor, despatch & responsibility could not be found
in three men, as well as in one man. The Executive ought to be
independent. It ought therefore in order to support its independence to consist of more than one.

Mr WILSON said that unity in the Executive, instead of being
the fetus of monarchy would be the best safeguard against
tyranny. He repeated that he was not governed by the British
Model which was inapplicable to the situation of this Country;
the extent of which was so great, and the manners so republican,
that nothing but a great confederated Republic would do for it.

Mr Wilson's motion for a single magistrate was postponed by
common consent, the Committee seeming unprepared for any
decision on it; and the first part of the clause agreed to, viz—
"that a National Executive be instituted."

Mr MADISON thought it would be proper, before a choice sh^d
be made between a unity and a plurality in the Executive, to fix
the extent of the Executive authority; that, as certain powers
were in their nature Executive and must be given to that de-
partm^t whether administered by one or more persons, a definition of their extent would assist the judgment in determining
how far they might be safely entrusted to a single officer. . . .

The next clause in Resolution 7, relating to the mode of appointing, & the duration of, the Executive being under consideration,

Mr WILSON said he was almost unwilling to declare the mode
which he wished to take place, being apprehensive that it might
appear chimerical. He would say, however, at least that in
theory he was for an election by the people. Experience, particularly in N. York & Mass^{ts}, shewed that an election of the first
magistrate by the people at large, was both a convenient & successful mode. The objects of choice in such cases must be persons whose merits have general notoriety.

Mr SHERMAN was for the appointment by the Legislature, and for making him absolutely dependent on that body, as it was the will of that which was to be executed. An independence of the Executive on the supreme Legislature, was in his opinion the very essence of tyranny if there was any such thing. . . .

Saturday, June 2. In Committee of the whole

William Saml Johnson from Connecticut, Daniel of St. Thomas Jennifer, from Mary^d & John Lansing J^r from N. York, took their seats.

. . . The mode of appoint^g ye Executive was resumed.

Mr WILSON made the following motion, to be substituted for the mode proposed by Mr Randolph's resolution, "that the Executive Magistracy shall be elected in the following manner: That the States be divided into   districts: & that the persons qualified to vote in each district for members of the first branch of the national Legislature elect   members for their respective districts to be electors of the Executive magistracy, that the said Electors of the Executive magistracy meet at   and they or any   of them so met shall proceed to elect by ballot, but not out of their own body,   person in whom the Executive authority of the national Government shall be vested."

Mr WILSON repeated his arguments in favor of an election without the intervention of the States. He supposed too that this mode would produce more confidence among the people in the first magistrate, than an election by the national Legislature.

Mr GERRY opposed the election by the national legislature. There would be a constant intrigue kept up for the appointment. The Legislature & the candidates w^d bargain & play into one another's hands, votes would be given by the former under promises or expectations from the latter, of recompensing them by services to members of the Legislature or to their friends. He liked the principle of Mr Wilson's motion, but fears it would alarm & give a handle to the State partisans, as tending to supersede altogether the State authorities. He thought the Community not yet ripe for stripping the States of their powers, even such as might not be requisite for local purposes. He was for waiting till people should feel more the necessity of it. He seemed to prefer the taking the suffrages of the States instead of Electors, or letting the Legislatures nominate, and the electors appoint. He was not clear that the people ought to act directly even in the choice of electors, being too little informed of personal characters in large districts, and liable to deceptions.

. . . .

On the question for agreeing to Mr Wilson's substitute, it was negatived: Mass^{ts} no. Con^t no. N. Y. no. P^a ay. Del. no. Mar^d ay. Virg^a no. N. C. no. S. C. no. Geo^a no. [Ayes, 2; noes, 8.]

On the question for electing the Executive by the national Legislature for the term of seven years, it was agreed to Mass^{ts} ay. Con^t ay. N. Y. ay. Pen^a no. Del. ay. Mary^d no. V^a ay. N. C. ay. S. C. ay. Geo. ay. [Ayes, 8; noes, 2.]

Here Franklin moved (in a paper read for him by Wilson) that the executive serve gratuitously except for necessary expenses. To make places of honor places of profit united the passions of ambition and avarice, contended Franklin, thus sowing seeds of discord. He cited historical examples, including Washington's refusal of salary as commander in chief, to show that candidates would seek office under these conditions. Hamilton seconded with the view of bringing a respectable proposal before the Committee, but no debate ensued. "It was treated with great respect," writes Madison, "but rather for the author of it, than from any apparent conviction of its expediency or practicability."

Mr DICKENSON moved "that the Executive be made removeable by the National Legislature on the request of a majority of the Legislatures of individual States." It was necessary he said to place the power of removing somewhere. He had no idea of abolishing the State Governments as some gentlemen seemed inclined to do. The happiness of this Country in his opinion required considerable powers to be left in the hands of the States.

. . .

Mr MASON. Some mode of displacing an unfit magistrate is

rendered indispensable by the fallibility of those who choose, as well as by the corruptibility of the man chosen. He opposed decidedly the making the Executive the mere creature of the Legislature as a violation of the fundamental principle of good Government.

Mr MADISON & Mr WILSON observed that it would leave an equality of agency in the small with the great States; that it would enable a minority of the people to prevent ye removal of an officer who had rendered himself justly criminal in the eyes of a majority; that it would open a door for intrigues agst him in States where his administration tho' just might be unpopular, and might tempt him to pay court to particular States whose leading partizans he might fear, or wish to engage as his partizans. They both thought it bad policy to introduce such a mixture of the State authorities, where their agency could be otherwise supplied.

Mr DICKENSON considered the business as so important that no man ought to be silent or reserved. He went into a discourse of some length, the sum of which was, that the Legislative, Executive, & Judiciary departments ought to be made as independent as possible; but that such an Executive as some seemed to have in contemplation was not consistent with a republic: that a firm Executive could only exist in a limited monarchy. In the British Gov^t itself the weight of the Executive arises from the attachments which the Crown draws to itself, & not merely from the force of its prerogatives. In place of these attachments we must look out for something else. One source of stability is the double branch of the Legislature. The division of the Country into distinct States formed the other principal source of stability. This division ought therefore to be maintained, and considerable powers to be left with the States. This was the ground of his consolation for the future fate of his Country. Without this, and in case of a consolidation of the States into one great Republic, we might read its fate in the history of smaller ones. A limited Monarchy he considered as *one* of the best Governments in the world. It was not *certain* that the same blessings were derivable from any other form. It was certain that equal blessings had never yet been derived from any of the republican form. A limited Monarchy however was out of the question. The spirit of the times—the state of our affairs, forbade the experiment, if it were desireable. Was it possible, moreover, in the nature of things to introduce it even if these obstacles were less insuperable. . . . No. They were the growth of ages, and could only arise under a complication of circumstances none of which existed in this Country. But though a form the most perfect *perhaps* in itself be unattainable, we must not despair. If antient republics have been found to flourish for a moment only & then vanish forever, it only proves that they were badly constituted; and that we ought to seek for every remedy for their diseases. One of these remedies he conceived to be the accidental lucky division of this Country into distinct States; a division which some seemed desirous to abolish altogether. As to the point of representation in the national Legislature as it might affect States of different sizes, he said it must probably end in mutual concession. He hoped that each State would retain an equal voice at least in one branch of the National Legislature, and supposed the sums paid within each State would form a better ratio for the other branch than either the number of inhabitants or the quantum of property.

.   .   .   .

On Mʳ DICKENSON's motion for making Executive removeable by Natˡ Legislature at request of majority of State Legislatures was . . . rejected—all the States being in the negative Except Delaware . . . .

Mʳ RUTLEDGE & Mʳ C. PINKNEY moved that the blank for the nº of persons in the Executive be filled with the words "one person." He supposed the reasons to be so obvious & conclusive in favor of one that no member would oppose the motion.

Mʳ RANDOLPH opposed it with great earnestness, declaring that he should not do justice to the Country which sent him if he were silently to suffer the establishmᵗ of a Unity in the Executive department. He felt an opposition to it which he believed he should continue to feel as long as he lived. He urged 1. that the permanent temper of the people was adverse to the very semblance of Monarchy. 2. that a unity was unnecessary, a plurality being equally competent to all the objects of the department. 3. that the necessary confidence would never be reposed in a single Magistrate. 4. that the appointments would generally be in favor of some inhabitant near the center of the Community, and consequently the remote parts would not be on an equal footing. He was in favor of three members of the Executive, to be drawn from different portions of the Country.

Mr BUTLER contended strongly for a single magistrate as most likely to answer the purpose of the remote parts. If one man should be appointed he would be responsible to the whole, and would be impartial to its interests. If three or more should be taken from as many districts, there would be a constant struggle for local advantages. In Military matters this would be particularly mischievous. . . .

Monday, June 4. In Committee of the whole

The Question was resumed . . . "shall the blank for the number of the Executive be filled with a single person?"

Mr WILSON was in favor of the motion. It had been opposed by the gentleman from Virg^a (Mr Randolph) but the arguments used had not convinced him. He observed that the objections of Mr R. were levelled not so much ag^st the measure itself, as ag^st its unpopularity. . . . On examination he could see no evidence of the alledged antipathy of the people. On the contrary, he was persuaded that it does not exist. . . . One fact has great weight with him. All the 13 States tho agreeing in scarce any other instance, agree in placing a single magistrate at the head of the Govern^t . . . In addition to his former reasons for preferring a unity, he would mention another. The *tranquility* not less than the vigor of the Gov^t he thought would be favored by it. Among three equal members, he foresaw nothing but uncontrouled, continued, & violent animosities; which would not only interrupt the public administration; but diffuse their poison thro' the other branches of Gov^t, thro' the States, and at length thro' the people at large. If the members were to be unequal in power the principle of the opposition to the unity was given up. If equal, the making them an odd number would not be a remedy. In Courts of Justice there are two sides only to a question. In the Legislative & Executive departm^{ts} questions have commonly many sides. Each member therefore might espouse a separate one & no two agree.

Mr SHERMAN. . . . Mr Wilson he said had observed that in each State a single magistrate was placed at the head of the Gov^t It was so he admitted, and properly so, and he wished the same policy to prevail in the federal Gov^t But then it should be also remarked that in all the States there was a Council of advice, without which the first magistrate could not act. A council he thought necessary to make the establishment acceptable to the people.

Mr WILLIAMSON asks Mr WILSON whether he means to annex a Council.

Mr WILSON means to have no Council, which oftener serves to cover, than prevent malpractices.

.   .   .   .

On the question for a single Executive it was agreed to Mass^{ts} ay. Con^t ay. N. Y. no. Pen^a ay. Del. no. Mary^d no. Virg. ay. (Mr R. & Mr Blair no—Doc^r M^{c}C^g Mr M. & Gen W. ay. Col. Mason being no, but not in house, Mr Wythe ay but gone home). N. C. ay. S. C. ay. Georg^a ay. [Ayes, 7; noes, 3.]

First Clause of Proposition 8 relating *to a Council of Revision* taken into consideration.

Mr GERRY doubts whether the Judiciary ought to form a part of it, as they will have a sufficient check agst encroachments on their own department by their exposition of the laws, which involved a power of deciding on their Constitutionality. In some States the Judges had actually set aside laws as being agst the Constitution. This was done too with general approbation. It was quite foreign from the nature of ye office to make them judges of the policy of public measures. He moves to postpone the clause in order to propose "that the National Executive shall have a right to negative any Legislative act which shall not be afterwards passed by   parts of each branch of the national Legislature."

Mʳ KING seconds the motion, observing that the Judges ought to be able to expound the law as it should come before them, free from the bias of having participated in its formation.

Mʳ WILSON thinks neither the original proposition nor the amendment go far enough. If the Legislative Exetv & Judiciary ought to be distinct & independent. The Executive ought to have an absolute negative. Without such a self-defense the Legislature can at any moment sink it into non-existence. He was for varying the proposition in such a manner as to give the Executive & Judiciary jointly an absolute negative.

. . . .

. . . Mʳ WILSON & Mʳ HAMILTON move that the last part of it (viz. "wᶜʰ sˡ not be afterwᵈˢ passed unless by   parts of each branch of the National legislature) be struck out, so as to give the Executive an absolute negative on the laws. There was no danger they thought of such a power being too much exercised. It was mentioned by Col: HAMILTON that the King of G. B. had not exerted his negative since the Revolution.

. . . .

Docʳ FRANKLIN said he was sorry to differ from his colleague for whom he had a very great respect, on any occasion, but he could not help it on this. He had had some experience of this check in the Executive on the Legislature, under the proprietary Government of Penˢ The negative of the Governor was constantly made use of to extort money. No good law whatever could be passed without a private bargain with him. . . . This was a mischievous sort of check. If the Executive was to have a Council, such a power would be less objectionable. It was true the King of G. B. had not, as was said, exerted his negative since the Revolution; but that matter was easily explained. The bribes and emoluments now given to the members of parliament rendered it unnecessary, everything being done according to the will of the Ministers. . . .

Mʳ SHERMAN was agᵗ enabling any one man to stop the will of the whole. No one man could be found so far above all the rest in wisdom. He thought we ought to avail ourselves of his wisdom in revising the laws, but not permit him to overule the decided and cool opinions of the Legislature.

Mʳ MADISON supposed that if a proper proportion of each branch should be required to overrule the objections of the Executive, it would answer the same purpose as an absolute negative. . . . To give such a prerogative would certainly be obnoxious to the temper of this Country; its present temper at least.

Mʳ WILSON believed as others did that this power would seldom be used. The Legislature would know that such a power existed, and would refrain from such laws, as it would be sure to defeat. Its silent operation would therefore preserve harmony and prevent mischief. . . .

Mʳ BUTLER had been in favor of a single Executive Magistrate; but could he have entertained an idea that a compleat negative on the laws was to be given him he certainly should have acted very differently. . . . Gentlemen seemed to think that we had nothing to apprehend from an abuse of the Executive power. But why might not a Cataline or a Cromwell arise in this Country as well as in others.

Mʳ BEDFORD was opposed to every check on the Legislative, even the Council of Revision first proposed. . . . The Representatives of the people were the best Judges of what was for their interest, and ought to be under no external controul whatever. The two branches would produce a sufficient controul within the Legislature itself.

Col. MASON observed that a vote had already passed he found (he was out at the time) for vesting the executive powers in a single person. Among these powers was that of appointing to offices in certain cases. The probable abuses of a negative had been well explained by Dʳ F. as proved by experience, the best of all tests. Will not the same door be opened here. The Executive may refuse its assent to necessary measures till new appointments shall be referred to him; and having by degrees engrossed all these into his own hands, the American Executive, like the British, will by bribery & influence, save himself the trouble & odium of exerting his negative afterwards. We are Mʳ Chairman going very far in this business. We are not indeed constituting a British Government, but a more dangerous monarchy, an elective one. We are introducing a new principle into our system, and not necessary as in the British Govᵗ where the Executive has greater rights to defend. Do gentlemen mean to pave the way to hereditary Monarchy? Do they flatter themselves that the people will ever consent to such an innovation? If they do I venture to tell them, they are mistaken. The people never will consent. And do gentlemen consider the danger of delay, and the still greater danger of a rejection, not for a moment but forever, of the plan which shall be proposed to them. Notwithstanding the oppressions & injustice experienced among us from democracy; the genius of the people is in favor of it, and the genius of the people must be consulted. He could not but consider the federal system as in effect dissolved by the appointment of this Convention to devise a better one. And do gentlemen look forward to the dangerous interval between the extinction of an old, and the establishment of a new Governmᵗ and to the scenes of confusion which may ensue. He hoped that nothing like a Monarchy would ever be attempted in this Country. A hatred to its oppressions had carried the people through the late Revolution. Will it not be eno' to enable the Executive to suspend offensive laws, till they shall be coolly revised, and the objections to them overruled by a greater majority than was required in the first instance. He never could agree to give up all the rights of the people to a single Magistrate. If more than one had been fixed on, greater powers might have been entrusted to the Executive. He hoped this attempt to give such powers would have its weight hereafter as an argument for increasing the number of the Executive.

. . . .

On the question for striking out so as to give Executive an absolute negative—Massᵗˢ no. Conᵗ no. N. Y. no. Pᵃ no. Dl. no. Mᵈ no. Vᵃ no. N. C. no. S. C. no. Georgᵃ no. [Ayes, 0; noes, 10.]

[A unanimous vote then withheld the power to suspend legislative acts.]

On a question for enabling *two thirds* of each branch of the Legislature to overrule the revisionary check: it passed in the affirmative sub silentio; and was inserted in the blank of Mʳ Gerry's motion.

On the question on Mʳ Gerry's motion which gave the Executive alone, without the Judiciary the revisionary controul on the laws unless overruled by 2/3 of each branch; Massᵗˢ ay. Conᵗ no. N. Y. ay. Pᵃ ay. Del. ay. Maryᵈ no. Vᵃ ay. N. C. ay. S. C. ay. Geo. ay. [Ayes, 8; noes, 2.] ...

It was then moved & 2ᵈᵉᵈ to proceed to the consideration of the 9ᵗʰ resolution submitted by Mʳ Randolph—when on motion to agree to the first clause namely "Resolved that a National Judiciary be established" It passed in the affirmative nem. con.

It was then moved & 2ᵈᵉᵈ to add these words to the first clause of the ninth resolution namely—"to consist of one supreme tribunal, and of one or more inferior tribunals," which passed in the affirmative—

The Commᵉ then rose and the House
Adjourned

Tuesday, June 5. In Committee of the whole

Governor Livingston from New Jersey, took his seat.

... The Clause—"that the National Judiciary be chosen by the National Legislature," being under consideration.

Mʳ WILSON opposed the appointmᵗ of Judges by the National Legisl: Experience shewed the impropriety of such appointmᵗˢ by numerous bodies. Intrigue, partiality, and concealment were the necessary consequences. A principal reason for unity in the Executive was that officers might be appointed by a single, responsible person.

Mʳ RUTLEDGE was by no means disposed to grant so great a power to any single person. The people will think we are leaning too much towards Monarchy. He was against establishing any national tribunal except a single supreme one. The State tribunals are most proper to decide in all cases in the first instance.

.   .   .   .

Mʳ MADISON disliked the election of the Judges by the Legislature or any numerous body. Besides, the danger of intrigue and partiality, many of the members were not judges of the requisite qualifications. . . . On the other hand he was not satisfied with referring the appointment to the Executive. He rather inclined to give it to the Senatorial branch, as numerous eno' to be confided in—as not so numerous as to be governed by the motives of the other branch; and as being sufficiently stable and independent to follow their deliberate judgments. He hinted this only and moved that the *appointment by the Legislature* might be struck out, & a blank left to be hereafter filled on maturer reflection. Mʳ WILSON seconds it. On the question for striking out. Massᵗˢ ay. Conᵗ no. N. Y. ay. N. J. ay. Penᵃ ay. Del. ay. Mᵈ ay. Vᵃ ay. N. C. ay. S. C. no. Geo. ay. [Ayes, 9; noes, 2.]

.   .   .   .

Resolution 10 was agreed to—viz—that provision ought to be made for the admission of States lawfully arising within the limits of the U. States, whether from a voluntary junction of Government & territory, or otherwise, with the consent of a number of voices in the National Legislature less than the whole.

The 11. propos: *"for guarantying to States Republican* Govᵗ & territory &c.,* being read, Mʳ PATTERSON wished the point of representation could be decided before this clause should be considered, and moved to postpone it: which was not opposed, and agreed to: . . .

Propos. 12 *"for continuing Congˢ till a given day and for fulfilling their engagements,"* produced no debate. . . .

Propos: 13. "that *provision ought to be made for hereafter amending the system now to be established, without requiring the assent of the Natˡ Legislature,"* being taken up,

M͟r PINKNEY doubted the propriety or necessity of it.

M͟r GERRY favored it. The novelty & difficulty of the experiment requires periodical revision. The prospect of such a revision would also give intermediate stability to the Gov͟t Nothing had yet happened in the States where this provision existed to prove its impropriety. The proposition was postponed for further consideration: . . .

Propos. 14. *"requiring oath from the State officers to support National Gov͟t"* was postponed after a short uninteresting conversation: . . .

Propos. 15 for *"recommending Conventions under appointment of the people to ratify the new Constitution"* &c. being taken up.

M͟r SHARMAN thought such a popular ratification unnecessary: the articles of Confederation providing for changes and alterations with the assent of Cong͟s and ratification of State Legislatures.

M͟r MADISON thought this provision essential. The articles of Confed͟n themselves were defective in this respect, resting in many of the States on the Legislative sanction only. Hence in conflicts between acts of the States, and of Cong͟s especially where the former are of posterior date, and the decision is to be made by State tribunals, an uncertainty must necessarily prevail, or rather perhaps a certain decision in favor of the State authority. He suggested also that as far as the articles of Union were to be considered as a Treaty only of a particular sort, among the Governments of Independent States, the doctrine might be set up that a breach of any one article, by any of the parties, absolved the other parties from the whole obligation. For these reasons as well as others he thought it indispensable that the new Constitution should be ratified in the most unexceptionable form, and by the supreme authority of the people themselves.

M͟r GERRY observed that in the Eastern States the Confed͟n had been sanctioned by the people themselves. He seemed afraid of referring the new system to them. The people in that quarter have at this time the wildest ideas of Government in the world.

They were for abolishing the Senate in Mass^ts and giving all the other powers of Gov^t to the other branch of the Legislature.

 Mr KING supposed that the last article of ye Confed^n rendered the legislature competent to the ratification. The people of the Southern States where the federal articles had been ratified by the Legislatures only, had since *impliedly* given their sanction to it. He thought notwithstanding that there might be policy in varying the mode. A Convention being a single house, the adoption may more easily be carried thro' it, than thro' the Legislatures where there are several branches. The Legislatures also being to lose power, will be most likely to raise objections. The people having already parted with the necessary powers it is immaterial to them, by which Government they are possessed, provided they be well employed.

Mr WILSON took this occasion to lead the Committee by a train of observations to the idea of not suffering a disposition in the plurality of States to confederate anew on better principles, to be defeated by the inconsiderate or selfish opposition of a few States. He hoped the provision for ratifying would be put on such a footing as to admit of such a partial union, with a door open for the acession of the rest.[7]

Mr PINKNEY hoped that in case the experiment should not unanimously take place nine States might be authorized to unite under the same Govern^t

The propos. 15. was postponed nem. con^t . . .

.   .   .   .

Mr RUTLIDGE hav^g obtained a rule for reconsideration of the clause for establishing *inferior* tribunals under the national authority, now moved that that part of the clause in propos. 9. should be expunged: arguing that the State Tribunals might and ought to be left in all cases to decide in the first instance the right of appeal to the supreme national tribunal being sufficient to secure the national rights & uniformity of Judgm^ts: that it was making an unnecessary encroachment on the jurisdiction

---

[7] This hint was probably meant in terrorem to the smaller States of N. Jersey & Delaware. Nothing was said in reply to it.

of the States and creating unnecessary obstacles to their adoption of the new system.—Mᵣ Sherman 2ᵈᵉᵈ the motion.

Mᵣ Madison observed that unless inferior tribunals were dispersed throughout the Republic with *final* jurisdiction in *many* cases, appeals would be multiplied to a most oppressive degree; that besides, an appeal would not in many cases be a remedy. . . . An effective Judiciary establishment commensurate to the legislative authority, was essential. A Government without a proper Executive & Judiciary would be the mere trunk of a body, without arms or legs to act or move.

. . . On the question for Mᵣ Rutlidge's motion to strike out "inferior tribunals"

Massᵗˢ divided. Conᵗ ay. N. Y. divᵈ N. J. ay. Pᵃ no. Del. no. Mᵈ no. Vᵃ no. N. C. ay. S. C. ay. Geo. ay. [Ayes, 5; noes, 4; divided, 2.]

Mᵣ Wilson & Mᵣ Madison then moved, . . . to add to Resol: 9. the words following "that the National Legislature be empowered to institute inferior tribunals." They observed that there was a distinction between establishing such tribunals absolutely, and giving a discretion to the Legislature to establish or not establish them. They repeated the necessity of some such provision.

Mᵣ Butler. The people will not bear such innovations. The States will revolt at such encroachments. Supposing such an establishment to be useful, we must not venture on it. We must follow the example of Solon who gave the Athenians not the best Govᵗ he could devise; but the best they wᵈ receive.

Mᵣ King remarked as to the comparative expence that the establishment of inferior tribunals wᵈ cost infinitely less than the appeals that would be prevented by them.

On this question as moved by Mᵣ W. & Mᵣ M.

Mass. ay. Cᵗ no. N. Y. divᵈ N. J. ay. Pᵃ ay. Del. ay. Mᵈ ay. Vᵃ ay. N. C. ay. S. C. no. Geo. ay. [Ayes, 8; noes, 2; divided 1.] . . .

Wednesday, June 6. In Committee of the whole

M![r]{.sup} PINKNEY . . . moved "that the first branch of the national Legislature be elected by the State Legislatures, and not by the people." contending that the people were less fit Judges in such a case, and that the Legislatures would be less likely to promote the adoption of the new Government, if they were to be excluded from all share in it.

M![r]{.sup} RUTLIDGE 2![ded]{.sup} the motion.

M![r]{.sup} GERRY. Much depends on the mode of election. In England, the people will probably lose their liberty from the smallness of the proportion having a right of suffrage. Our danger arises from the opposite extreme: hence in Mass![ts]{.sup} the worst men get into the Legislature. Several members of that Body had lately been convicted of infamous crimes. Men of indigence, ignorance & baseness, spare no pains, however dirty to carry their point ag![st]{.sup} men who are superior to the artifices practised. He was not disposed to run into extremes. He was as much principled as ever ag![st]{.sup} aristocracy and monarchy. It was necessary on the one hand that the people should appoint one branch of the Gov![t]{.sup} in order to inspire them with the necessary confidence. But he wished the election on the other to be so modified as to secure more effectually a just preference of merit. His idea was that the people should nominate certain persons in certain districts, out of whom the State Legislatures sh![d]{.sup} make the appointment.

M![r]{.sup} WILSON. He wished for vigor in the Gov![t]{.sup}, but he wished that vigorous authority to flow immediately from the legitimate source of all authority. The Gov![t]{.sup} ought to possess not only 1![st]{.sup} the *force,* but 2![dly]{.sup} the *mind or sense* of the people at large. The Legislature ought to be the most exact transcript of the whole Society. Representation is made necessary only because it is impossible for the people to act collectively. The opposition was to be expected he said from the *Governments,* not from the Citizens of the States. The latter had parted as was observed (by Mr King) with all the necessary powers; [8] and it was immaterial to them, by whom they were exercised, if well exercised. The State officers were to be the losers of power. The people he supposed would be rather more attached to the national Gov^t than to the State Gov^{ts} as being more important in itself, and more flattering to their pride. There is no danger of improper elections if made by *large* districts. Bad elections proceed from the smallness of the districts which give an opportunity to bad men to intrigue themselves into office.

Mr SHERMAN. If it were in view to abolish the State Gov^{ts} the elections ought to be by the people. If the State Gov^{ts} are to be continued, it is necessary in order to preserve harmony between the National & State Gov^{ts} that the elections to the former sh^d be made by the latter. The right of participating in the National Gov^t would be sufficiently secured to the people by their election of the State Legislatures. The objects of the Union, he thought were few. 1. defence agst foreign danger. 2. agst internal disputes & a resort to force. 3. Treaties with foreign nations. 4. regulating foreign commerce, & drawing revenue from it. These & perhaps a few lesser objects alone rendered a Confederation of the States necessary. All other matters civil & criminal would be much better in the hands of the States. The people are more happy in small than large States. States may indeed be too small as Rhode Island, & thereby be too subject to faction. Some others were perhaps too large, the powers of Gov^t not being able to pervade them. He was for giving the General Gov^t power to legislate and execute within a defined province.

COL. MASON. Under the existing Confederacy, Cong^s represent the *States* not the *people* of the States: their acts operate on the *States,* not on the individuals. The case will be changed in the new plan of Gov^t The people will be represented; they ought therefore to choose the Representatives. The requisites in actual representation are that the Rep^s should sympathize with their constituents; sh^d think as they think, & feel as they feel; and that for these purposes sh^d even be residents among them. Much

8 (The phrase "with all the necessary powers" is italicized in the transcript.)

he s^d had been alledged ag^st democratic elections. He admitted that much might be said; but it was to be considered that no Gov^t was free from imperfections & evils; and that improper elections in many instances, were inseparable from Republican Gov^ts But compare these with the advantage of this Form in favor of the rights of the people, in favor of human nature. He was persuaded there was a better chance for proper elections by the people, if divided into large districts, than by the State Legislatures. ...

Mr MADISON considered an election of one branch at least of the Legislature by the people immediately, as a clear principle of free Gov^t and that this mode under proper regulations had the additional advantage of securing better representatives, as well as of avoiding too great an agency of the State Governments in the General one.—He differed from the member from Connecticut (Mr Sharman) in thinking the objects mentioned to be all the principal ones that required a National Gov^t Those were certainly important and necessary objects; but he combined with them the necessity of providing more effectually for the security of private rights, and the steady dispensation of Justice. Interferences with these were evils which had more perhaps than any thing else, produced this convention. Was it to be supposed that republican liberty could long exist under the abuses of it practised in some of the States. The gentleman (Mr Sharman) had admitted that in a very small State, faction & oppression w^d prevail. It was to be inferred then that wherever these prevailed the State was too small. Had they not prevailed in the largest as well as the smallest tho' less than in the smallest; and were we not thence admonished to enlarge the sphere as far as the nature of the Gov^t would admit. This was the only defence ag^st the inconveniencies of democracy consistent with the democratic form of Gov^t All civilized Societies would be divided into different Sects, Factions, & interests, as they happened to consist of rich & poor, debtors & creditors, the landed, the manufacturing, the commercial interests, the inhabitants of this district or that district, the followers of this political leader or that political leader, the disciples of this religious Sect or that religious Sect. In all cases where a majority are united by a common interest or passion, the rights of the minority are in danger. What motives are to restrain them? A prudent regard to the maxim that honesty is the best policy is found by experience to be as little regarded by bodies of men as by individuals. Respect for character is always diminished in proportion to the number among whom the blame or praise is to be divided. Conscience, the only remaining tie, is known to be inadequate in individuals: In large numbers, little is to be expected from it. Besides, Religion itself may become a motive to persecution & oppression.—These observations are verified by the Histories of every Country antient & modern. In Greece & Rome the rich & poor, the creditors & debtors, as well as the patricians & plebians alternately oppressed each other with equal unmercifulness. What a source of oppression was the relation between the parent cities of Rome, Athens & Carthage, & their respective provinces: the former possessing the power, & the latter being sufficiently distinguished to be separate objects of it? Why was America so justly apprehensive of Parliamentary injustice? Because G. Britain had a separate interest real or supposed, & if her authority had been admitted, could have pursued that interest at our expence. We have seen the mere distinction of colour made in the most enlightened period of time, a ground of the most oppressive dominion ever exercised by man over man. What has been the source of those unjust laws complained of among ourselves? Has it not been the real or supposed interest of the major number? Debtors have defrauded their creditors. The landed interest has borne hard on the mercantile interest. The Holders of one species of property have thrown a disproportion of taxes on the holders of another species. The lesson we are to draw from the whole is that where a majority are united by a common sentiment, and have an opportunity, the rights of the minor party become insecure. In a Republican Gov^t the Majority if united have always an opportunity. The only remedy is to enlarge the sphere, & thereby divide the community into so great a number of interests & parties, that in the 1st place a majority will not be likely at the same moment to have a common interest separate from that of the whole or of the minority; and in the 2ᵈ place, that in case they shᵈ have such an interest, they may not be apt to unite in the pursuit of it. It was incumbent on us then to try this remedy, and with that view to frame a republican system on such a scale & in such a form as will controul all the evils wᶜʰ have been experienced.

Mʳ Dickenson considered it as essential that one branch of the Legislature shᵈ be drawn immediately from the people; and as expedient that the other shᵈ be chosen by the Legislatures of the States. This combination of the State Govᵗˢ with the national Govᵗ was as politic as it was unavoidable. ... He was for a strong National Govᵗ but for leaving the States a considerable agency in the System. . . .

Mʳ Read. Too much attachment is betrayed to the State Governᵗˢ We must look beyond their continuance. A national Govᵗ must soon of necessity swallow all of them up. ... The confederation was founded on temporary principles. It cannot last: it cannot be amended. If we do not establish a good Govᵗ on new principles, we must either go to ruin, or have the work to do over again. The people at large are wrongly suspected of being averse to a Genᶦ Govᵗ The aversion lies among interested men who possess their confidence.

. . . .

Mʳ Wilson, would not have spoken again, but for what had fallen from Mʳ Read; namely, that the idea of preserving the State Govᵗˢ ought to be abandoned. He saw no incompatibility between the National & State Govᵗˢ provided the latter were restrained to certain local purposes; nor any probability of their being devoured by the former. In all confederated Systems antient & modern the reverse had happened; the Generality being destroyed gradually by the usurpations of the parts composing it.

On the question for electing the 1ˢᵗ branch by the State Legislatures as moved by Mʳ Pinkney: it was negatived:

Mass. no. Cᵗ ay. N. Y. no. N. J. ay. Pᵃ no. Del. no. Mᵈ no. Vᵃ no. N. C. no. S. C. ay. Geo. no. [Ayes, 3; noes, 8.]

Mr WILSON moved to reconsider the vote excluding the Judiciary from a share in the revision of the laws, and to add after "National Executive" the words "with a convenient number of the national Judiciary"; remarking the expediency of reinforcing the Executive with the influence of that Department.

Mr MADISON 2^{ded} the motion. He observed that the great difficulty in rendering the Executive competent to its own defence arose from the nature of Republican Gov^t which could not give to an individual citizen that settled pre-eminence in the eyes of the rest, that weight of property, that personal interest agst betraying the national interest, which appertain to an hereditary magistrate. In a Republic personal merit alone could be the ground of political exaltation, but it would rarely happen that this merit would be so pre-eminent as to produce universal acquiescence. The Executive Magistrate would be envied & assailed by disappointed competitors: His firmness therefore w^d need support. . . .

Mr KING. If the Unity of the Executive was preferred for the sake of responsibility, the policy of it is as applicable to the revisionary as to the Executive power.

Mr PINKNEY had been at first in favor of joining the heads of the principal departm^{ts} the Secretary of War, of foreign affairs &—in the council of revision. He had however relinquished the idea from a consideration that these could be called in by the Executive Magistrate whenever he pleased to consult them. He was opposed to an introduction of the Judges into the business.

Mr DICKENSON. Secrecy, vigor & despatch are not the principal properties req^d in the Executive. Important as these are, that of responsibility is more so, which can only be preserved; by leaving it singly to discharge its functions. He thought too a junction of the judiciary to it, involved an improper mixture of powers.

Mr WILSON remarked, that the responsibility required belonged to his Executive duties. The revisionary duty was an extraneous one, calculated for collateral purposes. . . .

On the question for joining the Judges to the Executive in the revisionary business, Mass. no. Cont ay. N. Y. ay. N. J. no. Pª no. Del. no. Mᵈ no. Vª ay. N. C. no. S. C. No. Geo. no. [Ayes, 3; noes, 8.]

Thursday, June 7. In Committee of the whole

The Clause providing for yᵉ appointment of the 2ᵈ branch of the national Legislature, having lain blank since the last vote on the mode of electing it, to wit, by the 1ˢᵗ branch, Mʳ DICKENSON now moved "that the members of the 2ᵈ branch ought to be chosen by the individual Legislatures."

Mʳ SHARMAN seconded the motion; observing that the particular States would thus become interested in supporting the national Governmᵗ and that a due harmony between the two Governments would be maintained. He admitted that the two ought to have separate and distinct jurisdictions, but that they ought to have a mutual interest in supporting each other.

. . . .

Mʳ DICKENSON had two reasons for his motion. 1. because the sense of the States would be better collected through their Governments; than immediately from the people at large; 2. because he wished the Senate to consist of the most distinguished characters, distinguished for their rank in life and their weight of property, and bearing as strong a likeness to the British House of Lords as possible; and he thought such characters more likely to be selected by the State Legislatures, than in any other mode. The greatness of the number was no objection with him. . . . If their number should be small, the popular branch could not be balanced by them. The legislature of a numerous people ought to be a numerous body.

. . . .

Mʳ WILSON. If we are to establish a national Government, that Government ought to flow from the people at large. If one branch of it should be chosen by the Legislatures, and the other by the people, the two branches will rest on different foundations, and dissensions will naturally arise between them. He wished the Senate to be elected by the people as well as the other branch, and the people might be divided into proper districts for the purpose & moved to postpone the motion of Mr Dickenson, in order to take up one of that import.

Mr Morris 2^{ded} him.

Mr Read proposed "that the Senate should be appointed by the Executive Magistrate out of a proper number of persons to be nominated by the individual legislatures." . . . His proposition was not seconded nor supported.

Mr Madison, if the motion (of Mr. Dickenson) should be agreed to, we must either depart from the doctrine of proportional representation; or admit into the Senate a very large number of members. The first is inadmissible, being evidently unjust. The second is inexpedient. The use of the Senate is to consist in its proceeding with more coolness, with more system, & with more wisdom, than the popular branch. Enlarge their number and you communicate to them the vices which they are meant to correct. He differed from Mr D. who thought that the additional number would give additional weight to the body. On the contrary it appeared to him that their weight would be in an inverse ratio to their number. The example of the Roman Tribunes was applicable. . . . When the weight of a set of men depends merely on their personal characters; the greater the number the greater the weight. When it depends on the degree of political authority lodged in them the smaller the number the greater the weight. These considerations might perhaps be combined in the intended Senate; but the latter was the material one.

Mr Gerry. 4 modes of appointing the Senate have been mentioned. 1. by the 1st branch of the National Legislature. This would create a dependence contrary to the end proposed. 2. by the National Executive. This is a stride towards monarchy that few will think of. 3. by the people. The people have two great interests, the landed interest, and the commercial including the stockholders. To draw both branches from the people will leave no security to the latter interest; the people being chiefly composed of the landed interest, and erroneously supposing, that the other interests are adverse to it. 4. by the Individual Legislatures. The elections being carried thro' this refinement, will be most likely to provide some check in favor of the commercial interest agᵗ the landed; without which oppression will take place, and no free Govᵗ can last long where that is the case. He was therefore in favor of this last.

Mʳ DICKENSON.[9] The preservation of the States in a certain degree of agency is indispensable. It will produce that collision between the different authorities which should be wished for in order to check each other. To attempt to abolish the States altogether, would degrade the Councils of our Country, would be impracticable, would be ruinous. He compared the proposed National System to the Solar System, in which the States were the planets, and ought to be left to move freely in their proper orbits. The Gentleman from Pᵃ (Mʳ Wilson) wished he said to extinguish these planets. If the State Governments were excluded from all agency in the national one, and all power drawn from the people at large, the consequence would be that the national Govᵗ would move in the same direction as the State Govᵗˢ now do, and would run into all the same mischiefs. The reform would only unite the 13 small streams into one great current pursuing the same course without any opposition whatever. He adhered to the opinion that the Senate ought to be composed of a large number, and that their influence from family weight & other causes would be increased thereby. ... If the reasoning of (Mʳ Madison) was good it would prove that the number of the Senate ought to be reduced below ten, the highest nᵒ of the Tribunitial corps.

Mʳ WILSON. The subject it must be owned is surrounded with doubts and difficulties. But we must surmount them. The British Governmᵗ cannot be our model. We have no materials for a similar one. Our manners, our laws, the abolition of en-

---

[9] It will throw light on this discussion to remark that an election by the State Legislatures involved a surrender of the principle insisted on by the large States & dreaded by the small ones, namely that of a proportional representation in the Senate. Such a rule wᵈ make the body too numerous, as the smallest State must elect one member at least.

tails and of primogeniture, the whole genius of the people, are opposed to it. He did not see the danger of the States being devoured by the Nat[onl] Gov[t] On the contrary, he wished to keep them from devouring the national Gov[t] He was not however for extinguishing these planets as was supposed by M[r] D.— neither did he on the other hand, believe that they would warm or enlighten the Sun. Within their proper orbits they must still be suffered to act for subordinate purposes for which their existence is made essential by the great extent of our Country. He could not comprehend in what manner the landed interest w[d] be rendered less predominant in the Senate, by an election through the medium of the Legislatures than by the people themselves. If the Legislatures, as was now complained, sacrificed the commercial to the landed interest, what reason was there to expect such a choice from them as would defeat their own views. He was for an election by the people in large districts which w[d] be most likely to obtain men of intelligence & uprightness; subdividing the districts only for the accomodation of voters.

M[r] MADISON. ... The great evils complained of were that the State Legislatures run into schemes of paper money &c. whenever solicited by the people, & sometimes without even the sanction of the people. Their influence then, instead of checking a like propensity in the National Legislature, may be expected to promote it. Nothing can be more contradictory than to say that the Nat[l] Legislature with[t] a proper check, will follow the example of the State Legislatures, & in the same breath, that the State Legislatures are the only proper check.

.   .   .   .

COL. MASON. whatever power may be necessary for the Nat[l] Gov[t] a certain portion must necessarily be left in the States. It is impossible for one power to pervade the extreme parts of the U. S. so as to carry equal justice to them. The State Legislatures also ought to have some means of defending themselves ag[st] encroachments of the Nat[l] Gov[t] In every other department we have studiously endeavored to provide for its self-defence. Shall we leave the States alone unprovided with the means for this purpose? And what better means can we provide than the giving them some share in, or rather to make them a constituent part of, the Nat! Establishment. ...

On Mʳ DICKINSON's motion for an appointment of the Senate by the State-Legislatures.

Mass. ay. Cᵗ ay. N. Y. ay. Pᵃ ay. Del. ay. Mᵈ ay. Vᵃ ay. N. C. ay. S. C. ay. Geo. ay. [Ayes, 10; noes, 0.]

Still assumed to be proportional

Friday, June 8. In Committee of the whole

On a reconsideration of the clause giving the Nat! Legislature a negative on such laws of the States as might be contrary to the articles of Union, or Treaties with foreign nations,

Mʳ PINKNEY moved "that the National Legislature shᵈ have authority to negative all laws which they shᵈ judge to be improper." He urged that such a universality of the power was indispensably necessary to render it effectual; that the States must be kept in due subordination to the nation; that if the States were left to act of themselves in any case, it wᵈ be impossible to defend the national prerogatives, however extensive they might be on paper; that the acts of Congress had been defeated by this means; nor had foreign treaties escaped repeated violations; that this universal negative was in fact the corner stone of an efficient national Govᵗ; that under the British Govᵗ the negative of the Crown had been found beneficial, and the *States* are more one nation now, than the *Colonies* were then.

Mʳ MADISON seconded the motion. He could not but regard an indefinite power to negative legislative acts of the States as absolutely necessary to a perfect system. Experience had evinced a constant tendency in the States to encroach on the federal authority; to violate national Treaties; to infringe the rights & interests of each other; to oppress the weaker party within their respective jurisdictions. A negative was the mildest expedient that could be devised for preventing these mischiefs. The existence of such a check would prevent attempts to commit them.

Should no such precaution be engrafted, the only remedy w^d lie in an appeal to coercion. Was such a remedy eligible? was it practicable? Could the national resources, if exerted to the utmost enforce a national decree ag^st Mass^ts abetted perhaps by several of her neighbours? It w^d not be possible. A small proportion of the Community, in a compact situation, acting on the defensive, and at one of its extremities might at any time bid defiance to the National authority. Any Gov^t for the U. States formed on the supposed practicability of using force ag^st the unconstitutional proceedings of the States, w^d prove as visionary & fallacious as the Gov^t of Cong^s The negative w^d render the use of force unnecessary. The States c^d of themselves then pass no operative act, any more than one branch of a Legislature where there are two branches, can proceed without the other. But in order to give the negative this efficacy, it must extend to all cases. A discrimination w^d only be a fresh source of contention between the two authorities. In a word, to recur to the illustrations borrowed from the planetary system. This prerogative of the General Gov^t is the great pervading principle that must controul the centrifugal tendency of the States; which, without it, will continually fly out of their proper orbits and destroy the order & harmony of the political System.

Mr WILLIAMSON was ag^st giving a power that might restrain the States from regulating their internal police.

Mr GERRY c^d not see the extent of such a power, and was ag^st every power that was not necessary. He thought a remonstrance ag^st unreasonable acts of the States w^d reclaim them. If it sh^d not force might be resorted to. He had no objection to authorize a negative to paper money and similar measures. . . . He observed that the proposed negative w^d extend to the regulations of the Militia, a matter on which the existence of a State might depend. The Nat^l Legislature with such a power may enslave the States. Such an idea as this will never be acceded to. . . .

Mr SHERMAN thought the cases in which the negative ought to be exercised, might be defined. . . .

Mr WILSON would not say what modifications of the proposed

power might be practicable or expedient. But however novel it might appear the principle of it when viewed with a close & steady eye, is right. There is no instance in which the laws say that the individual sh^d be bound in one case, & at liberty to judge whether he will obey or disobey in another. The cases are parallel. Abuses of the power over the individual person may happen as well as over the individual States. Federal liberty is to States, what civil liberty, is to private individuals. And States are not more unwilling to purchase it, by the necessary concession of their political sovereignty, than the savage is to purchase civil liberty by the surrender of his personal sovereignty, which he enjoys in a State of nature. A definition of the cases in which the Negative should be exercised, is impracticable. A discretion must be left on one side or the other? will it not be most safely lodged on the side of the Nat^l Gov^t? Among the first sentiments expressed in the first Cong^s one was that Virg^a is no more, that Mas^ts is no, that P^a is no more &c. We are now one nation of brethren. We must bury all local interests & distinctions. This language continued for some time. The tables at length began to turn. No sooner were the State Gov^ts formed than their jealousy & ambition began to display themselves. ... Review the progress of the articles of Confederation thro' Congress & compare the first & last draught of it. To correct its vices is the business of this convention. One of its vices is the want of an effectual controul in the whole over its parts. What danger is there that the whole will unnecessarily sacrifice a part? But reverse the case, and leave the whole at the mercy of each part, and will not the general interest be continually sacrificed to local interests? ...

Mr BEDFORD. In answer to his colleague's question where w^d be the danger to the States from this power, would refer him to the smallness of his own State which may be injured at pleasure without redress. It was meant he found to strip the small States of their equal right of suffrage. In this case Delaware would have about 1/90 for its share in the General Councils, whilst P^a & V^a would possess 1/3 of the whole. Is there no difference of interests, no rivalship of commerce, of manufactures? Will not these large States crush the small ones whenever they stand in the way of their ambitious or interested views. This shews the impossibility of adopting such a system as that on the table, or any other founded on a change in the principle of representation. And after all, if a State does not obey the law of the new System, must not force be resorted to as the only ultimate remedy, in this as in any other system. It seems as if Pᵃ & Vᵃ by the conduct of their deputies wished to provide a system in which they would have an enormous & monstrous influence. Besides, How can it be thought that the proposed negative can be exercised? are the laws of the States to be suspended in the most urgent cases until they can be sent seven or eight hundred miles, and undergo the deliberations of a body who may be incapable of Judging of them? Is the National Legislature too to sit continually in order to revise the laws of the States?

Mʳ MADISON observed that the difficulties which had been started were worthy of attention and ought to be answered before the question was put. ... He asked Mʳ B. what would be the consequence to the small States of a dissolution of the Union wᶜʰ seemed likely to happen if no effectual substitute was made for the defective System existing, and he did not conceive any effectual system could be substituted on any other basis than that of a proportional suffrage? If the large States possessed the avarice & ambition with which they were charged, would the small ones in their neighbourhood, be more secure when all controul of a Genˡ Govᵗ was withdrawn.

. . .

On the question for extending the negative power to all cases as proposᵈ by (Mʳ P. & Mʳ M—) Mass. ay. Conᵗ no. N. Y. no. N. J. no. Pᵃ ay. Del. divᵈ Mʳ Read & Mʳ Dickenson ay. Mʳ Bedford & Mʳ Basset no. Maryᵈ no. Vᵃ ay. Mʳ R. Mʳ Mason no. Mʳ Blair, Docʳ Mᶜ ᵹ Mʳ M. ay. Genˡ W. not consulted. N. C. no. S. C. no. Geo. no. [Ayes, 3; noes, 7; divided, 1.]

Only limited negative on State Laws

Saturday, June 9. In Committee of the whole

Mr LUTHER MARTIN from Maryland took his seat.

Mr GERRY, ... moved "that the National Executive should be elected by the Executives of the States whose proportion of votes should be the same with that allowed to the States in the election of the Senate." If the appointm^t should be made by the Nat^l Legislature, it would lessen that independence of the Executive which ought to prevail, would give birth to intrigue and corruption between the Executive & Legislature previous to the election, and to partiality in the Executive afterwards to the friends who promoted him. ...

Mr RANDOLPH, urged strongly the inexpediency of Mr Gerry's mode of appointing the Nat^l Executive. ...

On the question for referring the appointment of the Nat^l Executive to the State Executives as prop^d by Mr Gerry Mass^{ts} no. Con^t no. N. Y. no. N. J. no. P^a no. Del. div^d M^d no. V^a no. S. C. no. Geo. no. [Ayes, 0; noes, 9; divided, 1.]

Mr PATTERSON moves that the Committee resume the clause relating to the rule of suffrage in the Nat^l Legislature.[10]

Mr BREARLY seconds him. He was sorry he said that any question on this point was brought into view. It had been much agitated in Cong^s at the time of forming the Confederation, and was then rightly settled by allowing to each sovereign State an equal vote. Otherwise the smaller States must have been destroyed instead of being saved. ... There will be 3. large states, and 10 small ones. The large States by which he meant Mass^{ts} Pen^a & Virg^a will carry every thing before them. It had been admitted, and was known to him from facts within N. Jersey that where large & small counties were united into a district for electing representatives for the district, the large counties always carried their point, and Consequently that the large States would do so. ... He had come to the convention with a view of being as useful as he could in giving energy and stability to

[10] [Postponed on May 30.]

the federal Government. When the proposition for destroying the equality of votes came forward, he was astonished, he was alarmed. Is it fair then it will be asked that Georgia should have an equal vote with Virg^s? He would not say it was. What remedy then? One only, that a map of the U. S. be spread out, that all the existing boundaries be erased, and that a new partition of the whole be made into 13 equal parts.

Mr PATTERSON considered the proposition for a proportional representation as striking at the existence of the lesser States. He w^d premise however to an investigation of this question some remarks on the nature structure and powers of the Convention. The Convention he said was formed in pursuance of an Act of Cong^s that this act was recited in several of the Commissions, particularly that of Mass^ts which he required to be read: that the amendment of the confederacy was the object of all the laws and commissions on the subject; that the articles of the Confederation were therefore the proper basis of all the proceedings of the Convention. We ought to keep within its limits, or we should be charged by our Constituents with usurpation, that the people of America were sharp-sighted and not to be deceived. But the Commissions under which we acted were not only the measure of our power, they denoted also the sentiments of the States on the subject of our deliberation. The idea of a national Gov^t as contradistinguished from a federal one, never entered into the mind of any of them, and to the public mind we must accomodate ourselves. We have no power to go beyond the federal scheme, and if we had the people are not ripe for any other. We must follow the people; the people will not follow us.—The *proposition* could not be maintained whether considered in reference to us as a nation, or as a confederacy. A confederacy supposes sovereignty in the members composing it & sovereignty supposes equality. If we are to be considered as a nation, all State distinctions must be abolished, the whole must be thrown into hotchpot, and when an equal division is made, then there may be fairly an equality of representation. He said there was no more reason that a great individual State contributing much, should have more votes than a small one contributing little, than that a rich individual citizen should have more votes than an indigent one. If the rateable property of A was to that of B as 40 to 1, ought A for that reason to have 40 times as many votes as B. Such a principle would never be admitted, and if it were admitted would put B entirely at the mercy of A. As A. has more to be protected than B so he ought to contribute more for the common protection. The same may be said of a large State wch has more to be protected than a small one. Give the large States an influence in proportion to their magnitude, and what will be the consequence? Their ambition will be proportionally increased, and the small States will have every thing to fear. . . . It has been said that if a Nat^l Gov^t is to be formed so as to operate on the people and not on the States, the representatives ought to be drawn from the people. But why so? May not a Legislature filled by the State Legislatures operate on the people who chuse the State Legislatures? or may not a practicable coercion be found. He admitted that there was none such in the existing System.— He was attached strongly to the plan of the existing confederacy, in which the people chuse their Legislative representatives; and the Legislatures their federal representatives. No other amendments were wanting than to mark the orbits of the States with due precision, and provide for the use of coercion, which was the great point. He alluded to the hint thrown out heretofore by Mr Wilson of the necessity to which the large States might be reduced of confederating among themselves, by a refusal of the others to concur. Let them unite if they please, but let them remember that they have no authority to compel the others to unite. N. Jersey will never confederate on the plan before the Committee. She would be swallowed up. He had rather submit to a monarch, to a despot, than to such a fate. He would not only oppose the plan here but on his return home do every thing in his power to defeat it there.

Mr Wilson hoped if the Confederacy should be dissolved, that a *majority*, that a *minority* [11] of the States would unite for their

[11] [The intended meaning here is: "that a majority, nay, that even a minority. . . ."]

safety. He entered elaborately into the defence of a proportional representation, stating for his first position that as all authority was derived from the people, equal numbers of people ought to have an equal n⁰ of representatives, and different numbers of people different numbers of representatives. This principle had been improperly violated in the Confederation, owing to the urgent circumstances of the time. As to the case of A. & B, stated by Mʳ Patterson, he observed that in districts as large as the States, the number of people was the best measure of their comparative wealth. Whether therefore wealth or numbers were to form the ratio it would be the same. Mʳ P. admitted persons, not property to be the measure of suffrage. Are not the Citizens of Penᵃ equal to those of N. Jersey? does it require 150 of the former to balance 50 of the latter? Representatives of different districts ought clearly to hold the same proportion to each other, as their respective Constituents hold to each other. If the small States will not confederate on this plan, Penᵃ & he presumed some other States, would not confederate on any other. We have been told that each State being sovereign, all are equal. So each man is naturally a sovereign over himself, and all men are therefore naturally equal. Can he retain this equality when he becomes a member of Civil Government? He can not. As little can a Sovereign State, when it becomes a member of a federal Governᵗ If N. J. will not part with her Sovereignty it is in vain to talk of Govᵗ A new partition of the States is desireable, but evidently & totally impracticable. . . .

The Question being about to be put Mʳ PATTERSON hoped that as so much depended on it, it might be thought best to postpone the decision till tomorrow, which was done nem. con.

The Comᵉ rose & the House adjourned.

Monday, June 11. In Committee of the whole

Mʳ ABRAHAM BALDWIN from Georgia took his seat.

The clause concerning the rule of suffrage in the natˡ Legislature postponed on Saturday was resumed.

Mʳ SHARMAN proposed that the proportion of suffrage in the 1ˢᵗ branch should be according to the respective numbers of free inhabitants; and that in the second branch or Senate, each State should have one vote and no more. He said as the States would remain possessed of certain individual rights, each State ought to be able to protect itself: otherwise a few large States will rule the rest. . . .

Mʳ RUTLIDGE proposed that the proportion of suffrage in the 1ˢᵗ branch should be according to the quotas of contribution. The justice of this rule he said could not be contested. Mʳ BUTLER urged the same idea: adding that money was power; and that the States ought to have weight in the Govᵗ in proportion to their wealth.

Mʳ KING & Mʳ WILSON, in order to bring the question to a point moved "that the right of suffrage in the first branch of the national Legislature ought not to be according the rule established in the articles of Confederation, but according to some equitable ratio of representation." The clause so far as it related to suffrage in the first branch was postponed in order to consider this motion.

Mʳ DICKENSON contended for the *actual* contributions of the States as the rule of their representation & suffrage in the first branch. By thus connecting the interest of the States with their duty, the latter would be sure to be performed.

The question being abᵗ to be put Docʳ FRANKLIN sᵈ he had thrown his ideas of the matter on a paper wᶜʰ Mʳ Wilson read to the Committee in the words following—
Mʳ CHAIRMAN

It has given me great pleasure to observe that till this point, the proportion of representation, came before us, our debates were carried on with great coolness & temper. If any thing of a contrary kind, has on this occasion appeared, I hope it will not be repeated; for we are sent here to *consult*, not to *contend*, with each other; and declarations of a fixed opinion, and of determined resolution, never to change it, neither enlighten nor convince us. Positiveness and warmth on one side, naturally beget their like on the other; and tend to create and augment discord & division in a great concern, wherein harmony & Union are extremely necessary to give weight to our Councils, and render them effectual in promoting & securing the common good.

Franklin added that decisions should be by majority of members rather than majority of states, since in America there was no disposition to have members of Congress represent the whole people but merely particular interests. Under this system he thought the greater would not swallow the smaller states, but demonstrated how at present the reverse could be the case. He found the proposal to equalize states fair but fraught with difficulties. Thus he proposed a system whereby decisions would be by majority of individual votes with all states equally represented in Congress. The weakest state was to determine what proportion of money or force it would give the Union, which other states were then to match.

My learned Colleague (Mr Wilson) has already mentioned that the present method of voting by States, was submitted to originally by Congress, under a conviction of its impropriety, inequality, and injustice. This appears in the words of their Resolution. It is of Sepr 6. 1774. The words are

"Resolved that in determining questions in this Congs each Colony or province shall have one vote: The Congs not being possessed of or at present able to procure materials for ascertaining the importance of each Colony."

On the question for agreeing to Mr Kings and Mr Wilsons motion it passed in the affirmative

Massts ay. Ct ay. N. Y. no. N. J. no. Pa ay. Del. no. Md divd. Va ay. N. C. ay. S. C. ay. Geo. ay. [Ayes, 7; noes, 3; divided, 1.]

It was then moved by Mr RUTLIDGE 2ded by Mr BUTLER to add to the words "equitable ratio of representation" at the end of the motion just agreed to, the words "according to the quotas of contribution." On motion of Mr WILSON seconded by Mr C. PINCKNEY, this was postponed; in order to add, after, after the words "equitable ratio of representation" the words following "in proportion to the whole number of white & other free Citizens & inhabitants of every age sex & condition including those bound to servitude for a term of years and three fifths of all other persons not comprehended in the foregoing description, except Indians not paying taxes, in each State," this being the rule in the Act of Congress agreed to by eleven States, for apportioning quotas of revenue on the States, and requiring a Census only every 5–7, or 10 years.

Mr GERRY thought property not the rule of representation. Why then sh^d the blacks, who were property in the South, be in the rule of representation more than the Cattle & horses of the North.

On the question,—Mass: Con: N. Y. Pen: Mary^d Virg^a N. C. S. C. & Geo: were in the affirmative: N. J. & Del: in the negative. [Ayes, 9; noes, 2.]

Mr SHARMAN moved that a question be taken whether each State shall have one vote in the 2^d branch. Every thing he said depended on this. The smaller States would never agree to the plan on any other principle than an equality of suffrage in this branch. Mr ELSWORTH seconded the motion. On the question for allowing each State one vote in the 2^d branch.

Mass^{ts} no. Con^t ay. N. Y. ay. N. J. ay. P^a no. Del. ay. M^d ay. V^a no. N. C. no. S. C. no. Geo. no. [Ayes, 5; noes, 6.]

Mr WILSON & Mr HAMILTON moved that the right of suffrage in the 2^d branch ought to be according to the same rule as in the 1st branch. On this question for making the ratio of representation the same in the 2^d as in the 1st branch it passed in the affirmative:

Mass^{ts} ay. Con^t no. N. Y. no. N. J. no. P^a ay. Del. no. M^d no. V^a ay. N. C. ay. S. C. ay. Geo. ay. [Ayes, 6; noes, 5.]

Members resumed discussion of various resolutions. After brief debate in which Sherman, Martin, and Gerry upheld state prerogative, the Convention approved by six to five a provision requiring an oath from state officials to observe the national constitution and laws. Six votes secured referral of the new system to the people of the states for ratification. Delegates fixed the term in both houses after considering one, two, and three years for the lower and three, five, and seven years for the upper branch. Debate turned on the issue of responsiveness to the public versus instability. A seven-to-four ballot fixed three years for the first house, with Gerry strongly favoring annual elections and Madison the higher limit. The term for the other house was set at seven years, after Randolph argued for a check on the "democratic licentiousness" of lower chambers and Madison lamented the lack of sufficient direct experience to guide deliberations. Pecuniary compensation was to be from the national treasury, thus precluding state influence.

Wednesday, June 13. In Committee of the whole

Resol: 9 [12] being resumed

. . . .

Mʳ RANDOLPH & Mʳ MADISON . . . moved the following resolution respecting a National Judiciary, viz "that the jurisdiction of the National Judiciary shall extend to cases, which respect the collection of the national revenue, impeachments of any national officers, and questions which involve the national peace and harmony" which was agreed to.

Mʳ PINKNEY & Mʳ SHERMAN moved to insert after the words "one supreme tribunal" the words "the Judges of which to be appointed by the national Legislature."

Mʳ MADISON, objected to an appᵗ by the whole Legislature. . . . He proposed that the appointment should be made by the Senate, which as a less numerous & more select body, would be more competent judges, and which was sufficiently numerous to justify such a confidence in them.

Mʳ SHARMAN & Mʳ PINKNEY withdrew their motion, and the appᵗ by the Senate was agᵈ to nem. con.

. . . .

Committee rose & Mʳ GHORUM made report, which was post-

12 [Relating to the national judiciary.]

poned till tomorrow, to give an opportunity for other plans to be proposed. The report was in the words following:

REPORT OF THE COMMITTEE OF WHOLE
ON Mʳ RANDOLPH'S PROPOSITIONS

1. Resᵈ that it is the opinion of this Committee that a National Governmᵗ ought to be established, consisting of a supreme Legislative, Executive & Judiciary.

2. Resolᵈ that the National Legislature ought to consist of two branches.

3. Resᵈ that the members of the first branch of the National Legislature ought to be elected by the people of the several States for the term of three years, to receive fixed Stipends by which they may be compensated for the devotion of their time to public service, to be paid out of the National Treasury: to be ineligible to any office established by a particular State, or under the authority of the U. States, (except those peculiarly belonging to the functions of the first branch), during the term of service, and under the national Government for the space of one year after its expiration.

4. Resᵈ that the members of the second branch of the Natˡ Legislature ought to be chosen by the individual Legislatures, to be of the age of 30 years at least, to hold their offices for a term sufficient to ensure their independency, namely, seven years, to receive fixed stipends by which they may be compensated for the devotion of their time to public service to be paid out of the National Treasury; to be ineligible to any office established by a particular State, or under the authority of the U. States, (except those peculiarly belonging to the functions of the second branch) during the term of service, and under the Natˡ Govᵗ for the space of one year after its expiration.

5. Resᵈ that each branch ought to possess the right of originating Acts.

6. Resᵈ that the Natˡ Legislature ought to be empowered to enjoy the Legislative rights vested in Congˢ by the Confederation, and moreover to legislate in all cases to which the separate States are incompetent; or in which the harmony of the U. S. may be interrupted by the exercise of individual legislation; to negative all laws passed by the several States contravening in

the opinion of the National Legislature the articles of Union, or any treaties subsisting under the authority of the Union.

7. Res^d that the rights of suffrage in the 1st branch of the National Legislature, ought not to be according to the rule established in the articles of confederation but according to some equitable ratio of representation, namely, in proportion to the whole number of white & other free citizens & inhabitants, of every age sex and condition, including those bound to servitude for a term of years, & three fifths of all other persons, not comprehended in the foregoing description, except Indians not paying taxes in each State:

8. Resolved that the right of suffrage in the 2^d branch of the National Legislature ought to be according to the rule established for the first.

9. Resolved that a National Executive be instituted to consist of a single person, to be chosen by the Nati^l Legislature for the term of seven years, with power to carry into execution the national laws, to appoint to offices in cases not otherwise provided for—to be ineligible a second time, & to be removeable on impeachment and conviction of malpractices or neglect of duty —to receive a fixed stipend by which he may be compensated for the devotion of his time to public service to be paid out of the national Treasury.

10. Resol^d that the Nat^l Executive shall have a right to negative any Legislative Act, which shall not be afterwards passed unless by two thirds of each branch of the National Legislature.

11. Resol^d that a Nat^l Judiciary be established, to consist of one supreme tribunal, the Judges of which to be appointed by the 2^d branch of the Nat^l Legislature, to hold their offices during good behaviour, & to receive punctually at stated times a fixed compensation for their services, in which no increase or diminution shall be made, so as to affect the persons actually in office at the time of such increase or diminution.

12. Resol^d that the Nat^l Legislature be empowered to appoint inferior Tribunals.

13. Res^d that the jurisdiction of the Nat^l Judiciary shall extend to all cases which respect the collection of the Nat^l revenue, impeachments of any Nat^l Officers, and questions which involve the national peace & harmony.

14. Res^d that provision ought to be made for the admission of

States lawfully arising within the limits of the U. States, whether from a voluntary junction of Government & territory or otherwise, with the consent of a number of voices in the Nat! Legislature less than the whole.

15. Res^d that provision ought to be made for the continuance of Congress and their authorities and privileges untill a given day after the reform of the articles of Union shall be adopted and for the completion of all their engagements.

16. Res^d that a Republican Constitution & its existing laws ought to be guaranteed to each State by the U. States.

17. Res^d that provision ought to be made for the amendment of the Articles of Union whensoever it shall seem necessary.

18. Res^d that the Legislative, Executive & Judiciary powers within the several States ought to be bound by oath to support the articles of Union.

19. Res^d that the amendments which shall be offered to the confederation by the Convention ought at a proper time or times after the approbation of Cong^s to be submitted to an Assembly or Assemblies recommended by the several Legislatures to be expressly chosen by the people to consider and decide thereon.

THE PLAN FOR NATIONAL GOVERNMENT ATTACKED: THE NEW JERSEY AND THE HAMILTON PLANS

Mounting opposition to national government as proposed by the Virginia Plan led to assaults on that scheme. From one quarter came the objection that it went too far. Hence several opponents combined to produce the New Jersey Plan, which aimed merely at strengthening the old Congress under the Articles of Confederation. However, this scheme did include an important provision for supremacy of the central government. From a different quarter came an assault on both of the foregoing alternatives. Hamilton condemned them for not going far enough to remedy existing defects. After spirited attack and defense, during which the central

issue was national government (either according to the Hamilton or Randolph measures) versus confederated government, the Virginia Plan was re-reported on June 19.

Thursday June 14. In Convention

M͏ͬ PATTERSON, observed to the Convention that it was the
wish of several deputations, particularly that of N. Jersey, that
further time might be allowed them to contemplate the plan
reported from the Committee of the Whole, and to digest one
purely federal, and contradistinguished from the reported plan.
He said they hoped to have such an one ready by tomorrow to be
laid before the Convention: And the Convention adjourned
that leisure might be given for the purpose.

Friday, June 15

M͏ͬ PATTERSON, laid before the Convention the plan which he
said several of the deputations wished to be substituted in place
of that proposed by M͏ͬ Randolph. After some little discussion
of the most proper mode of giving it a fair deliberation it was
agreed that it should be referred to a Committee of the whole,
and that in order to place the two plans in due comparison, the
other should be recommitted. At the earnest desire of M͏ͬ Lansing & some other gentlemen, it was also agreed that the Convention should not go into Committee of the whole on the subject
till tomorrow, by which delay the friends of the plan proposed
by M͏ͬ Patterson w͏ͩ be better prepared to explain & support it,
and all would have an opportu͏ʸ of taking copies.[1]

[1] this plan had been concerted among the deputations or members
thereof, from Cont N. Y. N. J. Del. and perhaps M͏ͬ Martin from Mary͏ͩ who
made with them a common cause on different principles Cont & N. Y. were
ag͏ˢͭ a departure from the principle of the Confederation, wishing rather to
add a few new powers to Cong͏ˢ than to substitute a National Gov͏ͭ The
States of N. J. & Del. were opposed to a National Gov͏ͭ because its patrons
considered a proportional representation of the States as the basis of it. The

The propositions from N. Jersey moved by Mr Patterson were in the words following.

1. Res^d that the articles of Confederation ought to be so revised, corrected & enlarged, as to render the federal Constitution adequate to the exigencies of Government, & the preservation of the Union.

2. Res^d that in addition to the powers vested in the U. States in Congress, by the present existing articles of Confederation, they be authorized to pass acts for raising a revenue, by levying a duty or duties on all goods or merchandizes of foreign growth or manufacture, imported into any part of the U. States, by Stamps on paper, vellum or parchment, and by a postage on all letters or packages passing through the general post-office, to be applied to such federal purposes as they shall deem proper & expedient; to make rules & regulations for the collection thereof; and the same from time to time, to alter & amend in such manner as they shall think proper: to pass Acts for the regulation of trade & commerce as well with foreign nations as with each other: provided that all punishments, fines, forfeitures & penalties to be incurred for contravening such acts rules and regulations shall be adjudged by the Common law Judiciaries of the State in which any offence contrary to the true intent & meaning of such Acts rules & regulations shall have been committed or perpetrated, with liberty of commencing in the first instance all suits & prosecutions for that purpose in the superior common law Judiciary in such State, subject nevertheless, for the correction of all errors, both in law & fact in rendering Judgment, to an appeal to the Judiciary of the U. States.

3. Res^d that whenever requisitions shall be necessary, instead

---

eagourness displayed by the members opposed to a Nat^l Gov^t from these different motives began now to produce serious anxiety for the result of the Convention. Mr Dickenson said to Mr Madison—You see the consequence of pushing things too far. Some of the members from the small States wish for two branches in the General Legislature, and are friends to a good National Government; but we would sooner submit to a foreign power than submit to be deprived of an equality of suffrage, in both branches of the legislature, and thereby be thrown under the domination of the large States.

of the rule for making requisitions mentioned in the articles of Confederation, the United States in Cong^s be authorized to make such requisitions in proportion to the whole number of white & other free citizens & inhabitants of every age sex and condition including those bound to servitude for a term of years & three fifths of all other persons not comprehended in the foregoing description, except Indians not paying taxes; that if such requisitions be not complied with, in the time specified therein, to direct the collection thereof in the non complying States & for that purpose to devise and pass acts directing & authorizing the same; provided that none of the powers hereby vested in the U. States in Cong^s shall be exercised without the consent of at least

States, and in that proportion if the number of Confederated States should hereafter be increased or diminished.

4. Res^d that the U. States in Cong^s be authorized to elect a federal Executive to consist of   persons, to continue in office for the term of   years, to receive punctually at stated times a fixed compensation for their services, in which no increase or diminution shall be made so as to affect the persons composing the Executive at the time of such increase or diminution, to be paid out of the federal treasury; to be incapable of holding any other office or appointment during their time of service and for   years thereafter; to be ineligible a second time, & removeable by Cong^s on application by a majority of the Executives of the several States; that the Executives besides their general authority to execute the federal acts ought to appoint all federal officers not otherwise provided for, & to direct all military operations; provided that none of the persons composing the federal Executive shall on any occasion take command of any troops, so as personally to conduct any enterprise as General or in other capacity.

5. Res^d that a federal Judiciary be established to consist of a supreme Tribunal the Judges of which to be appointed by the Executive, & to hold their offices during good behaviour, to receive punctually at stated times a fixed compensation for their services in which no increase or diminution shall be made, so as to affect the persons actually in office at the time of such increase

or diminution; that the Judiciary so established shall have authority to hear & determine in the first instance on all impeachments of federal officers, & by way of appeal in the dernier resort in all cases touching the rights of Ambassadors, in all cases of captures from an enemy, in all cases of piracies & felonies on the high Seas, in all cases in which foreigners may be interested, in the construction of any treaty or treaties, or which may arise on any of the Acts for regulation of trade, or the collection of the federal Revenue: that none of the Judiciary shall during the time they remain in office be capable of receiving or holding any other office or appointment during their time of service, or for thereafter.

6. Resd that all Acts of the U. States in Congs made by virtue & in pursuance of the powers hereby & by the articles of Confederation vested in them, and all Treaties made & ratified under the authority of the U. States shall be the supreme law of the respective States so far forth as those Acts or Treaties shall relate to the said States or their Citizens, and that the Judiciary of the several States shall be bound thereby in their decisions, any thing in the respective laws of the Individual States to the contrary notwithstanding; and that if any State, or any body of men in any State shall oppose or prevent ye carrying into execution such acts or treaties, the federal Executive shall be authorized to call forth ye power of the Confederated States, or so much thereof as may be necessary to enforce and compel an obedience to such Acts, or an observance of such Treaties.

7. Resd that provision be made for the admission of new States into the Union.

8. Resd the rule for naturalization ought to be the same in every State.

9. Resd that a Citizen of one State committing an offense in another State of the Union, shall be deemed guilty of the same offense as if it had been committed by a Citizen of the State in which the offense was committed.

Adjourned.

Saturday, June 16. In Committee of the whole

M͏ͬ LANSING called for the reading of the 1ˢᵗ resolution of each plan, which he considered as involving principles directly in contrast; that of M͏ͬ Patterson says he sustains the sovereignty of the respective States, that of M͏ͬ Randolph distroys it: the latter requires a negative on all the laws of the particular States; the former, only certain general powers for the general good. The plan of M͏ͬ R. in short absorbs all power except what may be exercised in the little local matters of the States which are not objects worthy of the supreme cognizance. He grounded his preference of M͏ͬ P.'s plan, chiefly on two objections ag͏ˢᵗ that of M͏ͬ R. 1. want of power in the Convention to discuss & propose it. 2. the improbability of its being adopted. . . .

M͏ͬ PATTERSON, said as he had on a former occasion given his sentiments on the plan proposed by M͏ͬ R. he would now avoiding repetition as much as possible give his reasons in favor of that proposed by himself. He preferred it because it accorded 1. with the powers of the Convention, 2. with the sentiments of the people. If the confederacy was radically wrong, let us return to our States, and obtain larger powers, not assume them of ourselves. . . . Our object is not such a Governm͏ᵗ as may be best in itself, but such a one as our Constituents have authorized us to prepare, and as they will approve. If we argue the matter on the supposition that no Confederacy at present exists, it can not be denied that all the States stand on the footing of equal sovereignty. All therefore must concur before any can be bound. If a proportional representation be right, why do we not vote so here? If we argue on the fact that a federal compact actually exists, and consult the articles of it we still find an equal Sovereignty to be the basis of it. He reads the 5ᵗʰ art: of Confederation giving each State a vote—& the 13ᵗʰ declaring that no alteration shall be made without unanimous consent. This is the nature of all treaties. What is unanimously done, must be unanimously undone. It was observed (by M͏ͬ Wilson) that the larger States gave up the point, not because it was right, but because the circumstances of the moment urged the concession. Be it so. Are they for that reason at liberty to take it back. Can the donor resume his gift without the consent of the donee. This doctrine may be convenient, but it is a doctrine that will sacrifice the lesser States. The large States acceded readily to the confederacy. It was the small ones that came in reluctantly and slowly. N.

Jersey & Maryland were the two last, the former objecting to the want of power in Congress over trade: both of them to the want of power to appropriate the vacant territory to the benefit of the whole.—If the sovereignty of the States is to be maintained, the Representatives must be drawn immediately from the States, not from the people: and we have no power to vary the idea of equal sovereignty. The only expedient that will cure the difficulty, is that of throwing the States into Hotchpot. To say that this is impracticable, will not make it so. Let it be tried, and we shall see whether the Citizens of Mass^{ts} Pen^a & V^a accede to it. It will be objected that Coercion will be impracticable. But will it be more so in one plan than the other? Its efficacy will depend on the quantum of power collected, not on its being drawn from the States, or from the individuals; and according to his plan it may be exerted on individuals as well as according that of Mr R. A distinct executive & Judiciary also were equally provided by his plan. It is urged that two branches in the Legislature are necessary. Why? for the purpose of a check. But the reason of the precaution is not applicable to this case. Within a particular State, where party heats prevail, such a check may be necessary. In such a body as Congress it is less necessary, and besides, the delegations of the different States are checks on each other. Do the people at large complain of Cong^s? No, what they wish is that Cong^s may have more power. If the power now proposed be not eno', the people hereafter will make additions to it. With proper powers Cong^s will act with more energy & wisdom than the proposed Nat^l Legislature; being fewer in number, and more secreted & refined by the mode of election. The plan of Mr R. will also be enormously expensive. Allowing Georgia & Del. two representatives each in the popular branch the aggregate number of that branch will be 180. Add to it half as many for the other branch and you have 270. members coming once at least a year from the most distant as well as the most central parts of the republic. In the present deranged state of our finances can so expensive a system be seriously thought of? By enlarging the powers of Cong⁵ the greatest part of this expence will be saved, and all purposes will be answered. At least a trial ought to be made.

Mʳ WILSON entered into a contrast of the principal points of the two plans so far he said as there had been time to examine the one last proposed. These points were 1. in the Virgᵃ plan there are 2 & in some degree 3 branches in the Legislature: in the plan from N. J. there is to be a *single* legislature only—2. Representation of the people at large is the basis of the one:— the State Legislatures, the pillars of the other—3. proportional representation prevails in one:—equality of suffrage in the other —4. A single Executive Magistrate is at the head of the one:—a plurality is held out in the other.—5. in the one the majority of the people of the U. S. must prevail:—in the other a minority may prevail. 6. the Natˡ Legislature is to make laws in all cases to which the separate States are incompetent &—:—in place of this Cong⁵ are to have additional power in a few cases only—7. A negative on the laws of the States:—in place of this coertion to be substituted—8. The Executive to be removeable on impeachment & conviction;—in one plan: in the other to be removeable at the instance of majority of the Executives of the States—9. Revision of the laws provided for in one:—no such check in the other—10. inferior national tribunals in one:— none such in the other. 11. In yᵉ one jurisdiction of Natˡ tribunals to extend &c—; an appellate jurisdiction only allowed in the other. 12. Here the jurisdiction is to extend to all cases affecting the Nationˡ peace & harmony: there, a few cases only are marked out. 13. finally yᵉ ratification is in this to be by the people themselves:—in that by the legislative authorities according to the 13 art: of Confederation.

With regard to the *power of the Convention,* he conceived himself authorized to *conclude nothing,* but to be at liberty to *propose any thing.* In this particular he felt himself perfectly indifferent to the two plans.

With *regard to the sentiments of the people,* he conceived it difficult to know precisely what they are. Those of the particular circle in which one moved, were commonly mistaken for the general voice. He could not persuade himself that the State Gov^{ts} & Sovereignties were so much the idols of the people, nor a Nat! Gov^t so obnoxious to them, as some supposed. Why s^d a Nat! Gov^t be unpopular? Has it less dignity? will each Citizen enjoy under it less liberty or protection? Will a Citizen of *Delaware* be degraded by becoming a Citizen of the *United States?* Where do the people look at present for relief from the evils of which they complain? Is it from an internal reform of their Gov^{ts}? no, Sir. It is from the Nat! Councils that relief is expected. For these reasons he did not fear, that the people would not follow us into a national Gov^t and it will be a further recommendation of Mr R.'s plan that it is to be submitted to *them,* and not to the *Legislatures,* for ratification.

proceeding now to the 1st point on which he had contrasted the two plans, he observed that anxious as he was for some augmentation of the federal powers, it would be with extreme reluctance indeed that he could ever consent to give powers to Cong^s he had two reasons either of wch was sufficient. 1. Cong^s as a Legislative body does not stand on the people. 2. it is a *single* body. 1. He would not repeat the remarks he had formerly made on the principles of Representation. he would only say that an inequality in it, has ever been a poison contaminating every branch of Gov^t . . . 2. *Congress is a single Legislature.* Despotism comes on Mankind in different Shapes, sometimes in an Executive, sometimes in a Military, one. Is there no danger of a Legislative despotism? Theory & practice both proclaim it. If the Legislative authority be not restrained, there can be neither liberty nor stability; and it can only be restrained by dividing it within itself, into distinct and independent branches. In a single House there is no check, but the inadequate one, of the virtue & good sense of those who compose it.

On another great point, the contrast was equally favorable to the plan reported by the Committee of the whole. It vested the Executive powers in a single Magistrate. The plan of N. Jersey, vested them in a plurality. In order to controul the Legislative authority, you must divide it. In order to controul the Executive you must unite it. One man will be more responsible than three. . . .

Mr PINKNEY, the whole comes to this, as he conceived. Give N. Jersey an equal vote, and she will dismiss her scruples, and concur in the Nati^l system. He thought the Convention authorized to go any length in recommending, which they found necessary to remedy the evils which produced this Convention.

.   .   .   .

Mr RANDOLPH, was not scrupulous on the point of power. When the salvation of the Republic was at stake, it would be treason to our trust, not to propose what we found necessary. He painted in strong colours, the imbecility of the existing Confederacy, & the danger of delaying a substantial reform. . . . There are certainly seasons of a peculiar nature where the ordinary cautions must be dispensed with; and this is certainly one of them. He w^d not as far as depended on him leave any thing that seemed necessary, undone. The present moment is favorable, and is probably the last that will offer.

The true question is whether we shall adhere to the federal plan, or introduce the national plan. The insufficiency of the former has been fully displayed by the trial already made. There are but two modes, by which the end of a Genl Gov^t can be attained: the 1st is by coercion as proposed by Mr P.s plan 2. by real legislation as prop^d by the other plan. Coercion he pronounced to be *impracticable, expensive, cruel to individuals.* It tended also to habituate the instruments of it to shed the blood & riot in the spoils of their fellow Citizens, and consequently trained them up for the service of ambition. We must resort therefor to a National *Legislation over individuals,* for which Cong^s are unfit. To vest such power in them, would be blending the Legislative with the Executive, contrary to the rec^d maxim on this subject: If the Union of these powers heretofore in Cong^s has been safe, it has been owing to the general impotency of that body. Cong⁸ are moreover not elected by the people, but by the Legislatures who retain even a power of recall. They have therefore no will of their own, they are a mere diplomatic body, and are always obsequious to the views of the States, who are always encroaching on the authority of the U. States. A provision for harmony among the States, as in trade, naturalization &c.—for crushing rebellion whenever it may rear its crest—and for certain other general benefits, must be made. The powers for these purposes, can never be given to a body, inadequate as Congress are in point of representation, elected in the mode in which they are, and possessing no more confidence than they do: for notwithstanding what has been said to the contrary, his own experience satisfied him that a rooted distrust of Congress pretty generally prevailed. A Nat¹ Gov⁴ alone, properly constituted, will answer the purpose; and he begged it to be considered that the present is the last moment for establishing one. After this select experiment, the people will yield to despair.

The Committee rose & the House adjourned.

Monday, June 18. In Committee of the whole

On motion of M⁓ DICKINSON to postpone the 1ˢᵗ Resolution in M⁓ Patterson's plan, in order to take up the following viz—"that the Articles of Confederation ought to be revised and amended, so as to render the Government of the U. S. adequate to the exigences, the preservation and the prosperity of the Union" the postponement was agreed to by 10 States, Pen: divided.

M⁓ HAMILTON, had been hitherto silent on the business before the Convention, partly from respect to others whose superior abilities age & experience rendered him unwilling to bring forward ideas dissimilar to theirs, and partly from his delicate situation with respect to his own State, to whose sentiments as expressed by his Colleagues, he could by no means accede. The crisis however which now marked our affairs, was too serious to

permit any scruples whatever to prevail over the duty imposed
on every man to contribute his efforts for the public safety &
happiness. He was obliged therefore to declare himself unfriendly to both plans. He was particularly opposed to that from
N. Jersey, being fully convinced, that no amendment of the
Confederation, leaving the States in possession of their Sovereignty could possibly answer the purpose. On the other hand he
confessed he was much discouraged by the amazing extent of
Country in expecting the desired blessings from any general
sovereignty that could be substituted.—As to the powers of the
Convention, he thought the doubts started on that subject had
arisen from distinctions & reasonings too subtle. A *federal* Gov^t
he conceived to mean an association of independent Communities into one. Different Confederacies have different
powers, and exercise them in different ways. In some instances
the powers are exercised over collective bodies; in others over
individuals, . . . Great latitude therefore must be given to the
signification of the term. The plan last proposed departs itself
from the *federal* idea, as understood by some, since it is to
operate eventually on individuals. He agreed moreover with the
Honble gentleman from V^a (Mr R.) that we owed it to our
Country, to do on this emergency whatever we should deem
essential to its happiness. The States sent us here to provide for
the exigences of the Union. To rely on & propose any plan not
adequate to these exigences, merely because it was not clearly
within our powers, would be to sacrifice the means to the end.
It may be said that the *States* can not *ratify* a plan not within
the purview of the article of Confederation providing for alterations & amendments. But may not the States themselves in which
no constitutional authority equal to this purpose exists in the
Legislatures, have had in view a reference to the people at
large.

.   .   .   .

The great question is what provision shall we make for the
happiness of our Country? He would first make a comparative
examination of the two plans—prove that there were essential
defects in both—and point out such changes as might render a

national one, efficacious.—The great & essential principles necessary for the support of Government are 1. an active & constant
interest in supporting it. This principle does not exist in the
States in favor of the federal Gov^t . . . They constantly pursue
internal interests adverse to those of the whole. . . . 2. The love
of power. Men love power. The same remarks are applicable to
this principle. The States have constantly shewn a disposition
rather to regain the powers delegated by them than to part with
more, or to give effect to what they had parted with. The ambition of their demagogues is known to hate the controul of the
Genl Government. It may be remarked too that the Citizens
have not that anxiety to prevent a dissolution of the Genl Gov^t
as of the particular Gov^ts A dissolution of the latter would be
fatal; of the former would still leave the purposes of Gov^t attainable to a considerable degree. . . . 3. An habitual attachment of the people. The whole force of this tie is on the side of
the State Gov^t Its sovereignty is immediately before the eyes of
the people: its protection is immediately enjoyed by them.
From its hand distributive justice, and all those acts which
familiarize & endear Gov^t to a people, are dispensed to them.
4. *Force* by which may be understood a *coertion of laws* or
coertion of arms. Cong^s have not the former except in few cases.
In particular States, this coercion is nearly sufficient; tho' he
held it in most cases, not entirely so. A certain portion of military force is absolutely necessary in large communities. Mass^s is
now feeling this necessity & making provision for it. But how
can this force be exerted on the States collectively. It is impossible. It amounts to a war between the parties. Foreign powers
also will not be idle spectators. They will interpose, the confusion will increase, and a dissolution of the Union ensue. 5.
 influence. he did not mean corruption, but a dispensation of
those regular honors & emoluments, which produce an attachment to the Gov^t Almost all the weight of these is on the side of
the States; and must continue so as long as the States continue
to exist. All the passions then we see, of avarice, ambition, interest, which govern most individuals, and all public bodies,
fall into the current of the States, and do not flow in the stream

of the Gen! Gov! The former therefore will generally be an overmatch for the Gen! Gov! and render any confederacy, in its very nature precarious. Theory is in this case fully confirmed by experience. [Here Hamilton cites the Amphictyonic Council, the German Confederacy and the German Diet, and the Swiss cantons.] How then are all these evils to be avoided? only by such a compleat sovereignty in the general Governm! as will turn all the strong principles & passions above mentioned on its side. Does the scheme of N. Jersey produce this effect? does it afford any substantial remedy whatever? On the contrary it labors under great defects, and the defect of some of its provisions will destroy the efficacy of others. It gives a direct revenue to Cong! but this will not be sufficient. The balance can only be supplied by requisitions: which experience proves can not be relied on. If States are to deliberate on the mode, they will also deliberate on the object of the supplies, and will grant or not grant as they approve or disapprove of it. The delinquency of one will invite and countenance it in others. Quotas too must in the nature of things be so unequal as to produce the same evil. To what standard will you resort? [Hamilton considers and rejects land, number of inhabitants, and geographical situation, and mentions commerce.] Another destructive ingredient in the plan, is that equality of suffrage which is so much desired by the small States. It is not in human nature that V! & the large States should consent to it, or if they did that they sh! long abide by it. It shocks too much the ideas of Justice, and every human feeling. Bad principles in a Gov! tho slow are sure in their operation and will gradually destroy it. ... If the powers proposed were adequate, the organization of Cong! is such that they could never be properly & effectually exercised. The members of Cong! being chosen by the States & subject to recall, represent all the local prejudices. Should the powers be found effectual, they will from time to time be heaped on them, till a tyrannic sway shall be established. The general power whatever be its form if it preserves itself, must swallow up the State powers. Otherwise it will be swallowed up by them. It is ag!t all the principles of a good Government to vest the requisite powers in such a body as

Cong⁸ Two Sovereignties can not co-exist within the same limits. Giving powers to Cong⁸ must eventuate in a bad Gov⁺ or in no Gov⁺ The plan of N. Jersey therefore will not do. What then is to be done? Here he was embarrassed. The extent of the Country to be governed, discouraged him. The expence of a general Gov⁺ was also formidable; unless there were such a diminution of expence on the side of the State Gov⁺⁸ as the case would admit. If they were extinguished, he was persuaded that great œconomy might be obtained by substituting a general Gov⁺ He did not mean however to shock the public opinion by proposing such a measure. On the other hand he saw no *other* necessity for declining it. They are not necessary for any of the great purposes of commerce, revenue, or agriculture. Subordinate authorities he was aware would be necessary. There must be district tribunals: corporations for local purposes. But cui bono, the vast & expensive apparatus now appertaining to the States. The only difficulty of a serious nature which occurred to him, was that of drawing representatives from the extremes to the center of the Community. What inducements can be offered that will suffice? The moderate wages for the 1st branch would only be a bait to little demagogues. Three dollars or thereabouts he supposed would be the utmost. The Senate he feared from a similar cause, would be filled by certain undertakers who wish for particular offices under the Gov⁺ This view of the subject almost led him to despair that a Republican Gov⁺ could be established over so great an extent. He was sensible at the same time that it would be unwise to propose one of any other form. In his private opinion he had no scruple in declaring, supported as he was by the opinions of so many of the wise & good, that the British Gov⁺ was the best in the world: and that he doubted much whether any thing short of it would do in America. He hoped Gentlemen of different opinions would bear with him in this, and begged them to recollect the change of opinion on this subject which had taken place and was still going on. It was once thought that the power of Cong⁸ was amply sufficient to secure the end of their institution. The error

was now seen by every one. The members most tenacious of republicanism, he observed, were as loud as any in declaiming agst the vices of democracy. This progress of the public mind led him to anticipate the time, when others as well as himself would join in the praise bestowed by Mr Neckar [2] on the British Constitution, namely, that it is the only Gov^t in the world "which unites public strength with individual security."—In every community where industry is encouraged, there will be a division of it into the few & the many.[3] Hence separate interests will arise. There will be debtors & creditors &c. Give all power to the many, they will oppress the few. Give all power to the few, they will oppress the many. Both therefore ought to have power, that each may defend itself agst the other. To the want of this check we owe our paper money, instalment laws &c. To the proper adjustment of it the British owe the excellence of their Constitution. Their house of Lords is a most noble institution. Having nothing to hope for by a change, and a sufficient interest by means of their property, in being faithful to the national interest, they form a permanent barrier agst every pernicious innovation, whether attempted on the part of the Crown or of the Commons. No temporary Senate will have firmness eno' to answer the purpose. . . . Gentlemen differ in their opinions concerning the necessary checks, from the different estimates they form of the human passions. They suppose seven years a sufficient period to give the senate an adequate firmness, from not duly considering the amazing violence & turbulence of the democratic spirit. When a great object of Gov^t is pursued, which seizes the popular passions, they spread like wild fire, and become irresistable. He appealed to the gentlemen from the N. England States whether experience had not there verified the remark.—As to the Executive, it seemed to be admitted that no

2 [Jacques Necker (1732-1804), Geneva-born, banker and neomercantilist, was primarily known as minister of finance in France prior to the Revolution. He wrote prodigiously on a number of subjects.]

3 [According to Yates, Hamilton added: "The first are the rich and well born, the other the mass of people." Farrand, *Records*, I, 299.]

good one could be established on Republican principles. Was not this giving up the merits of the question: for can there be a good Gov.^t without a good Executive. The English model was the only good one on this subject. The Hereditary interest of the King was so interwoven with that of the Nation, and his personal emoluments so great, that he was placed above the danger of being corrupted from abroad—and at the same time was both sufficiently independent and sufficiently controuled, to answer the purpose of the institution at home. one of the weak sides of Republics was their being liable to foreign influence & corruption. Men of little character, acquiring great power become easily the tools of intermedling Neibours. . . . What is the inference from all these observations? That we ought to go as far in order to attain stability and permanency, as republican principles will admit. Let one branch of the Legislature hold their places for life or at least during good behaviour. Let the Executive also be for life. He appealed to the feelings of the members present whether a term of seven years, would induce the sacrifices of private affairs which an acceptance of public trust would require, so so as to ensure the services of the best Citizens. On this plan we should have in the Senate a permanent will, a weighty interest, which would answer essential purposes. But is this a Republican Gov.^t, it will be asked? Yes if all the Magistrates are appointed, and vacancies are filled, by the people, or a process of election originating with the people. He was sensible that an Executive constituted as he proposed would have in fact but little of the power and independence that might be necessary. On the other plan of appointing him for 7 years, he thought the Executive ought to have but little power. He would be ambitious, with the means of making creatures; and as the object of his ambition w.^d be to *prolong* his power, it is probable that in case of a war, he would avail himself of the emergence, to evade or refuse a degradation from his place. An Executive for life has not this motive for forgetting his fidelity, and will therefore be a safer depository of power. It will be objected probably, that such an Executive will be an *elective Monarch,* and will give birth to the tumults which characterize that form of Gov^t He w^d reply that *Monarch* is an indefinite term. It marks not either the degree or duration of power. If this Executive Magistrate w^d be a monarch for life—the other prop^d by the Report from the Comtte of the whole, w^d be a monarch for seven years. The circumstance of being elective was also applicable to both. It had been observed by judicious writers that elective monarchies w^d be the best if they could be guarded agst the *tumults* excited by the ambition and intrigues of competitors. He was not sure that tumults were an inseparable evil. He rather thought this character of Elective Monarchies had been taken rather from particular cases than from general principles. ... Might not such a mode of election be devised among ourselves as will defend the community agst these effects in any dangerous degree? Having made these observations he would read to the Committee a sketch of a plan which he sh^d prefer to either of those under consideration. He was aware that it went beyond the ideas of most members. But will such a plan be adopted out of doors? In return he would ask will the people adopt the other plan? At present they will adopt neither. But he sees the Union dissolving or already dissolved—he sees evils operating in the States which must soon cure the people of their fondness for democracies—he sees that a great progress has been already made & is still going on in the public mind. He thinks therefore that the people will in time be unshackled from their prejudices; and whenever that happens, they will themselves not be satisfied at stopping where the plan of Mr R. w^d place them, but be ready to go as far at least as he proposes. He did not mean to offer the paper he had sketched as a proposition to the Committee. It was meant only to give a more correct view of his ideas, and to suggest the amendments which he should probably propose to the plan of Mr R. in the proper stages of its future discussion. He read his sketch in the words following: towit

I. "The Supreme Legislative power of the United States of America to be vested in two different bodies of men; the one to be called the Assembly, the other the Senate who together shall form the Legislature of the United States with power to pass all laws whatsoever subject to the Negative hereafter mentioned.

II. The Assembly to consist of persons elected by the people to serve for three years.

III. The Senate to consist of persons elected to serve during good behaviour; their election to be made by electors chosen for that purpose by the people: in order to this the States to be divided into election districts. On the death, removal or resignation of any Senator his place to be filled out of the district from which he came.

IV. The supreme Executive authority of the United States to be vested in a Governour to be elected to serve during good behaviour—the election to be made by Electors chosen by the people in the Election Districts aforesaid—The authorities & functions of the Executive to be as follows: to have a negative on all laws about to be passed, and the execution of all laws passed, to have the direction of war when authorized or begun; to have with the advice and approbation of the Senate the power of making all treaties; to have the sole appointment of the heads or chief officers of the departments of Finance, War and Foreign Affairs; to have the nomination of all other officers (Ambassadors to foreign Nations included) subject to the approbation or rejection of the Senate; to have the power of pardoning all offences except Treason; which he shall not pardon without the approbation of the Senate.

V. On the death, resignation or removal of the Governour his authorities to be exercised by the President of the Senate till a Successor be appointed.

VI. The Senate to have the sole power of declaring war, the power of advising and approving all Treaties, the power of approving or rejecting all appointments of officers except the heads or chiefs of the departments of Finance War and foreign affairs.

VII. The supreme Judicial authority to be vested in Judges to hold their offices during good behaviour with adequate and permanent salaries. This Court to have original jurisdiction in all causes of capture, and an appellative jurisdiction in all causes in which the revenues of the general Government or the Citizens of foreign Nations are concerned.

VIII. The Legislature of the United States to have power to institute Courts in each State for the determination of all matters of general concern.

IX. The Governour Senators and all officers of the United States to be liable to impeachment for mal- and corrupt conduct; and upon conviction to be removed from office, & disqualified for holding any place of trust or profit—All impeachments to be tried by a Court to consist of the Chief   or Judge of the superior Court of Law of each State, provided such Judge shall hold his place during good behavior, and have a permanent salary.

X. All laws of the particular States contrary to the Constitution or laws of the United States to be utterly void; and the better to prevent such laws being passed, the Governour or president of each State shall be appointed by the General Government and shall have a negative upon the laws about to be passed in the State of which he is Governour or President.

XI. No State to have any forces land or Naval; and the Militia of all the States to be under the sole and exclusive direction of the United States, the officers of which to be appointed and commissioned by them.

On these several articles he entered into explanatory observations corresponding with the principles of his introductory reasoning.   Committee rose & the House Adjourned.

Tuesday, June 19. In Committee of the whole

Dickinson's substitute motion of June 18 was rejected by the three largest states, Virginia, Massachusetts, and Pennsylvania, as well as the Carolinas and Georgia, with Maryland divided.

Mᶠ PATTERSON's plan was again at large before the Committee. Mᶠ MADISON. . . . It had been alledged (by Mᶠ PATTERSON), that the Confederation having been formed by unanimous consent, could be dissolved by unanimous Consent only. Does this doctrine result from the nature of compacts? does it arise from any particular stipulation in the articles of Confederation? If we consider the federal union as analogous to the fundamental compact by which individuals compose one Society, and which must in its theoretic origin at least, have been the unanimous act of the component members, it can not be said that no dissolution of the compact can be effected without unanimous consent. A breach of the fundamental principles of the compact by a part of the Society would certainly absolve the other part from their obligations to it. If the breach of *any* article by *any* of the parties, does not set the others at liberty, it is because, the contrary is *implied* in the compact itself, and particularly by that law of it, which gives an indifinite authority to the majority to bind the whole in all cases. This latter circumstance shews that we are not to consider the federal Union as analogous to the social compact of individuals: for if it were so, a Majority would have a right to bind the rest, and even to form a new Constitution for the whole, which the Gentⁿ from N. Jersey would be among the last to admit. If we consider the federal Union as analogous not to the social compacts among individual men: but to the conventions among individual States. What is the doctrine resulting from these conventions? Clearly, according to the Expositors of the law of Nations, that a breach of any one article, by any one party, leaves all the other parties at liberty, to consider the whole convention as dissolved, unless they choose rather to compel the delinquent party to repair the breach. In some treaties indeed it is expressly stipulated that a violation of particular articles shall not have this consequence, and even that particular articles shall remain in force during war, which in general is understood to dissolve all subsisting Treaties. But are there any exceptions of this sort to the Articles of confederation? So far from it that there is not even an express stipulation that force shall be used to compell an offending member of the Union to discharge its duty. He observed that the violations of the federal articles had been numerous & notorious. Among the most notorious was an act of N. Jersey herself; by which she *expressly refused* to comply with a constitutional requisition of Cong⁹ and yielded no farther to the expostulations of their deputies, than barely to rescind her vote of refusal without passing any positive act of compliance.[4] He did not wish to draw any rigid inferences from these observations. He thought it proper however that the true nature of the existing confederacy should be investigated, and he was not anxious to strengthen the foundations on which it now stands.

Proceeding to the consideration of M⁺ Patterson's plan, he stated the object of a proper plan to be twofold. 1. to preserve the Union. 2. to provide a Governm⁺ that will remedy the evils felt by the States both in their united and individual capacities. Examine M⁺ P.s plan, & say whether it promises satisfaction in these respects.[5]

[4] [Early in 1786 the lower house in New Jersey resolved not to comply with a September, 1785 requisition of Congress until certain grievances were corrected. One concerned the state's presumed inequality in the Confederation, and the other had to do with suffering at the hands of New York. That state, taking advantage of its port, did an active impost business which threw burdens on New Jersey (and Connecticut also) while preventing relief for its neighbors by blocking adoption of a federal tax. Although many other states failed to respond to congressional requisitions, New Jersey alone—and there only one chamber—openly refused obedience. Confronted with this independence, Congress dispatched a committee which included two later Convention delegates (Charles Pinckney and Gorham) and William Grayson of Virginia, for whom New Jersey rescinded on March 17. At that time Pinckney told the assembly that if the Confederation were dissolved the larger states would insist on greater influence, and Grayson was reported as saying that "in a new confederation you will be put in your proper place." See Edmund C. Burnett, *The Continental Congress* (New York, 1941), pp. 644-46.]

[5] [To illustrate his remarks Madison offers many examples not included here, most of which he drew from experience under the Articles of Confederation. Under his second point, for example, he mentions the following: Virginia and Maryland as well as Pennsylvania and New Jersey formed compacts without the consent of Congress; without permission

1. Will it prevent those violations of the law of nations & of Treaties which if not prevented must involve us in the calamities of foreign wars? The tendency of the States to these violations has been manifested in sundry instances. . . . The existing Confederacy does not sufficiently provide against this evil. The proposed amendment to it does not supply the omission. . . .

2. Will it prevent encroachments on the federal authority? A tendency to such encroachments has been sufficiently exemplified, among ourselves, as well in every other confederated republic antient and Modern. . . . He observed that the plan of Mr. Pat-son besides omitting a controul over the States as a general defence of the federal prerogatives was particularly defective in two of its provisions. 1. Its ratification was not to be by the people at large, but by the *legislatures*. It could not therefore render the Acts of Cong⁹ in pursuance of their powers, even legally *paramount* to the Acts of the States. 2. It gave to the federal Tribunal an appellate jurisdiction only—even in the criminal cases enumerated . . . . Besides in most if not all of the States, the Executives have by their respective *Constitutions* the right of pard⁶ How could this be taken from them by a *legislative* ratification only?

3. Will it prevent trespasses of the States on each other? Of these enough has been already seen. . . .The plan of Mᶠ Paterson, not giving even a negative on the acts of the States, left them as much at liberty as ever to execute their unrighteous projects ag⁵ᵗ each other.

4. Will it secure the internal tranquility of the States themselves? The insurrections in Massᵗˢ admonished all the States of the danger to which they were exposed. Yet the plan of Mᶠ P. contained no provisions for supplying the defect of the Confederation on this point. According to the Republican theory

Massachusetts raised a body of troops during Shays' Rebellion; Congress bribed Connecticut with the Western Reserve to gain her acquiescence in a decree against her claim to disputed territory in Pennsylvania. Also, Madison often refers to five of the six ancient and modern confederacies which he studied before journeying to Philadelphia.]

indeed, Right & power being both vested in the majority, are held to be synonimous. According to fact & experience, a minority may in an appeal to force be an overmatch for the majority. . . .

5. Will it secure a good internal legislation & administration to the particular States? In developing the evils which vitiate the political system of the U. S. it is proper to take into view those which prevail within the States individually as well as those which affect them collectively: Since the former indirectly affect the whole; and there is great reason to believe that the pressure of them had a full share in the motives which produced the present Convention. Under this head he enumerated and animadverted on 1. the multiplicity of the laws passed by the several States. 2. the mutability of their laws. 3. the injustice of them. 4. the impotence of them: observing that Mͬ Patterson's plan contained no remedy for this dreadful class of evils, and could not therefore be received as an adequate provision for the exigences of the Community.

6. Will it secure the Union ag͜ˢᵗ the influence of foreign powers over its members. He pretended not to say that any such influence had yet been tried: but it was naturally to be expected that occasions would produce it. . . . The plan of Mͬ Patterson, not giving to the general Councils any negative on the will of the particular States, left the door open for . . . pernicious machinations among ourselves.

7. He begged the smaller States which were most attached to Mͬ Pattersons plan to consider the situation in which it would leave them. In the first place they would continue to bear the whole expence of maintaining their Delegates in Congress. . . . As far as it led the small States to forbear keeping up a representation, by which the public business was delayed, it was evidently a matter of common concern. An examination of the minutes of Congress would satisfy every one that the public business had been frequently delayed by this cause; and that the States most frequently unrepresented in Cong͜ˢ were not the larger States. . . . In the 2ᵈ place The coercion, on

which the efficacy of the plan depends, can never be exerted but on themselves. The larger States will be impregnable, the smaller only can feel the vengeance of it. . . .

8. He begged them to consider the situation in which they would remain in case their pertinacious adherence to an inadmissible plan, should prevent the adoption of any plan. The contemplation of such an event was painful; but it would be prudent to submit to the task of examining it at a distance, that the means of escaping it might be the more readily embraced. Let the Union of the States be dissolved, and one of two consequences must happen. Either the States must remain individually independent & sovereign; or two or more Confederacies must be formed among them. In the first event would the small States be more secure agst the ambition & power of their larger neighbours, than they would be under a general Government pervading with equal energy every part of the Empire, and having an equal interest in protecting every part agst every other part? In the second, can the smaller expect that their larger neighbours would confederate with them on the principle of the present confederacy, which gives to each member, an equal suffrage; or that they would exact less severe concessions from the smaller States, than are proposed in the scheme of Mr Randolph?

The great difficulty lies in the affair of Representation; and if this could be adjusted, all others would be surmountable. It was admitted by both the gentlemen from N. Jersey (Mr Brearly and Mr Patterson) that it would not be *just to allow Virg^a* which was 16 times as large as Delaware an equal vote only. Their language was that it would not be *safe for Delaware* to allow Virg^a 16 times as many votes. The expedient proposed by them was that all the States should be thrown into one mass and a new partition be made into 13 equal parts. Would such a scheme be practicable? The dissimilarities existing in the rules of property, as well as in the manners, habits and prejudices of the different States, amounted to a prohibition of the attempt. . . . But admitting a general amalgamation and repartition of the States to be practicable, and the danger apprehended by the smaller States from a proportional representation to be real; would not a particular and voluntary coalition of these with their neighbours, be less inconvenient to the whole community, and equally effectual for their own safety. If N. Jersey or Delaware conceived that an advantage would accrue to them from an equalization of the States, in which case they would necessarily form a junction with their neighbours, why might not this end be attained by leaving them at liberty by the Constitution to form such a junction whenever they pleased? . . . The prospect of many new States to the Westward was another consideration of importance. If they should come into the Union at all, they would come when they contained but few inhabitants. If they sh⁴ be entitled to vote according to their proportions of inhabitants, all would be right & safe. Let them have an equal vote, and a more objectionable minority than ever might give law to the whole.

On a question for postponing generally the 1ˢᵗ proposition of Mʳ Patterson's plan, it was agreed to: N. Y. & N. J. only being no—

On the question moved by Mʳ King whether the Committee should rise & Mʳ Randolphs propositions be re-reported without alteration, which was in fact a question whether Mʳ R's should be adhered to as preferable to those of Mʳ Patterson:

Massᵗˢ ay. Conᵗ ay. N. Y. no. N. J. no. Pᵃ ay. Del no. M⁴ div⁴ Vᵃ ay. N. C. ay. S. C. ay. Geo. ay. [Ayes, 7; noes, 3; divided, 1.]

NATIONAL GOVERNMENT AND THE STRUGGLE FOR POWER

A detailed discussion of the proposal for national government lasted from June 19 through July 26, with a two-day recess over the anniversary of independence. Deepening controversy threatened, and for a time (one delegate reported) the Convention was "on the verge of dissolution, scarce held together by the strength of a hair." By July 5 small-state intransigence compelled the principal states with a majority of people to flirt with the idea of pushing through a just plan and letting others accede by degrees. Slavery occupied increasing attention. The great crisis was passed on July 16.

Tuesday, June 19 (cont'd.)

The first proposition of the Virginia Plan as reported from the Committee of the Whole House, "that a national government ought to be established consisting of a supreme Legislative, Executive, and Judiciary," was now taken up.

Mr WILSON observed that by a Nat^l Gov^t he did not mean one that would swallow up the State Gov^{ts} as seemed to be wished by some gentlemen. He was tenacious of the idea of preserving the latter. He thought, contrary to the opinion of (Col. Hamilton) that they might not only subsist but subsist on friendly terms with the former. They were absolutely necessary for certain purposes which the former could not reach. All large Governments must be subdivided into lesser jurisdictions. . . .

Col. HAMILTON coincided with the proposition as it stood in the Report. He had not been understood yesterday. By an abolition of the States, he meant that no boundary could be drawn between the National & State Legislatures; that the former must therefore have indefinite authority. If it were limited at all, the rivalship of the States would gradually subvert it. Even as Corporations the extent of some of them as V^a Mass^{ts} &c. would be formidable. As *States*, he thought they ought to be abolished. But he admitted the necessity of leaving in them, subordinate jurisdictions. . . .

Mr KING, wished as every thing depended on this proposition, that no objections might be improperly indulged agst the phraseology of it. He conceived that the import of the terms "States" "Sovereignty" "*national*" "federal," had been often used & applied in the discussions inaccurately & delusively. The States were not "Sovereigns" in the sense contended for by some. They did not possess the peculiar features of sovereignty, they could not make war, nor peace, nor alliances nor treaties.

Considering them as political Beings, they were dumb, for they could not speak to any foreign Sovereign whatever. They were deaf, for they could not hear any propositions from such Sovereign. They had not even the organs or faculties of defence or offence, for they could not of themselves raise troops, or equip vessels, for war. On the other side, if the Union of the States comprizes the idea of a confederation, it comprizes that also of consolidation. A Union of the States is a Union of the men composing them, from whence a *national* character results to the whole. Cong⁹ can act alone without the States—they can act & their acts will be binding ag⁹ᵗ the Instructions of the States. If they declare war: war is de jure declared—captures made in pursuance of it are lawful—No acts of the States can vary the situation, or prevent the judicial consequences. If the States therefore retained some portion of their sovereignty, they had certainly divested themselves of essential portions of it. If they formed a confederacy in some respects—they formed a Nation in others—The Convention could clearly deliberate on & propose any alterations that Cong⁹ could have done under yᵉ federal articles, and could not Cong⁹ propose by virtue of the last article, a change in any article whatever: and as well that relating to the equality of suffrage, as any other. He made these remarks to obviate some scruples which had been expressed. He doubted much the practicability of annihilating the States; but thought that much of their power ought to be taken from them.

Mʳ MARTIN, said he considered that the separation from G. B. placed the 13 States in a state of Nature towards each other; that they would have remained in that state till this time, but for the confederation; that they entered into the confederation on the footing of equality; that they met now to amend it on the same footing; and that he could never accede to a plan that would introduce an inequality and lay 10 States at the mercy of Vᵃ Massᵗˢ and Pennᵃ

Mʳ WILSON, could not admit the doctrine that when the Colonies became independent of G. Britain, they became independent also of each other. He read the declaration of Independence, observing thereon that the *United Colonies* were declared to be free & independent States; and inferring that they were independent, not *individually* but *Unitedly* and that they were confederated as they were independent, States.

Col. HAMILTON, assented to the doctrine of M[r] Wilson. He denied the doctrine that the States were thrown into a State of Nature. He was not yet prepared to admit the doctrine that the Confederacy, could be dissolved by partial infractions of it. He admitted that the States met now on an equal footing but could see no inference from that against concerting a change of the system in this particular. He took this occasion of observing for the purpose of appeasing the fears of the small States, that two circumstances would render them secure under a National Gov[t] in which they might lose the equality of rank they now held: one was the local situation of the 3 largest States Virg[a] Mas[ts] & P[a] They were separated from each other by distance of place, and equally so, by all the pecularities which distinguish the interests of one State from those of another. No combination therefore could be dreaded. In the second place, as there was a gradation in the States from V[a] the largest down to Delaware the smallest, it would always happen that ambitious combinations among a few States might & w[d] be counteracted by defensive combinations of greater extent among the rest. No combination has been seen among large Counties merely as such, ag[st] lesser Counties. The more close the Union of the States, and the more compleat the authority of the whole: the less opportunity will be allowed the stronger States to injure the weaker.

Adj[d]

Wednesday, June 20. In Convention

M[r] William Blount from N. Carolina took his seat.

1st propos: of the Report of Com[e] of the whole before the House.

M[r] ELSEWORTH 2[ded] by M[r] GORHAM, moves to alter it so as to run "that the Government of the United States ought to consist of a supreme legislative, Executive and Judiciary." This alteration he said would drop the word *national*, and retain the proper title "the United States." He could not admit the doctrine that a breach of any of the federal articles could dissolve the whole. It would be highly dangerous not to consider the Confederation as still subsisting. He wished also the plan of the Convention to go forth as an amendment to the articles of Confederation, since under this idea the authority of the Legislatures could ratify it. If they are unwilling, the people will be so too. If the plan goes forth to the people for ratification several succeeding Conventions within the States would be unavoidable. He did not like these conventions. They were better fitted to pull down than to build up Constitutions.   *M Engl, 1780s*

M? RANDOLPH, did not object to the change of expression, but apprised the gentlemen who wished for it that he did not admit it for the reasons assigned; particularly that of getting rid of a reference to the people for ratification. The motion of M? Ellsew^th was acquiesced in nem: con:

The 2^d Resol: "that the national Legislature ought to consist of two branches" taken up, the word "national" struck out as of course.

M? LANSING, observed that the true question here was, whether the Convention would adhere to or depart from the foundation of the present Confederacy; and moved instead of the 2^d Resolution, "that the powers of Legislation be vested in the U. States in Congress." . . .

Col. MASON, did not expect this point would have been reagitated. The essential differences between the two plans, had been clearly stated. The principal objections ag^st that of M? R. were the *want of power* & the *want of practicability*. There can be no weight in the first as the fiat is not to be *here*, but in the people. He thought with his colleague M? R. that there were besides certain crises, in which all the ordinary cautions yielded to public necessity. . . . The *impracticability* of gaining the public concurrence he thought was still more groundless. . . . He thought . . . that the plan . . . which proposed to augment the powers of Congress, never could be expected to succeed. He meant not to throw any reflections on Cong[s] as a body, much less on any particular members of it. He meant however to speak his sentiments without reserve on this subject; it was a privilege of Age, and perhaps the only compensation which nature had given for the privation of so many other enjoyments: and he should not scruple to exercise it freely. Is it to be thought that the people of America, so watchful over their interests; so jealous of their liberties, will give up their all, will surrender both the sword and the purse, to the same body, and that too not chosen immediately by themselves? They never will. They never ought. . . . Much has been said of the unsettled state of the mind of the people, he believed the mind of the people of America, as elsewhere, was unsettled as to some points; but settled as to others. In two points he was sure it was well settled. 1. in an attachment to Republican Government. 2. in an attachment to more than one branch in the Legislature. Their constitutions accord so generally in both these circumstances, that they seem almost to have been preconcerted. This must either have been a miracle, or have resulted from the genius of the people. . . . It was acknowledged by (M[r] Patterson) that his plan could not be enforced without military coertion. Does he consider the force of this concession. The most jarring elements of Nature; fire & water themselves are not more incompatible than such a mixture of civil liberty and military execution. Will the militia march from one State to another, in order to collect the arrears of taxes from the delinquent members of the Republic? Will they maintain an army for this purpose? Will not the Citizens of the invaded State assist one another till they rise as one Man, and shake off the Union altogether. Rebellion is the only case, in which the military force of the State can be properly exerted ag[st] its Citizens. . . . He took this occasion to repeat, that notwithstanding his solicitude to establish a national Government, he never would agree to abolish the State Gov[ts] or render them absolutely insignificant. They were as necessary as the Gen[l] Gov[t] and he would be equally careful to preserve them. He was aware of the difficulty of drawing the line between them, but hoped it was not insurmountable. The Convention, tho' comprising so many distinguished characters, could not be expected to make a faultless Gov^t And he would prefer trusting to posterity the amendment of its defects, rather than to push the experiment too far.

Mr LUTHER MARTIN agreed with (Col Mason) as to the importance of the State Gov^{ts} he would support them at the expence of the Genl Gov^t which was instituted for the purpose of that support. He saw no necessity for two branches, and if it existed Congress might be organized into two. . . . At the separation from the British Empire, the people of America preferred the establishment of themselves into thirteen separate sovereignties instead of incorporating themselves into one: to these they look up for the security of their lives, liberties & properties: to these they must look up. . . . He conceived also that the people of the States having already vested their powers in their respective Legislatures, could not resume them without a dissolution of their Governments. . . .

Mr SHERMAN 2^{ded} & supported Mr Lansings motion. He admitted two branches to be necessary in the State Legislatures, but saw no necessity for them in a Confederacy of States. The examples were all, of a single Council. . . . The complaints at present are not that the views of Cong^s are unwise or unfaithful; but that their powers are insufficient for the execution of their views. The national debt & the want of power somewhere to draw forth the National resources, are the great matters that press. . . . He saw no reason why the State Legislatures should be unfriendly as had been suggested, to Cong^s If they appoint Cong^s and approve of their measures, they would be rather favorable and partial to them. The disparity of the States in point of size he perceived was the main difficulty. But the large States had not yet suffered from the equality of votes enjoyed by the small ones. In all great and general points, the interests of all the States were the same. . . . To consolidate the States as some had proposed would dissolve our Treaties with foreign Nations, which had been formed with us, as *confederated* States. He did not however suppose that the creation of two branches in the Legislature would have such an effect. If the difficulty on the subject of representation can not be otherwise got over, he would agree to have two branches, and a proportional representation in one of them; provided each State had an equal voice in the other. This was necessary to secure the rights of the lesser States; otherwise three or four of the large States would rule the others as they please. . . .

Mʳ Wilson, urged the necessity of two branches; observed that if a proper model were not to be found in other Confederacies it was not to be wondered at. . . . He appealed to our own experience for the defects of our Confederacy. He had been 6 years in the 12 since the commencement of the Revolution, a member of Congress, and had felt all its weaknesses. He appealed to the recollection of others whether on many important occasions, the public interest had not been obstructed by the small members of the Union. The success of the Revolution was owing to other causes, than the Constitution of Congress. In many instances it went on even agˢᵗ the difficulties arising from Congˢ themselves. He admitted that the large States did accede . . . to the Confederation in its present form. But it was the effect of necessity not of choice. . . . The situation of things is now a little altered. He insisted that a jealousy would exist between the State Legislatures & the General Legislature: observing that the members of the former would have views & feelings very distinct in this respect from their constituents. A private Citizen of a State is indifferent whether power be exercised by the Genˡ or State Legislatures, provided it be exercised most for his happiness. His representative has an interest in its being exercised by the body to which he belongs. He will therefore view the National Legisl: with the eye of a jealous rival. He observed that the addresses of Congˢ to the people at large, had always been better received & produced greater effect, than those made to the Legislatures.

On the question for postponing in order to take up Mʳ Lansings proposition "to vest the powers of Legislation in Congˢ"

Mass^t no. Con^t ay. N. Y. ay. N. J. ay. P^a no. Del. ay. M^d div^d V^a no. N. C. no. S. C. no. Geo. no. [Ayes, 4; noes, 6; divided, 1.]

Thursday, June 21. In Convention

Mr Jonathan Dayton from N. Jersey took his seat.

Doc^r JOHNSON. On a comparison of the two plans which had been proposed from Virginia & N. Jersey, it appeared that the peculiarity which characterized the latter was its being calculated to preserve the individuality of the States. The plan from V^a did not profess to destroy this individuality altogether, but was charged with such a tendency. One Gentleman alone (Col. Hamilton) in his animadversions on the plan of N. Jersey, boldly and decisively contended for an abolition of the State Gov^ts Mr Wilson & the gentlemen from Virg^a who also were adversaries of the plan of N. Jersey held a different language. They wished to leave the States in possession of a considerable, tho' a subordinate jurisdiction. They had not yet however shewn how this c^d consist with, or be secured ag^st the general sovereignty & jurisdiction, which they proposed to give to the national Government. If this could be shewn in such a manner as to satisfy the patrons of the N. Jersey propositions, that the individuality of the States would not be endangered, many of their objections would no doubt be removed. If this could not be shewn their objections would have their full force. He wished it therefore to be well considered whether in case the States, as was proposed, sh^d retain some portion of sovereignty at least, this portion could be preserved, without allowing them to participate effectually in the Genl Gov^t, without giving them each a distinct and equal vote for the purpose of defending themselves in the general Councils.

Mr WILSON's respect for Doc^r Johnson, added to the importance of the subject led him to attempt, unprepared as he was, to solve the difficulty which had been started. It was asked how the Gen! Gov^t and individuality of the particular States could be reconciled to each other; and how the latter could be secured agst the former? Might it not, on the other side be asked how the former was to be secured agst the latter? It was generally admitted that a jealousy & rivalship would be felt between the Gen! & particular Gov^{ts} As the plan now stood, tho' indeed contrary to his opinion, one branch of the Gen! Gov^t (the Senate or second branch) was to be appointed by the State Legislatures. The State Legislatures, therefore, by this participation in the Gen! Gov^t would have an opportunity of defending their rights. Ought not a reciprocal opportunity to be given to the Gen! Gov^t of defending itself by having an appointment of some one constituent branch of the State Gov^{ts} If a security be necessary on one side, it w^d seem reasonable to demand it on the other. But taking the matter in a more general view, he saw no danger to the States from the Gen! Gov^t In case a combination should be made by the large ones it w^d produce a general alarm among the rest; and the project w^d be frustrated. But there was no temptation to such a project. The States having in general a similar interest, in case of any proposition in the National Legislature to encroach on the State Legislatures, he conceived a general alarm w^d take place in the National Legislature itself, that it would communicate itself to the State Legislatures, and w^d finally spread among the people at large. The Gen! Gov^t will be as ready to preserve the rights of the States as the latter are to preserve the rights of individuals; all the members of the former, having a common interest, as representatives of all the people of the latter, to leave the State Gov^{ts} in possession of what the people wish them to retain. He could not discover, therefore any danger whatever on the side from which it had been apprehended. On the contrary, he conceived that in spite of every precaution the general Gov^t would be in perpetual danger of encroachments from the State Gov^{ts}

Mr MADISON was of the opinion that there was 1. less danger of encroachment from the Gen! Gov^t than from the State Gov^{ts} 2. that the mischief from encroachments would be less fatal if made by the former, than if made by the latter. 1. All the examples of other confederacies prove the greater tendency in such systems to anarchy than to tyranny; to a disobedience of the members than to usurpations of the federal head. Our own experience had fully illustrated this tendency. . . . 2. Guards were more necessary agst encroachments of the State Gov^{ts} on the Genl Gov^{t} than of the latter on the former. The great objection made agst an abolition of the State Gov^{ts} was that the Genl Gov^{t} could not extend its care to all the minute objects which fall under the cognizance of the local jurisdictions. The objection as stated lay not agst the probable abuse of the general power, but agst the imperfect use that could be made of it throughout so great an extent of country, and over so great a variety of objects. As far as its operation would be practicable it could not in this view be improper; as far as it would be impracticable, the conveniency of the Genl Gov^{t} itself would concur with that of the people in the maintenance of subordinate Governments. Were it practicable for the Genl Gov^{t} to extend its care to every requisite object without the cooperation of the State Gov^{ts} the people would not be less free as members of one great Republic than as members of thirteen small ones. A Citizen of Delaware was not more free than a Citizen of Virginia: nor would either be more free than a Citizen of America. Supposing therefore a tendency in the Genl Government to absorb the State Gov^{ts} no fatal consequence could result. Taking the reverse of the supposition, that a tendency should be left in the State Gov^{ts} towards an independence on the General Gov^{t} and the gloomy consequences need not be pointed out. The imagination of them, must have suggested to the States the experiment we are now making to prevent the calamity, and must have formed the chief motive with those present to undertake the arduous task.

On the question for resolving "that the Legislature ought to consist of two Branches"

Mass. ay. Con^{t} ay. N. Y. no. N. Jersey no P^{a} ay. Del. no. M^{d} div^{d} V^{a} ay. N. C. ay. S. C. ay. Geo. ay. [Ayes, 7; noes, 3; divided, 1.]

Consideration of the third resolution may be summarized. South Carolina led an attempt to have state legislatures rather than the people elect representatives, with Rutledge contending that such "would be more likely to correspond with the sense of the whole community." Hamilton opposed the measure, which failed, with only Connecticut, New Jersey, Delaware, and South Carolina supporting. After debating the merits of frequency of election—state constitutions made the practice familiar; familiarity made the people listless—deputies fixed the term of service at two rather than three years. They prevented nest-feathering by agreeing that senators and representatives should be ineligible for executive offices created or whose emoluments were increased during their term of office.

Monday, June 25. In Convention

Resolution 4.[1] being taken up.

M[r] PINKNEY spoke as follows— The efficacy of the System will depend on this article. In order to form a right judgm[t] in the case, it will be proper to examine the situation of this Country more accurately than it has yet been done. The people of the U. States are perhaps the most singular of any we are acquainted with. Among them there are fewer distinctions of fortune & less of rank, than among the inhabitants of any other nation. Every freeman has a right to the same protection & security; and a very moderate share of property entitles them to the possession of all the honors and privileges the public can bestow: hence arises a greater equality, than is to be found among the people of any other country, and an equality which is more likely to continue—I say this equality is likely to continue, because in a new Country, possessing immense tracts of uncultivated lands, where every temptation is offered to emigration & where industry must be rewarded with competency, there will be few poor, and few dependent—Every member of the Society almost, will enjoy an equal power of arriving at the

1 [Relating to the second branch, and thus the crucial question of state equality.]

supreme offices & consequently of directing the strength & sentiments of the whole Community. None will be excluded by birth, & few by fortune, from voting for proper persons to fill the offices of Government—the whole community will enjoy in the fullest sense that kind of political liberty which consists in the power the members of the State reserve to themselves, of arriving at the public offices, or at least, of having votes in the nomination of those who fill them.

If this State of things is true & the prospect of its continuing probable, it is perhaps not politic to endeavour too close an imitation of a Government calculated for a people whose situation is, & whose views ought to be extremely different.

Much has been said of the Constitution of G. Britain. I will confess that I believe it to be the best Constitution in existence; but at the same time I am confident it is one that will not or can not be introduced into this Country, for many centuries.— If it were proper to go here into a historical dissertation on the British Constitution, it might easily be shewn that the peculiar excellence, the distinguishing feature of that Governm^t can not possibly be introduced into our System—that its balance between the Crown & the people can not be made a part of our Constitution.—that we neither have or can have the members to compose it, nor the rights, privileges & properties of so distinct a class of Citizens to guard.—that the materials for forming this balance or check do not exist, nor is there a necessity for having so permanent a part of our Legislative, until the Executive power is so constituted as to have something fixed & dangerous in its principle—By this I mean a sole, hereditary, though limited Executive.

That we cannot have a proper body for forming a Legislative balance between the inordinate power of the Executive and the people, is evident from a review of the accidents & circumstances which gave rise to the peerage of Great Britain. [Pinckney then briefly sketched the growth of the nobility and commons.]

I have said that such a body cannot exist in this Country for ages, and that untill the situation of our people is exceedingly changed no necessity will exist for so permanent a part of the

Legislature. To illustrate this I have remarked that the people of the United States are more equal in their circumstances than the people of any other Country—that they have very few rich men among them,—by rich men I mean those whose riches may have a dangerous influence, or such as are esteemed rich in Europe—perhaps there are not one hundred such on the Continent; that it is not probable this number will be greatly increased: that the genius of the people, their mediocrity of situation & the prospects which are afforded their industry in a Country which must be a new one for centuries are unfavorable to the rapid distinction of ranks. The destruction of the right of primogeniture & the equal division of the property of Intestates will also have an effect to preserve this mediocrity; for laws invariably affect the manners of a people. On the other hand that vast extent of unpeopled territory which opens to the frugal & industrious a sure road to competency & independence will effectually prevent for a considerable time the increase of the poor or discontented, and be the means of preserving that equality of condition which so eminently distinguishes us.

If equality is as I contend the leading feature of the U. States, where then are the riches & wealth whose representation & protection is the peculiar province of this permanent body. Are they in the hands of the few who may be called rich; in the possession of less than a hundred citizens? certainly not. They are in the great body of the people, among whom there are no men of wealth, and very few of real poverty.—Is it probable that a change will be created, and that a new order of men will arise? If under the British Government, for a century no such change was probable, I think it may be fairly concluded it will not take place while even the semblance of Republicanism remains.—How is this change to be effected? Where are the sources from whence it is to flow? From the landed interest? No. That is too unproductive & too much divided in most of the States. From the Monied interest? If such exists at present, little is to be apprehended from that source. Is it to spring from commerce? I believe it would be the first instance in which a nobility sprang from merchants. Besides, Sir, I apprehend that on this point the policy of the U. States has been much mistaken. We have unwisely considered ourselves as the inhabitants of an old instead of a new country. We have adopted the maxims of a State full of people & manufactures & established in credit. We have deserted our true interest, and instead of applying closely to those improvements in domestic policy which would have ensured the future importance of our commerce, we have rashly & prematurely engaged in schemes as extensive as they are imprudent. This however is an error which daily corrects itself & I have no doubt that a few more severe trials will convince us, that very different commercial principles ought to govern the conduct of these States.

The people of this country are not only very different from the inhabitants of any State we are acquainted with in the modern world; but I assert that their situation is distinct from either the people of Greece or Rome, or of any State we are acquainted with among the antients. ...

Our true situation appears to me to be this.—a new extensive Country containing within itself the materials for forming a Government capable of extending to its citizens all the blessings of civil & religious liberty—capable of making them happy at home. This is the great end of Republican Establishments. We mistake the object of our Government, if we hope or wish that it is to make us respectable abroad. Conquest or superiority among other powers is not or ought not ever to be the object of republican systems. If they are sufficiently active & energetic to rescue us from contempt & preserve our domestic happiness & security, it is all we can expect from them,—it is more than almost any other Government ensures to its citizens.

I believe this observation will be found generally true:—that no two people are so exactly alike in their situation or circumstances as to admit the exercise of the same Government with equal benefit: that a system must be suited to the habits & genius of the people it is to govern, and must grow out of them.

The people of the U. S. may be divided into three classes— *Professional men* who must from their particular pursuits always have a considerable weight in the Government while it remains popular—*Commercial men*, who may or may not have weight as a wise or injudicious commercial policy is pursued.— If that commercial policy is pursued which I conceive to be the true one, the merchants of this Country will not or ought not for a considerable time to have much weight in the political scale.—The third is the *landed interest*, the owners and cultivators of the soil, who are and ought ever to be the governing spring in the system.—These three classes, however distinct in their pursuits are individually equal in the political scale, and may be easily proved to have but one interest. The dependence of each on the other is mutual. The merchant depends on the planter. Both must in private as well as public affairs be connected with the professional men; who in their turn must in some measure depend upon them. Hence it is clear from this manifest connection, & the equality which I before stated exists, & must for the reasons then assigned, continue, that after all there is one, but one great & equal body of citizens composing the inhabitants of this Country among whom there are no distinctions of rank, and very few or none of fortune.

For a people thus circumstanced are we then to form a government & the question is what kind of Government is best suited to them.

Will it be the British Gov^t? No. Why? Because G. Britain contains three orders of people distinct in their situation, their possessions & their principles.—These orders combined form the great body of the Nation. ... Each therefore must of necessity be represented by itself, or the sign of itself; and this accidental mixture has certainly formed a Government admirably well balanced.

But the U. States contain but one order that can be assimilated to the British Nation,—this is the order of Commons. They will not surely then attempt to form a Government consisting of three branches, two of which shall have nothing to represent. They will not have an Executive & Senate (hereditary) because the King & Lords of England are so. The same reasons do not exist and therefore the same provisions are not necessary.

We must as has been observed suit our Governm^t to the

people it is to direct. These are I believe as active, intelligent &
susceptible of good Governm^t as any people in the world. The
Confusion which has produced the present relaxed State is not
owing to them. It is owing to the weakness & (defects) of a Gov^t
incapable of combining the various interests it is intended to
unite, and destitute of energy.—All that we have to do then is
to distribute the powers of Gov^t in such a manner, and for such
limited periods, as while it gives a proper degree of permanency
to the Magistrate, will reserve to the people, the right of election
they will not or ought not frequently to part with.—I am of
opinion that this may be easily done; and that with some
amendments the propositions before the Committee will fully
answer this end.

No position appears to me more true than this; that the General Gov^t can not effectually exist without reserving to the
States the possession of their local rights. They are the instruments upon which the Union must frequently depend for the
support & execution of their powers, however immediately
operating upon the people, and not upon the States.

Much has been said about the propriety of abolishing the distinction of State Governments, & having but one general System. Suffer me for a moment to examine this question.

Madison stops here, saying that the author did not furnish
him the residue of his speech. From the notes of Robert Yates
we know that Pinckney ended as follows (paraphrased): the
United States includes a territory about 1500 miles long and
400 broad, divided into states and districts. No legislature
could make good laws for the whole of this, hence state
governments must remain.   Thus he favored forming the
second branch differently from the Report. "I have considered the subject with great attention," Yates records Pinckney as saying, "and I propose this plan (reads it) and if no
better plan is proposed, I will then move its adoption." But
Yates gives no further details.[2]

2 [Farrand, *Records,* I, 411-12. Irving Brant comments on Pinckney's
speech as follows:
Ringing words! Spoken by a man who so feared the people that he
fought their right to vote from the beginning to the end of the con-

Mʳ WILSON. the question is shall the members of the 2ᵈ branch be chosen by the Legislatures of the States? When he considered the amazing extent of Country—the immense population which is to fill it, the influence which the Govᵗ we are to form will have, not only on the present generation of our people & their multiplied posterity, but on the whole Globe, he was lost in the magnitude of the object. The project of Henry the 4ᵗʰ & his Statesmen was but the picture in miniature of the great portrait to be exhibited.[3] He was opposed to an election by the State

---

vention. The derivation of the speech explains its incoherence. Pinckney was taking over the thought expressed by Wilson on June 7: . . .
From this the Carolinian moved to a dream-picture of equality by classifying the people as professional, commercial and landed. But these
were not the people of the United States. They were the people who
were people in the eyes of a planter aristocracy.

From Yates, Brant adds, we learn that he was arguing for "an ultracon-
servative Senate to protect the three groups which he regarded as the
people." Yates tells only that Pinckney read his plan, which (as we know
from this plan as later reconstructed, plus Pinckney's Convention remarks
of July 2) provided that states have from one through four senators according to their standing in the union, all to be elected by the lower house.
The crucial question in interpreting Pinckney's speech lies in his use
of the word "landed." Brant, who sees him as meaning only the wealthier
landed aristocrats, is in apparent agreement with historians who have
long contended that property qualifications actually disfranchised most
early Americans. But recent historical scholarship has tended to show
that white males (in most states, although less so in South Carolina and
perhaps Virginia) possessed sufficient landed property to vote. Pinckney's
remarks should be compared with Madison's July 26 speech. Convention
debate amply proves that delegates from different sections possessing diverse outlooks agreed in viewing the people as constituents who could
not be displeased. Brant, *Madison*, pp. 79-80; Farrand, *Records*, I, 412, 510-
12; III, 596-97.]

3 [Henry IV (1553-1610) became king of France in 1598 and appointed
his friend the Duke of Sully to high administrative posts. Sully imputed to
the king—who really nourished no such scheme—his Grand Design, a plan
he adumbrated for organizing Europe on a federal basis with a supreme
court of arbitration and a council presided over by France. In the eighteenth century the Abbé de St. Pierre similarly envisioned in his *Project for
Lasting Peace* a federation of states in Europe, the beauty of which was
"that it established a power of restraint amongst the States without setting

Legislatures. In explaining his reasons it was necessary to observe the twofold relation in which the people would stand. 1. as Citizens of the Gen! Gov! 2. as Citizens of their particular State. The Gen! Gov! was meant for them in the first capacity: the State Gov^ts in the second. Both Gov^ts were derived from the people—both meant for the people—both therefore ought to be regulated on the same principles. The same train of ideas which belonged to the relation of the Citizens to their State Gov^ts were applicable to their relation to the Gen! Gov! and in forming the latter, we ought to proceed, by abstracting as much as possible from the idea of State Gov^ts With respect to the province & objects of the Gen! Gov! they should be considered as having no existence. The election of the 2^d branch by the Legislatures, will introduce & cherish local interests & local prejudices. The Gen! Gov! is not an assemblage of States, but of individuals for certain political purposes—it is not meant for the States, but for the individuals composing them; the *individuals* therefore not the *States*, ought to be represented in it: A proportion in this representation can be preserved in the 2^d as

---

up any *particular* 'sovereign,' or dominating power." Rousseau was greatly influenced by St. Pierre, whose works he asked to edit. I owe to Professor Charles W. Hendel the suggestion that Wilson probably drew on Rousseau for the thought expressed here. Professor Hendel treats Rousseau and St. Pierre in his *Rousseau: Moralist,* from which I have taken the above quotation, I, 199. Although Rousseau was certainly not the primary influence in Wilson's thought, it is interesting to observe Franklin referring to the same plan. In sending a copy of the proposed Constitution to a friend in Europe shortly after the Convention adjourned, he said that if it succeeded

I do not see why you might not in Europe carry forward the Project of good Henry the 4th into Execution, by forming a Federal Union and One Grand Republick of all its different States & Kingdoms; by means of a like Convention; for we had many Interests to reconcile.

That the American experience should point the way to federal union in Europe and elsewhere has been a recurrent theme since 1787. One recent example is afforded by Carl Van Doren's book entitled *The Great Rehearsal* (New York, 1948). The Franklin letter is quoted in Gaillard Hunt and James Brown Scott, eds., *The Debates in the Federal Convention of 1787* (New York, 1920), p. xxx.]

well as in the 1ˢᵗ branch; and the election can be made by electors chosen by the people for that purpose. He moved an amendment to that effect which was not seconded.

Mʳ ELSEWORTH saw no reason for departing from the mode contained in the Report. Whoever chooses the member, he will be a Citizen of the State he is to represent & will feel the same spirit & act the same part whether he be appointed by the people or the Legislature. . . . Wisdom was one of the characteristics which it was in contemplation to give the second branch. Would not more of it issue from the Legislatures; than from an immediate election by the people. He urged the necessity of maintaining the existence & agency of the States. Without their co-operation it would be impossible to support a Republican Govᵗ over so great an extent of Country. . . . The largest States are the worst Governed. Virgᵃ is obliged to acknowledge her incapacity to extend her Govᵗ to Kentucky. Masᵗˢ can not keep the peace one hundred miles from her capitol and is now forming an army for its support. How long Penᵃ may be free from a like situation can not be foreseen. If the principles & materials of our Govᵗ are not adequate to the extent of these single States; how can it be imagined that they can support a single Govᵗ throughout the U. States. The only chance of supporting a Genˡ Govᵗ lies in engrafting it on that of the individual States.

. . . .

On the question to agree "that the members of the 2ᵈ branch be chosen by the indivˡ Legislatures" Masᵗˢ ay. Conᵗ ay. N. Y. ay. N. J. ay. Pᵃ no. Del. ay. Mᵈ ay. Vᵃ no. N. C. ay. S. C. ay. Geo. ay.[4] [Ayes, 9; noes, 2.] Mass. defects

. . .

---

[4] It must be kept in view that the largest States particularly Pennsylvania & Virginia always considered the choice of the 2ᵈ Branch by the State Legislatures as opposed to a proportional Representation to which they were attached as a fundamental principle of just Government. The smaller States who had opposite views, were reinforced by the members from the large States most anxious to secure the importance of the State Governments.

Tuesday, June 26. In Convention

The duration of the 2^d branch under consideration.

Mr GHORUM moved to fill the blank with "six years," one third of the members to go out every second year.

Mr WILSON 2^{ded} the motion.

Genl PINKNEY opposed six years in favor of four years. The States he said had different interests. ... If the Senators should be appointed for a long term, they w^d settle in the State where they exercised their functions; and would in a little time be rather the representatives of that than of the State appoint^g them.

Mr READ mov^d that the term be nine years. This w^d admit of a very convenient rotation, one third going out triennially. ...

Mr MADISON. In order to judge of the form to be given to this institution, it will be proper to take a view of the ends to be served by it. These were first to protect the people agst their rulers: secondly to protect the people agst the transient impressions into which they themselves might be led. A people deliberating in a temperate moment, and with the experience of other nations before them, on the plan of Gov^t most likely to secure their happiness, would first be aware, that those charg^d with the public happiness, might betray their trust. An obvious precaution agst this danger w^d be to divide the trust between different bodies of men, who might watch & check each other. In this they w^d be governed by the same prudence which has prevailed in organizing the subordinate departments of Gov^t, where all business liable to abuses is made to pass thro' separate hands, the one being a check on the other. It w^d next occur to such a people, that they themselves were liable to temporary errors, thro' want of information as to their true interest, and that men chosen for a short term, & employed but a small portion of that in public affairs, might err from the same cause. This reflection w^d naturally suggest that the Gov^t be so constituted, as that one of its branches might have an opp^y of acquiring a competent knowledge of the public interests. Another reflection equally becoming a people on such an occasion, w^d be that they themselves, as well as a numerous body of Representatives, were liable to err also, from fickleness and passion. A necessary fence agst this danger would be to select a portion of enlightened citizens, whose limited number, and firmness might seasonably interpose agst impetuous councils. It ought finally to occur to a people deliberating on a Gov^t for themselves, that as different interests necessarily result from the liberty meant to be^t secured, the major interest might under sudden impulses be tempted to commit injustice on the minority. In all civilized Countries the people fall into different classes hav^g a real or supposed difference of interests. There will be creditors & debtors, farmers, merch^{ts} & manufacturers. There will be particularly the distinction of rich & poor. It was true as had been observ^d (by Mr Pinkney) we had not among us those hereditary distinctions, of rank which were a great source of the contests in the ancient Gov^{ts} as well as the modern States of Europe, nor those extremes of wealth or poverty which characterize the latter. We cannot however be regarded even at this time, as one homogeneous mass, in which every thing that affects a part will affect in the same manner the whole. In framing a system which we wish to last for ages, we sh^d not lose sight of the changes which ages will produce. An increase of population will of necessity increase the proportion of those who will labour under all the hardships of life, & secretly sigh for a more equal distribution of its blessings. These may in time outnumber those who are placed above the feelings of indigence. According to the equal laws of suffrage, the power will slide into the hands of the former. No agrarian attempts have yet been made in this Country, but symtoms, of a leveling spirit, as we have understood, have sufficiently appeared in a certain quarter to give notice of the future danger. How is this danger to be guarded agst on republican principles? How is the danger in all cases of interested coalitions to oppress the minority to be guarded agst? Among other means by the establishment of a body in the Gov^t sufficiently respectable for its wisdom & virtue, to aid on such emergences, the preponderance of justice by throwing its weight into that scale. Such being the objects of the second branch in the proposed Gov.ᵗ he thought a considerable duration ought to be given to it. He did not conceive that the term of nine years could threaten any real danger; but in pursuing his particular ideas on the subject, he should require that the long term allowed to the 2.ᵈ branch should not commence till such a period of life, as would render a perpetual disqualification to be re-elected little inconvenient either in a public or private view. He observed that as it was more than probable we were now digesting a plan which in its operation w.ᵈ decide for ever the fate of Republican Gov.ᵗ we ought not only to provide every guard to liberty that its preservation c.ᵈ require, but be equally careful to supply the defects which our own experience had particularly pointed out.

M.ʳ SHERMAN. Gov.ᵗ is instituted for those who live under it. It ought therefore to be so constituted as not to be dangerous to their liberties. The more permanency it has the worse if it be a bad Gov.ᵗ Frequent elections are necessary to preserve the good behavior of rulers. They also tend to give permanency to the Government, by preserving that good behavior, because it ensures their re-election. . . . He wished to have provision made for steadiness & wisdom in the system to be adopted; but he thought six or four years would be sufficient. He sh.ᵈ be content with either.

.   .   .   .

M.ʳ HAMILTON. He did not mean to enter particularly into the subject. He concurred with M.ʳ Madison in thinking we were now to decide for ever the fate of Republican Government; and that if we did not give to that form due stability and wisdom, it would be disgraced & lost among ourselves, disgraced & lost to mankind for ever. He acknowledged himself not to think favorably of Republican Government; but addressed his remarks to those who did think favorably of it, in order to prevail on them to tone their Government as high as possible. He professed himself to be as zealous an advocate for liberty as any man whatever, and trusted he should be as willing a martyr to it though he

differed as to the form in which it was most eligible.—He concurred also in the general observations of (Mʳ Madison) on the
subject, which might be supported by others if it were necessary.
It was certainly true: that nothing like an equality of property
existed: that an inequality would exist as long as liberty existed,
and that it would unavoidably result from that very liberty
itself. This inequality of property constituted the great & fundamental distinction in Society. . . . He rose principally to remark
that (Mʳ Sherman) seemed not to recollect that one branch of
the proposed Govᵗ was so formed, as to render it particularly the
guardians of the poorer orders of Citizens. . . .

Mʳ GERRY. . . . He did not deny the position of Mʳ Madison,
that the majority will generally violate justice when they have
an interest in so doing; But did not think there was any such
temptation in this Country. Our situation was different from
that of G. Britain: and the great body of lands yet to be par-
celled out & settled would very much prolong the difference.
Notwithstanding the symptoms of injustice which had marked
many of our public Councils, they had not proceeded so far as
not to leave hopes, that there would be a sufficient sense of
justice & virtue for the purpose of Govᵗ He admitted the evils
arising from a frequency of elections: and would agree to give
the Senate a duration of four or five years. A longer term would
defeat itself. It never would be adopted by the people.

Mʳ WILSON did not mean to repeat what had fallen from
others, but wᵈ add an observation or two which he believed had
not yet been suggested. Every nation may be regarded in two
relations 1. to its own citizens. 2 to foreign nations. It is therefore not only liable to anarchy & tyranny within, but has wars to
avoid & treaties to obtain from abroad. The Senate will probably be the depositary of the powers concerning the latter objects. It ought therefore to be made respectable in the eyes of
foreign Nations. The true reason why G. Britain has not yet
listened to a commercial treaty with us has been, because she
had no confidence in the stability or efficacy of our Government.
9 years with a rotation, will provide these desirable qualities;
and give our Govᵗ an advantage in this respect over Monarchy

itself. ... [A]s ⅓ would go out triennially, there would be always three divisions holding their places for unequal terms, and consequently acting under the influence of different views, and different impulses—On the question for 9 years, ⅓ to go out triennially

Mass⁺ˢ no. Con⁺ no. N. Y. no. N. J. no. P⁺ ay. Del. ay. M⁺ no. V⁺ ay. N. C. no. S. C. no. Geo. no. [Ayes, 3; noes, 8.]

On the question for 6 years ⅓ to go out biennially

Mass⁺ˢ ay. Con⁺ ay. N. Y. no. N. J. no. P⁺ ay. Del. ay. M⁺ ay. V⁺ ay. N. C. ay. S. C. no. Geo. no. [Ayes, 7; noes, 4.]

circled are those who switched

Wednesday, June 27. In Convention

The sixth resolution, defining powers of Congress, was postponed in favor of the seventh and eighth, involving "most fundamental points," i.e., rules of suffrage in the two branches.

A question being proposed on Resol: 7: declaring that the suffrage in the first branch s⁺ be according to an equitable ratio.

M⁺ L. MARTIN contended at great length and with great eagerness that the General Gov⁺ was meant merely to preserve the State Govern⁺ˢ: not to govern individuals: that its powers ought to be kept within narrow limits; that if too little power was given to it, more might be added; but that if too much, it could never be resumed: that individuals as such have little to do but with their own States; that the Gen⁺ Gov⁺ has no more to apprehend from the States composing the Union, while it pursues proper measures, than a Gov⁺ over individuals has to apprehend from its subjects: that to resort to the Citizens at large for their sanction to a new Govern⁺ will be throwing them back into a State of Nature: that the dissolution of the State Gov⁺ˢ is involved in the nature of the process: that the people have no right to do this without the consent of those to whom they have delegated their power for State purposes: through their tongue only they can speak, through their ears, only, can hear: that the

States have shewn a good disposition to comply with the Acts, of Cong^s weak, contemptibly weak as that body has been; and have failed through inability alone to comply: that the heaviness of the private debts, and the waste of property during the war, were the chief causes of this inability: that he did not conceive the instances mentioned by Mr Madison of compacts between V^a & M^d between P^a & N. J. or of troops raised by Mass^{ts} for defence against the Rebels, to be violations of the articles of confederation—that an equal vote in each State was essential to the federal idea, and was founded in justice & freedom, not merely in policy: that tho' the States may give up this right of sovereignty, yet they had not, and ought not: that the States like individuals were in a State of nature equally sovereign & free. In order to prove that individuals in a State of nature are equally free & independent he read passages from Locke, Vattel, Lord Summers—Priestly. To prove that the case is the same with States till they surrender their equal sovereignty, he read other passages in Locke & Vattel, and also Rutherford: [5] that the

5 [John Locke, 1632-1704. See Introduction, p. xxviii.

Emmerich de Vattel (1714-67), Swiss diplomat and international jurist, whose *Le droit des gens* (1758) exercised wide influence. Holding that the ultimate basis of the natural law of nations was in notions of utility drawn from postulates of ideal reason, Vattel taught that each state was bound in conscience and justice to co-operate in preservation of other states and was justified in seeking its own preservation.

Lord John Somers (1651-1716), lord chancellor of England, achieved prominence during the climax of the Glorious Revolution. This associate of Locke, Newton, and Algernon Sidney either wrote or had a principal share in composing the Declaration of Rights, took part in the Parliamentary debate on the Bill of Rights, and in various political tracts written in 1681 (and perhaps 1689) defended similar ideas.

Joseph Priestley (1733-1804), a British nonconformist minister and chemist who emigrated to the United States in 1794, expressed his political theory systematically in his *Essay on . . . the Nature of Political, Civil and Religious Liberty* (1768), where he widened and gave contemporary emphasis to Locke's political doctrines. In surrendering natural liberty, he insisted, members of society obtained in return political and civil liberty.

Thomas Rutherforth (1712-71) was regius professor of divinity at Cambridge University. His writings included a two-volume work entitled *Insti-*

States being equal cannot treat or confederate so as to give up an equality of votes without giving up their liberty: that the propositions on the table were a system of slavery for 10 States: that as V^a Mas^ts & P^a have 42/90 of the votes they can do as they please without a miraculous Union of the other ten: that they will have nothing to do, but to gain over one of the ten to make them compleat masters of the rest: that they can then appoint an Execut^e & Judiciary & legislate [6] for them as they please: that there was & would continue a natural predilection & partiality in men for their own States; that the States, particularly the smaller, would never allow a negative to be exercised over their laws: that no State in ratifying the Confederation had objected to the equality of votes; that the complaints at present run not ag^st this equality but the want of power; that 16 members from V^a would be more likely to act in concert than a like number formed of members from different States; that instead of a junction of the small States as a remedy, he thought a division of the large States would be more eligible.—This was the substance of a speech which was continued more than three hours. He was too much exhausted he said to finish his remarks, and reminded the House that he should tomorrow, resume them.

Adj^d

Thursday, June 28. In Convention

Mr L. MARTIN resumed his discourse, contending that the Genl Gov^t ought to be formed for the States, not for individuals:

---

tutes of Natural Law (Cambridge, 1754-6), whose subtitle described it as the substance of a course of lectures on Grotius' famous *De Jure Belli ac Pacis.* However, it is remotely possible that Martin referred to Samuel Rutherford (*c.* 1600-1661). He was a Scottish ecclesiastic and political theorist who maintained that civil government had a natural origin, that sovereignty lay in the people, and that therefore law was above the king, whose power was fiduciary. His main work was *Rex Lex: The Law of the Prince* (1644). Rutherford had been quoted in the colonies in the seventeenth century.]

[6] (The word "legislature" is substituted in the transcript for "legislate.")

that if the States were to have votes in proportion to their numbers of people, it would be the same thing whether their representatives were chosen by the Legislatures or the people; the smaller States would be equally enslaved; that if the large States have the same interest with the smaller as was urged, there could be no danger in giving them an equal vote; they would not injure themselves, and they could not injure the large ones on that supposition without injuring themselves and if the interests, were not the same, the inequality of suffrage w^d be dangerous to the smaller States: that it will be in vain to propose any plan offensive to the rulers of the States, whose influence over the people will certainly prevent their adopting it: that the large States were weak at present in proportion to their extent: & could only be made formidable to the small ones, by the weight of their votes; that in case a dissolution of the Union should take place, the small States would have nothing to fear from their power; that if in such a case the three great States should league themselves together, the other ten could do so too: & that he had rather see partial confederacies take place, than the plan on the table.

This was the substance of the residue of his discourse which was delivered with much diffuseness & considerable vehemence.[7]

.   .   .   .

Mr MADISON, s^d he was much disposed to concur in any expedient not inconsistent with fundamental principles, that could remove the difficulty concerning the rule of representation. But he could neither be convinced that the rule contended for was just, nor necessary for the safety of the small States agst the large States. . . . The fallacy of the reasoning drawn from the equality of Sovereign States in the formation of compacts, lay in confounding mere Treaties, in which were specified

[7] [In an address to Martin printed in early 1788, Ellsworth (writing as "The Landholder") remarked that after taking his seat in the Convention the Marylander scarcely had time to read the propositions already agreed to before opening "a speech which held during two days, and which might have continued two months, but for those marks of fatigue and disgust you saw strongly expressed on whichever side of the house you turned your mortified eyes." Farrand, *Records*, III, 271-72.]

certain duties to which the parties were to be bound, and certain rules by which their subjects were to be reciprocally governed in their intercourse, with a compact by which an authority was created paramount to the parties, & making laws for the government of them. If France, England & Spain were to enter into a Treaty for the regulation of commerce &c with the Prince of Monacho & 4 or 5 other of the smallest sovereigns of Europe, they would not hesitate to treat as equals, and to make the regulations perfectly reciprocal. W^d the case be the same, if a Council were to be formed of deputies from each with authority and discretion, to raise money, levy troops, determine the value of coin &c? Would 30 or 40. million of people submit their fortunes into the hands, of a few thousands? . . . Why are Counties of the same states represented in proportion to their numbers? Is it because the representatives are chosen by the people themselves? So will be the representatives in the Nation^l Legislature. Is it because, the larger have more at stake than the smaller? The case will be the same with the larger & smaller States. Is it because the laws are to operate immediately on their persons & properties? The same is the case in some degree as the articles of confederation stand; the same will be the case in a far greater degree under the plan proposed to be substituted. In the cases of captures, of piracies, and of offences in a federal army; the property & persons of individuals depend on the laws of Cong^s By the plan proposed a compleat power of taxation, the highest prerogative of supremacy is proposed to be vested in the National Gov^t Many other powers are added which assimilate it to the Gov^t of individual States. The negative proposed on the State laws, will make it an essential branch of the State Legislatures & of course will require that it should be exercised by a body established on like principles with the other branches of those Legislatures.—That it is not necessary to secure the small States agst the large ones he conceived to be equally obvious: Was a combination of the large ones dreaded? this must arise either from some interest common to V^a Mas^{ts} & P^a & distinguishing them from the other States or from the mere circumstance of similarity of size. Did any such common interest exist? In point of situation they could not have been more effectually separated from each other by the most jealous citizen of the most jealous State. In point of manners, Religion, and the other circumstances which sometimes beget affection between different communities, they were not more assimilated than the other States.—In point of the staple productions they were as dissimilar as any three other States in the Union. The Staple of Mas^{ts} was *fish,* of P^a *flower,* of V^a *Tob^o.* Was a combination to be apprehended from the mere circumstance of equality of size? Experience suggested no such danger. . . . Experience rather taught a contrary lesson. Among individuals of superior eminence & weight in Society, rivalships were much more frequent than coalitions. Among independent nations, pre-eminent over their neighbours, the same remark was verified. . . . Were the large States formidable *singly* to their smaller neighbours? On this supposition the latter ought to wish for such a general Gov^t as will operate with equal energy on the former as on themselves. The more lax the band, the more liberty the larger will have to avail themselves of their superior force. Here again Experience was an instructive monitor. What is ye situation of the weak compared with the strong in those stages of civilization in which the violence of individuals is least controuled by an efficient Government? . . . Is not the danger to the former exactly in proportion to their weakness. . . . In a word; the two extremes before us are a perfect separation & a perfect incorporation, of the 13 States. In the first case they would be independent nations subject to no law, but the law of nations. In the last, they would be mere counties of one entire republic, subject to one common law. In the first case the smaller States would have every thing to fear from the larger. In the last they would have nothing to fear. The true policy of the small States therefore lies in promoting those principles & that form of Gov^t which will most approximate the States to the condition of counties. Another consideration may be added. If the Genl Gov^t be feeble, the large States distrusting its continuance, and foreseeing that their importance & security may depend on their own size & strength, will never submit to a partition. Give to the Gen! Gov! sufficient energy & permanency, & you remove the objection. Gradual partitions of the large, & junctions of the small States will be facilitated, and time may effect that equalization, which is wished for by the small States now, but can never be accomplished at once. . . .

Mr SHERMAN. The question is not what rights naturally belong to men; but how they may be most equally & effectually guarded in Society. And if some give up more than others in order to attain this end, there can be no room for complaint. To do otherwise, to require an equal concession from all, if it would create danger to the rights of some, would be sacrificing the end to the means. The rich man who enters into Society along with the poor man, gives up more than the poor man, yet with an equal vote he is equally safe. Were he to have more votes than the poor man in proportion to his superior stake, the rights of the poor man would immediately cease to be secure. This consideration prevailed when the articles of Confederation were formed.

.   .   .   .

[DR. FRANKLIN.] Mr President
The small progress we have made after 4 or five weeks close attendance & continual reasonings with each other—our different sentiments on almost every question, several of the last producing as many noes as ays, is methinks a melancholy proof of the imperfection of the Human Understanding. We indeed seem to feel our own want of political wisdom, since we have been running about in search of it. We have gone back to ancient history for models of Government, and examined the different forms of those Republics which having been formed with the seeds of their own dissolution now no longer exist. And we have viewed Modern States all round Europe, but find none of their Constitutions suitable to our circumstances.

In this situation of this Assembly, groping as it were in the dark to find political truth, and scarce able to distinguish it when presented to us, how has it happened, Sir, that we have not hitherto once thought of humbly applying to the Father of lights to illuminate our understandings? In the beginning of the Contest with G. Britain, when we were sensible of danger we had daily prayer in this room for the divine protection.— Our prayers, Sir, were heard, & they were graciously answered. All of us who were engaged in the struggle must have observed frequent instances of a superintending providence in our favor. To that kind providence we owe this happy opportunity of consulting in peace on the means of establishing our future national felicity. And have we now forgotten that powerful friend? or do we imagine that we no longer need his assistance? I have lived, Sir, a long time, and the longer I live, the more convincing proofs I see of this truth—*that God Governs in the affairs of men*. And if a sparrow cannot fall to the ground without his notice, is it probable that an empire can rise without his aid? We have been assured, Sir, in the sacred writings, that "except the Lord build the House they labour in vain that build it." I firmly believe this; and I also believe that without his concurring aid we shall succeed in this political building no better, than the Builders of Babel: We shall be divided by our little partial local interests; our projects will be confounded, and we ourselves shall become a reproach and bye word down to future ages. And what is worse, mankind may hereafter from this unfortunate instance, despair of establishing Governments by Human wisdom and leave it to chance, war and conquest.

I therefore beg leave to move—that henceforth prayers imploring the assistance of Heaven, and its blessings on our deliberations, be held in this Assembly every morning before we proceed to business, and that one or more of the Clergy of this City be requested to officiate in that Service—

Mr SHARMAN seconded the motion.

Mr HAMILTON & several others expressed their apprehensions that however proper such a resolution might have been at the beginning of the convention, it might at this late day, 1. bring on it some disagreeable animadversions. & 2. lead the public to believe that the embarrassments and dissensions within the Convention, had suggested this measure. It was answered by Doc^r F.

Mr SHERMAN & others, that the past omission of a duty could not justify a further omission—that the rejection of such a proposition would expose the Convention to more unpleasant animadversions than the adoption of it: and that the alarm out of doors that might be excited for the state of things within, would at least be as likely to do good as ill.

M͏ʳ WILLIAMSON, observed that the true cause of the omission could not be mistaken. The Convention had no funds.

M͏ʳ RANDOLPH proposed in order to give a favorable aspect to yᵉ measure, that a sermon be preached at the request of the convention on 4ᵗʰ of July, the anniversary of Independence; & thenceforward prayers be used in yᵉ Convention every morning. D͏ʳ FRANK͏ⁿ 2ᵈᵉᵈ this motion. After several unsuccessful attempts for silently postponing the matter by adjournᵍ the adjournment was at length carried, without any vote on the motion.

Friday, June 29. In Convention

Doct͏ʳ JOHNSON. The controversy must be endless whilst Gentlemen differ in the grounds of their arguments; Those on one side considering the States as districts of people composing one political Society; those on the other considering them as so many political societies. The fact is that the States do exist as political Societies, and a Gov͏ᵗ is to be formed for them in their political capacity, as well as for the individuals composing them. Does it not seem to follow, that if the States as such are to exist they must be armed with some power of self-defence. This is the idea of (Col. Mason) who appears to have looked to the bottom of this matter. Besides the Aristocratic and other interests, which ought to have the means of defending themselves, the States have their interests as such, and are equally entitled to like means. On the whole he thought that as in some respects the States are to be considered in their political capacity, and in others as districts of individual citizens, the two ideas embraced on different sides, instead of being opposed to each other, ought to be combined; that in *one* branch the *people*, ought to be represented; in the *other* the *States*.

M͏ʳ GHORUM. The States as now confederated have no doubt

a right to refuse to be consolidated, or to be formed into any new system. But he wished the small States which seemed most ready to object, to consider which are to give up most, they or the larger ones. He conceived that a rupture of the Union w^d be an event unhappy for all, but surely the large States would be least unable to take care of themselves, and to make connections with one another. The weak therefore were most interested in establishing some general system for maintaining order. If among individuals, composed partly of weak, and partly of strong, the former most need the protection of law & Government, the case is exactly the same with weak & powerful States. [If the states separated, he asked, would not Delaware lie at the mercy of Pennsylvania and the fate of New Jersey be worst of all? Moreover, despite previous apprehension, past incorporations, such as Plymouth, Maine and Massachusetts; the two Jersies; Connecticut and New Haven, had proved satisfactory. Also, he hinted, some of the larger states would in the future be divided.] On the whole he considered a Union of the States as necessary to their happiness, & a firm Genl Gov^t as necessary to their Union. . . .

.   .   .   .

Mr READ. He sh^d have no objection to the system if it were truly national, but it has too much of a federal mixture in it. The little States he thought had not much to fear. . . . Mass^ts was evidently labouring under her weakness and he believed Delaware w^d not be in much danger if in her neighbourhood. . . . He was not however so selfish as not to wish for a good Genl Gov^t In order to obtain one the whole States must be incorporated. If the States remain, the representatives of the large ones will stick together, and carry every thing before them. . . . These jealousies are inseparable from the scheme of leaving the States in existence. They must be done away. . . .

Mr MADISON agreed with Doc^r Johnson, that the mixed nature of the Gov^t ought to be kept in view; but thought too much stress was laid on the rank of the States as political societies. There was a gradation, he observed from the smallest corporation, with the most limited powers, to the largest empire with the most perfect sovereignty. He pointed out the limitations on the sovereignty of the States, as now confederated; their laws in relation to the paramount law of the Confederacy were analogous to that of bye laws to the supreme law within a State. Under the proposed Gov^t the powers of the States will be much farther reduced. According to the views of every member, the Genl Gov^t will have powers far beyond those exercised by the British Parliament, when the States were part of the British Empire.[8] It will in particular have the power, without the consent of the State Legislatures, to levy money directly on the people themselves; and therefore not to divest such *unequal* portions of the people as composed the several States, of an *equal* voice, would subject the system to the reproaches & evils which have resulted from the vicious representation in G. B.

He entreated the gentlemen representing the small States to renounce a principle wch was confessedly unjust, which c^d never be admitted, & if admitted must infuse mortality into a Constitution which we wished to last forever. He prayed them to ponder well the consequences of suffering the Confederacy to go to pieces. It had been s^d that the want of energy in the large states w^d be a security to the small. It was forgotten that this want of energy proceeded from the supposed security of the States agst all external danger. Let each state depend on itself for its security, & let apprehensions arise of danger, from distant powers or from neighbouring States, & the languishing condition of all the States, large as well as small, w^d soon be trans-

8 [Yates' notes on the relevant part of this speech illuminate Madison's views, which took on renewed importance after the Convention with the rise of state rights and opposition to consolidated government.

Some contend that States are sovereign, when, in fact, they are only political societies. There is a gradation of power in all societies, from the lowest corporation to the highest sovereign. The States never possessed the essential rights of sovereignty. These were always vested in congress. Their voting, as States, in congress, is no evidence of sovereignty. . . . The States, at present, are only great corporations, having the power of making by-laws, and these are effectual only if they are not contradictory to the general confederation. The States ought to be placed under the control of the general government—at least as much as they formerly were under the king and British parliament.

Farrand, *Records*, I, 471.]

formed into vigorous & high toned Gov⁺ˢ His great fear was that their Gov⁺ˢ wᵈ then have too much energy, that these might not only be formidable in the large to the small States, but fatal to the internal liberty of all. The same causes which have rendered the old world the Theatre of incessant wars, & have banished liberty from the face of it, wᵈ soon produce the same effects here. The weakness & jealousy of the small States wᵈ quickly introduce some regular military force agˢᵗ sudden danger from their powerful neighbours. The example wᵈ be followed by others, and wᵈ soon become universal. In time of actual war, great discretionary powers are constantly given to the Executive Magistrate. Constant apprehension of war, has the same tendency to render the head too large for the body. A standing military force, with an overgrown Executive will not long be safe companions to liberty. The means of defence agˢᵗ foreign danger, have been always the instruments of tyranny at home. ...

Mʳ HAMILTON observed that individuals forming political Societies modify their rights differently, with regard to suffrage. Examples of it are found in all the States. In all of them some individuals are deprived of the right altogether, not having the requisite qualification of property. In some of the States the right of suffrage is allowed in some cases and refused in others. To vote for a member in one branch, a certain quantum of property, to vote for a member in another branch of the Legislature, a higher quantum of property is required. In like manner States may modify their right of suffrage differently, the larger exercising a larger, the smaller a smaller share of it. But as States are a collection of individual men which ought we to respect most, the rights of the people composing them, or of the artificial beings resulting from the composition. Nothing could be more preposterous or absurd than to sacrifice the former to the latter. It has been sᵈ that if the smaller States renounce their *equality*, they renounce at the same time their *liberty*. The truth is it is a contest for power, not for liberty. Will the men composing the small States be less free than those composing the larger. The State of Delaware having 40,000 souls will *lose power,* if she has 1/10 only of the votes allowed to P⁹ having 400,000: but will the people of Del: *be less free,* if each citizen has an equal vote with each citizen of P⁹ . . .

M ͬ GERRY urged that we never were independent States, were not such now, & never could be even on the principles of the Confederation. The States & the advocates for them were intoxicated with the idea of their *sovereignty.* He was a member of Congress at the time the federal articles were formed. The injustice of allowing each State an equal vote was long insisted on. He voted for it, but it was ag ˢͭ his Judgment, and under the pressure of public danger, and the obstinacy of the lesser States. The present confederation he considered as dissolving. The fate of the Union will be decided by the Convention. If they do not agree on something, few delegates will probably be appointed to Cong ˢ If they do Cong ˢ will probably be kept up till the new System should be adopted. He lamented that instead of coming here like a band of brothers, belonging to the same family, we seemed to have brought with us the spirit of political negociators.

M ͬ L. MARTIN. remarked that the language of the States being *sovereign & independent,* was once familiar & understood; though it seemed now so strange & obscure. He read those passages in the articles of Confederation, which describe them in that language.

.   .   .   .

On the motion to agree to the clause as reported, "that the rule of suffrage in the 1 ˢͭ branch ought not to be according to that established by the articles of Confederation.

Mass. ay. Con ͭ no. N. Y. no. N. J. no. P⁹ ay. Del. no. M ͩ div ͩ V⁹ ay. N. C. ay. S. C. ay. Geo. ay. [Ayes, 6; noes, 4; divided, 1.]

.   .   .   .

M ͬ ELSEWORTH moved that the rule of suffrage in the 2 ͩ branch be the same with that established by the articles of confederation." He was not sorry on the whole he said that the vote just passed, had determined against this rule in the first branch. He hoped it would become a ground of compromise with regard to the 2 ͩ branch. We were partly national; partly federal. The proportional representation in the first branch was conformable to the national principle & would secure the large States agst the small. An equality of voices was conformable to the federal principle and was necessary to secure the Small States agst the large. He trusted that on this middle ground a compromise would take place. . . . And if no compromise should take place, our meeting would not only be in vain but worse than in vain. To the Eastward he was sure Mass^{ts} was the only State that would listen to a proposition for excluding the States as equal political Societies, from an equal voice in both branches. . . . The existing confederation was founded on the equality of the States in the article of suffrage: was it meant to pay no regard to this antecedent plighted faith. Let a strong Executive, a Judiciary & Legislative power be created; but Let not too much be attempted; by which all may be lost. He was not in general a half-way man, yet he preferred doing half the good we could, rather than do nothing at all. The other half may be added, when the necessity shall be more fully experienced.

. . . .

Saturday, June 30. In Convention

New Jersey sponsored a futile attempt to have the president write to the New Hampshire executive stating that Convention business required immediate attendance of deputies. Madison reported that the known object was to add this state to the bloc opposed to proportional representation, which presumably her relative size would insure.

The motion of Mr Elseworth resumed for allowing each State an equal vote in ye 2^d branch.

Mr WILSON . . . The Gentleman from Connecticut (Mr Elseworth) had pronounced that if the motion should not be acceded to, of all the States North of Pen^a one only would agree to any Genl Government. . . . If the minority of the people of

America refuse to coalesce with the majority on just and proper principles, if a separation must take place, it could never happen on better grounds. The votes of yesterday agst the just principle of representation, were as 22 to 90 of the people of America. ... [T]he question will be shall less than ¼ of the U. States withdraw themselves from the Union; or shall more than ¾. renounce the inherent, indisputable, and unalienable rights of men, in favor of the artificial systems of States. ... Such an equality [of votes in the second branch] will enable the minority to controul in all cases whatsoever, the sentiments and interests of the majority. Seven States will controul six: Seven States, according to the estimates that had been used, composed 24/90. of the whole people. It would be in the power then of less than ⅓ to overrule ⅔ whenever a question should happen to divide the States in that manner. Can we forget for whom we are forming a Government? Is it for *men,* or for the imaginary beings called *States?* Will our honest Constituents be satisfied with metaphysical distinctions? Will they, ought they to be satisfied with being told that the one third compose the greater number of States? The rule of suffrage ought on every principle to be the same in the 2^d as in the 1st branch. If the Government be not laid on this foundation, it can be neither solid nor lasting. Any other principle will be local, confined & temporary. ... Are the people of the three large States more aristocratic than those of the small ones? Whence then the danger of aristocracy from their influence? It is all a mere illusion of names. We talk of States, till we forget what they are composed of. ... If the motion should be agreed to, we shall leave the U. S. fettered precisely as heretofore; with the additional mortification of seeing the good purposes of ye fair representation of the people in the 1st branch, defeated in 2^d Twenty four will still controul sixty six. He lamented that such a disagreement should prevail on the point of representation, as he did not forsee that it would happen on the other point most contested, the boundary between the Genl & the local authorities. He thought the States necessary & valuable parts of a good system.

M^r E$_{LSEWORTH}$. The capital objection of Mr Wilson "that the minority will rule the majority" is not true. The power is given to the few to save them from being destroyed by the many. . . .

M^r M$_{ADISON}$ . . . It was urged, he said, continually that an equality of votes in the 2^d branch was not only necessary to secure the small, but would be perfectly safe to the large ones whose majority in the 1st branch was an effectual bulwark. But notwithstanding this apparent defence, the majority of States might still injure the majority of people. 1. they could *obstruct* the wishes and interests of the majority. 2. they could *extort* measures repugnant to the wishes & interest of the Majority. 3. they could *impose* measures adverse thereto; as the 2^d branch will probly exercise some great powers, in which the 1st will not participate. He admitted that every peculiar interest whether in any class of citizens, or any description of States, ought to be secured as far as possible. Wherever there is danger of attack there ought be given a constitutional power of defence. But he contended that the States were divided into different interests not by their difference of size, but by other circumstances; the most material of which resulted partly from climate, but principally from the effects of their having or not having slaves. These two causes concurred in forming the great division of interests in the U. States. It did not lie between the large & small States: It lay between the Northern & Southern, and if any defensive power were necessary, it ought to be mutually given to these two interests. He was so strongly impressed with this important truth that he had been casting about in his mind for some expedient that would answer the purpose. The one which had occurred was that instead of proportioning the votes of the States in both branches, to their respective numbers of inhabitants computing the slaves in the ratio of 5 to 3, they should be represented in one branch according to the number of free inhabitants only; and in the other according to the whole number counting the slaves as if free. By this arrangement the Southern Scale would have the advantage in one House, and the Northern in the other. He had been restrained from proposing this expedient by two considerations: one was his unwillingness to urge any diversity of interests on an occasion where it is but too apt to arise of itself—the other was, the inequality of powers that must be vested in the two branches, and which would destroy the equilibrium of interests.

. . . .

Mr DAVY was much embarrassed and wished for explanations. [If state legislatures chose the Senate according to proportional representation, it would be too large. Yet to make the Senate merely the representative of the states brought back Congress again.] Under this view of the subject he could not vote for any plan for the Senate yet proposed. He thought that in general there were extremes on both sides. We were partly federal, partly national in our Union, and he did not see why the Govt might not in some respects operate on the States, in others on the people.

Mr WILSON admitted the question concerning the number of Senators, to be embarrassing. If the smallest States be allowed one, and the others in proportion, the Senate will certainly be too numerous. He looked forward to the time when the smallest States will contain 100,000 souls at least. Let there be then one Senator in each for every 100,000 souls and let the States not having that n⁰ of inhabitants be allowed one. He was willing himself to submit to this temporary concession to the small States; and threw out the idea as a ground of compromise.

Docr FRANKLIN. The diversity of opinions turns on two points. If a proportional representation takes place, the small States contend that their liberties will be in danger. If an equality of votes is to be put in its place, the large States say their money will be in danger. When a broad table is to be made, and the edges of planks do not fit, the artist takes a little from both, and makes a good joint. In like manner here both sides must part with some of their demands, in order that they may join in some accomodating proposition. [Franklin read a proposal for equality of representation in the upper house with equal suffrage for certain questions and in proportion to money contributions for others.]

Mr KING observed that the simple question was whether each

State should have an equal vote in the 2ᵈ branch; . . . that if the adherence to an equality of votes was fixed & unalterable, there could not be less obstinacy on the other side, & that we were in fact cut insunder already, and it was in vain to shut our eyes against it: . . . that his feelings were more harrowed & his fears more agitated for his Country than he could express, that he conceived this to be the last opportunity of providing for its liberty & happiness: that . . . his mind was prepared for every event, rather than to sit down under a Govᵗ founded in a vicious principle of representation, and which must be as short lived as it would be unjust. He might prevail on himself to accede to some such expedient as had been hinted by Mʳ Wilson: but he never could listen to an equality of votes as proposed in the motion.

Mʳ DAYTON. When assertion is given for proof, and terror substituted for argument, he presumed they would have no effect however eloquently spoken. . . .

Mʳ MARTIN, wᵈ never confederate if it could not be done on just principles

Mʳ MADISON would acquiesce in the concession hinted by Mʳ Wilson, on condition that a due independence should be given to the Senate. The plan in its present shape makes the Senate absolutely dependent on the States. The Senate therefore is only another edition of Congˢ He knew the faults of that Body & had used a bold language agˢᵗ it. Still he wᵈ preserve the State rights, as carefully as the trials by jury.⁹

Mʳ BEDFORD, contended that there was no middle way between a perfect consolidation and a mere confederacy of the States. . . . If political Societies possess ambition avarice, and all

⁹ [The phrase "state rights" seems to contradict the thought of Madison on June 29. Yet it did not. Without entering into the complexities of this case, the speech should end as follows:

Make [the Senate] properly independent and it is of little consequence from what states the members may be taken. I mean, however, to preserve the state rights with the same care as I would trials by jury; and I am willing to go as far as my honorable colleague. (Brant, *Madison*, p. 89.)]

the other passions which render them formidable to each other, ought we not to view them in this light here? Will not the same motives operate in America as elsewhere? . . . [L]ook at the votes. Have they not been dictated by interest, by ambition? Are not the large States evidently seeking to aggrandize themselves at the expense of the small? They think no doubt that they have right on their side, but interest had blinded their eyes. Look at Georgia. Though a small State at present, she is actuated by the prospect of soon being a great one. S. Carolina is actuated both by present interest & future prospects. She hopes too to see the other States cut down to her own dimensions. N. Carolina has the same motives of present & future interest. Virgᵃ follows. Maryᵈ is not on that side of the Question. Penᵃ has a direct and future interest. Massᵗˢ has a decided and palpable interest in the part she takes. Can it be expected that the small States will act from pure disinterestedness. . . . Will it be said that an inequality of power will not result from an inequality of votes. Give the opportunity, and ambition will not fail to abuse it. The whole History of mankind proves it.[10]

. . . .

It is not true that the people will not agree to enlarge the powers of the present Congˢ . . . The little States are willing to observe their engagements, but will meet the large ones on no ground but that of the Confederation. We have been told with a dictatorial air that this is the last moment for a fair trial in favor of a good Governmᵗ It will be the last indeed if the propositions reported from the Committee go forth to the people. He was under no apprehensions. The Large States dare not dissolve the Confederation. If they do the small ones will find some foreign ally of more honor and good faith, who will take

10 [Yates reported Bedford as saying here (paraphrased): the large states insist that increasing the power of the general government will be for the good of the whole, and that they will not injure the lesser states. "I do not, gentlemen, trust you. If you possess the power," he continued, "the abuse of it could not be checked; and what then would prevent you from exercising it to our destruction?" Farrand, *Records*, I, 500.]

them by the hand and do them justice. He did not mean by this to intimidate or alarm.[11] It was a natural consequence; which ought to be avoided by enlarging the federal powers not annihilating the federal system. This is what the people expect. All agree in the necessity of a more efficient Gov[t] and why not make such an one; as they desire.

.   .   .   .

M[r] KING was for preserving the States in a subordinate degree .... In the establishm[t] of Societies the Constitution was to the Legislature what the laws were to individuals. As the fundamental rights of individuals are secured by express provisions in the State Constitutions; why may not a like security be provided for the Rights of States in the National Constitution. ... He was aware that this will be called a mere *paper security*. He thought it a sufficient answer to say that if fundamental articles of compact, are no sufficient defence against physical power, neither will there be any safety ag[st] it if there be no compact. He could not sit down, without taking some notice of the language of the honorable gentleman from Delaware (M[r] Bedford). It was not he that had uttered a dictatorial language. This intemperance had marked the honorable gentleman himself. It was not he who with a vehemence unprecedented in that House, had declared himself ready to turn his hopes from our common Country, and court the protection of some foreign hand. This too was the language of the Honbl member himself. He was grieved that such a thought had entered into his heart. He was more grieved that such an expression had dropped from his lips. The gentleman c[d] only excuse it to himself on the score of passion. For himself whatever might be his distress, he w[d] never court relief from a foreign power.

Adjourned

11 [Yates: "Sooner than be ruined, there are *foreign powers who will take us by the hand*. I say this not to threaten or intimidate, but that we should reflect seriously before we act." Farrand, *Records*, I, 501.]

Monday, July 2. In Convention

On the question for allowing each State one vote in the second branch as moved by Mʳ Elseworth, Massᵗˢ no. Conᵗ ay. N. Y. ay. N. J. ay. Pᵃ no. Del. ay. Mᵈ ay. Mʳ Jenifer being not present Mʳ Martin alone voted Vᵃ no. N. C. no. S. C. no. Geo. divᵈ Mʳ Houston no. Mʳ Baldwin ay. [Ayes, 5; noes, 5; divided, 1.]

. . . .

General PINKNEY. . . . Some compromise seemed to be necessary: the States being exactly divided on the question for an equality of votes in the 2ᵈ branch. He proposed that a Committee consisting of a member from each State should be appointed to devise & report some compromise.

. . . .

[12] Mʳ Govʳ MORRIS. thought a Comᵉ adviseable as the Convention had been equally divided. He had a stronger reason also. The mode of appointing the 2ᵈ branch tended he was sure to defeat the object of it. What is this object? to check the precipitation, changeableness, and excesses of the first branch. Every man of observation had seen in the democratic branches of the State Legislatures, precipitation—in Congress changeableness, in every department excesses agˢᵗ personal liberty private property & personal safety. What qualities are necessary to constitute a check in this case? *Abilities* and *virtue*, are equally necessary in both branches. Something more then is now wanted. 1. the checking branch must have a personal interest in checking the other branch, one interest must be opposed to another interest. Vices as they exist, must be turned agˢᵗ each other. 2. It must have great personal property, it must have the aristocratic spirit; it must love to lord it thro' pride, pride is indeed the great principle that actuates both the poor & the rich. It is this principle which in the former resists, in the latter abuses

[12] He had just returned from N. Y. havᵍ left yᵉ Convention a few days after it commenced business.

authority. 3. It should be independent. . . . The aristocratic body, should be as independent & as firm as the democratic. If the members of it are to revert to a dependence on the democratic choice, the democratic scale will preponderate. . . . To make it independent, it should be for life. It will then do wrong, it will be said. He believed so: He hoped so. The Rich will strive to establish their dominion & enslave the rest. They always did. They always will. The proper security agst them is to form them into a separate interest. The two forces will then controul each other. Let the rich mix with the poor and in a Commercial Country, they will establish an oligarchy. Take away commerce, and the democracy will triumph. Thus it has been all the world over. So it will be among us. Reason tells us we are but men: and we are not to expect any particular interference of Heaven in our favor. By thus combining & setting apart, the aristocratic interest, the popular interest will be combined agst it. There will be a mutual check and mutual security. 4. An independence for life, involves the necessary permanency. If we change our measures no body will trust us: and how avoid a change of measures, but by avoiding a change of men. . . . He perceived that the 1st branch was to be chosen by the people of the States: the 2^{d} by those chosen by the people. Is not here a Gov^{t} by the States. A Govern^{t} by Compact between Virg^{a} in the 1st & 2^{d} branch; Mas^{ts} in the 1st & 2^{d} branch &c. This is going back to mere treaty. It is no Gov^{t} at all. It is altogether dependent on the States, and will act over again the part which Cong^{s} has acted. A firm Govern^{t} alone can protect our liberties. He fears the influence of the rich. They will have the same effect here as elsewhere if we do not by such a Gov^{t} keep them within their proper sphere. We should remember that the people never act from reason alone. The Rich will take advantage of their passions & make these the instruments for oppressing them. The Result of the Contest will be a violent aristocracy, or a more violent despotism. The schemes of the Rich will be favored by the extent of the Country. The people in such distant parts can not communicate & act in concert. They will be the dupes of those who have more knowledge & intercourse. The only security agst encroachments will be a select & sagacious body of men, instituted to watch agst them on all sides. He meant only to hint these observations, without grounding any motion on them.

.   .   .   .

Mr WILSON objected to the Committee, because it would decide according to that very rule of voting which was opposed on one side. Experience in Cong^s had also proved the inutility of Committees consisting of members from each State.

.   .   .   .

The Committee elected by ballot, were Mr Gerry, Mr Elseworth, Mr Yates, Mr Patterson, Dr Franklin, Mr Bedford, Mr Martin, Mr Mason, Mr Davy, Mr Rutlidge, Mr Baldwin.[13]

That time might be given to the Committee, and to such as chose to attend to the celebrations on the anniversary of Independence, the Convention adjourned till Thursday.

Thursday, July 5. In Convention

Mr Gerry delivered in from the Committee appointed on Monday last the following Report.

"The Committee to whom was referred the 8th Resol. of the Report from the Committee of the whole House, and so much of the 7th as has not been decided on, submit the following Report: That the subsequent propositions be recommended to the Convention on condition that both shall be generally adopted. I. that in the 1st branch of the Legislature each of the States now in the Union shall be allowed 1 member for every 40,000 inhabitants of the description reported in the 7th Resolution of the Com^e of the whole House: that each State not containing that number shall be allowed 1 member: that all bills for raising

13 [The personnel of this Grand Committee show that the Convention had accepted the necessity of giving in to the small-state bloc. Madison and Wilson, the ablest nationalists, were kept off. In the vote that day Baldwin had just abandoned his large-state views to keep the parley from ending, and Davie would do the same. Others were unyielding small-state men, or ready for compromise. The report was founded on a motion by Franklin.]

or appropriating money, and for fixing the Salaries of the offi-
cers of the Govern^t of the U. States shall originate in the 1st
branch of the Legislature, and shall not be altered or amended
by the 2^d branch: and that no money shall be drawn from the
public Treasury. but in pursuance of appropriations to be
originated in the 1st branch" II. That in the 2^d branch each
State shall have an equal vote."

Mr Ghorum observed that as the report consisted of propositions mutually conditional he wished to hear some explanations touching the grounds on which the conditions were estimated.

Mr Gerry. The Committee were of different opinions as well
as the Deputations from which the Com^e were taken, and agreed
to the Report merely in order that some ground of accomodation might be proposed. Those opposed to the equality of votes
have only assented conditionally; and if the other side do not
generally agree will not be under any obligation to support the
Report.

.   .   .   .

Mr Madison. coulu not regard the exclusive privilege of originating money bills as any concession on the side of the small
States. Experience proved that it had no effect. If seven States
in the upper branch wished a bill to be originated, they might
surely find some member from some of the same States in the
lower branch who would originate it. The restriction as to
amendments was of as little consequence. Amendments could
be handed privately by the Senate to members in the other
house. . . . He conceived that the Convention was reduced to
the alternative of either departing from justice in order to con-
ciliate the smaller States, and the minority of the people of the
U. S. or of displeasing these by justly gratifying the larger States
and the majority of the people. He could not himself hesitate
as to the option he ought to make. . . . The merits of the System
alone can finally & effectually obtain the public suffrage. He was
not apprehensive that the people of the small States would ob-
stinately refuse to accede to a Gov^t founded on just principles,
and promising them substantial protection. . . . Harmony in

the Convention was no doubt much to be desired. Satisfaction to all the States, in the first instance still more so. But if the principal States comprehending a majority of the people of the U. S. should concur in a just & judicious plan, he had the firmest hopes, that all the other States would by degrees accede to it.

.   .   .   .

Mᵣ Govᵣ Morris. thought the form as well as the matter of the Report objectionable. . . . He conceived the whole aspect of it to be wrong. He came here as a Representative of America; he flattered himself he came here in some degree as a Representative of the whole human race; for the whole human race will be affected by the proceedings of this Convention. He wished gentlemen to extend their views beyond the present moment of time; beyond the narrow limits of place from which they derive their political origin. If he were to believe some things which he had heard, he should suppose that we were assembled to truck and bargain for our particular States. . . . Much has been said of the sentiments of the people. They were unknown. They could not be known. All that we can infer is that if the plan we recommend be reasonable & right; all who have reasonable minds and sound intentions will embrace it, notwithstanding what had been said by some gentlemen. Let us suppose that the larger States shall agree; and that the smaller refuse: and let us trace the consequences. The opponents of the system in the smaller States will no doubt make a party, and a noise for a time, but the ties of interest, of kindred & of common habits which connect them with the other States will be too strong to be easily broken. In N. Jersey particularly he was sure a great many would follow the sentiments of Penᵃ & N. York. This Country must be united. If persuasion does not unite it, the sword will. He begged that this consideration might have its due weight. The scenes of horror attending civil commotion can not be described, and the conclusion of them will be worse than the term of their continuance. The stronger party will then make traytors of the weaker; and the Gallows & Halter will finish the work of the sword. How far foreign powers would be ready to take part in the confusions he would not say. Threats that they will be invited have it seems been thrown out. ... But returning to the Report he could not think it in any respect calculated for the public good. ... State attachments, and State importance have been the bane of this Country. We can not annihilate; but we may perhaps take out the teeth of the serpents. He wished our ideas to be enlarged to the true interest of man, instead of being circumscribed within the narrow compass of a particular Spot. And after all how little can be the motive yielded by selfishness for such a policy. Who can say whether he himself, much less whether his children, will the next year be an inhabitant of this or that State.

Mͬ BEDFORD. He found that what he had said as to the small States being taken by the hand, had been misunderstood; and he rose to explain. He did not mean that the small States would court the aid & interposition of foreign powers. He meant that they would not consider the federal compact as dissolved untill it should be so by the Acts of the large States. In this case The consequence of the breach of faith on their part, and the readiness of the small States to fulfill their engagements, would be that foreign Nations having demands on this Country would find it their interest to take the small States by the hand, in order to do themselves justice. This was what he meant. But no man can foresee to what extremities the small States may be driven by oppression. He observed also in apology that some allowance ought to be made for the habits of his profession in which warmth was natural & sometimes necessary. ...

.   .   .   .

Mͬ PATTERSON ... complained of the manner in which Mͬ M[adison] & Mͬ Govͬ Morris had treated the small States.

Mͬ GERRY. Tho' he had assented to the Report in the Committee, he had very material objections to it. We were however in a peculiar situation. We were neither the same Nation nor different Nations. We ought not therefore to pursue the one or the other of these ideas too closely. If no compromise should take place what will be the consequence. A secession he foresaw would take place; for some gentlemen seem decided on it;

two different plans will be proposed; and the result no man could foresee. If we do not come to some agreement among ourselves some foreign sword will probably do the work for us.

Mʳ MASON. The Report was meant not as specific propositions to be adopted; but merely as a general ground of accomodation. There must be some accomodation on this point, or we shall make little further progress in the work. Accomodation was the object of the House in the appointment of the Committee; and of the Committee in the Report they had made. And however liable the Report might be to objections, he thought it preferable to an appeal to the world by the different sides, as had been talked of by some Gentlemen. It could not be more inconvenient to any gentleman to remain absent from his private affairs, than it was for him: but he would bury his bones in this City rather than expose his Country to the Consequences of a dissolution of the Convention without any thing being done.

The 1ˢᵗ proposition in the report for fixing the representation in the 1ˢᵗ branch, one member for every 40,000 inhabitants, being taken up.

Mʳ Govʳ MORRIS objected to that scale of apportionment. He thought property ought to be taken into the estimate as well as the number of inhabitants. Life & liberty were generally said to be of more value, than property. An accurate view of the matter would nevertheless prove that property was the main object of Society. The savage State was more favorable to liberty than the Civilized; and sufficiently so to life. It was preferred by all men who had not acquired a taste for property; it was only renounced for the sake of property which could only be secured by the restraints of regular Government. These ideas might appear to some new, but they were nevertheless just. If property then was the main object of Govᵗ certainly it ought to be one measure of the influence due to those who were to be affected by the Governmᵗ He looked forward also to that range of New States which wᵈ soon be formed in the West. He thought the rule of representation ought to be so fixed as to secure to the Atlantic States a prevalence in the National Councils. . . .

Saturday, July 7. In Convention

"Shall the clause allowing each State one vote in the 2ᵈ branch, stand as part of the Report"? being taken up—

Mʳ GERRY. This is the critical question. He had rather agree to it than have no accomodation. A Governᵗ short of a proper national plan, if generally acceptable, would be preferable to a proper one which if it could be carried at all, would operate on discontented States. . . .

Mʳ SHERMAN Supposed that it was the wish of every one that some Genˡ Govᵗ should be established. An equal vote in the 2ᵈ branch would, he thought, be most likely to give it the necessary vigor. The small States have more vigor in their Govᵗˢ than the large ones, the more influence therefore the large ones have, the weaker will be the Govᵗ In the large States it will be most difficult to collect the real & fair sense of the people. Fallacy & undue influence will be practiced with most success: and improper men will most easily get into office. If they vote by States in the 2ᵈ branch, and each State has an equal vote, there must be always a majority of States as well as a majority of the people on the side of public measures, & the Govᵗ will have decision and efficacy. If this be not the case in the 2ᵈ branch there may be a majority of the States agˢᵗ public measures, and the difficulty of compelling them to abide by the public determination, will render the Government feebler than it has ever yet been.

Mʳ WILSON was not deficient in a conciliating temper, but firmness was sometimes a duty of higher obligation. Conciliation was also misapplied in this instance. It was pursued here rather among the Representatives, than among the Constituents; and it wᵈ be of little consequence, if not established among the latter; and there could be little hope of its being established among them if the foundation should not be laid in justice and right.

On Question shall the words stand as part of the Report?

Mass^{ts} div^d Con^t ay. N. Y. ay. N. J. ay. P^a no. Del. ay. M^d ay. V^a no. N. C. ay. S. C. no. Geo. div^d [Ayes, 6; noes, 3; divided, 2.]

(Note. Several votes were given here in the affirmative or were div^d because another final question was to be taken on the whole report.)

Mr GERRY thought it would be proper to proceed to enumerate & define the powers to be vested in the Genl Gov^t before a question on the report should be taken, as to the rule of representation in the 2^d branch.

Mr MADISON, observed that it w^d be impossible to say what powers could be safely & properly vested in the Gov^t before it was known, in what manner the States were to be represented in it.

Mr PATTERSON would not decide whether the privilege concerning money bills were a valuable consideration or not: But he considered the mode & rule of representation in the 1st branch as fully so. and that after the establishment of that point, the small States would never be able to defend themselves without an equality of votes in the 2^d branch. There was no other ground of accomodation. His resolution was fixt. He would meet the large States on that Ground and no other. For himself he should vote agst the Report, because it yielded too much.

Mr Govr MORRIS. He had no resolution unalterably fixed except to do what should finally appear to him right. He was agst the Report because it maintained the improper Constitution of the 2^d branch. . . . It had been s^d . . . that the new Govern^t would be partly national, partly federal; that it ought in the first quality to protect individuals; in the second, the States. But in what quality was it to protect the aggregate interest of the whole. Among the many provisions which had been urged, he had seen none for supporting the dignity and splendor of the American Empire. . . . [T]he great objects of the nation had been sacrificed constantly to local views. . . . But particular States . . . were originally nothing more than colonial corporations. On the declaration of Independence, a Governm^t was to be formed. The small States aware of the necessity of preventing anarchy, and taking advantage of the moment, extorted from the large ones an equality of votes. Standing now on that ground, they demand under the new system greater rights as men, than their fellow Citizens of the large States. The proper answer to them is that the same necessity of which they formerly took advantage, does not now exist, and that the large States are at liberty now to consider what is right, rather than what may be expedient. We must have an efficient Gov^t and if there be an efficiency in the local Gov^{ts} the former is impossible. ... What if all the Charters & Constitutions of the States were thrown into the fire, and all their demagogues into the ocean. What would it be to the happiness of America. But he was ready to join in devising such an amendment of the plan, as will be most likely to secure our liberty & happiness.

Monday, July 9. In Convention

Mr. Daniel Carroll from Maryland took his Seat.

Mr Govr Morris delivered a report from the Com^e of 5 members . . . as follows viz

"The Committee to whom was referred the 1st clause of the 1st proposition reported from the grand Committee, beg leave to report

I. that in the 1st meeting of the Legislature the 1st branch thereof consist of 56. members of which Number, N. Hamshire shall have 2. Mass^{ts} 7. R. I^d 1. Con^t 4. N. Y. 5. N. J. 3. P^a 8. Del. 1. M^d 4. V^a 9. N. C. 5. S. C. 5. Geo. 2.—

II. But as the present situation of the States may probably alter as well in point of wealth as in the number of their inhabitants, that the Legislature be authorized from time to time to augment ye number of Representatives. And in case any of the States shall hereafter be divided, or any two or more States united, or any new States created within the limits of the United States, the Legislature shall possess authority to regulate the number of Representatives in any of the foregoing cases, upon the principles of their wealth and number of inhabitants."

Mr SHERMAN wished to know on what principles or calculations the Report was founded. It did not appear to correspond with any rule of numbers, or of any requisition hitherto adopted by Cong^s

Mr GORHAM. Some provision of this sort was necessary in the outset. The number of blacks & whites with some regard to supposed wealth was the general guide Fractions could not be observed. The Legisl^{re} is to make alterations from time to time as justice & propriety may require. . . .

.   .   .   .

Mr PATTERSON considered the proposed estimate for the future according to the Combined rule of numbers and wealth, as too vague. For this reason N. Jersey was agst it. He could regard negro slaves in no light but as property. They are no free agents, have no personal liberty, no faculty of acquiring property, but on the contrary are themselves property, & like other property entirely at the will of the Master. Has a man in Virg^a a number of votes in proportion to the number of his slaves? And if Negroes are not represented in the States to which they belong, why should they be represented in the Genl Gov^t What is the true principle of Representation? It is an expedient by which an assembly of certain individ^{ls} chosen by the people is substituted in place of the inconvenient meeting of the people themselves. If such a meeting of the people was actually to take place, would the slaves vote? They would not. Why then sh^d they be represented. He was also agst such an indirect encouragem^t of the slave trade; observing that Cong^s in their act relating to the change of the 8 art: of Confed^n had been ashamed to use the term "slaves" & had substituted a description.

Mr MADISON, reminded Mr Patterson that his doctrine of Representation which was in its principle the genuine one, must for ever silence the pretensions of the small States to an equality of votes with the large ones. They ought to vote in the same proportion in which their citizens would do, if the people of all the

States were collectively met. He suggested as a proper ground of compromise, that in the first branch the States should be represented according to their number of free inhabitants; and in the 2ᵈ which had for one of its primary objects the guardianship of property, according to the whole number, including slaves.

Tuesday, July 10. In Convention

Mʳ KING reported from the Comᵉ yesterday appointed that the States at the 1ˢᵗ meeting of the General Legislature, should be represented by 65 members in the following proportions, to wit. N. Hamshire by 3. Masᵗˢ 8. R. Isᵈ 1. Conᵗ 5. N. Y. 6. N. J. 4. Pᵃ 8. Del. 1. Mᵈ 6. Vᵃ 10. N. C. 5. S. C. 5. Georgia 3.

Mʳ KING. . . . He remarked that the four Eastern States having 800,000 souls, have ⅓ fewer representatives than the four Southern States, having not more than 700,000 souls rating the blacks, as 5 for 3. The Eastern people will advert to these circumstances, and be dissatisfied. . . . He was fully convinced that the question concerning a difference of interests did not lie where it had hitherto been discussed, between the great & small States; but between the Southern & Eastern. For this reason he had been ready to yield something in the proportion of representatives for the security of the Southern. No principle would justify the giving them a majority. They were brought as near an equality as was possible. He was not averse to giving them a still greater security, but did not see how it could be done.

Genˡ PINKNEY. The Report before it was committed was more favorable to the S. States than as it now stands. If they are to form so considerable a minority, and the regulation of trade is to be given to the Genˡ Government, they will be nothing more than overseers for the Northern States. He did not expect the S. States to be raised to a majority of representatives, but wished them to have something like an equality. . . .

.   .   .   .

On the question for agreeing to the apportionment of Rep⁸
as amended by the last committee, it passed in the affirmative
Mas. ay. Conᵗ ay. N. Y. ay. N. J. ay. P⁸ ay. Del. ay. Mᵈ ay.
V⁸ ay. N. C. ay. S. C. no. Geo. no. [Ayes, 9; noes, 2.]

.   .   .   .

Mᴿ RANDOLPH moved as an amendment to the report of the
Commᵉ of five "that in order to ascertain the alterations in the
population & wealth of the several States the Legislature should
be required to cause a census, and estimate to be taken within
one year after its first meeting; and every   years thereafter—and that the Legislʳᵉ arrange the Representation accordingly."

Wednesday, July 11. In Convention

Mᴿ WILLIAMSON . . . moved that Mᴿ Randolph's proposition
be postponᵈ in order to consider the following "that in order to
ascertain the alterations that may happen in the population
& wealth of the several States, a census shall be taken of the
free white inhabitants and 3/5ᵗʰˢ of those of other descriptions
on the 1ˢᵗ year after this Government shall have been adopted
and every   year thereafter; and that the Representation
be regulated accordingly."

Mᴿ RANDOLPH agreed that Mᴿ Williamson's proposition
should stand in the place of his. He observed that the ratio fixt
for the 1ˢᵗ meeting was a mere conjecture, that it placed the
power in the hands of that part of America, which could not
always be entitled to it, that this power would not be voluntarily renounced; and that it was consequently the duty of the
Convention to secure its renunciation when justice might so require; by some constitutional provisions. . . . If a fair representation of the people be not secured, the injustice of the Govᵗ
will shake it to its foundations. What relates to suffrage is justly
stated by the celebrated Montesquieu, as a fundamental article
in Republican Govᵗˢ . . .

Mᴿ BUTLER & Genˡ PINKNEY insisted that blacks be included

in the rule of Representation, *equally* with the Whites: and for that purpose moved that the words "three fifths" be struck out.

Mͬ GERRY thought that 3/5 of them was to say the least the full proportion that could be admitted.

.   .   .   .

On Mͬ Butlers motion for considering blacks as equal to Whites in the apportionmᵗ of Representation.

Massᵗˢ no. Conᵗ no. (N. Y. not on floor.) N. J. no. Pᵃ no. Del. ay. Mᵈ no. Vᵃ no N. C. no. S. C. ay. Geo. ay. [Ayes, 3; noes, 7.]

.   .   .   .

Mͬ RUTLIDGE contended for the admission of wealth in the estimate by which Representation should be regulated. The Western States will not be able to contribute in proportion to their numbers; they shᵈ not therefore be represented in that proportion. The Atlantic States will not concur in such a plan. . . .

Mͬ SHERMAN thought the number of people alone the best rule for measuring wealth as well as representation; and that if the Legislature were to be governed by wealth, they would be obliged to estimate it by numbers. . . .

.   .   .   .

Mͬ MADISON, . . . It was said that Representation & taxation were to go together; that taxation and wealth ought to go together, that population & wealth were not measures of each other. He admitted that in different climates, under different forms of Govᵗ and in different stages of civilization the inference was perfectly just. He would admit that in no situation, numbers of inhabitants were an accurate measure of wealth. He contended however that in the U. States it was sufficiently so for the object in contemplation. Altho' their climate varied considerably, yet as the Govᵗˢ the laws, and the manners of all were nearly the same, and the intercourse between different parts perfectly free, population, industry, arts, and the value of labour, would constantly tend to equalize themselves. . . .

.   .   .   .

On the question on the first clause of Mͬ Williamson's motion as to taking a census of the *free* inhabitants; it passed in the affirmative Mas^{ts} ay. Con^t ay. N. J. ay. P^a ay. Del. no. M^d no. V^a ay. N. C. ay. S. C. no. Geo. no. [Ayes, 6; noes, 4.]

the next clause as to 3/5 of the negroes considered.

Mr KING. being much opposed to fixing numbers as the rule of representation, was particularly so on account of the blacks. He thought the admission of them along with Whites at all, would excite great discontents among the States having no slaves. . . .

Mr SHERMAN. . . . In general the allotment might not be just, but considering all circumstances, he was satisfied with it.

.   .   .   .

Mr WILSON did not well see on what principle the admission of blacks in the proportion of three fifths could be explained. Are they admitted as Citizens? then why are they not admitted on an equality with White Citizens? are they admitted as property? then why is not other property admitted into the computation? These were difficulties however which he thought must be overruled by the necessity of compromise. . . .

M^r GOV^r MORRIS was compelled to declare himself reduced to the dilemma of doing injustice to the Southern States or to human nature, and he must therefore do it to the former. . . .

On Question for agreeing to include 3/5 of the blacks

Mass^{ts} no. Con^t ay. N. J. no. P^a no. Del. no. Mard. no. V^a ay. N. C. ay. S. C. no. Geo. ay. [Ayes, 4; noes, 6.]

Thursday, July 12. In Convention

M^r GOV^r MORRIS moved to add to the clause empowering the Legislature to vary the Representation according to the principles of wealth & number of inhab^{ts} a "proviso that taxation shall be in proportion to Representation."

.   .   .   .

Mr MASON . . . was afraid embarrassments might be occasioned to the Legislature by it. . . .

M^r GOV^r MORRIS, admitted that some objections lay agst his motion, but supposed they would be removed by restraining the rule to *direct* taxation. ...

. . . .

[Morris'] Motion . . . pass^d nem. con. as follows—"provided always that direct taxation ought to be proportioned to representation."

. . . .

Genl PINKNEY desired that the rule of wealth should be ascertained and not left to the pleasure of the Legislature; and that property in slaves should not be exposed to danger under a Gov^t instituted for the protection of property.

. . . .

Mr RANDOLPH . . . The danger will be revived that the ingenuity of the Legislature may evade or pervert the rule so as to perpetuate the power where it shall be lodged in the first instance. He proposed . . . "that in order to ascertain the alterations in Representation that may be required from time to time by changes in the relative circumstances of the States, a census shall be taken within two years from the 1st meeting of the Genl Legislature of the U. S., and once within the term of every   year afterwards, of all the inhabitants in the manner & according to the ratio recommended by Congress in their resolution of the 18th day of Ap^l 1783; (rating the blacks at 3/5 of their number) and, that the Legislature of the U. S. shall arrange the Representation accordingly."—He urged strenuously that express security ought to be provided for including slaves in the ratio of Representation. He lamented that such a species of property existed. But as it did exist the holders of it would require this security. It was perceived that the design was entertained by some of excluding slaves altogether; the Legislature therefore ought not to be left at liberty.

. . . .

Mr WILSON observed that less umbrage would perhaps be taken ag^st an admission of the slaves into the Rule of representation, if it should be so expressed as to make them indirectly only an ingredient in the rule, by saying that they should enter into the rule of taxation: and as representation was to be according to taxation, the end would be equally attained. He accordingly moved & was 2^{ded} so to alter the last clause adopted by the House, that together with the amendment proposed the whole should read as follows—provided always that the representation ought to be proportioned according to direct taxation, and in order to ascertain the alterations in the direct taxation which may be required from time to time by the changes in the relative circumstances of the States. Resolved that a census be taken within two years from the first meeting of the Legislature of the U. States, and once within the term of every years afterwards of all the inhabitants of the U. S. in the manner and according to the ratio recommended by Congress in their Resolution of April 18. 1783; and that the Legislature of the U. S. shall proportion the direct taxation accordingly."

.   .   .   .

On the question on ye whole proposition; as proportioning representation to direct taxation & both to the white & 3/5 of black inhabitants, & requiring a Census within six years—& within every ten years afterwards.

Mas. div^d Con^t ay. N. J. no. P^a ay. Del. no. M^d ay. V^a ay. N. C. ay. S. C. div^d Geo. ay. [Ayes, 6; noes, 2; divided, 2.]

Friday, July 13. In Convention

On the motion of Mr Randolph, the vote . . . authorising the Legisl^{re} to adjust from time to time, the representation upon the principles of *wealth* & numbers of inhabitants was reconsidered by common consent in order to strike out "Wealth" and adjust the resolution to that requiring periodical revisions according to the number of whites & three fifths of the blacks: the motion was in the words following—"But as the present situation of the States may probably alter in the number of their inhabitants, that the Legislature of the U. S. be authorized from time to time to apportion the number of representatives: and in case any of the States shall hereafter be divided or any two or more States united or new States created within the limits of the U. S. the Legislature of U. S. shall possess authority to regulate the number of Representatives in any of the foregoing cases, upon the principle of their number of inhabitants; according to the provisions hereafter mentioned."

Mr Govr Morris opposed the alteration as leaving still an incoherence. If Negroes were to be viewed as inhabitants, and the revision was to proceed on the principle of numbers of inhabts they ought to be added in their entire number, and not in the proportion of 3/5. If as property, the word wealth was right, and striking it out, would produce the very inconsistency which it was meant to get rid of.—The train of business & the late turn which it had taken, had led him he said, into deep meditation on it, and He wd candidly state the result. A distinction had been set up & urged, between the Nn & Southn States. He had hitherto considered this doctrine as heretical. He still thought the distinction groundless. He sees however that it is persisted in, and that the Southn Gentlemen will not be satisfied unless they see the way open to their gaining a majority in the public Councils. The consequence of such a transfer of power from the maritime to the interior & landed interest will he foresees be such an oppression of commerce, that he shall be obliged to vote for ye vicious principle of equality in the 2d branch in order to provide some defence for the N. States agst it. But to come more to the point; either this distinction is fictitious or real; if fictitious let it be dismissed & let us proceed with due confidence. If it be real, instead of attempting to blend incompatible things, let us at once take a friendly leave of each other. There can be no end of demands for security if every particular interest is to be entitled to it. The Eastern States may claim it for their fishery, and for other objects, as the Southn States claim it for their peculiar objects. In this struggle between the two ends of the Union, what part ought the middle States in point of policy to take: to join their Eastern brethren according to his ideas. . . .

Mr Butler. The security the Southn States want is that their negroes may not be taken from them, which some gentlemen within or without doors, have a very good mind to do. . . .

Mʳ WILSON. If a general declaration would satisfy any gentleman he had no indisposition to declare his sentiments. Conceiving that all men wherever placed have equal rights and are equally entitled to confidence, he viewed without apprehension the period when a few States should contain the superior number of people. The majority of people wherever found ought in all questions to govern the minority. If the interior Country should acquire this majority, it will not only have the right, but will avail themselves of it whether we will or no. . . . Further, if numbers be not a proper rule, why is not some better rule pointed out. No one has yet ventured to attempt it. Congˢ have never been able to discover a better. No State as far as he had heard, has suggested any other. In 1783, after elaborate discussion of a measure of wealth all were satisfied then as they are now that the rule of numbers, does not differ much from the combined rule of numbers & wealth. Again he could not agree that property was the sole or the primary object of Governᵗ & society. The cultivation & improvement of the human mind was the most noble object. With respect to this object, as well as to other *personal* rights, numbers were surely the natural & precise measure of Representation. And with respect to property, they could not vary much from the precise measure. In no point of view however could the establishmᵗ of numbers as the rule of representation in the 1ˢᵗ branch vary his opinion as to the impropriety of letting a vicious principle into the 2ᵈ branch. —On the Question to strike out *wealth,* & to make the change as moved by Mʳ Randolph, it passed in the affirmative—

Mas. ay. Conᵗ ay. N. J. ay. Pᵃ ay. Del. divᵈ Mᵈ ay. Vᵃ ay. N. C. ay. S. C. ay. Geo. ay. [Ayes, 9; noes, 0; divided, 1.]

Saturday, July 14. In Convention

Mʳ L. MARTIN called for the question on the whole report, including the parts relating to the origination of money bills, and the equality of votes in the 2ᵈ branch.

•   •   •   •   •   •   •   •   •   •   •   •   •   •

M⁬ RUTLIDGE proposed to reconsider the two propositions touching the originating of money bills in the first & the equality of votes in the second branch.

M⁬ SHERMAN was for the question on the whole at once. It was he said a conciliatory plan, . . . and if any part should now be altered, it would be necessary to go over the whole ground again.

.   .   .   .

M⁬ WILSON traced the progress of the report through its several stages, remarking yᵗ when on the question concerning an equality of votes, the House was divided, our Constituents had they voted as their representatives did, would have stood as ⅔ agˢᵗ the equality, and ⅓ only in favor of it. This fact would ere long be known, and it will appear that this fundamental point has been carried by ⅓ agˢᵗ ⅔. What hopes will our Constituents entertain when they find that the essential principles of justice have been violated in the outset of the Governmᵗ As to the privilege of originating money bills, it was not considered by any as of much moment, and by many as improper in itself. He hoped both clauses wᵈ be reconsidered. The equality of votes was a point of such critical importance, that every opportunity ought to be allowed, for discussing and collecting the mind of the Convention on it.

M⁬ L. MARTIN denies that there were ⅔ agˢᵗ the equality of votes. The States that please to call themselves large, are the weekest in the Union. Look at Masᵗˢ Look at Virgᵃ Are they efficient States? He was for letting a separation take place if they desired it. He had rather there should be two Confederacies, than one founded on any other principle than an equality of votes in the 2ᵈ branch at least.

.   .   .   .

M⁬ GERRY . . . favored the reconsideration with a view not of destroying the equality of votes; but of providing that the States should vote per capita, which he said would prevent the delays & inconveniences that had been experienced in Congˢ and would give a national aspect & Spirit to the management of business. He did not approve of a reconsideration of the clause relating to money bills. It was of great consequence. It was the corner stone of the accomodation. ... The Report was not altogether to his mind. But he would agree to it as it stood rather than throw it out altogether.

The reconsideration being tacitly agreed to.

Mr PINKNEY moved that instead of an equality of votes, the States should be represented in the 2^d branch as follows: N. H. by. 2. members. Mas. 4. R. I. 1. Con^t 3. N. Y. 3. N. J. 2. P^a 4. Del 1. M^d 3. Virg^a 5. N. C. 3. S. C. 3. Geo. 2. making in the whole 36.

Mr WILSON seconds the motion

Mr DAYTON. The smaller States can never give up their equality. For himself he would in no event yield that security for their rights.

Mr SHERMAN urged the equality of votes not so much as a security for the small States; as for the State Gov^{ts} which could not be preserved unless they were represented & had a negative in the Genl Government. He had no objection to the members in the 2^d b. voting per capita, as had been suggested by (Mr Gerry)

Mr MADISON concurred in this motion of Mr Pinkney as a reasonable compromise.

Mr GERRY said he should like the motion, but could see no hope of success. An accomodation must take place, and it was apparent from what had been seen that it could not do so on the ground of the motion. He was utterly against a partial confederacy, leaving other States to accede or not accede; as had been intimated.

Mr KING said it was always with regret that he differed from his colleagues, but it was his duty to differ from (Mr Gerry) on this occasion. He considered the proposed Government as substantially and formally, a General and National Government over the people of America. There never will be a case in which it will act as a federal Government on the States and not on the individual Citizens. And is it not a clear principle that in a free Gov^t those who are to be the objects of a Gov^t ought to influence the operations of it? What reason can be assigned why the same rule of representation s^d not prevail in the 2^d branch as in the

1ˢᵗ? He could conceive none. . . . He was sure that no Govᵗ
could last that was not founded on just principles. He prefer'd
the doing of nothing, to an allowance of an equal vote to all the
States. It would be better he thought to submit to a little more
confusion & convulsion, than to submit to such an evil. It was
difficult to say what the views of different Gentlemen might be.
Perhaps there might be some who thought no Governmᵗ coextensive with the U. States could be established with a hope of
its answering the purpose. Perhaps there might be other fixed
opinions incompatible with the object we were pursuing. If
there were, he thought it but candid that Gentlemen would
speak out that we might understand one another.

Mʳ STRONG. . . . It is agreed on all hands that Congress are
nearly at an end. If no Accomodation takes place, the Union
itself must soon be dissolved. . . . [H]e was compelled to give his
vote for the Report taken all together.

Mʳ MADISON expressed his apprehensions that if the proper
foundation of Govenmᵗ—was destroyed, by substituting an
equality in place of a proportional Representation, no proper
superstructure would be raised. . . . He reminded them of the
consequences of laying the existing confederation on improper
principles. . . . Representation was an expedient by which the
meeting of the ⸗people themselves was rendered unnecessary;
and . . . representatives ought therefore to bear a proportion to
the votes which their constituents if convened, would respectively have. Was not this remark as applicable to one branch
of the Representation as to the other? But it had been said that
the Governᵗ would in its operation be partly federal, partly
national; that altho' in the latter respect the Representatives of
the people ought to be in proportion to the people: yet in the
former it ought to be according to the number of States. If
there was any solidity in this distinction he was ready to abide
by it, if there was none it ought to be abandoned. In all cases
where the Genˡ Governmᵗ is to act on the people, let the people
be represented and the votes be proportional. In all cases where
the Governᵗ is to act on the States as such, in like manner as
Congˢ now act on them, let the States be represented & the votes

be equal. This was the true ground of compromise if there was any ground at all. But he denied that there was any ground. He called for a single instance in which the Genl Gov^t was not to operate on the people individually. The practicability of making laws, with coercive sanctions, for the States as Political bodies, had been exploded on all hands. He observed that the people of the large States would in some way or other secure to themselves a weight proportioned to the importance accruing from their superior numbers. If they could not effect it by a proportional representation in the Gov^t they would probably accede to no Gov^t which did not in great measure depend for its efficacy on their voluntary cooperation; in which case they would indirecty secure their object. ... He enumerated the objections agst an equality of votes in the 2^d branch, notwithstanding the proportional representation in the first. 1. the minority could negative the will of the majority of the people. 2. they could extort measures by making them a condition of their assent to other necessary measures. 3. they could obtrude measures on the majority by virtue of the peculiar powers which would be vested in the Senate. 4. the evil instead of being cured by time, would increase with every new State that should be admitted, as they must all be admitted on the principle of equality. 5. the perpetuity it would give to the preponderance of the North^n agst the South^n Scale was a serious consideration. It seemed now to be pretty well understood that the real difference of interests lay, not between the large & small but between the N. & South^n States. The institution of slavery & its consequences formed the line of discrimination. There were 5 States on the South, 8 on the North^n side of this line. Should a proport^l representation take place it was true, the N. side would still outnumber the other; but not in the same degree, at this time; and every day would tend towards an equilibrium.

Mr WILSON would add a few words only. ... The justice of the general principle of proportional representation has not in argument at least been yet contradicted. But it is said that a departure from it so far as to give the States an equal vote in one branch of the Legislature is essential to their preservation.

He had considered this position maturely, but could not see its application. That the States ought to be preserved he admitted. But does it follow that an equality of votes is necessary for the purpose? ... An equal vote then is not necessary as far as he can conceive: and is liable among other objections to this insuperable one: The great fault of the existing confederacy is its inactivity. It has never been a complaint agst Cong^s that they governed over-much. The complaint has been that they have governed too little. To remedy this defect we were sent here. Shall we effect the cure by establishing an equality of votes as is proposed? no: this very equality carries us directly to Congress: to the system which it is our duty to rectify. The small States cannot indeed act, by virtue of this equality, but they may controul the Gov^t as they have done in Cong^s This very measure is here prosecuted by a minority of the people of America. Is then the object of the Convention likely to be accomplished in this way? ... He knew there were some respectable men who preferred three confederacies, united by offensive & defensive alliances. Many things may be plausibly said, some things may be justly said, in favor of such a project. He could not however concur in it himself; but he thought nothing so pernicious as bad first principles.

Monday, July 16. In Convention

On the question for agreeing to the whole Report as amended & including the equality of votes in the 2^d branch. it passed in the Affirmative.

Mas. divided Mr Gerry, Mr Strong, ay. Mr King Mr Ghorum no. Con^t ay. N. J. ay. Pen^a no. Del. ay. M^d ay. V^a no. N. C. ay. Mr Spaight no. S. C. no. Geo. no. [Ayes, 5; noes, 4; divided, 1.]

On the morning following before the hour of the convention a number of the members from the larger States, by common agreement met for the purpose of consulting on the proper steps to be taken in consequence of the vote in favor of an equal Representation in the 2ᵈ branch, and the apparent inflexibility of the smaller States on that point. Several members from the latter States also attended. The time was wasted in vague conversation on the subject, without any specific proposition or agreement. It appeared indeed that the opinions of the members who disliked the equality of votes differed so much as to the importance of that point, and as to the policy of risking a failure of any general act of the Convention, by inflexibly opposing it. Several of them supposing that no good Governmᵗ could or would be built on that foundation, and that as a division of the Convention into two opinions was unavoidable; it would be better that the side comprising the principal States, and a majority of the people of America, should propose a scheme of Govᵗ to the States, than that a scheme should be proposed on the other side, would have concurred in a firm opposition to the smaller States, and in a separate recommendation, if eventually necessary. Others seemed inclined to yield to the smaller States, and to concur in such an act however imperfect & exceptionable, as might be agreed on by the Convention as a body, tho' decided by a bare majority of States and by a minority of the people of the U. States. It is probable that the result of this consultation satisfied the smaller States that they had nothing to apprehend from a union of the larger, in any plan whatever agˢᵗ the equality of votes in the 2ᵈ branch.

EMPOWERING THE NATIONAL GOVERNMENT

Tuesday, July 17. In Convention

The action of the preceding day, in giving equality of votes in the Senate, enabled delegates to turn for the first time to the question of powers for the central government, which had been postponed until it was determined who should control there. That problem decided, the Convention turned immediately to the sixth resolution from the Committee of the Whole:

> Resolved that the National Legislature ought to be empowered to enjoy the Legislative rights vested in Congress by the Confederation, and moreover to legislate in all cases to which the separate States are incompetent; or in which the harmony of the U.S. may be interrupted by the exercise of individual legislation; to negative all laws passed by the several States contravening in the opinion of the National Legislature the articles of Union, or any treaties subsisting under the authority of the Union.

They agreed unanimously to the first clause. Butler called for explanation of the extent of the power in the second, particularly of the word "incompeten.." Backing him, Rutledge moved to commit this so that "a specification of the powers comprised in the general terms might be reported." A tie vote indicated a deadlock on the question of granting general versus enumerated powers. For committal, and presumably thus largely for enumeration, were Connecticut, Maryland, Virginia, South Carolina, and Georgia. Opposed, and thus presumably favoring a general grant, were Massachusetts, New Jersey, Pennsylvania, Delaware, and North Carolina. Although this tie remained unbroken until the Committee of Detail reported on August 6, renewed attempts to find a solution were made on July 17. Sherman made the following motion, which only Connecticut and Maryland favored:

Mr SHERMAN observed that it would be difficult to draw the line between the powers of the Genⁱ Legislatures, and those to be left with the States; that he did not like the definition contained in the Resolution, and proposed in place of the words "of individual Legislation" line 4. inclusive, to insert "to make laws binding on the people of the United States in all cases which may concern the common interests of the Union; but not to interfere with the Government of the individual States in any matters of internal police which respect the Govt of such States only, and wherein the general welfare of the U. States is not concerned."

Thereupon Bedford's proposal, which, Randolph asserted, involved the power of violating state laws and constitutions and meddling with their police powers, passed by six to four.

Mᴿ BEDFORD moved that the 2ᵈ member of Resolution 6. be so altered as to read "and moreover to legislate in all cases for the general interests of the Union, and also in those to which the States are separately ¹ incompetent," or in which the harmony of the U. States may be interrupted by the exercise of individual Legislation." [Then members turned to the question of the negative.]

"To negative all laws passed by the several States contravening in the opinion of the Nat: Legislature the articles of Union, or any treaties subsisting under the authority of yᵉ Union"

Mᴿ Govᴿ MORRIS opposed this power as likely to be terrible to the States, and not necessary, if sufficient Legislative authority should be given to the Genˡ Government.

Mᴿ SHERMAN thought it unnecessary, as the Courts of the States would not consider as valid any law contravening the Authority of the Union, and which the legislature would wish to be negatived.

Mᴿ L. MARTIN considered the power as improper & inadmissible. Shall all the laws of the States be sent up to the Genˡ Legislature before they shall be permitted to operate?

Mᴿ MADISON, considered the negative on the laws of the States as essential to the efficacy & security of the Genˡ Govᵗ The necessity of a general Govᵗ proceeds from the propensity of the States to pursue their particular interests in opposition to the general interest. This propensity will continue to disturb the system, unless effectually controuled. Nothing short of a negative on their laws will controul it. They can pass laws which will accomplish their injurious objects before they can be repealed by the Genˡ Legislʳᵉ or be set aside by the National Tribunals. Confidence can not be put in the State Tribunals as guardians

---

1 (The word "severally" is substituted in the transcript for "separately.")

of the National authority and interests. In all the States these are more or less depend[t] on the Legislatures. . . .

M[r] Gov[r] MORRIS was more & more opposed to the negative. . . . A law that ought to be negatived will be set aside in the Judiciary departm[t] and if that security should fail; may be repealed by a Nation[l] law.

M[r] SHERMAN. Such a power involves a wrong principle, to wit, that a law of a State contrary to the articles of the Union, would if not negatived, be valid & operative.

.   .   .   .

On the question for agreeing to the power of negativing laws of States &c" it passed in the negative.

Mas. ay. C[t] no. N. J. no. P[a] no. Del. no. M[d] no. V[a] ay. N. C. ay. S. C. no. Geo. no. [Ayes, 3; noes, 7.]

M[r] LUTHER MARTIN moved the following resolution "that the Legislative acts of the U. S. made by virtue & in pursuance of the articles of Union, and all Treaties made & ratified under the authority of the U. S. shall be the supreme law of the respective States, as far as those acts or treaties shall relate to the said States, or their Citizens and inhabitants—& that the Judiciaries of the several States shall be bound thereby in their decisions, any thing in the respective laws of the individual States to the contrary notwithstanding" which was agreed to nem: con: [2]

9th Resol: "that Nat[l] Executive consist of a single person." Ag[d] to nem. con.

"To be chosen by the National Legisl:"

This initiated a brief discussion of one of the most troublesome points in the Convention. Since most of the arguments offered now are brought out below (July 19), they are omitted here. At this time unanimous agreement favored choice by the legislature. Then delegates made the executive eligible a second time.

"For the term of 7 years" resumed.

.   .   .   .

[2] [Note that state *constitutions* are at this time carefully excluded.]

Doc.ʳ M꜀Clurg moved [3] to strike out 7 years, and insert "during good behavior." By striking out the words declaring him not re-eligible, he was put into a situation that would keep him dependent for ever on the Legislature; and he conceived the independence of the Executive to be equally essential with that of the Judiciary department.

M.ʳ Gov.ʳ Morris 2.ᵈᵉᵈ the motion. He expressed great pleasure in hearing it. This was the way to get a good Government. . . .

. . . .

M.ʳ Madison [4] If it be essential to the preservation of liberty that the Legisl: Execut: & Judiciary powers be separate, it is essential to a maintenance of the separation, that they should be independent of each other. The Executive could not be independent of the Legislure, if dependent on the pleasure of that branch for a reappointment. . . . [A] dependence of the Executive on the Legislature, would render it the Executor as well as the maker of laws; & then according to the observation of Montesquieu, tyrannical laws may be made that they may be executed in a tyrannical manner. . . . [I]t might be more dangerous to suffer a union between the Executive & Legisl: powers, than between the Judiciary & Legislative powers. He conceived it to be absolutely necessary to a well constituted Republic that the two first sh.ᵈ be kept distinct & independent of each other. Whether the plan proposed by the motion was a proper one was another question, as it depended on the practicability of instituting a tribunal for impeachm.ᵗˢ as certain & as adequate in the one case as in the other. . . .

Col. Mason. . . . He considered an Executive during good behavior as a softer name only for an Executive for life. And that the next would be an easy step to hereditary Monarchy. . . .

3 The probable object of this motion was merely to enforce the argument against the re-eligibility of the Executive Magistrate, by holding out a tenure during good behaviour as the alternative for keeping him independent of the Legislature.

4 The view here taken of the subject was meant to aid in parrying the animadversions likely to fall on the motion of D.ʳ M꜀Clurg, for whom J. M. had a particular regard. The Doct.ʳ though possessing talents of the highest order, was modest & unaccustomed to exert them in public debate.

Mr MADISON, was not apprehensive of being thought to favor any step towards monarchy. The real object with him was to prevent its introduction. Experience had proved a tendency in our governments to throw all power into the Legislative vortex. The Executives of the States are in general little more than Cyphers; the legislatures omnipotent. If no effectual check be devised for restraining the instability & encroachments of the latter, a revolution of some kind or other would be inevitable. The preservation of Republican Gov^t therefore required some expedient for the purpose, but required evidently at the same time that in devising it, the genuine principles of that form should be kept in view.

．　．　．　．　．　．　．　．　．　．　．　．

On the question for inserting "during good behavior" in place of 7 years (with a re-eligibility) it passed in the negative. Mas. no. C^t no. N. J. ay. P^a ay. Del. ay. M^d no. V^a ay. N. C. no. S. C. no. Geo. no.[5] [Ayes, 4; noes, 6.]

On the motion "to strike out seven years" it passed in the negative.

Mas. ay. C^t no. N. J. no. P^a ay. Del. ay. M^d no. V^a no. N. C. ay. S. C. no. Geo. no.[6] [Ayes, 4; noes, 6.]

[5] This vote is not to be considered as any certain index of opinion, as a number in the affirmative probably had it chiefly in view to alarm those attached to a dependence of the Executive on the Legislature, & thereby facilitate some final arrangement of a contrary tendency. The avowed friends of an Executive, "during good behaviour" were not more than three or four, nor is it certain they would finally have adhered to such a tenure. An independence of the three great departments of each other, as far as possible, and the responsibility of all to the will of the community seemed to be generally admitted as the true basis of a well constructed government.

[6] There was no debate on this motion, the apparent object of many in the affirmative was to secure the re-eligibility by shortening the term, and of many in the negative to embarrass the plan of referring the appointment & dependence of the Executive to the Legislature.

Wednesday, July 18. In Convention

Resol. 11 "that a Nat! Judiciary be estab⁴ to consist of one supreme tribunal." ag⁴ to nem. con.

"The Judges of which to be appoint⁴ by the 2⁴ branch of the Nat! Legislature."

M⁺ GHORUM, w⁴ prefer an appointment by the 2⁴ branch to an appointm⁺ by the whole Legislature; but he thought even that branch too numerous, and too little personally responsible, to ensure a good choice. He suggested that the Judges be appointed by the Execu⁺ᵉ with the advice & consent of the 2⁴ branch, in the mode prescribed by the constitution of Mas⁺ˢ This mode had been long practised in that country, & was found to answer perfectly well.

M⁺ WILSON, still w⁴ prefer an appointm⁺ by the Executive; but if that could not be attained, w⁴ prefer in the next place, the mode suggested by M⁺ Ghorum. He thought it his duty however to move in the first instance "that the Judges be appointed by the Executive." M⁺ Gov⁺ MORRIS 2⁴ᵉᵈ the motion.

M⁺ L. MARTIN was strenuous for an app⁺ by the 2⁴ branch. Being taken from all the States it w⁴ be best informed of characters & most capable of making a fit choice.

.   .   .   .

M⁺ MASON. The mode of appointing the Judges may depend in some degree on the mode of trying impeachments of the Executive. If the Judges were to form a tribunal for that purpose, they surely ought not to be appointed by the Executive. ...

.   .   .   .

On the question for referring the appointment of the Judges to the Executive, instead of the 2⁴ branch

Mas. ay. Con⁺ no. P⁺ ay. Del. no. M⁴ no. V⁺ no. N. C. no. S. C. no.—Geo. absent. [Ayes, 2; noes, 6; absent, 1.]

.   .   .   .

12. Resol: "that Nat! Legislature be empowered to appoint inferior tribunals"

M⸍ BUTLER could see no necessity for such tribunals. The State Tribunals might do the business.

M⸍ L. MARTIN concurred. They will create jealousies & oppositions in the State tribunals, with the jurisdiction of which they will interfere.

.   .   .   .

M⸍ RANDOLPH observed that the Courts of the States can not be trusted with the administration of the National laws. The objects of jurisdiction are such as will often place the General & local policy at variance.

M⸍ GOV⸍ MORRIS urged also the necessity of such a provision

M⸍ SHERMAN was willing to give the power to the Legislature but wished them to make use of the State Tribunals whenever it could be done, with safety to the general interest.

Col. MASON thought many circumstances might arise not now to be foreseen, which might render such a power absolutely necessary.

On question for agreeing to 12. Resol: empowering the National Legislature to appoint "inferior tribunals." Ag⸍ to nem. con.

.   .   .   .

Resol. 16. "That a Republican Constitution & its. existing laws ought to be guarantied to each State by the U. States."

M⸍ GOV⸍ MORRIS—thought the Resol: very objectionable. He should be very unwilling that such laws as exist in R. Island should be guaranteid.

M⸍ WILSON. The object is merely to secure the States ag⸍ dangerous commotions, insurrections and rebellions.

Col. MASON. If the Gen⸍ Gov⸍ should have no right to suppress rebellions ag⸍ particular States, it will be in a bad situation indeed. As Rebellions ag⸍ itself originate in & ag⸍ individual States, it must remain a passive Spectator of its own subversion.

M⸍ RANDOLPH. The Resol⸍ has 2. objects. 1. to secure Republican Government. 2. to suppress domestic commotions. He urged the necessity of both these provisions.

.   .   .   .

Mͬ L. Martin was for leaving the States to suppress Rebellions themselves.

. . . .

Mͬ Wilson moved as a better expression of the idea, "that a Republican form of Governmͭ shall be guarantied to each State & that each State shall be protected agͤͭ foreign & domestic violence.

This seeming to be well received, . . . it passed nem. con.

Adjͩ

Thursday, July 19. In Convention

On reconsideration of the vote rendering the Executive re-eligible a 2ͩ time, Mͬ Martin moved to reinstate the words, "to be ineligible a 2ͩ time."

Mͬ Governeur Morris. It is necessary to take into one view all that relates to the establishment of the Executive; on the due formation of which must depend the efficacy & utility of the Union among the present and future States. It has been a maxim in Political Science that Republican Government is not adapted to a large extent of Country, because the energy of the Executive Magistracy can not reach the extreme parts of it. Our Country is an extensive one. We must either then renounce the blessings of the Union, or provide an Executive with sufficient vigor to pervade every part of it. This subject was of so much importance that he hoped to be indulged in an extensive view of it. One great object of the Executive is to controul the Legislature. The Legislature will continually seek to aggrandize & perpetuate themselves . . . . It is necessary then that the Executive Magistrate should be the guardian of the people, even of the lower classes, agͤͭ Legislative tyranny, against the Great & the wealthy who in the course of things will necessarily compose the Legislative body. . . . The check provided in the 2ͩ branch was not meant as a check on Legislative usurpations of power, but . . . on the propensity in the 1ͤͭ branch to legislate too much to run into projects of paper money & similar expedients. It is no check on Legislative tyranny. On the contrary it may favor it, and if the 1st branch can be seduced may find the means of success. The Executive therefore ought to be so constituted as to be the great protector of the Mass of the people.—It is the duty of the Executive to appoint the officers & to command the forces of the Republic .... . Who will be the best Judges whether these appointments be well made? The people at large, who will know, will see, will feel the effects of them. ... He finds too that the Executive is not to be re-eligible. What effect will this have? 1. it will destroy the great incitement to merit public esteem by taking away the hope of being rewarded with a reappointment. It may give a dangerous turn to one of the strongest passions in the human breast. The love of fame is the great spring to noble & illustrious actions. Shut the Civil road to Glory & he may be compelled to seek it by the sword. 2. It will tempt him to make the most of the short space of time allotted him, to accumulate wealth and provide for his friends. 3. It will produce violations of the very constitution it is meant to secure. In moments of pressing danger the tried abilities and established character of a favorite Magistrate will prevail over respect for the forms of the Constitution. The Executive is also to be impeachable. ... It will hold him in such dependence that he will be no check on the Legislature, will not be a firm guardian of the people and of the public interest. He will be the tool of a faction, of some leading demagogue in the Legislature. These then are the faults of the Executive establishment as now proposed. Can no better establishmt be devised? If he is to be the Guardian of the people let him be appointed by the people? If he is to be a check on the Legislature let him not be impeachable. Let him be of short duration, that he may with propriety be re-eligible. It has been said that the candidates for this office will not be known to the people. If they be known to the Legislature, they must have such a notoriety and eminence of Character, that they can not possibly be unknown to the people at large. It cannot be possible that a man shall have sufficiently distinguished himself to merit this high trust without having his character proclaimed by fame throughout the Empire. As to the danger from an unimpeachable magistrate he could not regard it as formidable. ... He suggested a biennial election of the Executive ... by the people at large. ... He saw no alternative for making the Executive independent of the Legislature but either to give him his office for life, or make him eligible by the people—Again, it might be objected that two years would be too short a duration. But he believes that as long as he should behave himself well, he would be continued in his place. The extent of the Country would secure his re-election agst the factions & discontents of particular States. It deserved consideration also that such an ingredient in the plan would render it extremely palatable to the people. These were the general ideas which occurred to him on the subject, and which led him to wish & move that the whole constitution of the Executive might undergo reconsideration.

Mr RANDOLPH urged the motion of Mr L. Martin for restoring the words making the Executive ineligible a 2^d time. If he ought to be independent, he should not be left under a temptation to court a re-appointment. ... He thought an election by the Legislature with an incapacity to be elected a second time would be more acceptable to the people than the plan suggested by Mr Govr Morris.

Mr KING. did not like the ineligibility. He thought ... that he who has proved himself to be most fit for an Office, ought not to be excluded by the constitution from holding it. He would therefore prefer any other reasonable plan that could be substituted. He was much disposed to think that in such cases the people at large would chuse wisely. There was indeed some difficulty arising from the improbability of a general concurrence of the people in favor of any one man. On the whole ne was of opinion that an appointment by electors chosen by the people for the purpose, would be liable to fewest objections.

.   .   .   .

Mr WILSON. It seems to be the unanimous sense that the Executive should not be appointed by the Legislature, unless he be rendered in-eligible a 2ᵈ time: he perceived with pleasure that the idea was gaining ground, of an election mediately or immediately by the people.

. . . .

Mᵣ GERRY. . . . He was agˢᵗ a popular election. The people are uninformed, and would be misled by a few designing men. He urged the expediency of an appointment of the Executive by Electors to be chosen by the State Executives. The people of the States will then choose the 1ˢᵗ branch: The legislatures of the States the 2ᵈ branch of the National Legislature, and the Executives of the States, the National Executive. This he thought would form a strong attachnᵗ in the States to the National System. The popular mode of electing the chief Magistrate would certainly be the worst of all. If he should be so elected & should do his duty, he will be turned out for it like Govᵣ Bowdoin in Massᵗˢ & President Sullivan in N. Hamshire.

On the question of Mᵣ Govᵣ Morris motion to reconsider generally the constitution of the Executive.

Mas. ay. Cᵗ ay. N. J. ay & all the others ay.

Mᵣ ELSEWORTH moved to strike out the appointmᵗ by the Natˡ Legislature, and insert "to be chosen by electors appointed, by the Legislatures of the States in the following ratio; towit— one for each State not exceeding 200,000 inhabᵗˢ two for each above yᵗ number & not exceeding 300,000. and three for each State exceeding 300,000."—Mᵣ BROOME 2ᵈᵉᵈ the motion.

. . . .

The question as moved by Mᵣ Elseworth being divided, on the 1ˢᵗ part shall yᵉ Natˡ Executive be appointed by Electors?

Mas. divᵈ Conᵗ ay. N. J. ay. Pᵃ ay. Del. ay. Mᵈ ay. Vᵃ ay. N. C. no. S. C. no. Geo. no. [Ayes, 6; noes, 3; divided, 1.]

On 2ᵈ part shall the Electors be chosen by State Legislatures? Mas. ay. Conᵗ ay. N. J. ay. Pᵃ ay. Del. ay. Mᵈ ay. Vᵃ no. N. C. ay. S. C. no. Geo. ay. [Ayes, 8; noes, 2.]

Members determined the ratio of electors for various states in appointing the magistrate and then considered whether that official should be "removeable on impeachment and conviction for mal practice or neglect of duty." Debate revealed they again steered between the Scylla of an incompetent and perfidious executive and the Charybdis of domination by the legislature. Franklin warned that, historically, lack of power to impeach had necessitated recourse to assassination. Morris, having opposed the measure at the outset, announced that his opinion had been changed by the argument.

Saturday, July 21. In Convention

Mr WILSON moved as an amendment to Resol^n 10. that the supreme Nat^l Judiciary should be associated with the Executive in the Revisionary power." [7] This proposition had been before made and failed: but he was so confirmed by reflection in the opinion of its utility, that he thought it incumbent on him to make another effort: The Judiciary ought to have an opportunity of remonstrating agst projected encroachments on the people as well as on themselves. It had been said that the Judges, as expositors of the Laws would have an opportunity of defending their constitutional rights. There was weight in this observation; but this power of the Judges did not go far enough. Laws may be unjust, may be unwise, may be dangerous, may be destructive; and yet may not be so unconstitutional as to justify the Judges in refusing to give them effect. Let them have a share in the Revisionary power, and they will have an opportunity of taking notice of these characters of a law, and of counteracting, by the weight of their opinions the improper views of the Legislature.—

Mr MADISON 2^{ded} the motion

Mr GHORUM did not see the advantage of employing the Judges in this way. As Judges they are not to be presumed to possess any peculiar knowledge of the mere policy of public measures. Nor can it be necessary as a security for their constitutional rights. The Judges in England have no such additional

---

[7] [On July 18 the executive received power to veto acts not subsequently passed by two thirds of each legislative house.]

provision for their defence, yet their jurisdiction is not invaded. He thought it would be best to let the Executive alone be responsible, and at most to authorize him to call on Judges for their opinions.

M︫ᴿ ELSEWORTH approved heartily of the motion. The aid of the Judges will give more wisdom & firmness to the Executive. They will possess a systematic and accurate knowledge of the Laws, which the Executive can not be expected always to possess. The law of Nations also will frequently come into question. Of this the Judges alone will have competent information.

M︫ᴿ MADISON considered the object of the motion as of great importance to the meditated Constitution. It would be useful to the Judiciary departm︫ᵗ by giving it an additional opportunity of defending itself ag︫ˢᵗ Legislative encroachments; It would be useful to the Executive, by inspiring additional confidence & firmness in exerting the revisionary power: It would be useful to the Legislature by the valuable assistance it would give in preserving a consistency, conciseness, perspicuity & technical propriety in the laws, qualities peculiarly necessary; & yet shamefully wanting in our republican Codes. It would moreover be useful to the Community at large as an additional check ag︫ˢᵗ a pursuit of those unwise & unjust measures which constituted so great a portion of our calamities. If any solid objection could be urged ag︫ˢᵗ the motion, it must be on the supposition that it tended to give too much strength either to the Executive or Judiciary. He did not think there was the least ground for this apprehension. It was much more to be apprehended that notwithstanding this co-operation of the two departments, the Legislature would still be an over-match for them. Experience in all the States had evinced a powerful tendency in the Legislature to absorb all power into its vortex. This was the real source of danger to the American Constitutions; & suggested the necessity of giving every defensive authority to the other departments that was consistent with republican principles.

.   .   .   .

Mr GERRY did not expect to see this point which had undergone full discussion, again revived. The object he conceived of the Revisionary power was merely to secure the Executive department agst legislative encroachment. The Executive therefore who will best know and be ready to defend his rights ought alone to have the defence of them. The motion was liable to strong objections. It was combining & mixing together the Legislative & the other departments. It was establishing an improper coalition between the Executive & Judiciary departments. It was making Statesmen of the Judges; and setting them up as the guardians of the Rights of the people. He relied for his part on the Representatives of the people as the guardians of their Rights & interests. It was making the Expositors of the Laws the Legislators, which ought never to be done. . . .

. . . .

Mr Govr MORRIS. Some check being necessary on the Legislature, the question is in what hands it should be lodged. On one side it was contended that the Executive alone ought to exercise it. He did not think that an Executive appointed for 6 years,[8] and impeachable whilst in office w^d be a very effectual check. On the other side it was urged that he ought to be reinforced by the Judiciary department. Agst this it was objected that Expositors of laws ought to have no hand in making them, and arguments in favor of this had been drawn from England. What weight was due to them might be easily determined by an attention to facts. The truth was that the Judges in England had a great share in ye Legislation. They are consulted in difficult & doubtful cases. They may be & some of them are members of the Legislature. They are or may be members of the privy Council, and can there advise the Executive as they will do with us if the motion succeeds. The influence the English Judges may have in the latter capacity in strengthening the Executive check can not be ascertained, as the King by his influence in a manner dictates the laws. There is one difference in the two Cases however

[8] [Reduced from seven on July 19.]

which disconcerts all reasoning from the British to our proposed Constitution. The British Executive has so great an interest in his prerogatives and such powerful means of defending them that he will never yield any part of them. The interest of our Executive is so inconsiderable & so transitory, and his means of defending it so feeble, that there is the justest ground to fear his want of firmness in resisting incroachments. He was extremely apprehensive that the auxiliary firmness & weight of the Judiciary would not supply the deficiency. He concurred in thinking the public liberty in greater danger from Legislative usurpations than from any other source. It had been said that the Legislature ought to be relied on as the proper Guardians of liberty. The answer was short and conclusive. Either bad laws will be pushed or not. On the latter supposition no check will be wanted. On the former a strong check will be necessary: And this is the proper supposition. Emissions of paper money, largesses to the people—a remission of debts and similar measures, will at some times be popular, and will be pushed for that reason. At other times such measures will coincide with the interests of the Legislature themselves, & that will be a reason not less cogent for pushing them. It may be thought that the people will not be deluded and misled in the latter case. But experience teaches another lesson. The press is indeed a great means of diminishing the evil, yet it is found to be unable to prevent it altogether.

Mr L. MARTIN. Considered the association of the Judges with the Executive as a dangerous innovation; as well as one which could not produce the particular advantage expected from it. A knowledge of Mankind, and of Legislative affairs cannot be presumed to belong in a higher degree to the Judges than to the Legislature. And as to the Constitutionality of laws, that point will come before the Judges in their proper official character. In this character they have a negative on the laws. Join them with the Executive in the Revision and they will have a double negative. It is necessary that the Supreme Judiciary should have the confidence of the people. This will soon be lost, if they are employed in the task of remonstrating agst popular measures of the Legislature. ...

Mr MADISON could not discover in the proposed association of the Judges with the Executive in the Revisionary check on the Legislative any violation of the maxim which requires the great departments of power to be kept separate & distinct. On the contrary he thought it an auxiliary precaution in favor of the maxim If a Constitutional discrimination of the departments on paper were a sufficient security to each agst encroachments of the others, all further provisions would indeed be superfluous. But experience had taught us a distrust of that security; and that it is necessary to introduce such a balance of powers and interests, as will guarantee the provisions on paper. Instead therefore of contenting ourselves with laying down the Theory in the Constitution that each department ought to be separate & distinct, it was proposed to add a defensive power to each which should maintain the Theory in practice. In so doing we did not blend the departments together. We erected effectual barriers for keeping them separate. The most regular example of this theory was in the British Constitution. Yet it was not only the practice there to admit the Judges to a seat in the legislature, and in the Executive Councils, and to submit to their previous examination all laws of a certain description, but it was a part of their Constitution that the Executive might negative any law whatever; a part of *their* Constitution which had been universally regarded as calculated for the preservation of the whole. The objection agst a union of the Judiciary & Executive branches in the revision of the laws, had either no foundation or was not carried far enough. If such a Union was an improper mixture of powers, or such a Judiciary check on the laws, was inconsistent with the Theory of a free Constitution, it was equally so to admit the Executive to any participation in the making of laws; and the revisionary plan ought to be discarded altogether.

. . . .

Mr WILSON. The separation of the departments does not require that they should have separate objects but that they should act separately tho' on the same objects. It is necessary that the two branches of the Legislature should be separate and distinct, yet they are both to act precisely on the same object.

Mr Gerry had rather give the Executive an absolute negative for its own defence than thus to blend together the Judiciary & Executive departments. It will bind them together in an offensive and defensive alliance ag^st the Legislature, and render the latter unwilling to enter into a contest with them.

. . . .

Mr Ghorum. All agree that a check on the Legislature is necessary. But there are two objections ag^st admitting the Judges to share in it which no observations on the other side seem to obviate. the 1st is that the Judges ought to carry into the exposition of the laws no prepossessions with regard to them. 2^d that as the Judges will outnumber the Executive, the revisionary check would be thrown entirely out of the Executive hands, and instead of enabling him to defend himself, would enable the Judges to sacrifice him.

Mr Wilson. The proposition is certainly not liable to all the objections which have been urged ag^st it. According (to Mr Gerry) it will unite the Executive & Judiciary in an offensive & defensive alliance ag^st the Legislature. According to Mr Ghorum it will lead to a subversion of the Executive by the Judiciary influence. To the first gentleman the answer was obvious; that the joint weight of the two departments was necessary to balance the single weight of the Legislature. To the 1st objection stated by the other Gentleman it might be answered that supposing the prepossession to mix itself with the exposition, the evil would be overbalanced by the advantages promised by the expedient. To the 2^d objection, that such a rule of voting might be provided in the detail as would guard ag^st it.

. . . .

On Question on Mr Wilson's motion for joining the Judiciary in the Revision of laws it passed in the negative—

Mas. no. Con^t ay. N. J. not present. P^a div^d Del. no. M^d ay V^a ay. N. C. no. S. C. no. Geo. div^d [Ayes, 3; noes, 4; divided, 2.]

Resol. 10, giving the Ex. a qualified veto, without the amend^t was then ag^d to nem. con.

Monday, July 23. In Convention

Mr John Langdon & Mr Nicholas Gilman from N. Hampshire, took their seats.

. . . .

Resol: 19. "referring the new Constitution to Assemblies to be chosen by the people for the express purpose of ratifying it" was next taken into consideration.

Mr ELSEWORTH moved that it be referred to the Legislatures of the States for ratification. Mr PATTERSON 2^{ded} the motion.

Col. MASON considered a reference of the plan to the authority of the people as one of the most important and essential of the Resolutions. The Legislatures have no power to ratify it. They are the mere creatures of the State Constitutions, and can not be greater than their creators. And he knew of no power in any of the Constitutions, he knew there was no power in some of them, that could be competent to this object. Whither then must we resort? To the people with whom all power remains that has not been given up in the Constitutions derived from them. It was of great moment he observed that this doctrine should be cherished as the basis of free Government. Another strong reason was that admitting the Legislatures to have a competent authority, it would be wrong to refer the plan to them, because succeeding Legislatures having equal authority could undo the acts of their predecessors; and the National Gov^t would stand in each State on the weak and tottering foundation of an Act of Assembly. There was a remaining consideration of some weight. In some of the States the Gov^{ts} were not derived from the clear & undisputed authority of the people. This was the case in Virginia. Some of the best & wisest citizens considered the Constitution as established by an assumed authority. A National Constitution derived from such a source would be exposed to the severest criticisms.

M͏ͬ RANDOLPH. One idea has pervaded all our proceedings, to wit, that opposition as well from the States as from individuals, will be made to the System to be proposed. Will it not then be highly imprudent, to furnish any unnecessary pretext by the mode of ratifying it. Added to other objections ag͏ˢᵗ a ratification by Legislative authority only, it may be remarked that there have been instances in which the authority of the Common law has been set up in particular States ag͏ˢᵗ that of the Confederation which has had no higher sanction than Legislative ratification.—Whose opposition will be most likely to be excited ag͏ˢᵗ the System? That of the local demagogues who will be degraded by it from the importance they now hold. These will spare no efforts to impede that progress in the popular mind which will be necessary to the adoption of the plan, and which every member will find to have taken place in his own, if he will compare his present opinions with those brought with him into the Convention. It is of great importance therefore that the consideration of this subject should be transferred from the Legislatures where this class of men, have their full influence to a field in which their efforts can be less mischievous. It is moreover worthy of consideration that some of the States are averse to any change in their Constitution, and will not take the requisite steps, unless expressly called upon to refer the question to the people.

M͏ͬ GERRY. The arguments of Col. Mason & M͏ͬ Randolph prove too much. they prove an unconstitutionality in the present federal system even in some of the State Gov͏ᵗˢ Inferences drawn from such a source must be inadmissible. Both the State Gov͏ᵗˢ & the federal Gov͏ᵗ have been too long acquiesced in, to be now shaken. He considered the Confederation to be paramount to any State Constitution. The last article of it authorizing alterations must consequently be so as well as the others, and every thing done in pursuance of the article must have the same high authority with the article.—Great confusion he was confident would result from a recurrence to the people. They would never agree on any thing. He could not see any ground to suppose that the people will do what their rulers will not. The rulers will either conform to, or influence the sense of the people.

Mr GHORUM was agst referring the plan to the Legislatures. 1. Men chosen by the people for the particular purpose, will discuss the subject more candidly than members of the Legislature who are to lose the power which is to be given up to the Genl Gov^t 2. Some of the Legislatures are composed of several branches. It will consequently be more difficult in these cases to get the plan through the Legislatures, than thro' a Convention. 3. in the States many of the ablest men are excluded from the Legislatures, but may be elected into a Convention. Among these may be ranked many of the Clergy who are generally friends to good Government. Their services were found to be valuable in the formation & establishment of the Constitution of Massach^{ts} 4. the Legislatures will be interrupted with a variety of little business, by artfully pressing which, designing men will find means to delay from year to year, if not to frustrate altogether, the national system. 5. If the last art: of the Confederation is to be pursued the unanimous concurrence of the States will be necessary. But will any one say, that all the States are to suffer themselves to be ruined, if Rho. Island should persist in her opposition to general measures. Some other States might also tread in her steps. The present advantage which N. York seems to be so much attached to, of taxing her neighbours by the regulation of her trade, makes it very probable, that she will be of the number. It would therefore deserve serious consideration whether provision ought not to be made for giving effect to the System without waiting for the unanimous concurrence of the States.

Mr ELSEWORTH. If there be any Legislatures who should find themselves incompetent to the ratification, he should be content to let them advise with their constitutents and pursue such a mode as w^d be competent. He thought more was to be expected from the Legislatures than from the people. . . . It was said by Col Mason 1. that the Legislatures have no authority in this case. 2. that their successors having equal authority could rescind their acts. As to the 2ᵈ point he could not admit it to be well founded. An Act to which the States by their Legislatures, make themselves parties, becomes a compact from which no one of the parties can recede of itself. As to the 1ˢᵗ point, he observed that a new sett of ideas seemed to have crept in since the articles of Confederation were established. Conventions of the people, or with power derived expressly from the people, were not then thought of. The Legislatures were considered as competent. Their ratification has been acquiesced in without complaint. To whom have Congˢ applied on subsequent occasions for further powers? To the Legislatures; not to the people. The fact is that we exist at present, and we need not enquire how, as a federal Society, united by a charter one article of which is that alterations therein may be made by the Legislative authority of the States. It has been said that if the confederation is to be observed, the States must *unanimously* concur in the proposed innovations. He would answer that if such were the urgency & necessity of our situation as to warrant a new compact among a part of the States, founded on the consent of the people; the same pleas would be equally valid in favor of a partial compact, founded on the consent of the Legislatures.

. . . .

Mʳ Govʳ Morris considered the inference of Mʳ Elseworth from the plea of necessity as applied to the establishment of a new System on yᵉ consent of the people of a part of the States, in favor of a like establishnᵗ on the consent of a part of the Legislatures as a non sequitur. If the Confederation is to be pursued no alteration can be made without the unanimous consent of the Legislatures: Legislative alterations not conformable to the federal compact, would clearly not be valid. The Judges would consider them as null & void. Whereas in case of an appeal to the people of the U. S., the supreme authority, the federal compact may be altered by a *majority of them;* in like manner as the Constitution of a particular State may be altered by a majority of the people of the State. The amendmᵗ moved by Mr Elseworth erroneously supposes that we are proceeding on the basis of the Confederation. This Convention is unknown to the Confederation.

Mr KING thought with Mr Elseworth that the Legislatures had a competent authority . . . . At the same time he preferred a reference to the authority of the people expressly delegated to Conventions, as the most certain means of obviating all disputes & doubts concerning the legitimacy of the new Constitution; as well as the most likely means of drawing forth the best men in the States to decide on it. . . .

Mr MADISON thought it clear that the Legislatures were incompetent to the proposed changes. These changes would make essential inroads on the State Constitutions, and it would be a novel & dangerous doctrine that a Legislature could change the constitution under which it held its existence. There might indeed be some Constitutions within the Union, which had given a power to the Legislature to concur in alterations of the federal Compact. But there were certainly some which had not; and in the case of these, a ratification must of necessity be obtained from the people. He considered the difference between a system founded on the Legislatures only, and one founded on the people, to be the true difference between a *league* or *treaty*, and a *Constitution*. The former in point of *moral obligation* might be as inviolable as the latter. In point of *political operation*, there were two important distinctions in favor of the latter. 1. A law violating a treaty ratified by a pre-existing law, might be respected by the Judges as a law, though an unwise or perfidious one. A law violating a constitution established by the people themselves, would be considered by the Judges as null & void. 2. The doctrine laid down by the law of Nations in the case of treaties is that a breach of any one article by any of the parties, frees the other parties from their engagements. In the case of a union of people under one Constitution, the nature of the pact has always been understood to exclude such an interpretation. Comparing the two modes in point of expediency he thought all the considerations which recommended this Convention in preference to Congress for pro-

posing the reform were in favor of State Conventions in preference to the Legislatures for examining and adopting it.

On question on Mᵣ Elseworth's motion to refer the plan to
the Legislatures of the States

N. H. no. Mas. no. Cᵗ ay. Pᵃ no. Del. ay. Mᵈ ay. Vᵃ no.
N. C. no. S. C. no. Geo. no. [Ayes, 3; noes, 8.]

Smallst bloc

.   .   .   .

Mᵣ GERRY moved that the proceedings of the Convention for
the establishment of a Natᵎ Govᵗ (except the part relating to the
Executive), be referred to a Committee to prepare & report a
Constitution conformable thereto.

Genᵎ PINKNEY reminded the Convention that if the Committee should fail to insert some security to the Southern States
agᵗ an emancipation of slaves, and taxes on exports, he shᵈ be
bound by duty to his State to vote agᵗ their Report—The
appᵗ of a Comᵉ as moved by Mᵣ Gerry. Agᵈ to nem. con.

Nothing re decision to have two senators /state

Tuesday, July 24. In Convention

After reconsideration, delegates voted seven to four to reinstate appointment of the executive magistrate by the national legislature. This necessitated opening anew the question of re-eligibility, consideration of which lasted until
Gerry declared, "We seem to be entirely at a loss on this
head." Among new methods of selection offered was one for
choosing electors from Congress by lot, which elicited the
response, "We ought to be governed by reason, not by
chance." The question was postponed.

On a ballot for a Committee to report a Constitution conformable to the Resolutions passed by the Convention, the
members chosen were

Mᵣ Rutlidge, Mᵣ Randolph, Mᵣ Ghorum, Mᵣ Elseworth,
Mᵣ Wilson—

Wednesday, July 25. In Convention

Clause relating to the Executive again under consideration.

. . . .

Mʳ MADISON. There are objections agˢᵗ every mode that has been, or perhaps can be proposed. The election must be made either by some existing authority under the Natⁱ or State Constitutions—or by some special authority derived from the people—or by the people themselves.—The two Existing authorities under the Natˡ Constitution wᵈ be the Legislative & Judiciary. The latter he presumed was out of the question. The former was in his Judgment liable to insuperable objections. . . . The existing authorities in the States are the Legislative, Executive & Judiciary. The appointment of the Natˡ Executive by the first, was objectionable in many points of view, some of which had been already mentioned. He would mention one which of itself would decide his opinion. The Legislatures of the States had betrayed a strong propensity to a variety of pernicious measures. One object of the Natˡ Legislʳᵉ was to controul this propensity. One object of the Natˡ Executive, so far as it would have a negative on the laws, was to controul the Natˡ Legislature, so far as it might be infected with a similar propensity. Refer the appointmᵗ of the Natˡ Executive to the State Legislatures, and this controuling purpose may be defeated. The Legislatures can & will act with some kind of regular plan, and will promote the appointmᵗ of a man who will not oppose himself to a favorite object. Should a majority of the Legislatures at the time of election have the same object, or different objects of the same kind, The Natˡ Executive would be rendered subservient to them.—An appointment by the State Executives, was liable among other objections to this insuperable one, that being standing bodies, they could & would be courted, and intrigued with by the Candidates, by their partizans, and by the Ministers of foreign powers. The State Judiciarys had not & he presumed wᵈ not be proposed as a proper source of appointment. The option before us then lay between an appointment by Electors chosen by the people—and an immediate appointment by the people. He thought the former mode free from many of the objections which had been urged agst it, and greatly preferable to an appointment by the Nat^l Legislature. As the electors would be chosen for the occasion, would meet at once, & proceed immediately to an appointment, there would be very little opportunity for cabal, or corruption. As a farther precaution, it might be required that they should meet at some place, distinct from the seat of Gov^t and even that no person within a certain distance of the place at the time sh^d be eligible. This Mode however had been rejected so recently & by so great a majority that it probably would not be proposed anew. The remaining mode was an election by the people or rather by the qualified part of them, at large: With all its imperfections he liked this best. . . .

.   .   .   .

Mr Govr Morris was agst a rotation in every case. It formed a political School, in wch we were always governed by the scholars, and not by the Masters. The evils to be guarded agst in this case are 1. the undue influence of the Legislature. 2. instability of Councils. 3. misconduct in office. To guard agst the first, we run into the second evil. We adopt a rotation which produces instability of Councils. To avoid Sylla we fall into Charibdis. A change of men is ever followed by a change of measures. . . . 2. the Rotation in office will not prevent intrigue and dependence on the Legislature. The man in office will look forward to the period at which he will become re-eligible. The distance of the period, the improbability of such a protraction of his life will be no obstacle. Such is the nature of man, formed by his benevolent author no doubt for wise ends, that altho' he knows his existence to be limited to a span, he takes his measures as if he were to live for ever. But taking another supposition, the inefficacy of the expedient will be manifest. If the magistrate does not look forward to his re-election to the Executive, he will be pretty sure to keep in view the opportunity of his going into the Legislature itself. He will have little objection then to an extension of power on a theatre where he expects to act a distinguished part; and will be very unwilling to take any step that may endanger his popularity with the Legislature, on his influence over which the figure he is to make will depend. 3. To avoid the third evil, impeachments will be essential, and hence an additional reason agst an election by the Legislature. He considered an election by the people as the best, by the Legislature as the worst, mode. . . .

Since a principal objection to popular election was the presumed disadvantage to smaller states arising from belief in the influence of a set of men (such as the Order of the Cincinnati) acting in concert in large states, a proposal arose (from Williamson and Morris) that each man vote for two persons, at least one of whom was to be from a state other than his own. Dickinson suggested that each state choose its best citizens, from whom the national legislature or electors appointed by it would select a chief executive.

Mr GERRY & Mr BUTLER moved to refer the resolution relating to the Executive (except the clause making it consist of a single person) to the Committee of detail.

Thursday, July 26. In Convention

Col. MASON. In every Stage of the Question relative to the Executive, the difficulty of the subject and the diversity of the opinions concerning it have appeared. Nor have any of the modes of constituting that department been satisfactory. 1. It has been proposed that the election should be made by the people at large; that is that an act which ought to be performed by those who know most of Eminent characters, & qualifications, should be performed by those who know least. 2. that the election should be made by the Legislatures of the States. 3. by the Executives of the States. Agst these modes also strong objections have been urged. 4. It has been proposed that the election should be made by Electors chosen by the people for that purpose. This was at first agreed to: But on further consideration has been rejected. 5. Since which, the mode of Mr Williamson, requiring each freeholder to vote for several candidates has been proposed. This seemed like many other propositions, to carry a plausible face, but on closer inspection is liable to fatal objections. A popular election in any form, as Mr Gerry has observed, would throw the appointment into the hands of the Cincinnati, a Society for the members of which he had a great respect; but which he never wished to have a preponderating influence in the Gov^t 6. Another expedient was proposed by Mr Dickenson, which is liable to so palpable & material an inconvenience that he had little doubt of its being by this time rejected by himself. It would exclude every man who happened not to be popular within his own State; tho' the causes of his local unpopularity might be of such a nature as to recommend him to the States at large. 7. Among other expedients, a lottery has been introduced. But as the tickets do not appear to be in much demand, it will probably, not be carried on, and nothing therefore need be said on that subject. After reviewing all these various modes, he was led to conclude, that an election by the Nat^l Legislature as originally proposed, was the best. If it was liable to objections, it was liable to fewer than any other. He conceived at the same time that a second election ought to be absolutely prohibited. Having for his primary object, for the polestar of his political conduct, the preservation of the rights of the people, he held it as an essential point, as the very palladium of Civil liberty, that the great officers of State, and particularly the Executive should at fixed periods return to that mass from which they were at first taken, in order that they may feel & respect those rights & interests, which are again to be personally valuable to them. He concluded with moving that the constitution of the Executive as reported by the Com^e of the whole be re-instated, viz. "that the Executive be appointed for seven years, & be ineligible a 2^d time"

Mr DAVIE seconded the motion

DOC^r FRANKLIN. It seems to have been imagined by some that the returning to the mass of the people was degrading the magistrate. This he thought was contrary to republican principles. In free Governments the rulers are the servants, and the people their superiors & sovereigns. For the former therefore to return among the latter was not to *degrade* but to *promote* them. And it would be imposing an unreasonable burden on them, to keep them always in a State of servitude, and not allow them to become again one of the Masters.

Question on Col Masons motion as above; which passed in the affirmative

N. H. ay. Mas^{ts} not on floor. C^t no. N. J. ay. P^a no. Del. no. M^d ay. V^a ay. N. C. ay. S. C. ay. Geo. ay. [Ayes, 7; noes, 3.]

Mr Govr Morris was now agst the whole paragraph. . . .

After adding the words "judiciary" and "executive" to a proposal that all members of the legislative branch possess landed property, delegates eliminated "landed" by a ten-to-one vote. Dickinson (who was of a different opinion on August 7) argued the impropriety of disabling any man of merit in a republic where merit was the "great title to public trust, honors and rewards." King affirmed that "landed" would exclude "the monied interest," and Madison stated that America was divided into landed, commercial, and manufacturing classes. The latter two, then proportionately small, would daily increase, he argued, and the interests of no one or two should be left to the care of a third.

The proceedings since Monday last were referred unanimously to the Com^e of detail, and the Convention then unanimously Adjourned till Monday, Augst 6. that the Com^e of detail might have time to prepare & report the Constitution.

The whole proceedings [9] as referred are as follow:—

June 20.	I. Resolved, That the Government of the United States ought to consist of a supreme legislative, judiciary, and executive.

[9] [Madison noted in the transcript that these twenty-three resolutions were copied from the official journal, where they are spread over the Convention proceedings from late June to late July. The dates in the margin show when the respective resolutions were adopted.]

June 21.

II. Resolved, That the legislature consist of two branches.

III. Resolved, That the members of the first branch of the legislature ought to be elected by the people of the

June 22.

several states for the term of two years; to be paid out of the publick treasury; to receive an adequate compensation for their serv-

June 23.

ices; to be of the age of twenty-five years at least; to be ineligible and incapable of holding any office under the authority of the United States (except those peculiarly belonging to the functions of the first branch) during the term of service of the first branch.

June 25.

IV. Resolved, That the members of the second branch of the legislature of the United States ought to be chosen by the individual legisla-

June 26.

tures; to be of the age of thirty years at least; to hold their offices for six years, one third to go out biennally; to receive a compensation for the devotion of their time to the publick service; to be ineligible to and incapable of holding any office, under the authority of the United States (except those peculiarly belonging to the functions of the second branch) during the term for which they are elected, and for one year thereafter.

V. Resolved, That each branch ought to possess the right of originating acts.

Postponed 27.
July 16.
July 17.

VI. Resolved, That the national legislature ought to possess the legislative rights vested in Congress by the confederation; and moreover, to legislate in all cases for the general interests of the union, and also in those to which the states are separately incompetent, or in

still no explicit taxing power

which the harmony of the United States may be interrupted by the exercise of individual legislation.

VII. RESOLVED, That the legislative acts of the United States, made by virtue and in pursuance of the articles of union, and all treaties made and ratified under the authority of the United States, shall be the supreme law of the respective states, as far as those acts or treaties shall relate to the said states, or their citizens and inhabitants; and that the judiciaries of the several states shall be bound thereby in their decisions, any thing in the respective laws of the individual states to the contrary, notwithstanding.

Not consts (NJ)

16.

VIII. RESOLVED, That in the original formation of the legislature of the United States, the first branch thereof shall consist of sixty-five members; of which number

New Hampshire shall send			three,
Massachusetts	.	.	eight,
Rhode Island	.	.	one,
Connecticut	.	.	five,
New York	.	.	six,
New Jersey	.	.	four,
Pennsylvania	.	.	eight,
Delaware	.	.	one,
Maryland	.	.	six,
Virginia	.	.	ten,
North Carolina	.	.	five,
South Carolina	.	.	five,
Georgia	.	.	three.

But as the present situation of the states may probably alter in the number of their inhabitants, the legislature of the United States shall be authorized, from time to time, to apportion the number of representatives; and in case any of the states shall hereafter be divided, or enlarged by addition of territory, or any two or more states united, or any new states created within the limits of the United States, the legislature of the United States shall possess authority to regulate the number of representatives, in any of the foregoing cases, upon the principle of their number of inhabitants according to the provisions hereafter mentioned, namely—Provided always, that representation ought to be proportioned according to direct taxation. And in order to ascertain the alteration in the direct taxation, which may be required from time to time by the changes in the relative circumstances of the states—

IX. RESOLVED, That a census be taken within six years from the first meeting of the legislature of the United States, and once within the term of every ten years afterwards, of all the inhabitants of the United States, in the manner and according to the ratio recommended by Congress in their resolution of April 18, 1783; and that the legislature of the United States shall proportion the direct taxation accordingly.

X. RESOLVED, That all bills for raising or appropriating money, and for fixing the salaries of the officers of the government of the United States, shall originate in the first branch of the legislature of the United States, and shall not be altered or amended by the second branch; and that no money shall be drawn from the publick treasury, but in pursuance of appropriations to be originated by the first branch.

XI. RESOLVED, That in the second branch of the legislature of the United States, each state shall have an equal vote.

July 26.

XII. RESOLVED, That a national executive be instituted, to consist of a single person; to be chosen by the national legislature, for the term of seven years; to be ineligible a second time; with power to carry into execution the national laws; to appoint to offices in cases not otherwise provided for; to be removable on impeachment, and conviction of malpractice or neglect of duty; to receive a fixed compensation for the devotion of his time to publick service; to be paid out of the publick treasury.

July 21.

XIII. RESOLVED, That the national executive shall have a right to negative any legislative act, which shall not be afterwards passed, unless by two third parts of each branch of the national legislature.

18.

July 21.

18.

XIV. RESOLVED, That a national judiciary be established, to consist of one supreme tribunal, the judges of which shall be appointed by the second branch of the national legislature; to hold their offices during good behaviour; to receive punctually, at stated times, a fixed compensation for their services, in which no diminution shall be made, so as to affect the persons actually in office at the time of such diminution.

XV. RESOLVED, That the national legislature be empowered to appoint inferior tribunals.

XVI. Resolved, That the jurisdiction of the national judiciary shall extend to cases arising under laws passed by the general legislature; and to such other questions as involve the national peace and harmony.

XVII. Resolved, That provision ought to be made for the admission of states lawfully arising within the limits of the United States, whether from a voluntary junction of government and territory, or otherwise, with the consent of a number of voices in the national legislature less than the whole.

XVIII. Resolved, That a republican form of government shall be guarantied to each state; and that each state shall be protected against foreign and domestick violence.

23.

XIX. Resolved, That provision ought to be made for the amendment of the articles of union, whensoever it shall seem necessary.

XX. Resolved, That the legislative, executive, and judiciary powers, within the several states, and of the national government, ought to be bound, by oath, to support the articles of union.

XXI. Resolved, That the amendments which shall be offered to the confederation by the convention ought, at a proper time or times after the approbation of Congress, to be submitted to an assembly or assemblies of representatives, recommended by the several legislatures, to be expressly chosen by the people to consider and decide thereon.

XXII. Resolved, That the representation in the second branch of the legisla-

ture of the United States [shall]
consist of two members from each
state, who shall vote per capita.

26.   XXIII. RESOLVED, That it be an instruction
to the committee, to whom were
referred the proceedings of the convention for the establishment of a
national government, to receive a
clause or clauses, requiring certain
qualifications of property and citizenship, in the United States, for
the executive, the judiciary, and
the members of both branches of
the legislature of the United
States.

With the above resolutions were referred the propositions
offered by Mr C. Pinckney on the 29th of May, & by Mr Patterson
on the 15th of June.

DETAILED EXAMINATION

Directed to report a Constitution, the five men of the
Committee [1] gained a unique opportunity to impress their
own interests and judgment on the proposals submitted to
them. Randolph prepared a draft which the Committee carefully studied and altered much. Wilson rewrote parts of Randolph's offering, made extracts from the New Jersey and
Pinckney plans, and then fused all into one complete whole.
The Committee thoroughly studied, slightly improved, and
submitted this document.

The August 6 Report drew on a variety of sources, among
which the Articles of Confederation were by far the most
important. The Committee dropped some of the national
supremacy features of the Virginia Plan, and substituted for
the Bedford proposal of general powers a grant of enumerated powers for Congress which often copied verbatim from
the Articles. Prohibitions on the states and interstate privileges also came from there. The New Jersey and Pinckney

1 [For the members of this Committee see July 24 (p. 246).]

plans also contributed, as did the state constitutions. Southern members added provisions concerning taxes on exports and importation of slaves, and navigation acts.

From August 6 through September 10 the Convention considered this Report in detail. Decisions of major importance alternate with controversy over the meaning of clauses and specific words.

Monday, August 6. In Convention

M⯑ John Francis Mercer from Maryland took his seat.

M⯑ RUTLIDGE delivered in the Report of the Committee of detail as follows: . . .

"We the people of the States of New Hampshire, Massachussetts, Rhode-Island and Providence Plantations, Connecticut, New-York, New-Jersey, Pennsylvania, Delaware, Maryland, Virginia, North-Carolina, South-Carolina, and Georgia, do ordain, declare, and establish the following Constitution for the Government of Ourselves and our Posterity.

ARTICLE I

The stile of the Government shall be, "The United States of America"

II

The Government shall consist of supreme legislative, executive; and judicial powers.

III

The legislative power shall be vested in a Congress, to consist of two separate and distinct bodies of men, a House of Representatives and a Senate; each of which shall in all cases have a negative on the other. The Legislature shall meet on the first Monday in December every year.

IV

Sect. 1. The members of the House of Representatives shall be chosen every second year, by the people of the several States comprehended within this Union. The qualifications of the electors shall be the same, from time to time, as those of the electors in the several States, of the most numerous branch of their own legislatures.

Sect. 2. Every member of the House of Representatives shall be of the age of twenty five years at least; shall have been a citizen in the United States for at least three years before his election; and shall be, at the time of his election, a resident of the State in which he shall be chosen.

Sect. 3. The House of Representatives shall, at its first formation, and until the number of citizens and inhabitants shall be taken in the manner herein after described, consist of sixty five Members, of whom three shall be chosen in New-Hampshire, eight in Massachusetts, one in Rhode-Island and Providence Plantations, five in Connecticut, six in New-York, four in New-Jersey, eight in Pennsylvania, one in Delaware, six in Maryland, ten in Virginia, five in North-Carolina, five in South-Carolina, and three in Georgia.

Sect. 4. As the proportions of numbers in different States will alter from time to time; as some of the States may hereafter be divided; as others may be enlarged by addition of territory; as two or more States may be united; as new States will be erected within the limits of the United States, the Legislature shall, in each of these cases, regulate the number of representatives by the number of inhabitants, according to the provisions herein after made, at the rate of one for every forty thousand.

Sect. 5. All bills for raising or appropriating money, and for fixing the salaries of the officers of Government, shall originate in the House of Representatives, and shall not be altered or amended by the Senate. No money shall be drawn from the Public Treasury, but in pursuance of appropriations that shall originate in the House of Representatives.

Sect. 6. The House of Representatives shall have the sole power of impeachment. It shall choose its Speaker and other officers.

Sect. 7. Vacancies in the House of Representatives shall be supplied by writs of election from the executive authority of the State in the representation from which it shall happen.

V

Sect. 1. The Senate of the United States shall be chosen by the Legislatures of the several States. Each Legislature shall chuse two members. Vacancies may be supplied by the Executive until the next meeting of the Legislature. Each member shall have one vote.

Sect. 2. The Senators shall be chosen for six years; but immediately after the first election they shall be divided, by lot, into three classes, as nearly as may be, numbered one, two and three. The seats of the members of the first class shall be vacated at the expiration of the second year, of the second class at the expiration of the fourth year, of the third class at the expiration of the sixth year, so that a third part of the members may be chosen every second year.

Sect. 3. Every member of the Senate shall be of the age of thirty years at least; shall have been a citizen in the United States for at least four years before his election; and shall be, at the time of his election, a resident of the State for which he shall be chosen.

Sect. 4. The Senate shall chuse its own President and other officers.

VI

Sect. 1. The times and places and manner of holding the elections of the members of each House shall be prescribed by the Legislature of each State; but their provisions concerning them may, at any time be altered by the Legislature of the United States.

Sect. 2. The Legislature of the United States shall have authority to establish such uniform qualifications of the members of each House, with regard to property, as to the said Legislature shall seem expedient.

Sect. 3. In each House a majority of the members shall constitute a quorum to do business; but a smaller number may adjourn from day to day.

Sect. 4. Each House shall be the judge of the elections, returns and qualifications of its own members.

Sect. 5. Freedom of speech and debate in the Legislature shall not be impeached or questioned in any Court or place out of the Legislature; and the members of each House shall, in all cases, except treason felony and breach of the peace, be privileged from arrest during their attendance at Congress, and in going to and returning from it.

Sect. 6. Each House may determine the rules of its proceedings; may punish its members for disorderly behaviour; and may expel a member.

Sect. 7. The House of Representatives, and the Senate, when it shall be acting in a legislative capacity, shall keep a journal of their proceedings, and shall, from time to time, publish them: and the yeas and nays of the members of each House, on any question, shall at the desire of one-fifth part of the members present, be entered on the journal.

Sect. 8. Neither House, without the consent of the other, shall adjourn for more than three days, nor to any other place than that at which the two Houses are sitting. But this regulation shall not extend to the Senate, when it shall exercise the powers mentioned in the   article.

Sect. 9. The members of each House shall be ineligible to, and incapable of holding any office under the authority of the United States, during the time for which they shall respectively be elected: and the members of the Senate shall be ineligible to, and incapable of holding any such office for one year afterwards.

Sect. 10. The members of each House shall receive a compensation for their services, to be ascertained and paid by the State, in which they shall be chosen.

Sect. 11. The enacting stile of the laws of the United States shall be. "Be it enacted by the Senate and Representatives in Congress assembled." [2]

2 (Section 11 is copied in the transcript as originally printed. In Section 11 of Article VI, as it was printed, it appeared: "The enacting stile of the laws of the United States shall be. 'Be it enacted, and it is hereby enacted by the House of Representatives, and by the Senate of the United States, in Congress assembled.' " which Madison altered to read: "The enacting stile of the law of the United States shall be. 'Be it enacted by the Senate & representatives in Congress assembled.' " The printed copy among the Madison papers is a duplicate of the copy filed by General Washington with the papers of the Constitution, and Section 11 is there given as actually printed. Madison accurately transcribed the Report for his notes and it is this copy which is used in the text. [This note integrates two notes contained in Gaillard Hunt and James Brown Scott, eds., *The Debates in the Federal Convention of 1787*, Washington, 1920.])

Sect. 12. Each House shall possess the right of originating bills, except in the cases beforementioned.

Sect. 13. Every bill, which shall have passed the House of Representatives and the Senate, shall, before it become a law, be presented to the President of the United States for his revision: if, upon such revision, he approve of it, he shall signify his approbation by signing it: But if, upon such revision, it shall appear to him improper for being passed into a law, he shall return it, together with his objections against it, to that House in which it shall have originated, who shall enter the objections at large on their journal and proceed to reconsider the bill. But if after such reconsideration, two thirds of that House shall, notwithstanding the objections of the President, agree to pass it, it shall together with his objections, be sent to the other House, by which it shall likewise be reconsidered, and if approved by two thirds of the other House also, it shall become a law. But in all such cases, the votes of both Houses shall be determined by yeas and nays; and the names of the persons voting for or against the bill shall be entered on the journal of each House respectively. If any bill shall not be returned by the President within seven days after it shall have been presented to him, it shall be a law, unless the legislature, by their adjournment, prevent its return; in which case it shall not be a law.

VII

Sect. 1. The Legislature of the United States shall have the power to lay and collect taxes, duties, imposts and excises;

To regulate commerce with foreign nations, and among the several States;

To establish an uniform rule of naturalization throughout the United States;

To coin money;

To regulate the value of foreign coin;

To fix the standard of weights and measures;

To establish Post-offices;

To borrow money, and emit bills on the credit of the United States;

To appoint a Treasurer by ballot;

To constitute tribunals inferior to the Supreme Court;

To make rules concerning captures on land and water;

To declare the law and punishment of piracies and felonies committed on the high seas, and the punishment of counterfeiting the coin of the United States, and of offenses against the law of nations;

To subdue a rebellion in any State, on the application of its legislature;

To make war;

To raise armies;

To build and equip fleets;

To call forth the aid of the militia, in order to execute the laws of the Union, enforce treaties, suppress insurrections, and repel invasions;

And to make all laws that shall be necessary and proper for carrying into execution the foregoing powers, and all other powers vested, by this Constitution, in the government of the United States, or in any department or officer thereof;

Sect. 2. Treason against the United States shall consist only in levying war against the United States, or any of them; and in adhering to the enemies of the United States, or any of them. The Legislature of the United States shall have power to declare the punishment of treason. No person shall be convicted of treason, unless on the testimony of two witnesses. No attainder of treason shall work corruption of blood, nor forfeiture, except during the life of the person attainted.

Sect. 3. The proportions of direct taxation shall be regulated by the whole number of white and other free citizens and inhabitants of every age, sex and condition, including those bound to servitude for a term of years, and three fifths of all other persons not comprehended in the foregoing description, (except Indians not paying taxes) which number shall, within six years after the first meeting of the Legislature, and within the term of every ten years afterwards, be taken in such manner as the said Legislature shall direct.

Sect. 4. No tax or duty shall be laid by the Legislature on articles exported from any State; nor on the migration or importation of such persons as the several States shall think proper to admit; nor shall such migration or importation be prohibited.

Sect. 5. No capitation tax shall be laid, unless in proportion to the Census hereinbefore directed to be taken.

Sect. 6. No navigation act shall be passed without the assent of two thirds of the members present in the each House.

Sect. 7. The United States shall not grant any title of Nobility.

VIII

The Acts of the Legislature of the United States made in pursuance of this Constitution, and all treaties made under the authority of the United States shall be the supreme law of the several States, and of their citizens and inhabitants; and the judges in the several States shall be bound thereby in their decisions; any thing in the Constitutions or laws of the several States to the contrary notwithstanding.

IX

Sect. 1. The Senate of the United States shall have power to make treaties, and to appoint Ambassadors, and Judges of the Supreme Court.

Sect. 2. In all disputes and controversies now subsisting, or that may hereafter subsist between two or more States, respecting jurisdiction or territory, the Senate shall possess the following powers. Whenever the Legislature, or the Executive authority, or lawful agent of any State, in controversy with another, shall by memorial to the Senate, state the matter in question, and apply for a hearing; notice of such memorial and application shall be given by order of the Senate, to the Legislature or the Executive authority of the other State in Controversy. The Senate shall also assign a day for the appearance of the parties, by their agents, before the House. The Agents shall be directed to appoint, by joint consent, commissioners or judges to constitute a Court for hearing and determining the matter in question. But if the Agents cannot agree, the Senate shall name three persons out of each of the several States; and from the list of such persons each party shall alternately strike out one, until the number shall be reduced to thirteen; and from that number not less than seven nor more than nine names, as the Senate shall direct, shall in their presence, be drawn out by lot; and the persons whose names shall be so drawn, or any five of them shall be commissioners or Judges to hear and finally determine the controversy; provided a majority of the Judges, who shall hear the cause, agree in the determination. If either party shall neglect to attend at the day assigned, without shewing sufficient reasons for not attending, or being present shall refuse to strike, the Senate shall proceed to nominate three persons out of each State, and the Clerk of the Senate shall strike in behalf of the party absent or refusing. If any of the parties shall refuse to submit to the authority of such Court; or shall not appear to prosecute or defend their claim or cause, the Court shall nevertheless proceed to pronounce judgment. The judgment shall be final and conclusive. The proceedings shall be transmitted to the President of the Senate, and shall be lodged among the public records, for the security of the parties concerned. Every Commissioner shall, before he sit in judgment, take an oath, to be administred by one of the Judges of the Supreme or Superior Court of the State where the cause shall be tried, "well and truly to hear and determine the matter in question according to the best of his judgment, without favor, affection, or hope of reward."

Sect. 3. All controversies concerning lands claimed under different grants of two or more States, whose jurisdictions, as they respect such lands shall have been decided or adjusted subsequent to such grants, or any of them, shall, on application to the Senate, be finally determined, as near as may be, in the same manner as is before prescribed for deciding controversies between different States.

X

Sect. 1. The Executive Power of the United States shall be vested in a single person. His stile shall be, "The President of the United States of America;" and his title shall be, "His Excellency." He shall be elected by ballot by the Legislature. He shall hold his office during the term of seven years; but shall not be elected a second time.

Sect. 2. He shall, from time to time, give information to the Legislature, of the state of the Union: he may recommend to their consideration such measures as he shall judge necessary, and expedient: he may convene them on extraordinary occasions. In case of disagreement between the two Houses, with regard to the time of adjournment, he may adjourn them to such time as he thinks proper: he shall take care that the laws of the United States be duly and faithfully executed: he shall commission all the officers of the United States; and shall appoint officers in all cases not otherwise provided for by this Constitution. He shall receive Ambassadors, and may correspond with the supreme Executives of the several States. He shall have power to grant reprieves and pardons; but his pardon shall not be pleadable in bar of an impeachment. He shall be commander in chief of the Army and Navy of the United States, and of the Militia of the several States. He shall, at stated times, receive for his services, a compensation, which shall neither be increased nor diminished during his continuance in office. Before he shall enter on the duties of his department, he shall take the following oath or affirmation, "I ———— solemnly swear, (or affirm) that I will faithfully execute the office of President of the United States of America." He shall be removed from his office on impeachment by the House of Representatives, and conviction in the supreme Court, of treason, bribery, or corruption. In case of his removal as aforesaid, death, resignation, or disability to discharge the powers and duties of his office, the President of the Senate shall exercise those powers and duties, until another President of the United States be chosen, or until the disability of the President be removed.

XI

Sect. 1. The Judicial Power of the United States shall be vested in one Supreme Court, and in such inferior Courts as shall, when necessary, from time to time, be constituted by the Legislature of the United States.

Sect. 2. The Judges of the Supreme Court, and of the Inferior Courts, shall hold their offices during good behaviour. They shall, at stated times, receive for their services, a compensation, which shall not be diminished during their continuance in office.

Sect. 3. The Jurisdiction of the Supreme Court shall extend to all cases arising under laws passed by the Legislature of the United States; to all cases affecting Ambassadors, other Public Ministers and Consuls; to the trial of impeachments of officers of the United States; to all cases of Admiralty and maritime jurisdiction; to controversies between two or more States, (except such as shall regard Territory or Jurisdiction) between a State and Citizens of another State, between Citizens of different States, and between a State or the Citizens thereof and foreign States, citizens or subjects. In cases of impeachment, cases affecting Ambassadors, other Public Ministers and Consuls, and those in which a State shall be party, this jurisdiction shall be original. In all the other cases beforementioned, it shall be appellate, with such exceptions and under such regulations as the Legislature shall make. The Legislature may assign any part of the jurisdiction abovementioned (except the trial of the President of the United States) in the manner, and under the limitations which it shall think proper, to such Inferior Courts, as it shall constitute from time to time.

Sect. 4. The trial of all criminal offences (except in cases of impeachments) shall be in the State where they shall be committed; and shall be by Jury.

Sect. 5. Judgment, in cases of Impeachment, shall not extend further than to removal from office, and disqualification to hold and enjoy any office of honour, trust or profit, under the United States. But the party convicted shall, nevertheless be liable and subject to indictment, trial, judgment and punishment according to law.

XII

No State shall coin money; nor grant letters of marque and reprisal; nor enter into any Treaty, alliance, or confederation; nor grant any title of Nobility.

XIII

No State, without the consent of the Legislature of the United States, shall emit bills of credit, or make any thing but specie a tender in payment of debts; nor lay imposts or duties on imports; nor keep troops or ships of war in time of peace; nor enter into any agreement or compact with another State, or with any foreign power; nor engage in any war, unless it shall be actually invaded by enemies, or the danger of invasion be so imminent, as not to admit of delay, until the Legislature of the United States can be consulted.

XIV

The Citizens of each State shall be entitled to all privileges and immunities of citizens in the several States.

XV

Any person charged with treason, felony or high misdemeanor in any State, who shall flee from justice, and shall be found in any other State, shall, on demand of the Executive power of the State from which he fled, be delivered up and removed to the State having jurisdiction of the offence.

XVI

Full faith shall be given in each State to the acts of the Legislatures, and to the records and judicial proceedings of the Courts and magistrates of every other State.

XVII

New States lawfully constituted or established within the limits of the United States may be admitted, by the Legislature, into this Government; but to such admission the consent of two thirds of the members present in each House shall be necessary. If a new State shall arise within the limits of any of the present States, the consent of the Legislatures of such States shall be also necessary to its admission. If the admission be consented to, the new States shall be admitted on the same terms with the original States. But the Legislature may make conditions with the new States, concerning the public debt which shall be then subsisting.

XVIII

The United States shall guaranty to each State a Republican form of Government; and shall protect each State against foreign invasions, and, on the application of its Legislature, against domestic violence.

XIX

On the application of the Legislatures of two thirds of the States in the Union, for an amendment of this Constitution, the Legislature of the United States shall call a Convention for that purpose.

XX

The members of the Legislatures, and the Executive and Judicial officers of the United States, and of the several States, shall be bound by oath to support this Constitution.

XXI

The ratifications of the Conventions of   States shall be
sufficient for organizing this Constitution.

XXII

This Constitution shall be laid before the United States in
Congress assembled, for their approbation; and it is the opinion
of this Convention, that it should be afterwards submitted to a
Convention chosen [in each State], under the recommendation
of its legislature, in order to receive the ratification of such Convention.

XXIII

To introduce this government, it is the opinion of this Convention, that each assenting Convention should notify its assent
and ratification to the United States in Congress assembled;
that Congress, after receiving the assent and ratification of the
Conventions of   States, should appoint and publish a day,
as early as may be, and appoint a place for commencing proceedings under this Constitution; that after such publication, the
Legislatures of the several States should elect members of the
Senate, and direct the election of members of the House of
Representatives; and that the members of the Legislature should
meet at the time and place assigned by Congress, and should, as
soon as may be, after their meeting, choose the President of the
United States, and proceed to execute this Constitution."

Tuesday, August 7. In Convention

The Report of the Committee of detail being taken up,

.   .   .   .

"Art IV. Sect. 1.[3] taken up."

Mr Govr Morris moved to strike out the last member of the
section beginning with the words "qualifications of Electors,"

3 [Relating to selection of representatives. See pp. 258-9.]

in order that some other provision might be substituted which w^d restrain the right of suffrage to freeholders.

. . . .

Mr WILSON. This part of the Report was well considered by the Committee, and he did not think it could be changed for the better. It was difficult to form any uniform rule of qualifications for all the States. Unnecessary innovations he thought too should be avoided. It would be very hard & disagreeable for the same persons at the same time, to vote for representatives in the State Legislature and to be excluded from a vote for those in the Nat^l Legislature.

Mr Govr MORRIS. Such a hardship would be neither great nor novel. The people are accustomed to it and not dissatisfied with it, in several of the States. In some the qualifications are different for the choice of the Govr & Representatives; In others for different Houses of the Legislature. Another objection ag^st the clause as it stands is that it makes the qualifications of the Nat^l Legislature depend on the will of the States, which he thought not proper.

Mr ELSEWORTH. thought the qualifications of the electors stood on the most proper footing. The right of suffrage was a tender point, and strongly guarded by most of the State Constitutions. The people will not readily subscribe to the Nat^l Constitution if it should subject them to be disfranchised. The States are the best Judges of the circumstances & temper of their own people.

COL. MASON. The force of habit is certainly not attended to by those gentlemen who wish for innovations on this point. Eight or nine States have extended the right of suffrage beyond the freeholders, what will the people there say, if they should be disfranchised. A power to alter the qualifications would be a dangerous power in the hands of the Legislature.

Mr BUTLER. There is no right of which the people are more jealous than that of suffrage. . . .

Mr DICKINSON. had a very different idea of the tendency of vesting the right of suffrage in the freeholders of the Country. He considered them as the best guardians of liberty; And the restriction of the right to them as a necessary defence agst the dangerous influence of those multitudes without property & without principle with which our Country like all others, will in time abound. As to the unpopularity of the innovation it was in his opinion chemirical. The great mass of our Citizens is composed at this time of freeholders, and will be pleased with it.

Mr ELSEWORTH. How shall the freehold be defined? Ought not every man who pays a tax, to vote for the representative who is to levy & dispose of his money? Shall the wealthy merchants & manufacturers, who will bear a full share of the public burdens be not allowed a voice in the imposition of them—taxation & representation ought to go together.

Mr Govr MORRIS. He had long learned not to be the dupe of words. The sound of Aristocracy therefore had no effect on him. It was the thing, not the name, to which he was opposed, and one of his principal objections to the Constitution as it is now before us, is that it threatens this Country with an Aristocracy. The aristocracy will grow out of the House of Representatives. Give the votes to people who have no property, and they will sell them to the rich who will be able to buy them. We should not confine our attention to the present moment. The time is not distant when this Country will abound with mechanics & manufacturers who will receive their bread from their employers. Will such men be the secure & faithful Guardians of liberty? Will they be the impregnable barrier agst aristocracy?— He was as little duped by the association of the words "taxation & Representation." The man who does not give his vote freely is not represented. It is the man who dictates the vote. Children do not vote . . . because they have no will of their own. The ignorant & the dependent can be as little trusted with the public interest. He did not conceive the difficulty of defining "freeholders" to be insuperable. Still less that the restriction could be unpopular. 9/10 of the people are at present freeholders and these will certainly be pleased with it. As to Merch^{ts} &c. if they have wealth & value the right they can acquire it. If not they don't deserve it.

Col. MASON. We all feel too strongly the remains of antient

prejudices, and view things too much through a British medium. A Freehold is the qualification in England, & hence it is imagined to be the only proper one. The true idea in his opinion was that every man having evidence of attachment to & permanent common interest with the Society ought to share in all its rights & privileges. Was this qualification restrained to freeholders? Does no other kind of property but land evidence a common interest in the proprietor? does nothing besides property mark a permanent attachment. Ought the merchant, the monied man, the parent of a number of children whose fortunes are to be pursued in his own Country, to be viewed as suspicious characters, and unworthy to be trusted with the common rights of their fellow Citizens

Mᴿ MADISON. the right of suffrage is certainly one of the fundamental articles of republican Government, and ought not to be left to be regulated by the Legislature. A gradual abridgment of this right has been the mode in which Aristocracies have been built on the ruins of popular forms. Whether the Constitutional qualification ought to be a freehold, would with him depend much on the probable reception such a change would meet with in States where the right was now exercised by every description of people. In several of the States a freehold was now the qualification. Viewing the subject in its merits alone, the freeholders of the Country would be the safest despositories of Republican liberty. In future times a great majority of the people will not only be without landed, but any other sort of, property. These will either combine under the influence of their common situation; in which case, the rights of property & the public liberty, will not be secure in their hands: or which is more probable, they will become the tools of opulence & ambition, in which case there will be equal danger on another side. . . .

Docᴿ FRANKLIN. It is of great consequence that we shᵈ not depress the virtue & public spirit of our common people; of which they displayed a great deal during the war, and which contributed principally to the favorable issue of it. He related the honorable refusal of the American seamen who were carried in great numbers into the British Prisons during the war, to redeem themselves from misery or to seek their fortunes, by entering on board the Ships of the Enemies to their Country; contrasting their patriotism with a contemporary instance in which the British seamen made prisoners by the Americans, readily entered on the ships of the latter on being promised a share of the prizes that might be made out of their own Country. This proceeded he said from the different manner in which the common people were treated in America & G. Britain. He did not think that the elected had any right in any case to narrow the privileges of the electors. . . . He was persuaded also that such a restriction as was proposed would give great uneasiness in the populous States. The sons of a substantial farmer, not being themselves freeholders, would not be pleased at being disfranchised, and there are a great many persons of that description.

.   .   .   .

On the question for striking out as moved by Mr Govr Morris, from the word "qualifications" to the end of the III article.

N. H. no. Mas. no. C^t no. P^a no. Del. ay. M^d div^d V^a no. N. C. no. S. C. no. Geo. not pres^t [Ayes, 1; noes, 7; divided, 1.]

Article IV, Section 1, after brief discussion on the following day, passed unanimously.

Thursday, August 9. In Convention

Art: V. Sect. 3.[4] taken up.

Mr Govr Morris moved to insert 14 instead of 4 years citizenship as a qualification for Senators: urging the danger of admitting strangers into our public Councils. . . .

Mr Elseworth. was opposed to the motion as discouraging meritorious aliens from emigrating to this Country.

Col. Mason highly approved of the policy of the motion. Were it not that many not natives of this Country had acquired

[4] [Relating to qualifications for senators. See p. 260.]

great merit [5] during the revolution, he should be for restraining the eligibility into the Senate, to natives.

Mr PINKNEY. As the Senate is to have the power of making treaties & managing our foreign affairs, there is peculiar danger and impropriety in opening its door to those who have foreign attachments. . . .

Mr MADISON, was not averse to some restrictions on this subject; but could never agree to the proposed amendment. He thought any restriction however in the *Constitution* unnecessary, and improper. . . . Should the proposed Constitution have the intended effect of giving stability & reputation to our Gov^{ts} great numbers of respectable Europeans: men who love liberty and wish to partake its blessings, will be ready to transfer their fortunes hither. All such would feel the mortification of being marked with suspicious incapacitations though they s^d not covet the public honors. . . .

Mr BUTLER was decidedly opposed to the admission of foreigners without a long residence in the Country. They bring with them, not only attachments to other Countries; but ideas of Gov^t so distinct from ours that in every point of view they are dangerous. . . .

Doc^r FRANKLIN was not agst a reasonable time, but should be very sorry to see any thing like illiberality inserted in the Constitution. The people in Europe are friendly to this Country. Even in the Country with which we have been lately at war, we have now & had during the war, a great many friends not only among the people at large but in both houses of Parliament. In every other Country in Europe all the people are our friends. We found in the course of the Revolution that many strangers served us faithfully—and that many natives took part agst their Country. When foreigners after looking about for some other Country in which they can obtain more happiness, give a preference to ours it is a proof of attachment which ought to excite our confidence & affection.

Mr RANDOLPH . . . reminded the Convention of the language held by our patriots during the Revolution, and the principles

5 (The word "credit" is substituted in the transcript for "merit.")

laid down in all our American Constitutions. Many foreigners may have fixed their fortunes among us under the faith of these invitations. All persons under this description, with all others who would be affected by such a regulation, would enlist themselves under the banners of hostility to the proposed System. He would go as far as seven years, but no farther.

Mʳ WILSON said he rose with feelings which were perhaps peculiar; mentioning the circumstance of his not being a native, and the possibility, if the ideas of some gentlemen should be pursued, of his being incapacitated from holding a place under the very Constitution, which he had shared in the trust of making. He remarked the illiberal complexion which the motion would give to the System, & the effect which a good system would have in inviting meritorious foreigners among us, and the discouragement & mortification they must feel from the degrading discrimination, now proposed. He had himself experienced this mortification. On his removal into Maryland, he found himself, from defect of residence, under certain legal incapacities which never ceased to produce chagrin, though he assuredly did not desire & would not have accepted the offices to which they related. To be appointed to a place may be matter of indifference. To be incapable of being appointed, is a circumstance grating and mortifying.

Mʳ GOVʳ MORRIS. The lesson we are taught is that we should be governed as much by our reason, and as little by our feelings as possible. What is the language of Reason on this subject? That we should not be polite at the expence of prudence. There was a moderation in all things. . . . He ran over the privileges which emigrants would enjoy among us, though they should be deprived of that of being eligible to the great offices of Government; observing that they exceeded the privileges allowed to foreigners in any part of the world; and that as every Society from a great nation down to a club had the right of declaring the conditions on which new members should be admitted, there could be no room for complaint. As to those philosophical gentlemen, those Citizens of the World as they call themselves, He owned he did not wish to see any of them in our public

Councils. He would not trust them. The men who can shake off their attachments to their own Country can never love any other. These attachments are the wholesome prejudices which uphold all Governments . . . .

The Convention rejected fourteen, thirteen, and ten years before favoring a nine-year term of citizenship as a qualification for senators. On August 8 they had raised the requirement for representatives from three to seven years. Reconsidering these provisions on August 13, Wilson and Hamilton (both foreign born) and Madison tried to secure a lowering of these periods. Madison pleaded for the national government to maintain the liberal faith pledged by states to foreigners during the Revolution, but in vain.

Friday, August 10. In Convention

Art. VI. Sect. 2.[6] taken up.

Mʳ PINKNEY. The Committee as he had conceived were instructed to report the proper qualifications of property for the members of the Natˡ Legislature; instead of which they have referred the task to the Natˡ Legislature itself. Should it be left on this footing, the first Legislature will meet without any particular qualifications of property: and if it should happen to consist of rich men they might fix such qualifications as may be too favorable to the rich; if of poor men, an opposite extreme might be run into. He was opposed to the establishment of an undue aristocratic influence in the Constitution but he thought it essential that the members of the Legislature, the Executive, and the Judges, should be possessed of competent property to make them independent & respectable. ... Were he to fix the quantum of property which should be required, he should not think of less than one hundred thousand dollars for the President, half of that sum for each of the Judges, and in

[6] [Relating to property qualifications for members of each House. See p. 260.]

like proportion for the members of the Nat! Legislature. He would however leave the sums blank. . . .

Mr RUTLIDGE seconded the motion; observing that the Committee . . . could not agree on any among themselves, being embarrassed by the danger on one side of displeasing the people by making them high, and on the other of rendering them nugatory by making them low.

Mr ELSEWORTH. The different circumstances of different parts of the U. S. and the probable difference between the present and future circumstances of the whole, render it improper to have either *uniform or fixed* qualifications. . . . [I]t was better to leave this matter to the Legislative discretion than to attempt a provision for it in the Constitution.

Doct^r FRANKLIN expressed his dislike of every thing that tended to debase the spirit of the common people. If honesty was often the companion of wealth, and if poverty was exposed to peculiar temptation, it was not less true that the possession of property increased the desire of more property. Some of the greatest rogues he was ever acquainted with, were the richest rogues. . . . This Constitution will be much read and attended to in Europe, and if it should betray a great partiality to the rich, will not only hurt us in the esteem of the most liberal and enlightened men there, but discourage the common people from removing into this Country.

. . . .

Mr MADISON was opposed to the Section as vesting an improper & dangerous power in the Legislature. The qualifications of electors and elected were fundamental articles in a Republican Gov^t and ought to be fixed by the Constitution. If the Legislature could regulate those of either, it can by degrees subvert the Constitution. A Republic may be converted into an aristocracy or oligarchy as well by limiting the number capable of being elected, as the number authorised to elect. . . .

. . . .

Mr Govr MORRIS moved to strike out "with regard to property" in order to leave the Legislature entirely at large.

Mʳ WILLIAMSON. This could surely never be admitted. Should a majority of the Legislature be composed of any particular description of men, of lawyers for example, which is no improbable supposition, the future elections might be secured to their own body.

. . . .

Question on the motion to strike out with regard to property
N. H. no. Mas. no. Cᵗ ay. N. J. ay. Pᵃ ay. Del. no. Mᵈ no. Vᵃ no. N. C. no. S. C. no. Geo. ay. [Ayes, 4; noes, 7.]

. . . .

On the question for agreeing to Art. VI. Sect. 2ᵈ
N. H. ay. Mas. ay. Cᵗ no. N. J. no. Pᵃ no. Mᵈ no. Vᵃ no. N. C. no. S. C. no. Geo. ay. [Ayes, 3; noes, 7.]

NAVIGATION ACTS AND SLAVERY

The important compromise dealing with navigation acts and importation of slaves must be followed from August 21 through August 29. The basis of this dispute lay in contradictory sectional attitudes which the report of the Committee of Detail challenged. North and South differed on the requirement (Art. VII, Sect. 4) that navigation acts receive a two thirds majority, since the former wanted to build up shipping and the latter desired low rates for moving staples. Congress at this time was empowered to tax imports (VII, 1) but not exports (VII, 4). It could not, however, interfere with the importation of slaves (VII, 4). Besides many humanitarian objections to the latter, the slave-breeding states of the upper South saw in this restriction loss of a market in the deep South. Thus beginning on August 21, just after an attempt to make it easier for Congress to tax exports passed negatively, a Marylander and a Virginian raised the question of slavery. Hoping for accommodation on control of navigation acts, Northern delegates threatened the South to the point where disruption was feared. Morris candidly saw the ingredients of a bargain, which emerged from the Grand Committee on August 29. Nevertheless Charles Pinckney, Martin, and Mason tried to prevent the compromise, which passed on August 29.

Tuesday, August 21. In Convention

Mr L. MARTIN, proposed to vary the Sect: 4. art VII. so as to allow a prohibition or tax on the importation of slaves. 1. as five slaves are to be counted as 3 free men in the apportionment of Representatives, such a clause w^d leave an encouragement to this trafic. 2. slaves weakened one part of the Union which the other parts were bound to protect: the privilege of importing them was therefore unreasonable. 3. it was inconsistent with the principles of the revolution and dishonorable to the American character to have such a feature in the Constitution.

Mr RUTLIDGE did not see how the importation of slaves could be encouraged by this Section. He was not apprehensive of insurrections and would readily exempt the other States from the obligation to protect the Southern against them.—Religion & humanity had nothing to do with this question. Interest alone is the governing principle with nations. The true question at present is whether the Southⁿ States shall or shall not be parties to the Union. If the Northern States consult their interest, they will not oppose the increase of Slaves which will increase the commodities of which they will become the carriers.

Wednesday, August 22. In Convention

Art VII sect 4. resumed. Mr SHERMAN was for leaving the clause as it stands. He disapproved of the slave trade; yet as the States were now possessed of the right to import slaves, as the public good did not require it to be taken from them, & as it was expedient to have as few objections as possible to the proposed scheme of Government, he thought it best to leave the matter as we find it. He observed that the abolition of Slavery seemed to be going on in the U. S. & that the good sense of the several States would probably by degrees compleat it. He urged on the Convention the necessity of despatching its business.

Col. MASON. . . . The present question concerns not the importing States alone but the whole Union. The evil of having slaves was experienced during the late war. . . . Maryland & Virginia he said had already prohibited the importation of slaves expressly. N. Carolina had done the same in substance. All this would be in vain if S. Carolina & Georgia be at liberty to import. The Western people are already calling out for slaves for their new lands, and will fill that Country with slaves if they can be got thro' S. Carolina & Georgia. Slavery discourages arts & manufactures. The poor despise labor when performed by slaves. They prevent the immigration of Whites, who really enrich & strengthen a Country. They produce the most pernicious effect on manners. Every master of slaves is born a petty tyrant. They bring the judgment of heaven on a Country. As nations can not be rewarded or punished in the next world they must be in this. By an inevitable chain of causes & effects providence punishes national sins, by national calamities. He lamented that some of our Eastern brethren had from a lust of gain embarked in this nefarious traffic. As to the States being in possession of the Right to import, this was the case with many other rights, now to be properly given up. He held it essential in every point of view that the Genl Govt should have power to prevent the increase of slavery.

Mr ELSWORTH. As he had never owned a slave could not judge of the effects of slavery on character: He said however that if it was to be considered in a moral light we ought to go farther and free those already in the Country.—As slaves also multiply so fast in Virginia & Maryland that it is cheaper to raise than import them, whilst in the sickly rice swamps foreign supplies are necessary, if we go no farther than is urged, we shall be unjust towards S. Carolina & Georgia. Let us not intermeddle. As population increases poor laborers will be so plenty as to render slaves useless. Slavery in time will not be a speck in our Country. Provision is already made in Connecticut for abolishing it. And the abolition has already taken place in Massachusetts. . . .

Mr PINKNEY. If slavery be wrong, it is justified by the example of all the world. . . . In all ages one half of mankind have been slaves. If the S. States were let alone they will probably of themselves stop importations. . . . An attempt to take away the right as proposed will produce serious objections to the Constitution which he wished to see adopted.

General PINKNEY declared it to be his firm opinion that if himself & all his colleagues were to sign the Constitution & use their personal influence, it would be of no avail towards obtaining the assent of their Constituents. S. Carolina & Georgia cannot do without slaves. As to Virginia she will gain by stopping the importations. Her slaves will rise in value, & she has more than she wants. It would be unequal to require S. C. & Georgia to confederate on such unequal terms. . . . He contended that the importation of slaves would be for the interest of the whole Union. The more slaves, the more produce to employ the carrying trade; The more consumption also, and the more of this, the more of revenue for the common treasury. He admitted it to be reasonable that slaves should be dutied like other imports, but should consider a rejection of the clause as an exclusion of S. Carolᵃ from the Union.

. . . .

Mʳ WILSON . . . As the Section now stands all articles imported are to be taxed. Slaves alone are exempt. This is in fact a bounty on that article.

Mʳ GERRY thought we had nothing to do with the conduct of the States as to Slaves, but ought to be careful not to give any sanction to it.

Mʳ DICKENSON considered it as inadmissible on every principle of honor & safety that the importation of slaves should be authorised to the States by the Constitution. . . .

. . . .

Mʳ RUTLIDGE. If the Convention thinks that N.C. S.C. & Georgia will ever agree to the plan, unless their right to import slaves be untouched, the expectation is vain. The people of those States will never bé such fools as to give up so important an interest. He was strenuous agˢᵗ striking out the Section, and seconded the motion of Genˡ Pinkney for a commitment.

Mʳ Govʳ MORRIS wished the whole subject to be committed

including the clauses relating to taxes on exports & to a navigation act. These things may form a bargain among the Northern & Southern States.

. . . .

Mʳ PINKNEY & Mʳ LANGDON moved to commit Sect. 6. as to navigation act by two thirds of each House

Mʳ GORHAM did not see the propriety of it. Is it meant to require a greater proportion of votes? He desired it to be remembered that the Eastern States had no motive to Union but a commercial one. They were able to protect themselves. They were not afraid of external danger, and did not need the aid of the Southⁿ States.

Mʳ WILSON wished for a commitment in order to reduce the proportion of votes required.

Mʳ ELSWORTH was for taking the plan as it is. This widening of opinions has a threatening aspect. If we do not agree on this middle & moderate ground he was afraid we should lose two States, with such others as may be disposed to stand aloof, should fly into a variety of shapes & directions, and most probably into several confederations and not without bloodshed.

On Question for committing 6 Sect. as to navigation act to a member from each State—N. H. ay. Mas. ay. Cᵗ no. N. J. no. Pᵃ ay. Del. ay. Mᵈ ay. Vᵃ ay. N. C. ay. S. C. ay. Geo. ay. [Ayes, 9; noes, 2.]

The Committee appointed were Mʳ Langdon, King, Johnson, Livingston, Clymer, Dickenson, L. Martin, Madison, Williamson, C. C. Pinkney, & Baldwin.

To this committee were referred also the two clauses abovementioned, of the 4 & 5. Sect: of Art. 7.

Friday, August 24. In Convention

Governour Livingston, from the Committee of Eleven, to whom were referred the two remaining clauses of the 4ᵗʰ Sect & the 5 & 6 Sect: of the 7ᵗʰ art: delivered in the following Report:

"Strike out so much of the 4ᵗʰ Sect: as was referred to the

Committee and insert—"The migration or importation of such persons as the several States now existing shall think proper to admit, shall not be prohibited by the Legislature prior to the year 1800, but a tax or duty may be imposed on such migration or importation at a rate not exceeding the average of the duties laid on imports."

"The 5 Sect: to remain as in the Report"

"The 6 Sect to be stricken out"

Saturday, August 25. In Convention

The Report of the Committee of eleven (see friday the 24th instant) being taken up,

Gen[l] PINKNEY moved to strike out the words "the year eighteen hundred" as the year limiting the importation of slaves, and to insert the words "the year eighteen hundred and eight"

M[r] GHORUM 2[ded] the motion

M[r] MADISON. Twenty years will produce all the mischief that can be apprehended from the liberty to import slaves. So long a term will be more dishonorable to the National [1] character than to say nothing about it in the Constitution.

On the motion; which passed in the affirmative.

N. H. ay. Mas. ay. C[t] ay. N. J. no. P[a] no. Del. no. M[d] ay. V[a] no. N. C. ay. S. C. ay. Geo. ay. [Ayes, 7; noes, 4.]

.   .   .   .

It was finally agreed nem: contrad: to make the clause read "but a tax or duty may be imposed on such importation not exceeding ten dollars for each person," and then the 2[d] part as amended was agreed to. ...

Wednesday, August 29. In Convention

Art. VII Sect. 6 by y[e] Committee of eleven reported to be struck out (see the 24 instant) being now taken up,

M[r] PINKNEY moved to postpone the Report in favor of the

1 (The word "American" is substituted in the transcript for "National.")

following proposition—"That no act of the Legislature for the purpose of regulating the commerce of the U-S. with foreign powers, or among the several States, shall be passed without the assent of two thirds of the members of each House." He remarked that there were five distinct commercial interests. 1. the fisheries & W. India trade, which belonged to the N. England States. 2. the interest of N. York lay in a free trade. 3. Wheat & flour the Staples of the two Middle States (N. J. & Penn^a). 4 Tob^o the staple of Mary^d & Virginia & partly of N. Carolina. 5. Rice & Indigo, the staples of S. Carolina & Georgia. These different interests would be a source of oppressive regulations if no check to a bare majority should be provided. States pursue their interests with less scruple than individuals. The power of regulating commerce was a pure concession on the part of the S. States. They did not need the protection of the N. States at present.

Mr MARTIN 2^{ded} the motion

Genl PINKNEY said it was the true interest of the S. States to have no regulation of commerce; but considering the loss brought on the commerce of the Eastern States by the revolution, their liberal conduct towards the views [2] of South Carolina, and the interest the weak South^n States had in being united with the strong Eastern States, he thought it proper that no fetters should be imposed on the power of making commercial regulations; and that his constituents though prejudiced against the Eastern States, would be reconciled to this liberality. He had himself, he said, prejudices agst the Eastern States before he came here, but would acknowledge that he had found them as liberal and candid as any men whatever.

Mr CLYMER. . . . The Northern & middle States will be ruined, if not enabled to defend themselves against foreign regulations.

.   .   .   .

[2] he meant the permission to import slaves. An understanding on the two subjects of *navigation* and *slavery,* had taken place between those parts of the Union, which explains the vote on the motion depending, as well as the language of Genl Pinkney & others.

Mᵣ Govᵣ MORRIS, opposed the object of the motion as highly injurious. Preferences to American ships will multiply them, till they can carry the Southern produce cheaper than it is now carried.—A navy was essential to security, particularly of the S. States, and can only be had by a navigation act encouraging American bottoms & seamen. In those points of view then alone, it is the interest of the S. States that navigation acts should be facilitated. Shipping he said was the worst & most precarious kind of property, and stood in need of public patronage.

.   .   .   .

Mᵣ SPAIGHT was against the motion. The Southern States could at any time save themselves from oppression, by building ships for their own use.

Mᵣ BUTLER differed from those who considered the rejection of the motion as no concession on the part of the S. States. He considered the interests of these and of the Eastern States, to be as different as the interests of Russia and Turkey. Being notwithstanding desirous of conciliating the affections of the East: States. he should vote agˢᵗ requiring ⅔ instead of a majority.

Col. MASON. . . . The Southern States are the *minority* in both Houses. Is it to be expected that they will deliver themselves bound hand & foot to the Eastern States, and enable them to exclaim, in the words of Cromwell on a certain occasion—"the lord hath delivered them into our hands.

.   .   .   .

Mᵣ MADISON, went into a pretty full view of the subject. He observed that the disadvantage to the S. States from a navigation act, lay chiefly in a temporary rise of freight, attended however with an increase of Southⁿ as well as Northern Shipping—with the emigration of Northern Seamen & merchants to the Southern States—& with a removal of the existing & injurious retaliations among the States on each other. The power of foreign nations to obstruct our retaliating measures on them by a corrupt influence would also be less if a majority shᵈ be made competent than if ⅔ of each House shᵈ be required to Legislative acts in this case. An abuse of the power would be qualified with all these good effects. But he thought an abuse was rendered improbable by the provision of 2 branches—by the independence of the Senate, by the negative of the Executive, by the interest of Connecticut & N: Jersey which were agricultural, not commercial States; by the interior interest which was also agricultural in the most commercial States, by the accession of Western States which w⁴ be altogether agricultural. He added that the Southern States would derive an essential advantage in the general security afforded by the increase of our maritime strength. He stated the vulnerable situation of them all, and of Virginia in particular. The increase of the coasting trade, and of seamen, would also be favorable to the S. States, by increasing, the consumption of their produce. If the Wealth of the Eastern should in a still greater proportion be augmented, that wealth w⁴ contribute the more to the public wants, and be otherwise a national benefit.

M⁻ RUTLIDGE was ag⁵ᵗ the motion of his colleague. It did not follow from a grant of the power to regulate trade, that it would be abused. At the worst a navigation act could bear hard a little while only on the S. States. As we are laying the foundation for a great empire, we ought to take a permanent view of the subject and not look at the present moment only. He reminded the House of the necessity of securing the West India trade to this country. That was the great object, and a navigation Act was necessary for obtaining it.

M⁻ RANDOLPH said that there were features so odious in the constitution as it now stands, that he doubted whether he should be able to agree to it. A rejection of the motion would compleat the deformity of the system. He took notice of the argument in favor of giving the power over trade to a majority, drawn from the opportunity foreign powers would have of obstructing retaliating measures, if two thirds were made requisite. He did not think there was weight in that consideration. The difference between a majority & two thirds did not afford room for such an opportunity. Foreign influence would also be more likely to be exerted on the President who could require three fourths by his negative. He did not mean however to enter into the merits. What he had in view was merely to pave the way for a declaration which he might be hereafter obliged to make if an accumulation of obnoxious ingredients should take place, that he could not give his assent to the plan.

M⸢ʳ⸣ GORHAM. If the Government is to be so fettered as to be unable to relieve the Eastern States what motive can they have to join in it, and thereby tie their own hands from measures which they could otherwise take for themselves. The Eastern States were not led to strengthen the Union by fear for their own safety. He deprecated the consequences of disunion, but if it should take place it was the Southern part of the Continent that had the most reason to dread them. He urged the improbability of a combination against the interest of the Southern States, the different situations of the Northern & Middle States being a security against it. It was moreover certain that foreign ships would never be altogether excluded especially those of Nations in treaty with us.

.   .   .   .

The Report of the Committee for striking out sect: 6. requiring two thirds of each House to pass a navigation act was then agreed to, nem: con:

OTHER IMPORTANT PROVISIONS

Delegates continued working through the report of the Committee of Detail. Since many clauses were interrelated, they wove back and forth, accepting, postponing, and recommitting. A word of explanation may illuminate the debate and action which follow. The Convention placed restrictions on the powers of the national and state legislatures, both separately and jointly. Some of these, such as those pertaining to bills of attainder and religious tests, incorporated in the body of the Constitution guarantees often found in separate state bills of rights. Restrictions on state financial excesses (of the type which roiled pre-Convention waters) were taken from congressional prerogative and made absolute. This action has often been viewed as the economic heart of the Constitution. Although the supreme-law-of-the-land clause was heightened so as to include state constitutions (previously omitted), a renewed bid for a federal veto followed. If this motion showed the persistence with which nationalists labored to insure supremacy, the reception of it revealed that equality in the Senate made bitter defense of state rights unnecessary. But the question of equality of states—for new ones to be created and for old ones with respect to disposition of the West—revived old antagonisms. After renewed threats of rupture, three states suffered final defeat as the Convention decided how frontier land should be converted into states. The question of ratification raised both fundamental and practical issues. After August 23 Madison flagged under his heavy burdens and the quantity of his notes diminished.

Wednesday, August 22. In Convention

Mᵣ GERRY & Mᵣ MᶜHENRY moved to insert after the 2ᵈ sect. Art: 7,[1] the Clause following, to wit, "The Legislature shall pass no bill of attainder [2] nor any ex post facto law."

Mᵣ GERRY urged the necessity of this prohibition, which he said was greater in the National than the State Legislature, because the number of members in the former being fewer were on that account the more to be feared.

Mᵣ GOVᵣ MORRIS thought the precaution as to ex post facto laws unnecessary; but essential as to bills of attainder.

Mᵣ ELSEWORTH contended that there was no lawyer, no civilian who would not say that ex post facto laws were void of themselves. It can not then be necessary to prohibit them.

Mᵣ WILSON was against inserting any thing in the Constitution as to ex post facto laws. It will bring reflexions on the Constitution—and proclaim that we are ignorant of the first principles of Legislation, or are constituting a Government which will be so.

---

1 [Article VII deals with the powers of Congress. See pp. 262-4.]

2 [A bill of attainder is a legislative act designed to inflict penalties on a person. On the whole subject see Zechariah Chafee, Jr., *Three Human Rights in the Constitution of 1787* (Lawrence, Kansas, 1956), pp. 90-161.]

The question being divided, The first part of the motion relating to bills of attainder was agreed to nem. contradicente.

On the second part relating to ex post facto laws—

Mr CARROL remarked that experience overruled all other calculations. It had proved that in whatever light they might be viewed by civilians or others, the State Legislatures had passed them, and they had taken effect.

Mr WILSON. If these prohibitions in the State Constitutions have no effect, it will be useless to insert them in this Constitution. Besides, both sides will agree to the principle, & will differ as to its application.

Mr WILLIAMSON. Such a prohibitory clause is in the Constitution of N. Carolina, and tho it has been violated, it has done good there & may do good here, because the Judges can take hold of it.

Doc^r JOHNSON thought the clause unnecessary, and implying an improper suspicion of the National Legislature.

Mr RUTLIDGE was in favor of the clause.

On the question for inserting the prohibition of ex post facto laws.

N. H. ay. Mas. ay. Con^t no. N. J. no. P^a no. Del. ay. M^d ay. Virg^a ay. N. C. div^d S. C. ay. Geo. ay. [Ayes, 7; noes, 3; divided, 1.]

Thursday, August 23. In Convention

Mr RUTLIDGE moved to amend Art: VIII [3] to read as follows,

"This Constitution & the laws of the U. S. made in pursuance thereof, and all Treaties made under the authority of the U. S. shall be the supreme law of the several States and of their citizens and inhabitants; and the Judges in the several States shall be bound thereby in their decisions, any thing in the Constitutions or laws of the several States, to the contrary notwithstanding."

[3] [Relating to the supremacy of national laws and treaties. See p. 264.]

which was agreed to nem: contrad:

. . .

Mʳ C- PINKNEY moved to add as an additional power to be vested in the Legislature of the U. S. "To negative all laws passed by the several States interfering in the opinion of the Legislature with the general interests and harmony of the Union; provided that two thirds of the members of each House assent to the same"

This principle he observed had formerly been agreed to. He considered the precaution as essentially necessary: The objection drawn from the predominance of the large States had been removed by the equality established in the Senate. . . .

Mʳ SHERMAN thought it unnecessary; the laws of the General Government being Supreme & paramount to the State laws according to the plan, as it now stands.

. . . .

Mʳ WILSON considered this as the key-stone wanted to compleat the wide arch of Government, we are raising. The power of self-defence had been urged as necessary for the State Governments. It was equally necessary for the General Government. The firmness of Judges is not of itself sufficient. Something further is requisite. It will be better to prevent the passage of an improper law, than to declare it void when passed.

Mʳ RUTLIDGE. If nothing else, this alone would damn and ought to damn the Constitution. Will any State ever agree to be bound hand & foot in this manner. . . .

. . . .

On the question for commitment, it passed in the negative.

N. H. ay. Masᵗˢ no. Conᵗ no. N. J. no. Pᵃ ay. Del: ay. Mᵈ ay. Vᵃ ay. N. C. no. S. C. no. Geo. no. [Ayes, 5; noes, 6.]

Mʳ PINKNEY then withdrew his proposition.

Sections 2 and 3 of Article IX, perpetuating the method for deciding controversies found in the Articles of Confederation, were struck out on August 24.

Tuesday, August 28. In Convention

Sect. 4.[4] was so amended nem: con: as to read "The trial of all crimes (except in cases of impeachment) shall be by jury, and such trial shall be held in the State where the said crimes shall have been committed; but when not committed within any State, then the trial shall be at such place or places as the Legislature may direct." The object of this amendment was to provide for trial by jury of offences committed out of any State.

Mr PINKNEY, urging the propriety of securing the benefit of the Habeas corpus in the most ample manner, moved "that it should not be suspended but on the most urgent occasions, & then only for a limited time, not exceeding twelve months"

Mr RUTLIDGE was for declaring the Habeas Corpus inviolable. He did not conceive that a suspension could ever be necessary at the same time through all the States.

M^r GOV^r MORRIS moved that "The privilege of the writ of Habeas Corpus shall not be suspended; unless where in cases of Rebellion or invasion the public safety may require it."

Mr WILSON doubted whether in any case a suspension could be necessary, as the discretion now exists with Judges, in most important cases to keep in Gaol or admit to Bail.

The first part of Mr Govr Morris' motion, to the word "unless" was agreed to nem: con:—on the remaining part;

N. H. ay. Mas. ay. C^t ay. P^a ay. Del. ay. M^d ay. V^a ay. N. C. no. S. C. no. Geo. no.: [Ayes, 7; noes, 3.]

. . . .

Art: XII.[5] being taken up.

Mr WILSON & Mr SHERMAN moved to insert after the words "coin money" the words "nor emit bills of credit, nor make any thing but gold & silver coin a tender in payment of debts" making these prohibitions absolute, instead of making the meas-

---

[4] [Section 4 of Article XI, relating to the judicial power. See p. 267.]
[5] [Relating to absolute prohibitions on state legislatures. See p. 267.]

ures allowable (as in the XIII art:) [6] *with the consent of the Legislature of the U. S.*

M[r] GHORUM thought the purpose would be as well secured by the provision of art: XIII which makes the consent of the Gen[l] Legislature necessary, and that in that mode, no opposition would be excited; whereas an absolute prohibition of paper money would rouse the most desperate opposition from its partizans.

M[r] SHERMAN thought this a favorable crisis for crushing paper money. If the consent of the Legislature could authorise emissions of it, the friends of paper money, would make every exertion to get into the Legislature in order to licence it.

The question being divided; on the 1st part—"nor emit bills of credit"

N. H. ay. Mas. ay. C[t] ay. P[a] ay. Del. ay. M[d] div[d] V[a] no. N. C. ay. S. C. ay. Geo. ay. [Ayes, 8; noes, 1; divided, 1.]

The remaining part of M[r] Wilson's & Sherman's motion was agreed to nem: con:

M[r] KING moved to add, in the words used in the Ordinance of Cong[s] establishing new States,[7] a prohibition on the States to interfere in private contracts.

M[r] GOV[r] MORRIS. This would be going too far. There are a thousand laws, relating to bringing actions—limitations of actions & which affect contracts. The Judicial power of the U. S. will be a protection in cases within their jurisdiction; and within the State itself a majority must rule, whatever may be the mischief done among themselves.

M[r] SHERMAN. Why then prohibit bills of credit?

M[r] WILSON was in favor of M[r] King's motion.

M[r] MADISON admitted that inconveniences might arise from such a prohibition but thought on the whole it would be over-

[6] [Relating to qualified prohibitions on state legislatures. See p. 267.]

[7] [The Northwest Ordinance of 1787. Article II provided: "And, in the just preservation of rights and property, it is understood and declared, that no law ought ever to be made or have force in the said territory, that shall, in any manner whatever, interfere with or affect private contracts, or engagements, *bona fide*, and without fraud previously formed."]

balanced by the utility of it. He conceived however that a negative on the State laws could alone secure the effect. Evasions might and would be devised by the ingenuity of Legislatures.

Col: MASON. This is carrying the restraint too far. Cases will happen that can not be foreseen, where some kind of interference will be proper & essential. . . .

Mr WILSON. The answer to these objections is that *retrospective* interferences only are to be prohibited.

Mr MADISON. Is not that already done by the prohibition of ex post facto laws, which will oblige the Judges to declare such interferences null & void.

Mr RUTLIDGE moved instead of Mr King's Motion to insert—"nor pass bills of attainder nor retrospective laws" on which motion

N. H. ay. C^t no. N. J. ay. P^a ay. Del. ay. M^d no. Virg^a no. N.C. ay. S. C. ay. Geo. ay. [Ayes, 7; noes, 3.]

Madison was incorrect, as the action of August 22 shows. Having searched Blackstone's *Commentaries*, Dickinson announced on the following day that the terms "ex post facto" related to criminal cases only. Therefore they would not, without further provision, restrain the states from retrospective laws in civil cases. Later (September 14) Gerry tried unsuccessfully to have the provision extended to such cases. Consequently where the Constitution lacks specific restraints, restrospective civil laws are forbidden to neither Congress nor the states.

Wednesday, August 29. In Convention

Art: XVII [8] being taken up, Mr Govr MORRIS moved to strike out the two last sentences, to wit "If the admission be consented to, the new States shall be admitted on the same terms with the original States. But the Legislature may make conditions with the new States, concerning the public debt, which shall be then subsisting."—He did not wish to bind down the Legislature to admit Western States on the terms here stated.

[8] [Relating to the admission of new states. See p. 268.]

Mr MADISON opposed the motion, insisting that the Western States neither would nor ought to submit to a union which degraded them from an equal rank with other States.

Col: MASON. If it were possible by just means to prevent emigrations to the Western Country, it might be good policy. But go the people will as they find it for their interest, and the best policy is to treat them with that equality which will make them friends not enemies.

Mr Govr MORRIS, did not mean to discourage the growth of the Western Country. He knew that to be impossible. He did not wish however to throw the power into their hands.

.   .   .   .

On Mr Govr Morris's motion for striking out.

N. H. ay. Mas. ay. Ct ay. N. J. ay. Pa ay. Del. ay. Md no. Va no. N. C. ay. S. C. ay. Geo. ay. [Ayes, 9; noes, 2.]

.   .   .   .

Mr Govr MORRIS moved the following proposition as a substitute for the XVII art:

"New States may be admitted by the Legislature into this Union: but no new State shall be erected within the limits of any of the present States, without the consent of the Legislature of such State, as well as of the Genl Legislature"

The first part to Union inclusive was agreed to nem: con:

Mr L. MARTIN opposed the latter part. Nothing he said would so alarm the limited States as to make the consent of the large States claiming the Western lands, necessary to the establishment of new States within their limits. ...

.   .   .   .

Mr LANGDON thought there was great weight in the argument of Mr Luther Martin, and that the proposition substituted by Mr Govr Morris would excite a dangerous opposition to the plan.

Mr Govr MORRIS thought on the contrary that the small States would be pleased with the regulation, as it holds up the idea of dismembering the large States.

.   .   .   .

Mr DICKINSON hoped the article would not be agreed to. He

dwelt on the impropriety of requiring the small States to secure the large ones in their extensive claims of territory.

Mr WILSON. When the *majority* of a State wish to divide they can do so. The aim of those in opposition to the article, he perceived, was that the Genl Government should abet the *minority*, & by that means divide a State against its own consent.

Mr Govr MORRIS. If the forced division of States is the object of the new System, and is to be pointed agst one or two States, he expected, the Gentleman from these would pretty quickly leave us.

Thursday, August 30. In Convention

Mr CARROL moved to strike out so much of the article as requires the consent of the State to its being divided. He was aware that the object of this prerequisite might be to prevent domestic disturbances, but such was our situation with regard to the Crown lands, and the sentiments of Maryland on that subject, that he perceived we should again be at sea, if no guard was provided for the right of the U. States to the back lands. He suggested that it might be proper to provide that nothing in the Constitution should affect the Right of the U. S. to lands ceded by G. Britain in the Treaty of peace, and proposed a committment to a member from each State. He assured the House that this was a point of a most serious nature. It was desirable above all things that the act of the Convention might be agreed to unanimously. But should this point be disregarded, he believed that all risks would be run by a considerable minority, sooner than give their concurrence.

.   .   .   .

Mr WILSON was against the committment. Unanimity was of great importance, but not to be purchased by the majority's yielding to the minority. He should have no objection to leaving the case of new States as heretofore. He knew of nothing that would give greater or juster alarm than the doctrine, that a political society is to be torne asunder without its own consent.

On Mr Carrol's motion for commitment

N. H. no. Mas. no. C^t no. N. J. ay. P^a no. Del. ay. M^d ay. V^a no. N. C. no. S. C. no. Geo. no. [Ayes, 3; noes, 8.]

.   .   .   .

Mr L. Martin, urged the unreasonableness of forcing & guaranteeing the people of Virginia beyond the Mountains, the Western people, of N. Carolina, & of Georgia, & the people of Maine, to continue under the States now governing them, without the consent of those States to their separation. ... It was said yesterday by Mr Govr Morris, that if the large States were to be split to pieces without their consent, their representatives here would take their leave. If the Small States are to be required to guarantee them in this manner, it will be found that the Representatives of other States will with equal firmness take their leave of the Constitution on the table.

It was moved by Mr L. Martin to postpone the substituted article, in order to take up the following.

"The Legislature of the U. S. shall have power to erect New States within as well as without the territory claimed by the several States or either of them, and admit the same into the Union: provided that nothing in this constitution shall be construed to affect the claim of the U. S. to vacant lands ceded to them by the late treaty of peace. which passed in the negative: N. J. Del. & M^d only ay.

On the question to agree to Mr Govr Morris's substituted article [of the preceding day]

N. H. ay. Mas. ay. C^t ay. N. J. no. P^a ay. Del. no. M^d no. V^a ay. N. C. ay. S. C. ay. Geo. ay. [Ayes, 8; noes, 3.]

Art: XX.^9 taken up.—"or affirmation" was added after "oath."

Mr Pinkney moved to add to the art:—"but no religious test shall ever be required as a qualification to any office or public trust under the authority of the U. States"

Mr Sherman thought it unnecessary, the prevailing liberality being a sufficient security ag^st such tests.

Mr Govr Morris & Genl Pinkney approved the motion.

9 [Relating to oaths to support the Constitution. See p. 268.]

The motion was agreed to nem: con: and then the whole Article; N. C. only no—& M^d divided

Art: XXI. taken up. viz: The ratifications of the Conventions of   States shall be sufficient for organizing this Constitution."

Mr WILSON proposed to fill the blank with "seven" that being a majority of the whole number & sufficient for the commencement of the plan.

.   .   .   .

M^r GOV^r MORRIS thought the blank ought to be filled in a twofold way, so as to provide for the event of the ratifying States being contiguous which would render a smaller number sufficient, and the event of their being dispersed, which w^d require a greater number for the introduction of the Government.

.   .   .   .

Mr DICKINSON asked whether the concurrence of Congress is to be essential to the establishment of the system, whether the refusing States in the Confederacy could be deserted—and whether Congress could concur in contravening the system under which they acted?

Mr MADISON, remarked that if the blank should be filled with "seven" eight, or "nine"—the Constitution as it stands might be put in force over the whole body of the people, tho' less than a majority of them should ratify it.

Mr WILSON. As the Constitution stands, the States only which ratify can be bound. We must he said in this case go to the original powers of Society. The House on fire must be extinguished, without a scrupulous regard to ordinary rights.

Mr BUTLER was in favor of "nine." He revolted at the idea, that one or two States should restrain the rest from consulting their safety.

Mr CARROL moved to fill the blank with "the thirteen," unanimity being necessary to dissolve the existing confederacy which had been unanimously established.

Friday, August 31. In Convention

M.̲r̲ KING moved to add to the end of art: XXI the words "between the said States" so as to confine the operation of the Gov.̲t̲ to the States ratifying it.

On the question

N. H. ay. Mas. ay. C.̲t̲ ay. N. J. ay. P.̲a̲ ay. M.̲d̲ no. Virg.̲a̲ ay. N. C. ay. S. C. ay. Geo. ay. [Ayes, 9; noes, 1.]

.   .   .   .

M.̲r̲ GOV.̲r̲ MORRIS moved to strike out "Conventions of the" after "ratifications," leaving the States to pursue their own modes of ratification.

.   .   .   .

M.̲r̲ MADISON considered it best to require Conventions; among other reasons, for this, that the powers given to the Gen.̲l̲ Gov.̲t̲ being taken from the State Gov.̲ts̲ the Legislatures would be more disinclined than conventions composed in part at least of other men; and if disinclined, they could devise modes apparently promoting, but really, thwarting the ratification. The difficulty in Maryland [10] was no greater than in other States, where no mode of change was pointed out by the Constitution, and all officers were under oath to support it. The people were in fact, the fountain of all power, and by resorting to them, all difficulties were got over. They could alter constitutions as they pleased. It was a principle in the Bills of rights, that first principles might be resorted to.

M.̲r̲ M.̲c̲HENRY said that the officers of Gov.̲t̲ in Maryland were under oath to support the mode of alteration prescribed by the Constitution.

.   .   .   .

[10] [The Maryland Constitution of 1776 (Article LIX) provided for amendment as follows: the proposed alteration was to be placed in a bill which, after passing in the General Assembly, was to be published three months before a new election, after which the General Assembly was to act on it. Nothing in the Constitution relating to the eastern shore was to be altered unless two thirds of each branch concurred. See Thorpe, ed., *Federal and State Constitutions*, III, 1701.]

Mr L. MARTIN insisted on a reference to the State Legislatures. He urged the danger of commotions from a resort to the people & to first principles in which the Governments might be on one side & the people on the other. He was apprehensive of no such consequences however in Maryland, whether the Legislature or the people should be appealed to. Both of them would be generally against the Constitution. . . .

Mr KING observed that the Constitution of Massachussets was made unalterable till the year 1790, yet this was no difficulty with him. The State must have contemplated a recurrence to first principles before they sent deputies to this Convention.

.   .   .   .

On question for "nine"

N. H. ay. Mas. ay. C^t ay. N. J. ay. P^a ay. Del. ay. M^d ay. V^a no. N. C. no. S. C. no. Geo. ay [Ayes, 8; noes, 3.]

Art: XXI. as amended was then agreed to by all the States, Maryland excepted, & Mr Jenifer being, ay.

Art. XXII [11] taken up, . . .

Mr Govr MORRIS & Mr PINKNEY . . . moved to amend the art: so as to read

"This Constitution shall be laid before the U. S. in Congress assembled; and it is the opinion of this Convention that it should afterwards be submitted to a Convention chosen in each State, in order to receive the ratification of such Convention: to which end the several Legislatures ought to provide for the calling Conventions within their respective States as speedily as circumstances will permit."—Mr Govr MORRIS said his object was to impress in stronger terms the necessity of calling Conventions in order to prevent enemies to the plan, from giving it the go by. When it first appears, with the sanction of this Convention, the people will be favorable to it. By degrees the State officers, & those interested in the State Gov^{ts} will intrigue & turn the popular current against it.

Mr L. MARTIN believed Mr Morris to be right, that after a while the people would be agst it, but for a different reason from

[11] [Relating to laying the Constitution before Congress for approval. See p. 269.]

that alledged. He believed they would not ratify it unless hurried into it by surprize.

Mʳ GERRY enlarged on the idea of Mʳ L. Martin in which he concurred, represented the system as full of vices, and dwelt on the impropriety of distroying the existing Confederation, without the unanimous consent of the parties to it.

Question on Mʳ Govʳ Morris's & Mʳ Pinkney's motion

N. H. ay. Mas. ay. Cᵗ no. N. J. no. Pᵃ ay. Del. ay. Mᵈ no. Vᵃ no. N. C. no. S. C. no. Geo. no. [Ayes, 4; noes, 7.]

Mʳ GERRY moved to postpone art: XXII.

Col: MASON 2ᵈᵉᵈ the motion, declaring that he would sooner chop off his right hand than put it to the Constitution as it now stands. He wished to see some points not yet decided brought to a decision, before being compelled to give a final opinion on this article. Should these points be improperly settled, his wish would then be to bring the whole subject before another general Convention.

Mʳ Govʳ MORRIS was ready for a postponement. He had long wished for another Convention, that will have the firmness to provide a vigorous Government, which we are afraid to do.

Mʳ RANDOLPH stated his idea to be, in case the final form of the Constitution should not permit him to accede to it, that the State Conventions should be at liberty to propose amendments to be submitted to another General Convention which may reject or incorporate them, as shall be judged proper.

On the question for postponing

N. H. no. Mas. no. Cᵗ no. N. J. ay. Pᵃ no. Del. no. Mᵈ ay. Vᵃ no. N. C. ay. S. C. no. Geo. no. [Ayes, 3; noes, 8.]

On the question on Art: XXII

N. H. ay. Mas. ay. Cᵗ ay. N. J. ay. Pᵃ ay. Del. ay. Mᵈ no. Vᵃ ay. N. C. ay. S. C. ay. Geo. ay. [Ayes, 10; noes, 1.]

On August 31 members referred all unfinished parts to an able committee on which King, Morris, and Madison from large states took places alongside Sherman, Brearly, and Dickinson from the small-state bloc. Also included were Gilman and Carroll, and from the lower South Williamson,

Butler, and Baldwin. These men received eleven proposals, five of which—the only important ones—centered in some way on the question of "high-mounted government." [12] From this committee, for which Chairman Brearly reported on September 1, 4, and 5 (the essential parts of which follow here), emerged decisions of first importance to the structure of the Constitution. Persistent and complicated problems finally found solution as lack of fresh alternatives combined with political bargaining to yield agreement. Only upon examination of their roots do these matters become understandable.

Of the five important proposals before the Committee on Unfinished Parts three concerned the powers of Congress. One of these raised the fundamental problem of a general as opposed to an enumerated grant. Introduced in the Virginia Plan (first and sixth resolutions), this issue took second place while control of the government was being contested. But the moment all states won equal footing in the Senate (July 16), the Convention immediately raised the point again —and quickly boggled, as a tie vote reveals. Sherman on the following day pointed a path which his colleagues spurned, after which they accepted Bedford's route (a motion empowering Congress "to legislate in all cases for the general interests of the Union, and also in those to which the States are separately incompetent . . ."). But since delegates failed to resolve their impasse on the basic question the Committee of Detail without further direction decided for an enumeration of specific powers in Article VII of its August 6 report.

Subsequently there appeared several new proposals designed to invigorate Congress. Madison, Charles Pinckney, Gerry, Morris, Rutledge, and Mason offered two score suggestions, of which some were duplicates. Among other things these empowered the general legislature to exercise exclusive authority over the seat of government; grant charters of incorporation, patents, and copyrights; establish a university and a Council of State to assist the President; guarantee certain civil rights, and restrain perpetual revenue. Upon acceptance each went for consideration to the Committee of Detail. Faced with a threatening prospect of being submerged, that

[12] [In tracing what was before this committee I have followed Irving Brant, who states that "For more than a hundred years, the proceedings of this committee have been a cause of high controversy and bafflement . . . . Nobody looked to see what was actually before the committee, though every postponement was by vote and every action on a committee report was recorded." Brant, *Madison*, pp. 134-37.]

body struck through to higher ground by investing Congress with indefinite power in its recommendation of August 22:

At the end of the sixteenth clause of the second section, seventh article, add, "and to provide, as may become necessary, from time to time, for the well managing and securing the common property and general interests and welfare of the United States in such manner as shall not interfere with the governments of individual states, in matters which respect only their internal police, or for which their individual authorities may be competent."

This bold provision for strong government drew on the Virginia Plan and the July 17 motions of Sherman and Bedford. On August 31 this "general welfare" clause went to the Brearly Committee.

Closely connected was a second measure dealing with taxes and debts, which emerged out of an intricate past. The issue of assumption of state debts by the national government appeared repeatedly in the debates. Related to this were two of the supplementary proposals referred to the Committee of Detail: one prohibiting the diversion to other purposes of funds appropriated to public creditors; another restraining perpetual revenue. Governor Livingston reported for the Grand Committee to which the debt problem was referred a recommendation that: "The Legislature of the U. S. shall have power to fulfil the engagements which have been entered into by Congress, and to discharge as well the debts of the U. S. as the debts incurred by the several States during the late war, for the common defence and general welfare." But in altering this so as to drop state debts and make payment mandatory the Convention elicited protest against speculators and stockjobbers. On reconsideration Sherman moved to add to the clause for laying taxes the explanation that it was "for the payment of said debts and for the defraying the expences that shall be incurred for the common defence and general welfare." This "general welfare" motion failed, and the Livingston draft found its way to the Brearly committee.

A third proposal before that group concerned the power of Congress over money bills. Members actually sent along Article VI, Section 12: "Each house shall possess the right of originating bills, except in the cases before-mentioned." But the "before-mentioned" clause (Article IV, Section 5: "All bills for raising or appropriating money, and for the fixing the salaries of the officers of Government, shall originate in the House of Representatives, and shall not be altered or amended by the Senate") had already been struck out. Why then did the Committee on Unfinished Parts become a new battleground for this third most troublesome problem in the Convention? What was at stake and who were the protagonists?

Confronted with the crisis over proportional representation in both branches, a grand committee reported on July 5 a plan to resolve the deadlock by allowing equality of votes in the second house, in return for which the large states received exclusive power over appropriations. Five large states—Massachusetts, Pennsylvania, Virginia, North and South Carolina—suffered a common defeat with the triumph of minority rule in the Senate, after which they fell out over the presumed concession.

One camp—whose most vocal supporters were Mason, Gerry, Randolph, and Williamson—continued to demand this privilege. Repeatedly these republican purists offered arguments which refought the seventeenth-century English revolution and the American Revolution as well. The popular branch was most immediately in touch with the people, and since the state-chosen Senate was, like the House of Lords, a haven for aristocrats, and the President a monarch, the people would insist on controlling the purse. "Taxation and representation are strongly associated in the minds of the people," asserted Gerry in the secrecy of the deliberative chamber, "and they will not agree that any but their immediate representatives shall meddle with their purses." Spoken at large, Gerry's opponents must have realized, here was a wind which would fan to a blaze the coals of '76.

But privacy enabled more flexible minds to escape the rigors of consistency. From three of the five large states came leaders—Madison, Wilson and Morris, King, Butler—who wrenched themselves free from the Old World to look the New squarely in the face. They accepted as inevitable a wrongly constituted Senate but saw no reason to multiply the vices of the Constitution with another evil. They charged that the money-bill discrimination had been transcribed through blind adherence to British models into several state constitutions, where upon examination it would prove to be "a trifle light as air." "Experience must be our only guide," countered Dickinson. "Reason may mislead us." Had not experience "verified the utility" of restraining such bills to the immediate representatives of the people? No, came the answer. It had not worked in the states and would palsy the national government. Either the Senate would be rendered impotent (since all important acts pertained to money in some way), or there would be perpetual contention as the Senate blocked other measures in order to influence appropriations. The restriction was a "mere tub to the whale." To mollify Mason and Randolph, Washington voted against his convictions to reinstate the omitted clause. Although this failed, the Brearly committee had to contend with these strong pressures.

Two of the items sent to the Committee on Unfinished Parts concerned machinery of government. Each dug into vital power relationships and touched on fundamental questions of principle. On the method of electing a president delegates continually changed their minds as they struggled to create a new type of office which would satisfy the various interests present and square with dominant theories concerning the proper structure of government. The latest provision was for a president to be chosen by the national legislature, which of course meant that he could not be re-eligible. Thus he was awarded one seven-year term. Closely connected but much less troublesome had been the problem of where to lodge the power of making treaties and appointing ambassadors and judges of the Supreme Court. As of August 31, although after many changes, the small states registered a victory in Article IX, Section 1, which gave these duties to the Senate.

This, then, is the background to the important issues before the Brearly committee. The report of that group is largely self-explanatory. It dropped the grant of indefinite powers to Congress and moved the general welfare provision to the first clause, thus enabling Congress only to *spend* for the general welfare. Portentous for the future, this vital decision apparently occasioned no great struggle. The "necessary and proper" clause of Article VII, the elastic clause of the Constitution, previously adopted on August 20 without debate or opposition, gave advocates of strong government a handle with which to reopen the issue after 1789.

The settlement from the Committee of Eleven contained something for everyone, as Madison's footnote hints. The new method of selecting a President conciliated republicans who feared aristocracy in the election of an executive, while awarding small states an advantage in the composition of presidential electors and in case the ballot went to the legislature. "High-mounted" men supported a money-bill provision with which they disagreed in return for aid from its partisans in making the government more powerful. This meant giving the President rather than the Senate the greater authority in making treaties, and appointing ambassadors and Supreme Court judges, all of which whittled down the strength of the small states which dominated the upper chamber. Undoubtedly the nationalists got the better of their bargain with the archrepublicans. As subsequent experience has shown, the final clause on money bills was all bark and no bite. The men who saw that European experience counted for little in the New World were in this instance—as in others —the men of vision.

Tuesday, September 4. In Convention

M⸢ʳ⸣ BREARLY from the Committee of eleven made a further partial Report as follows

"The Committee of Eleven to whom sundry resolutions &c were referred on the 31ˢᵗ of August, report that in their opinion the following additions and alterations should be made to the Report before the Convention, viz

(1.) The first clause of sect: 1. art. 7. to read as follow—'The Legislature shall have power to lay and collect taxes duties imposts & excises, to pay the debts and provide for the common defence & general welfare, of the U. S.'

. . .

(4) After the word 'Excellency' in sect. 1. art. 10. to be inserted. 'He shall hold his office during the term of four years, and together with the vice-President, chosen for the same term, be elected in the following manner, viz. Each State shall appoint in such manner as its Legislature may direct, a number of electors equal to the whole number of Senators and members of the House of Representatives to which the State may be entitled in the Legislature. The Electors shall meet in their respective States, and vote by ballot for two persons, of whom one at least shall not be an inhabitant of the same State with themselves; and they shall make a list of all the persons voted for, and of the number of votes for each, which list they shall sign and certify and transmit sealed to the Seat of the Genᴵ Government, directed

to the President of the Senate—The President of the Senate shall in that House open all the certificates; and the votes shall be then & there counted. The Person having the greatest number of votes shall be the President, if such number be a majority of that of the electors; and if there be more than one who have such majority, and have an equal number of votes, then the Senate shall immediately choose by ballot one of them for President: but if no person have a majority, then from the five highest on the list, the Senate shall choose by ballot the President. And in every case after the choice of the President, the person having the greatest number of votes shall be vice-president: but if there should remain two or more who have equal votes, the Senate shall choose from them the vice-President. The Legislature may determine the time of choosing and assembling the Electors, and the manner of certifying and transmitting their votes.'

. . . .

(7) 'Sect. 4. The President by and with the advice and Consent of the Senate, shall have power to make Treaties; and he shall nominate and by and with the advice and consent of the Senate shall appoint ambassadors, and other public Ministers, Judges of the Supreme Court, and all other Officers of the U. S., whose appointments are not otherwise herein provided for. But no Treaty shall be made without the consent of two thirds of the members present.'

. . . .

The (1ˢᵗ) clause of the Report was agreed to, nem. con.

. . . .

The (4) clause was accordingly taken up.

. . . .

Mʳ RANDOLPH & Mʳ PINKNEY wished for a particular explanation & discussion of the reasons for changing the mode of electing the Executive.

Mʳ Govʳ MORRIS said he would give the reasons of the Committee and his own. The 1ˢᵗ was the danger of intrigue & faction if the appointmᵗ should be made by the Legislature. 2. the inconveniency of an ineligibility required by that mode in order to lessen its evils. 3. The difficulty of establishing a Court of

Impeachments, other than the Senate which would not be so proper for the trial nor the other branch for the impeachment of the President, if appointed by the Legislature, 4. No body had appeared to be satisfied with an appointment by the Legislature. 5. Many were anxious even for an immediate choice by the people. 6. the indispensible necessity of making the Executive independent of the Legislature.—As the Electors would vote at the same time throughout the U. S. and at so great a distance from each other, the great evil of cabal was avoided. It would be impossible also to corrupt them. A conclusive reason for making the Senate instead of the Supreme Court the Judge of impeachments, was that the latter was to try the President after the trial of the impeachment.

Col: MASON confessed that the plan of the Committee had removed some capital objections, particularly the danger of cabal and corruption. It was liable however to this strong objection, that nineteen times in twenty the President would be chosen by the Senate, an improper body for the purpose.

.   .   .   .

Mr PINKNEY stated as objections to the mode 1. that it threw the whole appointment in fact into the hands of the Senate. 2. The Electors will be strangers to the several candidates and of course unable to decide on their comparative merits. 3. It makes the Executive reeligible which will endanger the public liberty. 4. It makes the same body of men which will in fact elect the President his Judges in case of an impeachment.

.   .   .   .

Mr WILSON. This subject has greatly divided the House, and will also divide people out of doors. It is in truth the most difficult of all on which we have had to decide. He had never made up an opinion on it entirely to his own satisfaction. He thought the plan on the whole a valuable improvement on the former. It gets rid of one great evil, that of cabal & corruption; & Continental Characters will multiply as we more & more coalesce, so as to enable the electors in every part of the Union to know & judge of them. It clears the way also for a discussion of the question of reeligibility on its own merits, which the former mode of election seems to forbid. He thought it might be better however to refer the eventual appointment to the Legislature than to the Senate, and to confine it to a smaller number than five of the Candidates. The eventual election by the Legislature w^d not open cabal anew, as it would be restrained to certain designated objects of choice, and as these must have had the previous sanction of a number of the States: and if the election be made as it ought as soon as the votes of the electors are opened & it is known that no one has a majority of the whole, there can be little danger of corruption. Another reason for preferring the Legislature to the Senate in this business, was that the House of Rep^s will be so often changed as to be free from the influence & faction to which the permanence of the Senate may subject that branch.

Wednesday, September 5. In Convention

Mr BREARLEY from the Committee of Eleven made a farther report as follows,

.   .   .   .

(3) Instead of sect: 12. art 6. say—"All bills for raising revenue shall originate in the House of Representatives, and shall be subject to alterations and amendments by the Senate: no money shall be drawn from the Treasury, but in consequence of appropriations made by law."

.   .   .   .

The (3) clause, Mr Govr MORRIS moved to postpone. It had been agreed to in the Committee on the ground of compromise, and he should feel himself at liberty to dissent to it, if on the whole he should not be satisfied with certain other parts to be settled.—

.   .   .   .

The Report made yesterday as to the appointment of the Executive being taken up. ...

Mr RUTLIDGE was much opposed to the plan reported by the

Committee. It would throw the whole power into the Senate. He was also against a re-eligibility. . . .

.   .   .   .

M![r](r) WILSON moved to strike out "Senate" and insert the word "Legislature"

M![r](r) MADISON considered it as a primary object to render an eventual resort to any part of the Legislature improbable. He was apprehensive that the proposed alteration would turn the attention of the large States too much to the appointment of candidates, instead of aiming at an effectual appointment of the officer, as the large States would predominate in the Legislature which would have the final choice out of the Candidates. Whereas if the Senate in which the small States predominate should have this final choice, the concerted effort of the large States would be to make the appointment in the first instance conclusive.

M![r](r) RANDOLPH. We have in some revolutions of this plan made a bold stroke for Monarchy. We are now doing the same for an aristocracy. He dwelt on the tendency of such an influence in the Senate over the election of the President in addition to its other powers, to convert that body into a real & dangerous Aristocracy.

.   .   .   .

On the question moved by M![r](r) Wilson

N. H. div![d](d) Mas. no. C![t](t) no. N. J. no. P![a](a) ay. Del. no. M![d](d) no. V![a](a) ay. N. C. no. S. C. ay. Geo. no. [Ayes, 3; noes, 7; divided, 1.]

.   .   .   .

M![r](r) GERRY suggested that the eventual election should be made by six Senators and seven Representatives chosen by joint ballot of both Houses.

M![r](r) KING observed that the influence of the Small States in the Senate was somewhat balanced by the influence of the large States in bringing forward the candidates; [13] and also by the

[13] This explains the compromise mentioned above by M![r](r) Gov![r](r) Morris. Col. Mason M![r](r) Gerry & other members from large States set great value on this privilege of originating money bills. Of this the members from the small States, with some from the large States who wished a high mounted Gov![t](t) en-

Concurrence of the small States in the Committee in the clause vesting the exclusive origination of Money bills in the House of Representatives.

.   .   .   .

Col: MASON. As the mode of appointment is now regulated, he could not forbear expressing his opinion that it is utterly inadmissible. He would prefer the Government of Prussia to one which will put all power into the hands of seven or eight men, and fix an Aristocracy worse than absolute monarchy.

Thursday, September 6. In Convention

Mᵣ WILSON said that he had weighed carefully the report of the Committee for remodelling the constitution of the Executive; and on combining it with other parts of the plan, he was obliged to consider the whole as having a dangerous tendency to aristocracy; as throwing a dangerous power into the hands of the Senate. They will have in fact, the appointment of the President, and through his dependence on them, the virtual appointment to offices; among others the offices of the Judiciary Department. They are to make Treaties; and they are to try all impeachments. In allowing them thus to make the Executive & Judiciary appointments, to be the Court of impeachments, and to make Treaties which are to be laws of the land, the Legislative, Executive & Judiciary powers are all blended in one branch of the Government. The power of making Treaties involves the case of subsidies, and here as an additional evil, foreign influence is to be dreaded. According to the plan as it now stands, the President will not be the man of the people as he ought to be, but the Minion of the Senate. He cannot even appoint a tide-waiter without the Senate. He had always thought the Senate too numerous a body for making appointments to office. The

---

deavored to avail themselves, by making that privilege, the price of arrangements in the constitution favorable to the small States, and to the elevation of the Government.

Senate, will moreover in all probability be in constant Session. They will have high salaries. And with all those powers, and the President in their interest, they will depress the other branch of the Legislature, and aggrandize themselves in proportion. Add to all this, that the Senate sitting in conclave, can by holding up to their respective States various and improbable candidates, contrive so to scatter their votes, as to bring the appointment of the President ultimately before themselves. Upon the whole, he thought the new mode of appointing the President, with some amendments, a valuable improvement; but he could never agree to purchase it at the price of the ensuing parts of the Report, nor befriend a system of which they make a part.

Mr Govr Morris expressed his wonder at the observations of Mr Wilson so far as they preferred the plan in the printed Report [14] to the new modification of it before the House, and entered into a comparative view of the two, with an eye to the nature of Mr Wilsons objections to the last. By the first the Senate he observed had a voice in appointing the President out of all the Citizens of the U. S: by this they were limited to five candidates previously nominated to them, with a probability of being barred altogether by the successful ballot of the Electors. Here surely was no increase of power. They are now to appoint Judges nominated to them by the President. Before they had the appointment without any agency whatever of the President. Here again was surely no additional power. If they are to make Treaties as the plan now stands, the power was the same in the printed plan. If they are to try impeachments, the Judges must have been triable by them before. Wherein then lay the dangerous tendency of the innovations to establish an aristocracy in the Senate? As to the appointment of officers, the weight of sentiment in the House, was opposed to the exercise of it by the President alone; though it was not the case with himself. If the Senate would act as was suspected, in misleading the States into a fallacious disposition of their votes for a President,

14 [The Report of the Committee of Detail presented by Rutledge on August 6, a printed copy of which had been furnished each member.]

they would, if the appointment were withdrawn wholly from them, make such representations in their several States where they have influence, as would favor the object of their partiality.

M͟ʳ WILLIAMSON. replying to M͟ʳ Morris: observed that the aristocratic complexion proceeds from the change in the mode of appointing the President which makes him dependent on the Senate.

M͟ʳ CLYMER said that the aristocratic part to which he could never accede was that in the printed plan, which gave the Senate the power of appointing to offices.

M͟ʳ HAMILTON said that he had been restrained from entering into the discussions by his dislike of the Scheme of Gov͟ᵗ in General; but as he meant to support the plan to be recommended, as better than nothing, he wished in this place to offer a few remarks. He liked the new modification, on the whole, better than that in the printed Report. . . .

. . . .

M͟ʳ WILLIAMSON suggested as better than an eventual choice by the Senate, that this choice should be made by the Legislature, voting *by States* and not *per capita*.

M͟ʳ SHERMAN suggested the House of Rep͟ˢ as preferable to the Legislature, and moved, accordingly,

To strike out the words "The Senate shall immediately choose &c." and insert "The House of Representatives shall immediately choose by ballot one of them for President, the members from each State having one vote."

Col: MASON liked the latter mode best as lessening the aristocratic influence of the Senate.

On the Motion of M͟ʳ Sherman

N. H. ay. Mas. ay. C͟ᵗ ay. N. J. ay. P͟ᵃ ay. Del. no. M͟ᵈ ay. V͟ᵃ ay. N. C. ay. S. C. ay. Geo. ay. [Ayes, 10; noes, 1.]

Subsequently four years was agreed on as the presidential term.

Saturday, September 8. In Convention

A Committee was . . . appointed by Ballot to revise the stile of and arrange the articles which had been agreed to by the House. The committee consisted of M͏ʳ Johnson, M͏ʳ Hamilton, M͏ʳ Gov͏ʳ Morris, M͏ʳ Madison and M͏ʳ King.

Monday, September 10. In Convention

M͏ʳ GERRY moved to reconsider Art XIX.[15] . . .

This Constitution he said is to be paramount to the State Constitutions. It follows, hence, from this article that two thirds of the States may obtain a Convention, a majority of which can bind the Union to innovations that may subvert the State-Constitutions altogether. He asked whether this was a situation proper to be run into.

M͏ʳ HAMILTON 2ᵈᵉᵈ the motion, but he said with a different view from M͏ʳ Gerry. He did not object to the consequence stated by M͏ʳ Gerry. There was no greater evil in subjecting the people of the U. S. to the major voice than the people of a particular State. It had been wished by many and was much to have been desired that an easier mode for introducing amendments had been provided by the articles of Confederation. It was equally desireable now that an easy mode should be established for supplying defects which will probably appear in the New System. The mode proposed was not adequate. The State Legislatures will not apply for alterations but with a view to increase their own powers. The National Legislature will be the first to perceive and will be most sensible to the necessity of amendments, and ought also to be empowered, whenever two thirds of each branch should concur to call a Convention.

[15] [Relating to the method of amendment. See p. 268.]

There could be no danger in giving this power, as the people would finally decide in the case.

.   .   .   .

On the motion of Mr Gerry to reconsider

N. H. div^d Mas. ay. C^t ay. N. J. no. P^a ay. Del. ay. M^d ay. V^a ay. N. C. ay. S. C. ay. GEO ay. [Ayes, 9; noes, 1; divided, 1.]

.   .   .   .

Mr MADISON moved to postpone . . . in order to take up the following,

"The Legislature of the U. S. whenever two thirds of both Houses shall deem necessary, or on the application of two thirds of the Legislatures of the several States, shall propose amendments to this Constitution, which shall be valid to all intents and purposes as part thereof, when the same shall have been ratified by three fourths at least of the Legislatures of the several States, or by Conventions in three fourths thereof, as one or the other mode of ratification may be proposed by the Legislature of the U S:"

Mr HAMILTON 2^ded the motion.

Mr RUTLIDGE said he never could agree to give a power by which the articles relating to slaves might be altered by the States not interested in that property and prejudiced against it. In order to obviate this objection, these words were added to the proposition: "provided that no amendments which may be made prior to the year 1808, shall in any manner affect the 4 & 5 sections of the VII article"—The postponement being agreed to,

On the question on the proposition of Mr Madison & Mr Hamilton as amended

N. H. div^d Mas. ay. C^t ay. N. J. ay. P^a ay. Del. no. M^d ay. V^a ay. N. C. ay. S. C. ay. Geo. ay. [Ayes, 9; noes, 1; divided, 1.]

Mr GERRY moved to reconsider art: XXI [16] and XXII.[17] from

16 [Relating to the number of state ratifications needed to implement the Constitution. See p. 269.]

17 [Relating to laying the Constitution before Congress for approval. See p. 269.]

the latter of which "for the approbation of Cong⁹" had been struck out. He objected to proceeding to change the Government without the approbation of Congress, as being improper and giving just umbrage to that body. He repeated his objections also to an annulment of the confederation with so little scruple or formality.

Mʳ HAMILTON concurred with Mʳ Gerry as to the indecorum of not requiring the approbation of Congress. He considered this as a necessary ingredient in the transaction. He thought it wrong also to allow nine States as provided by art XXI. to institute a new Government on the ruins of the existing one. He wᵈ propose as a better modification of the two articles (XXI & XXII) that the plan should be sent to Congress in order that the same if approved by them, may be communicated to the State Legislatures, to the end that they may refer it to State Conventions; each Legislature declaring that if the Convention of the State should think the plan ought to take effect among nine ratifying States, the same shᵈ take effect accordingly.

Mʳ GORHAM. Some States will say that nine States shall be sufficient to establish the plan, others will require unanimity for the purpose. And the different and conditional ratifications will defeat the plan altogether.

Mʳ HAMILTON. No Convention convinced of the necessity of the plan will refuse to give it effect on the adoption by nine States. He thought this mode less exceptionable than the one proposed in the article, and would attain the same end.

Mʳ FITZIMMONS remarked that the words "for their approbation" had been struck out in order to save Congress from the necessity of an Act inconsistent with the Articles of Confederation under which they held their authority.

Mʳ RANDOLPH declared, if no change should be made in the this part of the plan, he should be obliged to dissent from the whole of it. He had from the beginning he said been convinced that radical changes in the system of the Union were necessary. Under this conviction he had brought forward a set of republican propositions as the basis and outline of a reform. These Republican propositions had however, much to his regret, been widely, and in his opinion, irreconcileably departed from. In this state of things it was his idea and he accordingly meant to propose, that the State Conventions sh⁴ be at liberty to offer amendments to the plan; and that these should be submitted to a second General Convention, with full power to settle the Constitution finally. He did not expect to succeed in this proposition, but the discharge of his duty in making the attempt, would give quiet to his own mind.

. . . .

M⁺ KING thought it would be more respectful to Congress to submit the plan generally to them; than in such a form as expressly and necessarily to require their approbation or disapprobation. The assent of nine States he considered as sufficient; and that it was more proper to make this a part of the Constitution itself, than to provide for it by a supplemental or distinct recommendation.

M⁺ GERRY urged the indecency and pernicious tendency of dissolving in so slight a manner, the solemn obligations of the articles of confederation. If nine out of thirteen can dissolve the compact, Six out of nine will be just as able to dissolve the new one hereafter.

. . . .

On the question for reconsidering the two articles, XXI & XXII—

N. H. div⁴ Mas. no. C⁺ ay. N. J. ay. P⁴ no. Del. ay. M⁴ ay. V⁴ ay. N. C. ay. S. C. no. Geo. ay. [Ayes, 7; noes, 3; divided, 1.]

M⁺ HAMILTON then moved to postpone art XXI in order to take up the following, containing the ideas he had above expressed, viz

Resolved that the foregoing plan of a Constitution be transmitted to the U. S. in Congress assembled, in order that if the same shall be agreed to by them, it may be communicated to the Legislatures of the several States, to the end that they may provide for its final ratification by referring the same to the Consideration of a Convention of Deputies in each State to be chosen by the people thereof, and that it be recommended to the said Legislatures in their respective acts for organizing such convention to declare, that if the said Convention shall approve of the said Constitution, such approbation shall be binding and conclusive upon the State, and further that if the said Convention should be of opinion that the same upon the assent of any nine States thereto, ought to take effect between the States so assenting, such opinion shall thereupon be also binding upon such State, and the said Constitution shall take effect between the States assenting thereto"

Mr GERRY 2^{ded} the motion.

Mr WILSON. This motion being seconded, it is necessary now to speak freely. He expressed in strong terms his disapprobation of the expedient proposed, particularly the suspending the plan of the Convention on the approbation of Congress. He declared it to be worse than folly to rely on the concurrence of the Rhode Island members of Cong^s in the plan. Maryland has voted on this floor; for requiring the unanimous assent of the 13 States to the proposed change in the federal System. N. York has not been represented for a long time past in the Convention. Many individual deputies from other States have spoken much against the plan. Under these circumstances can it be safe to make the assent of Congress necessary. After spending four or five months in the laborious & arduous task of forming a Government for our Country, we are ourselves at the close throwing insuperable obstacles in the way of its success.

Mr CLYMER thought that the mode proposed by Mr Hamilton would fetter & embarrass Cong^s as much as the original one, since it equally involved a breach of the articles of Confederation.

Mr KING concurred with Mr Clymer. If Congress can accede to one mode, they can to the other. If the approbation of Congress be made necessary, and they should not approve, the State Legislatures will not propose the plan to Conventions; or if the States themselves are to provide that nine States shall suffice to establish the System, that provision will be omitted, every thing will go into confusion, and all our labor be lost.

Mr RUTLIDGE viewed the matter in the same light with Mr King.

On the question to postpone in order to take up Col: Hamilton's motion

N. H. no. Mas. no. C⁺ ay. N. J. no. Pᵃ no. Del. no. Mᵈ no. Vᵃ no. N. C. no. S. C. no. Geo. no. [Ayes, 1; noes, 10.]

A Question being then taken on the article XXI. It was agreed to unanimously.

.   .   .   .

Mᶠ WILLIAMSON & Mᶠ GERRY moved to re-instate the words "for the approbation of Congress" in art: XXII which was disagreed to nem: con:

Mᶠ RANDOLPH took this opportunity to state his objections to the System. They turned on the Senate's being made the Court of Impeachment for trying the Executive—on the necessity of ¾ instead of ⅔ of each house to overrule the negative of the President—on the smallness of the number of the Representative branch,—on the want of limitation to a standing army—on the general clause concerning necessary and proper laws—on the want of some particular restraint on navigation acts—on the power to lay duties on exports—on the Authority of the General Legislature to interpose on the application of the *Executives* of the States—on the want of a more definite boundary between the General .& State Legislatures—and between the General and State Judiciaries—on the the unqualified power of the President to pardon treasons—on the want of some limit to the power of the Legislature in regulating their own compensations. With these difficulties in his mind, what course he asked was he to pursue? Was he to promote the establishment of a plan which he verily believed would end in Tyranny? He was unwilling he said to impede the wishes and Judgment of the Convention, but he must keep himself free, in case he should be honored with a seat in the Convention of his State, to act according to the dictates of his judgment. The only mode in which his embarrassments could be removed, was that of submitting the plan to Congᵗ to go from them to the State Legislatures, and from these to State Conventions having power to adopt reject or amend; the process to close with another General Convention with full power to adopt or reject the alterations proposed by the State

Conventions, and to establish finally the Government. He accordingly proposed a Resolution to this effect.

Doc⸢ FRANKLIN 2ᵈᵉᵈ the motion

Col: MASON urged & obtained that the motion should lie on the table for a day or two to see what steps might be taken with regard to the parts of the system objected to by M⸢ Randolph.

COMPLETING THE CONSTITUTION

Gouverneur Morris undoubtedly gave final literary form to the Constitution. He reported faithfully, but took some liberty in shaping clauses his way. He admitted that with Article IV, Section 3 he went as far as he could to establish the exclusion without fear of raising objections. The semicolon in Article I, Section 8, clause 2 established an independent general welfare power, which was in accordance with Morris's views but was not what the Convention had adopted. The comma was restored in the engrossed Constitution.

Wednesday, September 12. In Convention

Doc⸢ JOHNSON from the Committee of stile &c. reported a digest of the plan, of which printed copies were ordered to be furnished to the members. He also reported a letter to accompany the plan, to Congress.[1]

[PREAMBLE]

WE, THE PEOPLE OF THE UNITED STATES, IN ORDER TO FORM a more perfect union, to establish justice, insure domestic tranquility, provide for the common defence, promote the general

[1] [See pp. 363-4. The draft of this letter accompanied, but was not printed with, the draft of the Constitution reported on this date. It does not seem to have caused debate, being read once throughout and afterwards agreed to by paragraphs. After acceptance it was printed with the final Constitution on September 17 and forwarded to Congress by Washington.]

welfare, and secure the blessings of liberty to ourselves and our posterity, do ordain and establish this Constitution for the United States of America.

ARTICLE I

Sect. 1. ALL legislative powers herein granted shall be vested in a Congress of the United States, which shall consist of a Senate and House of Representatives.

Sect. 2. The House of Representatives shall be composed of members chosen every second year by the people of the several states, and the electors in each state shall have the qualifications requisite for electors of the most numerous branch of the state legislature.

No person shall be a representative who shall not have attained to the age of twenty-five years, and been seven years a citizen of the United States, and who shall not, when elected, be an inhabitant of that state in which he shall be chosen.

Representatives and direct taxes shall be apportioned among the several states which may be included within this Union, according to their respective numbers, which shall be determined by adding to the whole number of free persons, including those bound to servitude for a term of years, and excluding Indians not taxed, three-fifths of all other persons. The actual enumeration shall be made within three years after the first meeting of the Congress of the United States, and within every subsequent term of ten years, in such manner as they shall by law direct. The number of representatives shall not exceed one for every forty thousand, but each state shall have at least one representative: and until such enumeration shall be made, the state of New-Hampshire shall be entitled to chuse three, Massachusetts eight, Rhode-Island and Providence Plantations one, Connecticut five, New-York six, New-Jersey four, Pennsylvania eight, Delaware one, Maryland six, Virginia ten, North-Carolina five, South-Caroline five, and Georgia three.

When vacancies happen in the representation from any state, the Executive authority thereof shall issue writs of election to fill such vacancies.

The House of Representatives shall choose their Speaker and

other officers; and they shall have the sole power of impeachment.

Sect. 3. The Senate of the United States shall be composed of two senators from each state, chosen by the legislature thereof, for six years: and each senator shall have one vote.

Immediately after they shall be assembled in consequence of the first election, they shall be divided (by lot) [2] as equally as may be into three classes. The seats of the senators of the first class shall be vacated at the expiration of the second year, of the second class at the expiration of the fourth year, and of the third class at the expiration of the sixth year, so that one-third may be chosen every second year: and if vacancies happen by resignation, or otherwise, during the recess of the Legislature of any state, the Executive thereof may make temporary appointments until the next meeting of the Legislature.

No person shall be a senator who shall not have attained to the age of thirty years, and been nine years a citizen of the United States, and who shall not, when elected, be an inhabitant of that state for which he shall be chosen.

The Vice-President of the United States shall be, ex officio President of the senate, but shall have no vote, unless they be equally divided.

The Senate shall choose their other officers, and also a President pro tempore, in the absence of the Vice-President, or when he shall exercise the office of President of the United States.

The Senate shall have the sole power to try all impeachments. When sitting for that purpose, they shall be on oath. When the President of the United States is tried, the Chief Justice shall preside: And no person shall be convicted without the concurrence of two-thirds of the members present.

Judgment in cases of impeachment shall not extend further than to removal from office, and disqualification to hold and enjoy any office of honor, trust or profit under the United States: but the party convicted shall nevertheless be liable and subject to indictment, trial, judgment and punishment, according to law.

Sect. 4. The times, places and manner of holding elections

[2] [The words "by lot" were not in the Report as printed but were inserted in manuscript. On September 14 they were struck out.]

for senators and representatives, shall be prescribed in each state by the legislature thereof: but the Congress may at any time by law make or alter such regulations.

The Congress shall assemble at least once in every year, and such meeting shall be on the first Monday in December, unless they shall by law appoint a different day.

Sect. 5. Each house shall be the judge of the elections, returns and qualifications of its own members, and a majority of each shall constitute a quorum to do business: but a smaller number may adjourn from day to day, and may be authorised to compel the attendance of absent members, in such manner, and under such penalties as each house may provide.

Each house may determine the rules of its proceedings; punish its members for disorderly behaviour, and, with the concurrence of two-thirds, expel a member.

Each house shall keep a journal of its proceedings, and from time to time publish the same, excepting such parts as may in their judgment require secrecy; and the yeas and nays of the members of either house on any question shall, at the desire of one-fifth of those present, be entered on the journal.

Neither house, during the session of Congress, shall, without the consent of the other, adjourn for more than three days, nor to any other place than that in which the two houses shall be sitting.

Sect. 6. The senators and representatives shall receive a compensation for their services, to be ascertained by law, and paid out of the treasury of the United States. They shall in all cases, except treason, felony and breach of the peace, be privileged from arrest during their attendance at the session of their respective houses, and in going to and returning from the same; and for any speech or debate in either house, they shall not be questioned in any other place.

No senator or representative shall, during the time for which he was elected, be appointed to any civil office under the authority of the United States, which shall have been created, or the emoluments whereof shall have been encreased during such time; and no person holding any office under the United States, shall be a member of either house during his continuance in office.

Sect. 7. The enacting stile of the laws shall be, "Be it enacted by the senators and representatives in Congress assembled."

All bills for raising revenue shall originate in the house of representatives: but the senate may propose or concur with amendments as on other bills.

Every bill which shall have passed the house of representatives and the senate, shall, before it become a law, be presented to the president of the United States. If he approve he shall sign it, but if not he shall return it, with his objections to that house in which it shall have originated, who shall enter the objections at large on their journal, and proceed to reconsider it. If after such reconsideration two-thirds of that house shall agree to pass the bill, it shall be sent, together with the objections, to the other house, by which it shall likewise be reconsidered, and if approved by two-thirds of that house, it shall become a law. But in all such cases the votes of both houses shall be determined by yeas and nays, and the names of the persons voting for and against the bill shall be entered on the journal of each house respectively. If any bill shall not be returned by the President within ten days (Sundays excepted) after it shall have been presented to him, the same shall be a law, in like manner as if he had signed it, unless the Congress by their adjournment prevent its return, in which case it shall not be a law.

Every order, resolution, or vote to which the concurrence of the Senate and House of Representatives may be necessary (except on a question of adjournment) shall be presented to the President of the United States; and before the same shall take effect, shall be approved by him, or, being disapproved by him, shall be repassed by three-fourths [3] of the Senate and House of Representatives, according to the rules and limitations prescribed in the case of a bill.

Sect. 8. The Congress may by joint ballot appoint a treasurer. They shall have power

To lay and collect taxes, duties, imposts and excises; to pay the debts and provide for the common defence and general welfare of the United States.

To borrow money on the credit of the United States.

To regulate commerce with foreign nations, among the several states, and with the Indian tribes.

To establish an uniform rule of naturalization, and uniform

---

3 [Changed to two thirds on September 12.]

laws on the subject of bankruptcies throughout the United States.

To coin money, regulate the value thereof, and of foreign coin, and fix the standard of weights and measures.

To provide for the punishment of counterfeiting the securities and current coin of the United States.

To establish post offices and post roads.

To promote the progress of science and useful arts, by securing for limited times to authors and inventors the exclusive right to their respective writings and discoveries.

To constitute tribunals inferior to the supreme court.

To define and punish piracies and felonies committed on the high seas, and [4] (punish) offences against the law of nations.

To declare war, grant letters of marque and reprisal, and make rules concerning captures on land and water.

To raise and support armies: but no appropriation of money to that use shall be for a longer term than two years.

To provide and maintain a navy.

To make rules for the government and regulation of the land and naval forces.

To provide for calling forth the militia to execute the laws of the union, suppress insurrections and repel invasions.

To provide for organizing, arming and disciplining the militia, and for governing such part of them as may be employed in the service of the United States, reserving to the States respectively, the appointment of the officers, and the authority of training the militia according to the discipline prescribed by Congress.

To exercise exclusive legislation in all cases whatsoever, over such district (not exceeding ten miles square) as may, by cession of particular States, and the acceptance of Congress, become the seat of the government of the United States, and to exercise like authority over all places purchased by the consent of the legislature of the state in which the same shall be, for the erection of forts, magazines, arsenals, dock-yards, and other needful buildings—And

To make all laws which shall be necessary and proper for carrying into execution the foregoing powers, and all other

[4] ["Punish" was omitted in the printed Report.]

powers vested by this constitution in the government of the United States, or in any department or officer thereof.

Sect. 9. The migration or importation of such persons as the several states now existing shall think proper to admit, shall not be prohibited by the Congress prior to the year one thousand eight hundred and eight, but a tax or duty may be imposed on such importation, not exceeding ten dollars for each person.

The privilege of the writ of habeas corpus shall not be suspended, unless when in cases of rebellion or invasion the public safety may require it.

No bill of attainder shall be passed, nor any ex post facto law.

No capitation tax shall be laid, unless in proportion to the census herein before directed to be taken.

No tax or duty shall be laid on articles exported from any state.

No money shall be drawn from the treasury, but in consequence of appropriations made by law.

No title of nobility shall be granted by the United States. And no person holding any office of profit or trust under them, shall, without the consent of the Congress, accept of any present, emolument, office, or title, of any kind whatever, from any king, prince, or foreign state.

Sect. 10. No state shall coin money, nor emit bills of credit, nor make any thing but gold or silver coin a tender in payment of debts, nor pass any bill of attainder, nor ex post facto laws, nor laws altering or impairing the obligation of contracts; nor grant letters of marque and reprisal, nor enter into any treaty, alliance, or confederation, nor grant any title of nobility.

No state shall, without the consent of Congress, lay imposts or duties on imports or exports, nor with such consent, but to the use of the treasury of the United States. Nor keep troops nor ships of war in time of peace, nor enter into any agreement or compact with another state, nor with any foreign power. Nor engage in any war, unless it shall be actually invaded by enemies, or the danger of invasion be so imminent, as not to admit of delay until the Congress can be consulted.

II

Sect. 1. The executive power shall be vested in a president of the United States of America. He shall hold his office during the term of four years, and, together with the vice-president, chosen for the same term, be elected in the following manner:

Each state shall appoint, in such manner as the legislature thereof may direct, a number of electors, equal to the whole number of senators and representatives to which the state may be entitled in Congress: but no senator or representative shall be appointed an elector, nor any person holding an office of trust or profit under the United States.

The electors shall meet in their respective states, and vote by ballot for two persons, of whom one at least shall not be an inhabitant of the same state with themselves. And they shall make a list of all the persons voted for, and of the number of votes for each; which list they shall sign and certify, and transmit sealed to the seat of the general government, directed to the president of the senate. The president of the senate shall in the presence of the senate and house of representatives open all the certificates, and the votes shall then be counted. The person having the greatest number of votes shall be the president, if such number be a majority of the whole number of electors appointed; and if there be more than one who have such majority, and have an equal number of votes, then the house of representatives shall immediately chuse by ballot one of them for president; and if no person have a majority, then from the five highest on the list the said house shall in like manner choose the president. But in choosing the president, the votes shall be taken by states and not per capita, the representation from each state having one vote. A quorum for this purpose shall consist of a member or members from two-thirds of the states, and a majority of all the states shall be necessary to a choice. In every case, after the choice of the president by the representatives, the person having the greatest number of votes of the electors shall be the vice-president. But if there should remain two or more who have equal votes, the senate shall choose from them by ballot the vice-president.

The Congress may determine the time of chusing the electors, and the time in which they shall give their votes; but the election shall be on the same day throughout the United States.

No person except a natural born citizen, or a citizen of the United States, at the time of the adoption of this constitution, shall be eligible to the office of president; neither shall any person be eligible to that office who shall not have attained to the age of thirty-five years, and been fourteen years a resident within the United States.

In case of the removal of the president from office, or of his death, resignation, or inability to discharge the powers and duties of the said office, the same shall devolve on the vice-president, and the Congress may by law provide for the case of removal, death, resignation or inability, both of the president and vice-president, declaring what officer shall then act as president, and such officer shall act accordingly, until the disability be *r*emoved, or the period for chusing another president arrive.

The president shall, at stated times, receive a fixed compensation for his services, which shall neither be encreased nor diminished during the period for which he shall have been elected.

Before he enter on the execution of his office, he shall take the following oath or affirmation: "I ———, do solemnly swear (or affirm) that I will faithfully execute the office of president of the United States, and will to the best of my judgment and power, preserve, protect and defend the constitution of the United States."

Sect. 2. The president shall be commander in chief of the army and navy of the United States, and of the militia of the several States: [5] he may require the opinion, in writing, of the principal officer in each of the executive departments, upon any subject relating to the duties of their respective offices, when called into the actual service of the United States,[6] and he shall have power to grant reprieves and pardons for offences against the United States, except in cases of impeachment.

He shall have power, by and with the advice and consent of the senate, to make treaties, provided two-thirds of the senators present concur; and he shall nominate, and by and with the advice and consent of the senate, shall appoint ambassadors, other public ministers and consuls, judges of the supreme court, and all other officers of the United States, whose appointments are not herein otherwise provided for.

[5] (The phrase "when called into the actual service of the United States" is transposed in the transcript so that it follows the words "several States.")

[6] [Same change as noted in preceding footnote.]

The president shall have power to fill up all vacancies that may happen during the recess of the senate, by granting commissions which shall expire at the end of their next session.

Sect. 3. He shall from time to time give to the Congress information of the state of the union, and recommend to their consideration such measures as he shall judge necessary and expedient: he may, on extraordinary occasions, convene both houses, or either of them, and in case of disagreement between them, with respect to the time of adjournment, he may adjourn them to such time as he shall think proper: he shall receive ambassadors and other public ministers: he shall take care that the laws be faithfully executed, and shall commission all the officers of the United States.

Sect. 4. The president, vice-president and all civil officers of the United States, shall be removed from office on impeachment for, and conviction of treason, bribery, or other high crimes and misdemeanors.

III

Sect. 1. The judicial power of the United States, both in law and equity, shall be vested in one supreme court, and in such inferior courts as the Congress may from time to time ordain and establish. The judges, both of the supreme and inferior courts, shall hold their offices during good behaviour, and shall, at stated times, receive for their services, a compensation, which shall not be diminished during their continuance in office.

Sect. 2. The judicial power shall extend to all cases, both in law and equity, arising under this constitution, the laws of the United States, and treaties made, or which shall be made, under their authority. To all cases affecting ambassadors, other public ministers and consuls. To all cases of admiralty and maritime jurisdiction. To controversies to which the United States shall be a party. To controversies between two or more States; between a state and citizens of another state; between citizens of different States; between citizens of the same state claiming lands under grants of different States, and between a state, or the citizens thereof, and foreign States, citizens or subjects.

In cases affecting ambassadors, other public ministers and consuls, and those in which a state shall be party, the supreme court shall have original jurisdiction. In all the other cases before mentioned, the supreme court shall have appellate jurisdiction, both as to law and fact, with such exceptions, and under such regulations as the Congress shall make.

The trial of all crimes, except in cases of impeachment, shall be by jury; and such trial shall be held in the state where the said crimes shall have been committed; but when not committed within any state, the trial shall be at such place or places as the Congress may by law have directed.

Sect. 3. Treason against the United States, shall consist only in levying war against them, or in adhering to their enemies, giving them aid and comfort. No person shall be convicted of treason unless on the testimony of two witnesses to the same overt act, or on confession in open court.

The Congress shall have power to declare the punishment of treason, but no attainder of treason shall work corruption of blood nor forfeiture, except during the life of the person attainted.

IV

Sect. 1. Full faith and credit shall be given in each state to the public acts, records, and judicial proceedings of every other state. And the Congress may by general laws prescribe the manner in which such acts, records and proceedings shall be proved, and the effect thereof.

Sect. 2. The citizens of each state shall be entitled to all privileges and immunities of citizens in the several states.

A person charged in any state with treason, felony, or other crime, who shall flee from justice, and be found in another state, shall on demand of the executive authority of the state from which he fled be delivered up, and removed to the state having jurisdiction of the crime.

No person legally held to service or labour in one state, escaping into another, shall in consequence of regulations subsisting therein be discharged from such service or labor, but shall be delivered up on claim of the party to whom such service or labour may be due.

Sect. 3. New states may be admitted by the Congress into this union; but no new state shall be formed or erected within the jurisdiction of any other state; nor any state be formed by the junction of two or more states, or parts of states, without the consent of the legislatures of the states concerned as well as of the Congress.

The Congress shall have power to dispose of and make all needful rules and regulations respecting the territory or other property belonging to the United States: and nothing in this Constitution shall be so construed as to prejudice any claims of the United States, or of any particular state.

Sect. 4. The United States shall guarantee to every state in this union a Republican form of government, and shall protect each of them against invasion; and on application of the legislature or executive, against domestic violence.

V

The Congress, whenever two-thirds of both houses shall deem necessary, or on the application of two-thirds of the legislatures of the several states, shall propose amendments to this constitution, which shall be valid to all intents and purposes, as part thereof, when the same shall have been ratified by three-fourths at least of the legislatures of the several states, or by conventions in three-fourths thereof, as the one or the other mode of ratification may be proposed by the Congress: Provided, that no amendment which may be made prior to the year 1808 shall in any manner affect the   and   section of   article

VI

All debts contracted and engagements entered into before the adoption of this Constitution shall be as valid against the United States under this Constitution as under the confederation.

This constitution, and the laws of the United States which shall be made in pursuance thereof; and all treaties made, or which shall be made, under the authority of the United States, shall be the supreme law of the land; and the judges in every state shall be bound thereby, any thing in the constitution or laws of any state to the contrary notwithstanding.

The senators and representatives beforementioned, and the members of the several state legislatures, and all executive and judicial officers, both of the United States and of the several States, shall be bound by oath or affirmation, to support this constitution; but no religious test shall ever be required as a qualification to any office or public trust under the United States.

VII

The ratification of the conventions of nine States, shall be sufficient for the establishment of this constitution between the States so ratifying the same.

.   .   .   .

Mʳ WILLIAMSON, observed to the House that no provision was yet made for juries in Civil cases and suggested the necessity of it.

Mʳ GORHAM. It is not possible to discriminate equity cases from those in which juries are proper. The Representatives of the people may be safely trusted in this matter.

Mʳ GERRY urged the necessity of Juries to guard agˢᵗ corrupt Judges. He proposed that the Committee last appointed should be directed to provide a clause for securing the trial by Juries.

Col: MASON perceived the difficulty mentioned by Mʳ Gorham. The jury cases can not be specified. A general principle laid down on this and some other points would be sufficient. He wished the plan had been prefaced with a Bill of Rights, & would second a Motion if made for the purpose. It would give great quiet to the people; and with the aid of the State declarations, a bill might be prepared in a few hours.

Mʳ GERRY concurred in the idea & moved for a Committee to prepare a Bill of Rights. Col: MASON 2ᵈᵉᵈ the motion.

Mʳ SHERMAN, was for securing the rights of the people where requisite. The State Declarations of Rights are not repealed by this Constitution; and being in force are sufficient. There are many cases where juries are proper which can not be discriminated. The Legislature may be safely trusted.

Col: MASON. The Laws of the U. S. are to be paramount to State Bills of Rights.

On the question for a Comᵉ to prepare a Bill of Rights

N. H. no. Mas. absᵗ Cᵗ no. N. J. no. Pᵃ no. Del no. Mᵈ no. Vᵃ no. N. C. no. S. C. no. Geo. no. [Ayes, 0; noes, 10.]

Friday, September 14. In Convention

Mʳ PINKNEY & Mʳ GERRY, moved to insert a declaration "that the liberty of the Press should be inviolably observed."

Mʳ SHERMAN. It is unnecessary. The power of Congress does not extend to the Press. On the question, it passed in the negative

N. H. no. Mas. ay. Cᵗ no. N. J. no. Pᵃ no. Del. no. Mᵈ ay. Vᵃ ay. N. C. no. S. C. ay. Geo. no. [Ayes, 4; noes, 7.]

Saturday, September 15. In Convention

Art. V. . . .

Mʳ SHERMAN expressed his fears that three fourths of the States might be brought to do things fatal to particular States, as abolishing them altogether or depriving them of their equality in the Senate. He thought it reasonable that the proviso in favor of the States importing slaves should be extended so as to provide that no State should be affected in its internal police, or deprived of its equality in the Senate.

Col: MASON thought the plan of amending the Constitution exceptionable & dangerous. As the proposing of amendments is in both the modes to depend, in the first immediately, in the second, ultimately, on Congress, no amendments of the proper kind would ever be obtained by the people, if the Government should become oppressive, as he verily believed would be the case.

Mʳ Govʳ MORRIS & Mʳ GERRY moved to amend the article so as to require a Convention on application of ⅔ of the Sts.

Mʳ MADISON did not see why Congress would not be as much bound to propose amendments applied for by two thirds of the States as to call a Convention on the like application. He saw no objection however against providing for a Convention for the purpose of amendments, except only that difficulties might arise as to the form, the quorum &c. which in Constitutional regulations ought to be as much as possible avoided.

The motion of Mr Govr Morris & Mr Gerry was agreed to nem: con: ...

. . . .

Mr Sherman moved according to his idea ... to annex to the end of the article a further proviso "that no State shall without its consent be affected in its internal police, or deprived of its equal suffrage in the Senate."

Mr Madison. Begin with these special provisos, and every State will insist on them, for their boundaries, exports &c.

On the motion of Mr Sherman

N. H. no. Mas. no. C^t ay. N. J. ay. P^a no. Del. ay. M^d no. V^a no. N. C. no. S. C. no. Geo. no. [Ayes, 3; noes, 8.]

. . . .

Mr Govr Morris moved to annex a further proviso—"that no State, without its consent shall be deprived of its equal suffrage in the Senate"

This motion being dictated by the circulating murmurs of the small States was agreed to without debate, no one opposing it, or on the question, saying no.

. . . .

Mr Randolph animadverting on the indefinite and dangerous power given by the Constitution to Congress, expressing the pain he felt at differing from the body of the Convention, on the close of the great & awful subject of their labours, and anxiously wishing for some accomodating expedient which would relieve him from his embarrassments, made a motion importing "that amendments to the plan might be offered by the State Conventions, which should be submitted to and finally decided on by another general Convention" Should this proposition be disregarded, it would he said be impossible for him to put his name to the instrument. Whether he should oppose it afterwards he would not then decide but he would not deprive himself of the freedom to do so in his own State, if that course should be prescribed by his final judgment.

Col: Mason 2^ded & followed Mr Randolph in animadversions

on the dangerous power and structure of the Government, concluding that it would end either in monarchy, or a tyrannical aristocracy; which, he was in doubt, but one or other, he was sure. This Constitution had been formed without the knowledge or idea of the people. A second Convention will know more of the sense of the people, and be able to provide a system more consonant to it. It was improper to say to the people, take this or nothing. As the Constitution now stands, he could neither give it his support or vote in Virginia; and he could not sign here what he could not support there. With the expedient of another Convention as proposed, he could sign.

Mᵣ PINKNEY. These declarations from members so respectable at the close of this important scene, give a peculiar solemnity to the present moment. He descanted on the consequences of calling forth the deliberations & amendments of the different States on the subject of Government at large. Nothing but confusion & contrariety could spring from the experiment. The States will never agree in their plans, and the Deputies to a second Convention coming together under the discordant impressions of their Constituents, will never agree. Conventions are serious things, and ought not to be repeated. He was not without objections as well as others to the plan. He objected to the contemptible weakness & dependence of the Executive. He objected to the power of a majority only of Congˢ over Commerce. But apprehending the danger of a general confusion, and an ultimate decision by the sword, he should give the plan his support.

Mᵣ GERRY, stated the objections which determined him to withhold his name from the Constitution. 1. the duration and re-eligibility of the Senate. 2. the power of the House of Representatives to conceal their journals. 3. the power of Congress over the places of election. 4 the unlimited power of Congress over their own compensations. 5. Massachusetts has not a due share of Representatives allotted to her. 6. 3/5 of the Blacks are to be represented as if they were freemen. 7. Under the power over commerce, monopolies may be established. 8. The vice president being made head of the Senate. He could however he said get over all these, if the rights of the Citizens were not rendered insecure 1. by the general power of the Legislature to make what laws they may please to call necessary and proper. 2. raise armies and money without limit. 3. to establish a tribunal without juries, which will be a Star-chamber as to Civil cases. Under such a view of the Constitution, the best that could be done he conceived was to provide for a second general Convention.

On the question on the proposition of Mr Randolph. All the States answered—no

On the question to agree to the Constitution, as amended. All the States ay.

The Constitution was then ordered to be engrossed.

MASON'S OBJECTIONS

Mason wrote his "Objections to this Constitution of Government" on the blank pages of his copy of the draft of September 12, and communicated these ideas to several people. The material in parentheses below indicates changes made before this statement was printed in pamphlet form.[1]

There is no Declaration of Rights, and the laws of the general government being paramount to the laws and constitution of the several States, the Declaration of Rights in the separate States are no security. Nor are the people secured even in the enjoyment of the benefit of the common law (which stands here upon no other foundation than its having been adopted by the respective acts forming the constitutions of the several States).

In the House of Representatives there is not the substance but the shadow only of representation; which can never produce proper information in the legislature, or inspire confidence in the people; the laws will therefore be generally made by men

[1] [Farrand, *Records*, II, 637-40, quoting from Kate Mason Rowland, *The Life of George Mason, 1725-1792* (2 vols., New York and London, 1892), II, 387-90.]

little concerned in, and unacquainted with their effects and consequences. (This objection has been in some degree lessened by an amendment, often before refused and at last made by an erasure, after the engrossment upon parchment of the word forty and inserting thirty, in the third clause of the second section of the first article.)

The Senate have the power of altering all money bills, and of originating appropriations of money, and the salaries of the officers of their own appointment, in conjunction with the president of the United States, although they are not the representatives of the people or amenable to them.

These with their other great powers, viz.: their power in the appointment of ambassadors and all public officers, in making treaties, and in trying all impeachments, their influence upon and connection with the supreme Executive from these causes, their duration of office and their being a constantly existing body, almost continually sitting, joined with their being one complete branch of the legislature, will destroy any balance in the government, and enable them to accomplish what ursurpations they please upon the rights and liberties of the people.

The Judiciary of the United States is so constructed and extended, as to absorb and destroy the judiciaries of the several States; thereby rendering law as tedious intricate and expensive, and justice as unattainable, by a great part of the community, as in England, and enabling the rich to oppress and ruin the poor.

The President of the United States has no Constitutional Council, a thing unknown in any safe and regular government. He will therefore be unsupported by proper information and advice, and will generally be directed by minions and favorites; or he will become a tool to the Senate—or a Council of State will grow out of the principal officers of the great departments; the worst and most dangerous of all ingredients for such a Council in a free country; (for they may be induced to join in any dangerous or oppressive measures, to shelter themselves, and prevent an inquiry into their own misconduct in office. Whereas, had a constitutional council been formed (as was proposed) of six members, viz.: two from the Eastern, two from the Middle, and two from the Southern States, to be appointed by vote of the States in the House of Representatives, with the same duration and rotation of office as the Senate, the executive would always have had safe and proper information and advice; the president of such a council might have acted as Vice-President of the United States pro tempore, upon any vacancy or disability of the chief magistrate; and long continued sessions of the Senate, would in a great measure have been prevented.) From this fatal defect has arisen the improper power of the Senate in the appointment of public officers, and the alarming dependence and connection between that branch of the legislature and the supreme Executive.

Hence also sprung that unnecessary (and dangerous) officer the Vice-President, who for want of other employment is made president of the Senate, thereby dangerously blending the executive and legislative powers, besides always giving to some one of the States an unnecessary and unjust preeminence over the others.

The President of the United States has the unrestrained power of granting pardons for treason, which may be sometimes exercised to screen from punishment those whom he had secretly instigated to commit the crime, and thereby prevent a discovery of his own guilt.

By declaring all treaties supreme laws of the land, the Executive and the Senate have, in many cases, an exclusive power of legislation; which might have been avoided by proper distinctions with respect to treaties, and requiring the assent of the House of Representatives, where it could be done with safety.

By requiring only a majority to make all commercial and navigation laws, the five Southern States, whose produce and circumstances are totally different from that of the eight Northern and Eastern States, may (will) be ruined, for such rigid and premature regulations may be made as will enable the merchants of the Northern and Eastern States not only to demand an exorbitant freight, but to monopolize the purchase of the commodities at their own price, for many years, to the great injury of the landed interest, and (the) impoverishment of the people; and the danger is the greater as the gain on one side will be in proportion to the loss on the other. Whereas requiring two-thirds of the members present in both Houses would have produced mutual moderation, promoted the general interest, and removed an insuperable objection to the adoption of this (the) government.

Under their own construction of the general clause, at the end of the enumerated powers, the Congress may grant monopolies in trade and commerce, constitute new crimes, inflict unusual and severe punishments, and extend their powers (power) as far as they shall think proper; so that the State legislatures have no security for the powers now presumed to remain to them, or the people for their rights.

There is no declaration of any kind, for preserving the liberty of the press, or the trial by jury in civil causes (cases); nor against the danger of standing armies in time of peace.

The State legislatures are restrained from laying export duties on their own produce.

Both the general legislature and the State legislature are expressly prohibited making ex post facto laws; though there never was nor can be a legislature but must and will make such laws, when necessity and the public safety require them; which will hereafter be a breach of all the constitutions in the Union, and afford precedents for other innovations.

This government will set out (commence) a moderate aristocracy: it is at present impossible to foresee whether it will, in its operation, produce a monarchy or a corrupt, tyrannical (oppressive) aristocracy; it will most probably vibrate some years between the two, and then terminate in the one or the other.

The general legislature is restrained from prohibiting the further importation of slaves for twenty odd years; though such importations render the United States weaker, more vulnerable, and less capable of defence.

THE LAST DAY OF THE CONVENTION

Monday, September 17. In Convention

The engrossed Constitution being read,

Doc.ʳ FRANKLIN rose with a speech in his hand, which he had reduced to writing for his own conveniency, and which Mʳ Wilson read in the words following.

Mʳ President

I confess that there are several parts of this constitution which I do not at present approve, but I am not sure I shall never approve them: For having lived long, I have experienced many instances of being obliged by better information, or fuller consideration, to change opinions even on important subjects, which I once thought right, but found to be otherwise. It is therefore that the older I grow, the more apt I am to doubt my own judgment, and to pay more respect to the judgment of others. Most men indeed as well as most sects in Religion, think themselves in possession of all truth, and that wherever others differ from them it is so far error. ... But though many private persons think almost as highly of their own infallibility as of that of their sect, few express it so naturally as a certain french lady, who in a dispute with her sister, said "I don't know how it happens, Sister but I meet with no body but myself, that's always in the right—*Il n'y a que moi qui a toujours raison.*"

In these sentiments, Sir, I agree to this Constitution with all its faults, if they are such; because I think a general Government necessary for us, and there is no form of Government but what may be a blessing to the people if well administered, and believe farther that this is likely to be well administered for a course of years, and can only end in Despotism, as other forms have done before it, when the people shall become so corrupted as to need despotic Government, being incapable of any other. I doubt too whether any other Convention we can obtain, may be able to make a better Constitution. For when you assemble a number of men to have the advantage of their joint wisdom, you inevitably assemble with those men, all their prejudices, their passions, their errors of opinion, their local interests, and their selfish views. From such an assembly can a perfect production be expected? It therefore astonishes me, Sir, to find this system approaching so near to perfection as it does; and I think it will astonish our enemies, who are waiting with confidence to hear that our councils are confounded like those of the Builders of Babel; and that our States are on the point of separation, only to meet hereafter for the purpose of cutting one another's throats. Thus I consent, Sir, to this Constitution because I expect no better, and because I am not sure, that it is not the best. The opinions I have had of its errors, I sacrifice to the public good. I have never whispered a syllable of them abroad. Within these walls they were born, and here they shall die. If every one of us in returning to our Constituents were to report the objections he has had to it, and endeavor to gain partizans in support of them, we might prevent its being generally received, and thereby lose all the salutary effects & great advantages resulting naturally in our favor among foreign Nations as well as among ourselves, from our real or apparent unanimity. Much of the strength & efficiency of any Government in procuring and securing happiness to the people, depends, on opinion, on the general opinion of the goodness of the Government, as well as of the wisdom and integrity of its Governors. I hope therefore that for our own sakes as a part of the people, and for the sake of posterity, we shall act heartily and unanimously in recommending this Constitution (if approved by Congress & confirmed by the Conventions) wherever our influence may extend, and turn our future thoughts & endeavors to the means of having it well administred.

On the whole, Sir, I can not help expressing a wish that every member of the Convention who may still have objections to it, would with me, on this occasion doubt a little of his own infallibility, and to make manifest our unanimity, put his name to this instrument.—

He then moved that the Constitution be signed by the members and offered the following as a convenient form viz. "Done in Convention by the unanimous consent of *the States* present the 17th of Sepr &c—In Witness whereof we have hereunto subscribed our names."

This ambiguous form had been drawn up by Mr G. M. in order to gain the dissenting members, and put into the hands of Docr Franklin that it might have the better chance of success.

Mr GORHAM said if it was not too late he could wish, for the purpose of lessening objections to the Constitution, that the clause declaring "the number of Representatives shall not exceed one for every forty thousand" which had produced so much discussion, might be yet reconsidered, in order to strike out 40,000 & insert "thirty thousand." . . .

.   .   .   .

When the PRESIDENT rose, for the purpose of putting the question, he said that although his situation had hitherto restrained him from offering his sentiments on questions depending in the House, and it might be thought, ought now to impose silence on him, yet he could not forbear expressing his wish that the alteration proposed might take place. It was much to be desired that the objections to the plan recommended might be made as few as possible. The smallness of the proportion of Representatives had been considered by many members of the Convention an insufficient security for the rights & interests of the people. He acknowledged that it had always appeared to himself among the exceptionable parts of the plan, and late as the present moment was for admitting amendments, he thought this of so much consequence that it would give much satisfaction to see it adopted [1]

No opposition was made to the proposition of Mr Gorham and it was agreed to unanimously.

On the question to agree to the Constitution enrolled in order to be signed. It was agreed to all the States answering ay.

Mr RANDOLPH then rose and with an allusion to the obser-

[1] This was the only occasion on which the President entered at all into the discussions of the Convention.

vations of Doc.ʳ Franklin apologized for his refusing to sign the Constitution notwithstanding the vast majority & venerable names that would give sanction to its wisdom and its worth. He said however that he did not mean by this refusal to decide that he should oppose the Constitution without doors. He meant only to keep himself free to be governed by his duty as it should be prescribed by his future judgment. He refused to sign, because he thought the object of the Convention would be frustrated by the alternative which it presented to the people. Nine States will fail to ratify the plan and confusion must ensue. With such a view of the subject he ought not, he could not, by pledging himself to support the plan, restrain himself from taking such steps as might appear to him most consistent with the public good.

M.ʳ Gov.ʳ Morris said that he too had objections, but considering the present plan as the best that was to be attained, he should take it with all its faults. The majority had determined in its favor and by that determination he should abide. The moment this plan goes forth all other considerations will be laid aside, and the great question will be, shall there be a national Government or not? and this must take place or a general anarchy will be the alternative. He remarked that the signing in the form proposed related only to the fact that the *States* present were unanimous.

M.ʳ Williamson suggested that the signing should be confined to the letter accompanying the Constitution to Congress, which might perhaps do nearly as well, and would he found be satisfactory to some members who disliked the Constitution. For himself he did not think a better plan was to be expected and had no scruples against putting his name to it.

M.ʳ Hamilton expressed his anxiety that every member should sign. A few characters of consequence, by opposing or even refusing to sign the Constitution, might do infinite mischief by kindling the latent sparks which lurk under an enthusiasm in favor of the Convention which may soon subside. No man's ideas were more remote from the plan than his were known to be; but is it possible to deliberate between anarchy and Convulsion on one side, and the chance of good to be expected from the plan on the other.

. . . .

Mr RANDOLPH could not but regard the signing in the proposed form, as the same with signing the Constitution. The change of form therefore could make no difference with him. He repeated that in refusing to sign the Constitution, he took a step which might be the most awful of his life, but it was dictated by his conscience, and it was not possible for him to hesitate, much less, to change. He repeated also his persuasion, that the holding out this plan with a final alternative to the people, of accepting or rejecting it in toto, would really produce the anarchy & civil convulsions which were apprehended from the refusal of individuals to sign it.

Mr GERRY described the painful feelings of his situation, and the embarrassment under which he rose to offer any further observations on the subject wch had been finally decided. Whilst the plan was depending, he had treated it with all the freedom he thought it deserved. He now felt himself bound as he was disposed to treat it with the respect due to the Act of the Convention. He hoped he should not violate that respect in declaring on this occasion his fears that a Civil war may result from the present crisis of the U. S. In Massachussetts, particularly he saw the danger of this calamitous event—In that State there are two parties, one devoted to Democracy, the worst he thought of all political evils, the other as violent in the opposite extreme. From the collision of these in opposing and resisting the Constitution, confusion was greatly to be feared. He had thought it necessary, for this & other reasons that the plan should have been proposed in a more mediating shape, in order to abate the heat and opposition of parties. As it has been passed by the Convention, he was persuaded it would have a contrary effect. He could not therefore by signing the Constitution pledge himself to abide by it at all events. The proposed form made no difference with him. But if it were not otherwise apparent, the refusals to sign should never be known from him. Alluding to the remarks of Doc^r Franklin, he could not he said but view them as levelled at himself and the other gentlemen who meant not to sign;

Gen! PINKNEY. We are not likely to gain many converts by the ambiguity of the proposed form of signing. He thought it best to be candid and let the form speak the substance. If the meaning of the signers be left in doubt, his purpose would not be answered. He should sign the Constitution with a view to support it with all his influence, and wished to pledge himself accordingly.

.   .   .   .

M͏ͬ INGERSOL did not consider the signing, either as a mere attestation of the fact, or as pledging the signers to support the Constitution at all events; but as a recommendation, of what, all things considered, was the most eligible.

On the motion of Doc͏ͬ Franklin

N. H. ay. Mas. ay. C͏ͭ ay. N. J. ay. P͏ͣ ay. Del. ay. M͏ͩ ay. V͏ͣ ay. N. C. ay. S. C. div͏ͩ ² Geo. ay. [Ayes, 10; noes, 0; divided, 1.]

.   .   .   .

The members then proceeded to sign the instrument.

Whilst the last members were signing it Doct͏ͬ FRANKLIN looking towards the Presidents Chair, at the back of which a rising sun happened to be painted, observed to a few members near him, that Painters had found it difficult to distinguish in their art a rising from a setting sun. I have said he, often and often in the course of the Session, and the vicisitudes of my hopes and fears as to its issue, looked at that behind the President without being able to tell whether it was rising or setting: But now at length I have the happiness to know that it is a rising and not a setting Sun.

The Constitution being signed by all the members except M͏ͬ Randolph, M͏ͬ Mason, and M͏ͬ Gerry who declined giving it the sanction of their names, the Convention dissolved itself by an Adjournment sine die—

---

² Gen! Pinkney & M͏ͬ Butler disliked the equivocal form of the signing, and on that account voted in the negative.

IV

THE CONSTITUTION
AND THE RATIFICATION

THE CONSTITUTION OF THE UNITED STATES

We the People of the United States, in Order to form a more perfect Union, establish Justice, insure domestic Tranquility, provide for the common defence, promote the general Welfare, and secure the Blessings of Liberty to ourselves and our Posterity, do ordain and establish this Constitution for the United States of America.

Article. I.

Section. I. All legislative Powers herein granted shall be vested in a Congress of the United States, which shall consist of a Senate and House of Representatives.

Section. 2. The House of Representatives shall be composed of Members chosen every second Year by the People of the several States, and the Electors in each State shall have ∧ the Qualifications requisite for Electors of the most numerous Branch of the State Legislature.

No person shall be a Representative who shall not have attained to the Age of twenty five Years, and been seven Years a Citizen of the United States, and who shall not, when elected, be an Inhabitant of that State in which he shall be chosen.

Representatives and direct Taxes shall be apportioned among the several States which may be included within this Union, according to their respective Numbers, which shall be determined by adding to the whole Number of free Persons, including those bound to Service for a Term of Years, and excluding Indians not taxed, three fifths of all other Persons. The actual Enumeration shall be made within three Years after the first Meeting of the Congress of the United States, and within every subsequent

Term of ten Years, in such Manner as they shall by Law direct. The Number of Representatives shall not exceed one for every thirty Thousand, but each State shall have at Least one Representative; and until such enumeration shall be made, the State of New Hampshire shall be entitled to chuse three, Massachusetts eight, Rhode-Island and Providence Plantations one, Connecticut five, New-York six, New Jersey four, Pennsylvania eight, Delaware one, Maryland six, Virginia ten, North Carolina five, South Carolina five, and Georgia three.

When vacancies happen in the Representation from any State, the Executive Authority thereof shall issue Writs of Election to fill such Vacancies.

The House of Representatives shall chuse their Speaker and other Officers; and shall have the sole Power of Impeachment.

Section. 3. The Senate of the United States shall be composed of two Senators from each State, chosen by the Legislature thereof, for six Years; and each Senator shall have one Vote.

Immediately after they shall be assembled in Consequence of the first Election, they shall be divided as equally as may be into three Classes. The Seats of the Senators of the first Class shall be vacated at the Expiration of the second Year, of the second Class at the Expiration of the fourth Year, and of the third Class at the Expiration of the sixth Year, so that one third may be chosen every second Year; and if Vacancies happen by Resignation, or otherwise, during the Recess of the Legislature of any State, the Executive thereof may make temporary Appointments until the next Meeting of the Legislature, which shall then fill such Vacancies.

No Person shall be a Senator who shall not have attained to the Age of thirty Years, and been nine Years a Citizen of the United States, and who shall not, when elected, be an Inhabitant of that State for which he shall be chosen.

The Vice President of the United States shall be President of the Senate, but shall have no Vote, unless they be equally divided.

The Senate shall chuse their other Officers, and also a President pro tempore, in the Absence of the Vice President, or when he shall exercise the Office of President of the United States.

The Senate shall have the sole Power to try all Impeachments. When sitting for that Purpose, they shall be on Oath or Affirmation. When the President of the United States ⋀ the Chief
is tried.
Justice shall preside: And no Person shall be convicted without the Concurrence of two thirds of the Members present.

Judgment in Cases of Impeachment shall not extend further than to removal from Office, and disqualification to hold and enjoy any Office of honor, Trust or Profit under the United States: but the Party convicted shall nevertheless be liable and subject to Indictment, Trial, Judgment and Punishment, according to Law.

Section. 4. The Times, Places and Manner of holding Elections for Senators and Representatives, shall be prescribed in each State by the Legislature thereof; but the Congress may at any time by Law make or alter such Regulations, except as to the Places of chusing Senators.

The Congress shall assemble at least once in every Year, and such Meeting shall be on the first Monday in December, unless they shall by Law appoint a different Day.

Section. 5. Each House shall be the Judge of the Elections, Returns and Qualifications of its own Members, and a Majority of each shall constitute a Quorum to do Business; but a smaller Number may adjourn from day to day, and may be authorized to compel the Attendance of absent Members, in such Manner, and under such Penalties as each House may provide.

Each House may determine the Rules of its Proceedings, punish its Members for disorderly Behaviour, and, with the Concurrence of two thirds, expel a Member.

Each House shall keep a Journal of its Proceedings, and from time to time publish the same, excepting such Parts as may in their Judgment require Secrecy; and the Yeas and Nays of the Members of either House on any question shall, at the Desire of one fifth of those Present, be entered on the Journal.

Neither House, during the Session of Congress, shall, without the Consent of the other, adjourn for more than three days, nor to any other Place than that in which the two Houses shall be sitting.

Section. 6. The Senators and Representatives shall receive a Compensation for their Services, to be ascertained by Law, and paid out of the Treasury of the United States. They shall in all Cases, except Treason, Felony and Breach of the Peace, be privileged from Arrest during their Attendance at the Session of their respective Houses, and in going to and returning from the same; and for any Speech or Debate in either House, they shall not be questioned in any other Place.

No Senator or Representative shall, during the Time for which he was elected, be appointed to any civil Office under the Authority of the United States, which shall have been created, or the Emoluments whereof shall have been encreased during such time; and no Person holding any Office under the United States, shall be a Member of either House during his Continuance in Office.

Section. 7. All Bills for raising Revenue shall originate in the House of Representatives; but the Senate may propose or concur with Amendments as on other Bills.

Every Bill which shall have passed the House of Representatives and the Senate, shall, before it become a Law, be presented to the President of the United States; If he approve he shall sign it, but if not he shall return it, with his Objections to that House in which it shall have originated, who shall enter the Objections at large on their Journal, and proceed to reconsider it. If after such Reconsideration two thirds of that House shall agree to pass the Bill, it shall be sent, together with the Objections, to the other House, by which it shall likewise be reconsidered, and if approved by two thirds of that House, it shall become a Law. But in all such Cases the Votes of both Houses shall be determined by yeas and Nays, and the Names of the Persons voting for and against the Bill shall be entered on the Journal of each House respectively. If any Bill shall not be returned by the President within ten days (Sundays excepted) after it shall have been presented to him, the Same shall be a Law, in like Manner as if he had signed it, unless the Congress by their Adjournment prevent its Return in which Case it shall not be a Law.

Every Order, Resolution, or Vote to which the Concurrence of the Senate and House of Representatives may be necessary (except on a question of Adjournment) shall be presented to the President of the United States; and before the Same shall take Effect, shall be approved by him, or being disapproved by him, shall be repassed by two thirds of the Senate and House of Representatives, according to the Rules and Limitations prescribed in the Case of a Bill.

Section. 8. The Congress shall have Power To lay and collect Taxes, Duties, Imposts and Excises, to pay the Debts and provide for the common Defence and general Welfare of the United States; but all Duties, Imposts and Excises shall be uniform throughout the United States;

To borrow Money on the credit of the United States;

To regulate Commerce with foreign Nations, and among the several States, and with the Indian Tribes;

To establish an uniform Rule of Naturalization, and uniform Laws on the subject of Bankruptcies throughout the United States;

To coin Money, regulate the Value thereof, and of foreign Coin, and fix the Standard of Weights and Measures;

To provide for the Punishment of counterfeiting the Securities and current Coin of the United States;

To establish Post Offices and post Roads;

To promote the Progress of Science and useful Arts, by securing for limited Times to Authors and Inventors the exclusive Right to their respective Writings and Discoveries;

To constitute Tribunals inferior to the supreme Court;

To define and punish Piracies and Felonies committed on the high Seas, and Offences against the Law of Nations;

To declare War, grant Letters of Marque and Reprisal, and make Rules concerning Captures on Land and Water;

To raise and support Armies, but no Appropriation of Money to that Use shall be for a longer Term than two Years;

To provide and maintain a Navy;

To make Rules for the Government and Regulation of the land and naval Forces;

To provide for calling forth the Militia to execute the Laws of the Union, suppress Insurrections and repel Invasions;

To provide for organizing, arming, and disciplining, the Militia, and for governing such Part of them as may be employed in the Service of the United States, reserving to the States respectively, the Appointment of the Officers, and the Authority of training the Militia according to the discipline prescribed by Congress;

To exercise exclusive Legislation in all Cases whatsoever, over such District (not exceeding ten Miles square) as may, by Cession of particular States, and the Acceptance of Congress, become the Seat of the Government of the United States, and to exercise like Authority over all Places purchased by the Consent of the Legislature of the State in which the Same shall be, for the Erection of Forts, Magazines, Arsenals, dock-Yards, and other needful Buildings;—And

To make all Laws which shall be necessary and proper for carrying into Execution the foregoing Powers, and all other Powers vested by this Constitution in the Government of the United States, or in any Department or Officer thereof.

Section. 9. The Migration or Importation of such Persons as any of the States now existing shall think proper to admit, shall not be prohibited by the Congress prior to the Year one thousand eight hundred and eight, but a Tax or duty may be imposed on such Importation, not exceeding ten dollars for each Person.

The Privilege of the Writ of Habeas Corpus shall not be suspended, unless when in Cases of Rebellion or Invasion the public Safety may require it.

No Bill of Attainder or ex post facto Law shall be passed.

No Capitation, or other direct, Tax shall be laid, unless in

Proportion to the Census or Enumeration herein before directed to be taken.

No Tax or Duty shall be laid on Articles exported from any State.

No Preference shall be given by any Regulation of Commerce or Revenue to the Ports of one State over those of another: nor shall Vessels bound to, or from, one State, be obliged to enter, clear, or pay Duties in another.

No Money shall be drawn from the Treasury, but in Consequence of Appropriations made by Law; and a regular Statement and Account of the Receipts and Expenditures of all public Money shall be published from time to time.

No Title of Nobility shall be granted by the United States: And no Person holding any Office of Profit or Trust under them, shall, without the Consent of the Congress, accept of any present, Emolument, Office, or Title, of any kind whatever, from any King, Prince, or foreign State.

Section. 10. No State shall enter into any Treaty, Alliance, or Confederation; grant Letters of Marque and Reprisal; coin Money; emit Bills of Credit; make any Thing but gold and silver Coin a Tender in Payment of Debts; pass any Bill of Attainder, ex post facto Law, or Law impairing the Obligation of Contracts, or grant any Title of Nobility.

No State shall, without the Consent of $\overset{\text{the}}{\wedge}$ Congress, lay any Imposts or Duties on Imports or Exports, except what may be absolutely necessary for executing it's inspection Laws: and the net Produce of all Duties and Imposts, laid by any State on Imports or Exports, shall be for the Use of the Treasury of the United States; and all such Laws shall be subject to the Revision and Controul of $\overset{\text{the}}{\wedge}$ Congress.

No State shall, without the Consent of Congress, lay any Duty of Tonnage, keep Troops, or Ships of War in time of Peace, enter into any Agreement or Compact with another State, or with a foreign Power, or engage in War, unless actually invaded, or in such imminent Danger as will not admit of delay.

Article. II.

Section. I. The executive Power shall be vested in a President of the United States of America. He shall hold his Office during the Term of four Years, and, together with the Vice President, chosen for the same Term, be elected as follows

Each State shall appoint, in such Manner as the Legislature thereof may direct, a Number of Electors, equal to the whole Number of Senators and Representatives to which the State may be entitled in the Congress: but no Senator or Representative, or Person holding an Office of Trust or Profit under the United States, shall be appointed an Elector.

The Electors shall meet in their respective States, and vote by Ballot for two Persons, of whom one at least shall not be an Inhabitant of the same State with themselves. And they shall make a List of all the Persons voted for, and of the Number of Votes for each; which List they shall sign and certify, and transmit sealed to the Seat of the Government of the United States, directed to the President of the Senate. The President of the Senate shall, in the Presence of the Senate and House of Representatives, open all the Certificates, and the Votes shall then be counted. The Person having the greatest Number of Votes shall be the President, if such Number be a Majority of the whole Number of Electors appointed; and if there be more than one who have such Majority, and have an equal Number of Votes, then the House of Representatives shall immediately chuse by Ballot one of them for President; and if no Person have a Majority, then from the five highest on the List the said House shall in like Manner chuse the President. But in chusing the President, the Votes shall be taken by States, the Representation from each State having one Vote; A quorum for this Purpose shall consist of a Member or Members from two thirds of the States, and a Majority of all the States shall be necessary to a Choice. In every Case, after the Choice of the President, the Person having the greatest Number of Votes of the Electors shall be the Vice President. But if there should remain two or more who have equal Votes, the Senate shall chuse from them by Ballot the Vice President.

The Congress may determine the Time of chusing the Electors, and the Day on which they shall give their Votes; which Day shall be the same throughout the United States.

No Person except a natural born Citizen, or a Citizen of the United States, at the time of the Adoption of this Constitution, shall be eligible to the Office of President; neither shall any Person be eligible to that Office who shall not have attained to the Age of thirty five Years, and been fourteen Years a Resident within the United States.

In Case of the Removal of the President from Office, or of his Death, Resignation, or Inability to discharge the Powers and Duties of the said Office, the Same shall devolve on the Vice President, and the Congress may by Law provide for the Case of Removal, Death, Resignation or Inability, both of the President and Vice President, declaring what Officer shall then act as President, and such Officer shall act accordingly, until the Disability be removed, or a President shall be elected.

The President shall, at stated Times, receive for his Services, a Compensation, which shall neither be encreased nor diminished during the Period for which he shall have been elected, and he shall not receive within that Period any other Emolument from the United States, or any of them.

Before he enter on the Execution of his Office, he shall take the following Oath or Affirmation:—"I do solemnly swear (or affirm) that I will faithfully execute the Office of President of the United States, and will to the best of my Ability, preserve, protect and defend the Constitution of the United States."

Section. 2. The President shall be Commander in Chief of the Army and Navy of the United States, and of the Militia of the several States, when called into the actual Service of the United States; he may require the Opinion, in writing, of the principal Officer in each of the executive Departments, upon any Subject relating to the Duties of their respective Offices, and he shall have Power to grant Reprieves and Pardons for Offences against the United States, except in Cases of Impeachment.

He shall have Power, by and with the Advice and Consent of the Senate, to make Treaties, provided two thirds of the Senators present concur; and he shall nominate, and by and with the Advice and Consent of the Senate, shall appoint Ambassadors, other public Ministers and Consuls, Judges of the supreme Court, and all other Officers of the United States, whose Appointments are not herein otherwise provided for, and which shall be established by Law: but the Congress may by Law vest the Appointment of such inferior Officers, as they think proper, in the President alone, in the Courts of Law, or in the Heads of Departments.

The President shall have Power to fill up all Vacancies that may happen during the Recess of the Senate, by granting Commissions which shall expire at the End of their next Session.

Section. 3. He shall from time to time give to the Congress Information of the State of the Union, and recommend to their Consideration such Measures as he shall judge necessary and expedient; he may, on extraordinary Occasions, convene both Houses, or either of them, and in Case of Disagreement between them, with Respect to the Time of Adjournment, he may adjourn them to such Time as he shall think proper; he shall receive Ambassadors and other public Ministers; he shall take Care that the Laws be faithfully executed, and shall Commission all the Officers of the United States.

Section. 4. The President, Vice President and all civil Officers of the United States, shall be removed from Office on Impeachment for, and Conviction of, Treason, Bribery, or other high Crimes and Misdemeanors.

Article III.

Section. 1. The judicial Power of the United States, shall be vested in one supreme Court, and in such inferior Courts as the Congress may from time to time ordain and establish. The Judges, both of the supreme and inferior Courts, shall hold their Offices during good Behaviour, and shall, at stated Times, receive for their Services, a Compensation, which shall not be diminished during their Continuance in Office.

Section. 2. The judicial Power shall extend to all Cases, in Law and Equity, arising under this Constitution, the Laws of the United States, and Treaties made, or which shall be made, under their Authority;—to all Cases affecting Ambassadors, other public Ministers and Consuls;—to all Cases of admiralty and maritime Jurisdiction;—to Controversies to which the United States shall be a Party;—to Controversies between two or more States;—between a State and Citizens of another State; —between Citizens of different States,—between Citizens of the same State claiming Lands under Grants of different States, and between a State, or the Citizens thereof, and foreign States, Citizens or Subjects.

In all Cases affecting Ambassadors, other public Ministers and Consuls, and those in which a State shall be Party, the supreme Court shall have original Jurisdiction. In all the other Cases before mentioned, the supreme Court shall have appellate Jurisdiction, both as to Law and Fact, with such Exceptions, and under such Regulations as the Congress shall make.

The Trial of all Crimes, except in Cases of Impeachment, shall be by Jury; and such Trial shall be held in the State where the said Crimes shall have been committed; but when not committed within any State, the Trial shall be at such Place or Places as the Congress may by Law have directed.

Section. 3. Treason against the United States, shall consist only in levying War against them, or in adhering to their Enemies, giving them Aid and Comfort. No Person shall be convicted of Treason unless on the Testimony of two Witnesses to the same overt Act, or on Confession in open Court.

The Congress shall have Power to declare the Punishment of Treason, but no Attainder of Treason shall work Corruption of Blood, or Forfeiture except during the Life of the Person attainted.

Article. IV.

Section. 1. Full Faith and Credit shall be given in each State to the public Acts, Records, and judicial Proceedings of every other State. And the Congress may by general Laws prescribe the Manner in which such Acts, Records and Proceedings shall be proved, and the Effect thereof.

Section. 2. The Citizens of each State shall be entitled to all Privileges and Immunities of Citizens in the several States.

A Person charged in any State with Treason, Felony, or other Crime, who shall flee from Justice, and be found in another State, shall on Demand of the executive Authority of the State from which he fled, be delivered up, to be removed to the State having Jurisdiction of the Crime.

No Person held to Service or Labour in one State, under the Laws thereof, escaping into another, shall, in Consequence of any Law or Regulation therein, be discharged from such Service or Labour, but shall be delivered up on Claim of the Party to whom such Service or Labour may be due.

Section. 3. New States may be admitted by the Congress into this Union; but no new State shall be formed or erected within the Jurisdiction of any other State; nor any State be formed by the Junction of two or more States, or Parts of States, without the Consent of the Legislatures of the States concerned as well as of the Congress.

The Congress shall have Power to dispose of and make all needful Rules and Regulations respecting the Territory or other Property belonging to the United States; and nothing in this Constitution shall be so construed as to Prejudice any Claims of the United States, or of any particular State.

Section. 4. The United States shall guarantee to every State in this Union a Republican Form of Government, and shall protect each of them against Invasion; and on Application of the Legislature, or of the Executive (when the Legislature cannot be convened) against domestic Violence.

Article. V.

The Congress, whenever two thirds of both Houses shall deem it necessary, shall propose Amendments to this Constitution, or, on the Application of the Legislatures of two thirds of the several States, shall call a Convention for proposing Amendments, which, in either Case, shall be valid to all Intents and Purposes, as Part of this Constitution, when ratified by the Legislatures of three fourths of the several States, or by Conventions in three fourths thereof, as the one or the other Mode of Ratification may be proposed by the Congress; Provided that no Amendment which may be made prior to the Year One thousand eight hundred and eight shall in any Manner affect the first and fourth Clauses in the Ninth Section of the first Article; and that no State, without its Consent, shall be deprived of it's equal Suffrage in the Senate.

Article. VI.

All Debts contracted and Engagements entered into, before the Adoption of this Constitution, shall be as valid against the United States under this Constitution, as under the Confederation.

This Constitution, and the Laws of the United States which shall be made in Pursuance thereof; and all Treaties made, or which shall be made, under the Authority of the United States, shall be the supreme Law of the Land; and the Judges in every State shall be bound thereby, any Thing in the Constitution or Laws of any State to the Contrary notwithstanding.

The Senators and Representatives before mentioned, and the Members of the several State Legislatures, and all executive and judicial Officers, both of the United States and of the several States, shall be bound by Oath or Affirmation, to support this Constitution; but no religious Test shall ever be required as a Qualification to any Office or public Trust under the United States.

Article. VII

The Ratification of the Conventions of nine States, shall be sufficient for the Establishment of this Constitution between the States so ratifying the Same.

The Word, "the," being interlined between the seventh and eighth Lines of the first Page, The Word "Thirty" being partly written on an Erazure in the fifteenth Line of the first Page, The Words "is tried" being interlined between the thirty second and thirty third Lines of the first Page and the Word "the" being interlined between the forty third and forty fourth Lines of the second Page.
Attest WILLIAM JACKSON
Secretary

done in Convention by the Unanimous Consent of the States present the Seventeenth Day of September in the Year of our Lord one thousand seven hundred and Eighty seven and of the Independance of the United States of America the Twelfth In witness whereof We have hereunto subscribed our Names,

G⁰ WASHINGTON—Presidᵗ and deputy from Virginia

New Hampshire	{ JOHN LANGDON NICHOLAS GILMAN }
Massachusetts	{ NATHANIEL GORHAM RUFUS KING
Connecticut	{ WᴹSAMᴸ JOHNSON ROGER SHERMAN
New York	ALEXANDER HAMILTON
New Jersey	{ WIL: LIVINGSTON DAVID BREARLEY. WᴹPATERSON. JONA: DAYTON

Pensylvania	B Franklin
	Thomas Mifflin
	Rob^T Morris
	Geo. Clymer
	Thos FitzSimons
	Jared Ingersoll
	James Wilson
	Gouv Morris
Delaware	Geo: Read
	Gunning Bedford jun
	John Dickinson
	Richard Bassett
	Jaco: Broom
Maryland	James McHenry
	Dan of S^T Thos Jenifer
	Dan^L Carroll
Virginia	John Blair—
	James Madison Jr.
North Carolina	Wm Blount
	Rich^D Dobbs Spaight.
	Hu Williamson
South Carolina	J. Rutledge
	Charles Cotesworth Pinckney
	Charles Pinckney
	Pierce Butler.
Georgia	William Few
	Abr Baldwin

RESOLUTION OF THE FEDERAL CONVEN-
TION SUBMITTING THE CONSTITUTION
TO THE CONTINENTAL CONGRESS

In Convention Monday September 17th 1787.

Present

The States of

New Hampshire, Massachusetts, Connecticut, Mr Hamilton from New York, New Jersey, Pennsylvania, Delaware, Maryland, Virginia, North Carolina, South Carolina and Georgia. Resolved,

That the preceeding Constitution be laid before the United States in Congress assembled, and that it is the Opinion of this Convention, that it should afterwards be submitted to a Convention of Delegates, chosen in each State by the People thereof, under the Recommendation of its Legislature, for their Assent and Ratification; and that each Convention assenting to, and ratifying the Same, should give Notice thereof to the United States in Congress assembled.

Resolved, That it is the Opinion of this Convention, that as soon as the Conventions of nine States shall have ratified this Constitution, the United States in Congress assembled should fix a Day on which Electors should be appointed by the States which shall have ratified the same, and a Day on which the Electors should assemble to vote for the President, and the Time and Place for commencing Proceedings under this Constitution. That after such Publication the Electors should be appointed, and the Senators and Representatives elected: That the Electors should meet on the Day fixed for the Election of the President, and should transmit their Votes certified, signed, sealed and directed, as the Constitution requires, to the Secretary of the United States in Congress assembled, that the Senators and Representatives should convene at the Time and Place assigned; that the Senators should appoint a President of the Senate, for the sole Purpose of receiving, opening and counting the Votes for President; and, that after he shall be chosen, the Congress, together with the President, should, without Delay, proceed to execute this Constitution.

By the Unanimous Order of the Convention

G⁰ WASHINGTON Presid^t

W. JACKSON Secretary.

LETTER OF THE PRESIDENT OF THE FEDERAL CONVENTION TO THE PRESIDENT OF CONGRESS, TRANSMITTING THE CONSTITUTION

September 17, 1787

Sir,

We have now the honor to submit to the consideration of the United States in Congress assembled, that Constitution which has appeared to us the most adviseable.

The friends of our country have long seen and desired, that the power of making war, peace, and treaties, that of levying money and regulating commerce, and the correspondent executive and judicial authorities should be fully and effectually vested in the general government of the Union: But the impropriety of delegating such extensive trust to one body of men is evident—Hence results the necessity of a different organization.

It is obviously impracticable in the federal government of these states, to secure all rights of independent sovereignty to each, and yet provide for the interest and safety of all: Individuals entering into society, must give up a share of liberty to preserve the rest. The magnitude of the sacrifice must depend as well on situation and circumstance, as on the object to be obtained. It is at all times difficult to draw with precision the line between those rights which must be surrendered, and those which may be reserved; and on the present occasion this difficulty was encreased by a difference among the several states as to their situation, extent, habits, and particular interests.

In all our deliberations on this subject we kept steadily in our view, that which appears to us the greatest interest of every true American, the consolidation of our Union, in which is involved our prosperity, felicity, safety, perhaps our national existence. This important consideration, seriously and deeply impressed on our minds, led each state in the Convention to be less rigid on points of inferior magnitude, than might have been otherwise expected; and thus the Constitution, which we now present, is the result of a spirit of amity, and of that mutual deference and concession which the peculiarity of our political situation rendered indispensible.

That it will meet the full and entire approbation of every state is not perhaps to be expected; but each will doubtless consider, that had her interest been alone consulted, the consequences might have been particularly disagreeable or injurious to others; that it is liable to as few exceptions as could reasonably have been expected, we hope and believe; that it may promote the lasting welfare of that country so dear to us all, and secure her freedom and happiness, is our most ardent wish.

With great respect, We have the honor to be, Sir,
    Your Excellency's
        most obedient and humble servants,
            GEORGE WASHINGTON, *President.*
            By unanimous Order of the Convention.
His Excellency the PRESIDENT of CONGRESS.

RESOLUTION OF CONGRESS SUBMITTING THE CONSTITUTION TO THE STATES

September 28, 1787

Congress assembled present New Hampshire Massachusetts Connecticut New York New Jersey Pennsylvania, Delaware Virginia North Carolina South Carolina and Georgia and from Maryland Mr Ross.

Congress having received the report of the Convention lately assembled in Philadelphia

Resolved Unanimously that the said Report with the resolutions and letter accompanying the same be transmitted to the several legislatures in Order to be submitted to a convention of Delegates chosen in each state by the people thereof in conformity to the resolves of the Convention made and provided in that case.

RATIFICATION

The ratification struggle began with Federalists and Anti-federalists marshaling forces as soon as Congress submitted the Constitution to the states. The latter possessed able leaders and arguments which met widespread support. Most important of these were fear of the taxing power, lack of a bill of rights, and the scale of representation. In vain did Federalists iterate a position implied in Convention debates —that no bill of rights was needed, since all powers not delegrated to Congress were reserved—to the people or the states. Antifederalists gained by insisting on explicit guarantees demanded by those who believed popular rights could not be over protected. Likewise, anxiety over national collapse arising from the notion that republicanism could not endure in a large territory led to insistence that government be brought closer to the governed. This meant reducing the scale of representation and increasing the number of representatives.

Despite several spirited contests the requisite number of states adopted the Constitution within nine months after submission to them. The first five accepted in short statements, often of one paragraph, which imposed no qualification. To achieve this in Pennsylvania necessitated force to obtain a quorum and buying up of opposition newspapers. However, Federalists preferred to accept amendments rather than risk ruin or a second convention, and in ratifying and at the same time recommending improvements Massachusetts discovered a formula which was used in all subsequent cases except Maryland.

Since there could be no hope of firm union without Virginia and New York, attention focused on the close struggles pending in these states when New Hampshire, the ninth state, completed the bond. After prolonged debate the Virginia Convention facilitated adoption of the Constitution by using the Massachusetts technique. Since this instrument of assent best exemplifies all that was involved in ratification it is the only one to appear here.

We the Delegates of the People of Virginia duly elected in pursuance of a recommendation from the General Assembly and now met in Convention having fully and freely investigated and discussed the proceedings of the Fœderal Convention and being prepared as well as the most mature deliberation hath enabled us to decide thereon Do in the name and in behalf of the People of Virginia declare and make known that the powers granted under the Constitution being derived from the People of the United States may be resumed by them whensoever the same shall be perverted to their injury or oppression and that every power not granted thereby remains with them and at their will: that therefore no right of any denomination can be cancelled abridged restrained or modified by the Congress by the Senate or House of Representatives acting in any Capacity by the President or any Department or Officer of the United States except in those instances in which power is given by the Constitution for those purposes: & that among other essential rights the liberty of Conscience and of the Press cannot be cancelled abridged restrained or modified by any authority of the United States. With these impressions with a solemn appeal to the Searcher of hearts for the purity of our intentions and under the conviction that whatsoever imperfections may exist in the Constitution ought rather to be examined in the mode prescribed therein than to bring the Union into danger by a delay with a hope of obtaining Amendments previous to the Ratification, We the said Delegates in the name and in behalf of the People of Virginia do by these presents assent to and ratify the Constitution recommended on the seventeenth day of September one thousand seven hundred and eighty seven by the Fœderal Convention for the Government of the United States hereby announcing to all those whom it may concern that the said Constitution is binding upon the said People according to an authentic Copy hereto annexed in the Words following; . . .

Done in Convention this twenty Sixth day of June one thousand seven hundred and eighty eight

By Order of the Convention

EDM^D PENDLETON President [SEAL.] . . .

Virginia towit:

Subsequent Amendments agreed to in Convention as necessary to the proposed Constitution of Government for the United States, recommended to the consideration of the Congress which shall first assemble under the said Constitution to be acted upon according to the mode prescribed in the fifth article thereof:

Videlicet;

That there be a Declaration or Bill of Rights asserting and securing from encroachment the essential and unalienable Rights of the People in some such manner as the following;

First, That there are certain natural rights of which men, when they form a social compact cannot deprive or divest their posterity, among which are the enjoyment of life and liberty, with the means of acquiring, possessing and protecting property, and pursuing and obtaining happiness and safety. Second. That all power is naturally vested in and consequently derived from the people; that Magistrates, therefore, are their trustees and agents and at all times amenable to them. Third, That Government ought to be instituted for the common benefit, protection and security of the People; and that the doctrine of nonresistance against arbitrary power and oppression is absurd slavish, and destructive of the good and happiness of mankind. Fourth, That no man or set of Men are entitled to exclusive or seperate public emoluments or privileges from the community, but in Consideration of public services; which not being descendible, neither ought the offices of Magistrate, Legislator or Judge, or any other public office to be hereditary. Fifth, That the legislative, executive, and judiciary powers of Government should be seperate and distinct, and that the members of the two first may be restrained from oppression by feeling and participating the public burthens, they should, at fixt periods be reduced to a private station, return into the mass of the people; and the vacancies be supplied by certain and regular elections; in which all or any part of the former members to be elegible or ineligible, as the rules of the Constitution of Government, and the laws shall direct. Sixth, That elections of representatives in the legislature ought to be free and frequent, and all men having sufficient evidence of permanent common interest with and attachment to the Community ought to have the right of suffrage: and no aid, charge, tax or fee can be set, rated, or levied upon the people without their own consent, or that of their representatives so elected, nor can they be bound by any law to which they have not in like manner assented for the public good. Seventh, That all power of suspending laws or the execution of laws by any authority, without the consent of the representatives of the people in the legislature is injurious to their rights, and ought not to be exercised. Eighth, That in all capital and criminal prosecutions, a man hath a right to demand the cause and nature of his accusation, to be confronted with the accusers and witnesses, to call for evidence and be allowed counsel in his favor, and to a fair and speedy trial by an impartial Jury of his vicinage, without whose unanimous consent he cannot be found guilty, (except in the government of the land and naval forces) nor can he be compelled to give evidence against himself. Ninth, That no freeman ought to be taken, imprisoned, or disseised of his freehold, liberties, privileges or franchises, or outlawed or exiled, or in any manner destroyed or deprived of his life, liberty or property but by the law of the land. Tenth, That every freeman restrained of his liberty is entitled to a remedy to enquire into the lawfulness thereof, and to remove the same, if unlawful, and that such remedy ought not to be denied nor delayed. Eleventh. That in controversies respecting property, and in suits between man and man, the ancient trial by Jury is one of the greatest Securities to the rights of the people, and ought to remain sacred and inviolable. Twelfth. That every freeman ought to find a certain remedy by recourse to the laws for all injuries and wrongs he may receive in his person, property or character. He ought to obtain right and justice freely without sale, compleatly and without denial, promptly and without delay, and that all establishments or regulations contravening these rights, are oppressive and unjust. Thirteenth, That excessive Bail ought not be required, nor excessive fines imposed, nor cruel and unusual punishments inflicted. Fourteenth, That every freeman has a right to be secure from all unreasonable searches and siezures of his person, his papers and his property; all warrants, therefore, to search suspected places, or sieze any freeman, his papers or property, without information upon Oath (or affirmation of a person religiously scrupulous of taking an oath) of legal and sufficient cause, are grievous and oppressive; and all general Warrants to search suspected places, or to apprehend any suspected person, without specially naming or describing the place or person, are dangerous and ought not to be granted. Fifteenth, That the people have a right peaceably to assemble together to consult for the common good, or to instruct their Representatives; and that every freeman has a right to petition or apply to the legislature for redress of grievances. Sixteenth, That the people have a right to freedom of speech, and of writing and publishing their Sentiments; but the freedom of the press is one of the greatest bulwarks of liberty and ought not to be violated. Seventeenth, That the people have a right to keep and bear arms; that a well regulated Militia composed of the body of the people trained to arms is the proper, natural and safe defence of a free State. That standing armies in time of peace are dangerous to liberty, and therefore ought to be avoided, as far as the circumstances and protection of the Community will admit; and that in all cases the military should be under strict subordination to and governed by the Civil power. Eighteenth, That no Soldier in time of peace ought to be quartered in any house without the consent of the owner, and in time of war in such manner only as the laws direct. Nineteenth, That any person religiously scrupulous of bearing arms ought to be exempted upon payment of an equivalent to employ another to bear arms in his stead. Twentieth, That religion or the duty which we owe to our Creator, and the manner of discharging it can be directed only by reason and conviction, not by force or violence, and therefore all men have an equal, natural and unalienable right to the free exercise of religion according to the dictates of conscience, and that no particular religious sect or society ought to be favored or established by Law in preference to others.

AMENDMENTS TO THE BODY OF THE CONSTITUTION

First, That each State in the Union shall respectively retain every power, jurisdiction and right which is not by this Constitution delegated to the Congress of the United States or to the departments of the Fœderal Government. Second, That there shall be one representative for every thirty thousand, according to the Enumeration or Census mentioned in the Constitution, until the whole number of representatives amounts to two hundred; after which that number shall be continued or encreased as the Congress shall direct, upon the principles fixed by the Constitution by apportioning the Representatives of each State to some greater number of people from time to time as population encreases. Third, When Congress shall lay direct taxes or excises, they shall immediately inform the Executive power of each State of the quota of such state according to the Census herein directed, which is proposed to be thereby raised; And if the Legislature of any State shall pass a law which shall be effectual for raising such quota at the time required by Congress, the taxes and excises laid by Congress shall not be collected, in such State. Fourth, That the members of the Senate and House of Representatives shall be ineligible to, and incapable of holding, any civil office under the authority of the United States, during the time for which they shall respectively be elected. Fifth, That the Journals of the proceedings of the Senate and House of Representatives shall be published at least once in every year, except such parts thereof relating to treaties, alliances or military operations, as in their judgment require secrecy. Sixth, That a regular statement and account of the receipts and expenditures of all public money shall be published at least once in every year. Seventh, That no commercial treaty shall be ratified without the concurrence of two thirds of the whole number of the members of the Senate; and no Treaty ceding, contracting, restraining or suspending the territorial rights or claims of the United States, or any of them or their, or any of their rights or claims to fishing in the American seas, or navigating the American rivers shall be but in cases of the most urgent and extreme necessity, nor shall any such treaty be ratified without the concurrence of three fourths of the whole number of the members of both houses respectively. Eighth, That no navigation law, or law regulating Commerce shall be passed without the consent of two thirds of the Members present in both houses. Ninth, That no standing army or regular troops shall be raised or kept up in time of peace, without the consent of two thirds of the members present in both houses. Tenth, That no soldier shall be inlisted for any longer term than four years, except in time of war, and then for no longer term than the continuance of the war. Eleventh, That each State respectively shall have the power to provide for organizing, arming and disciplining it's own Militia, whensoever Congress shall omit or neglect to provide for the same. That the Militia shall not be subject to Martial law, except when in actual service in time of war, invasion, or rebellion; and when not in the actual service of the United States, shall be subject only to such fines, penalties and punishments as shall be directed or inflicted by the Laws of its own State. Twelfth That the exclusive power of legislation given to Congress over the Fœderal Town and its adjacent District and other places purchased or to be purchased by Congress of any of the States shall extend only to such regulations as respect the police and good government thereof. Thirteenth, That no person shall be capable of being President of the United States for more than eight years in any term of sixteen years. Fourteenth That the judicial power of the United States shall be vested in one supreme Court, and in such courts of Admiralty as Congress may from time to time ordain and establish in any of the different States: The Judicial power shall extend to all cases in Law and Equity arising under treaties made, or which shall be made under the authority of the United States; to all cases affecting ambassadors other foreign ministers and consuls; to all cases of Admiralty and maritime jurisdiction; to controversies to which the United States shall be a party; to controversies between two or more States, and between parties claiming lands under the grants of different

States. In all cases affecting ambassadors, other foreign ministers and Consuls, and those in which a State shall be a party,
the supreme court shall have original jurisdiction; in all other
cases before mentioned the supreme Court shall have appellate
jurisdiction as to matters of law only: except in cases of equity,
and of admiralty and maritime jurisdiction, in which the
Supreme Court shall have appellate jurisdiction both as to law
and fact, with such exceptions and under such regulations as
the Congress shall make. But the judicial power of the United
States shall extend to no case where the cause of action shall
have originated before the ratification of this Constitution; except in disputes between States about their Territory, disputes
between persons claiming lands under the grants of different
States, and suits for debts due to the United States. Fifteenth,
That in criminal prosecutions no man shall be restrained in the
exercise of the usual and accustomed right of challenging or excepting to the Jury. Sixteenth, That Congress shall not alter,
modify or interfere in the times, places, or manner of holding
elections for Senators and Representatives or either of them,
except when the legislature of any State shall neglect, refuse or
be disabled by invasion or rebellion to prescribe the same.
Seventeenth, That those clauses which declare that Congress
shall not exercise certain powers be not interpreted in any manner whatsoever to extend the powers of Congress. But that they
may be construed either as making exceptions to the specified
powers where this shall be the case, or otherwise as inserted
merely for greater caution. Eighteenth, That the laws ascertaining the compensation to Senators and Representatives for their
services be postponed in their operation, until after the election
of Representatives immediately succeeding the passing thereof;
that excepted, which shall first be passed on the Subject. Nineteenth, That some Tribunal other than the Senate be provided
for trying impeachments of Senators. Twentieth, That the
Salary of a Judge shall not be encreased or diminished during
his continuance in Office, otherwise than by general regulations
of Salary which may take place on a revision of the subject at
stated periods of not less than seven years to commence from the

time such Salaries shall be first ascertained by Congress. And the Convention do, in the name and behalf of the People of this Commonwealth enjoin it upon their Representatives in Congress to exert all their influence and use all reasonable and legal methods to obtain a Ratification of the foregoing alterations and provisions in the manner provided by the fifth article of the said Constitution; and in all Congressional laws to be passed in the mean time, to conform to the spirit of those Amendments as far as the said Constitution will admit.

Done in Convention this twenty seventh day of June in the year of our Lord one thousand seven hundred and eighty eight.

By order of the Convention.

EDM^D PENDLETON President [SEAL.]

THE PROGRESS OF RATIFICATION

The following information reveals the action in the various state conventions on the ratification of the Constitution.

ORDER OF RATIFICATION	DATE OF RATIFICATION	VOTE ON RATIFICATION	
		FOR	AGAINST
1. Delaware	Dec. 7, 1787	Unanimous	
2. Pennsylvania	Dec. 12	46	23
3. New Jersey	Dec. 18	Unanimous	
4. Georgia	Jan. 2, 1788	Unanimous	
5. Connecticut	Jan. 9	128	40
6. Massachusetts (incl. Maine)	Feb. 7	187	168
7. Maryland	Apr. 28	63	11
8. South Carolina	May 23	149	73
9. New Hampshire	June 21	57	46
Total Vote of 9 States		*725*	*361*
10. Virginia	June 26	89	79
11. New York	~~June~~ July 26	30	27
Total Vote of 11 States		*844*	*467*
12. North Carolina	Nov. 21, 1789	195	77
13. Rhode Island	May 29, 1790	34	32
Total Vote		*1073*	*576*

AMENDMENTS TO THE CONSTITUTION

The First Congress under the Constitution moved quickly to fulfill the promise made in state conventions. In the House Madison drew on the Virginia statement (especially the Declaration) and reports of what people elsewhere had demanded to fashion proposals which he wished to place within the body of the frame of government. After Senate modification a joint conference committee (which included Sherman, Ellsworth, and Paterson) submitted to the states twelve resolutions as amendments to follow the text of the Constitution. This action induced North Carolina and Rhode Island, which had earlier withheld ratification, to make acceptance of the basic law unanimous. As for the amendments, the states rejected the first two, which are included separately below, and the last ten, known as the Bill of Rights, became part of the Constitution on December 15, 1791. Not until the sesquicentennial year of 1941 did Connecticut, Georgia, and Massachusetts formally ratify these.

REJECTED PROPOSALS

Article the first ... After the first enumeration required by the first Article of the Constitution, there shall be one Representative for every thirty thousand, until the number shall amount to one hundred, after which, the proportion shall be so regulated by Congress, that there shall be not less than one hundred Representatives, nor less than one Representative for every forty thousand persons, until the number of Representatives shall amount to two hundred, after which the proportion shall be so regulated by Congress, that there shall not be less than two hundred Representatives, nor more than one Representative for every fifty thousand persons.

Article the second ... No law, varying the compensation for the services of the Senators and Representatives, shall take effect, until an election of Representatives shall have intervened.

THE FIRST TEN AMENDMENTS TO THE CONSTITUTION

Article I

Congress shall make no law respecting an establishment of religion, or prohibiting the free exercise thereof; or abridging the freedom of speech, or of the press; or the right of the people peaceably to assemble, and to petition the Government for a redress of grievances.

Article II

A well regulated Militia, being necessary to the security of a free State, the right of the people to keep and bear Arms, shall not be infringed.

Article III

No Soldier shall, in time of peace be quartered in any house, without the consent of the Owner, nor in time of war, but in a manner to be prescribed by law.

Article IV

The right of the people to be secure in their persons, houses, papers, and effects, against unreasonable searches and seizures, shall not be violated, and no Warrants shall issue, but upon probable cause, supported by Oath or affirmation, and particularly describing the place to be searched, and the persons or things to be seized.

Article V

No person shall be held to answer for a capital, or otherwise infamous crime, unless on a presentment or indictment of a Grand Jury, except in cases arising in the land or naval forces, or in the Militia, when in actual service in time of War or public danger; nor shall any person be subject for the same offence to be twice put in jeopardy of life or limb; nor shall be compelled in any criminal case to be a witness against himself, nor be deprived of life, liberty, or property, without due process of law; nor shall private property be taken for public use, without just compensation.

Article VI

In all criminal prosecutions, the accused shall enjoy the right to a speedy and public trial, by an impartial jury of the State and district wherein the crime shall have been committed, which district shall have been previously ascertained by law, and to be informed of the nature and cause of the accusation; to be confronted with the witnesses against him; to have compulsory process for obtaining witnesses in his favor, and to have the Assistance of Counsel for his defence.

Article VII

In Suits at common law, where the value in controversy shall exceed twenty dollars, the right of trial by jury shall be preserved, and no fact tried by a jury, shall be otherwise re-examined in any Court of the United States, than according to the rules of the common law.

Article VIII

Excessive bail shall not be required, nor excessive fines imposed, nor cruel and unusual punishments inflicted.

Article IX

The enumeration in the Constitution, of certain rights, shall not be construed to deny or disparage others retained by the people.

Article X

The powers not delegated to the United States by the Constitution, nor prohibited by it to the States, are reserved to the States respectively, or to the people.

LATER AMENDMENTS

Article XI

[January 8, 1798]

The Judicial power of the United States shall not be construed to extend to any suit in law or equity, commenced or prosecuted against one of the United States by Citizens of another State, or by Citizens or Subjects of any Foreign State.

Article XII

[September 25, 1804]

The Electors shall meet in their respective states, and vote by ballot for President and Vice-President, one of whom, at least, shall not be an inhabitant of the same state with themselves; they shall name in their ballots the person voted for as President, and in distinct ballots the person voted for as Vice-President, and they shall make distinct lists of all persons voted for as President, and of all persons voted for as Vice-President, and of the number of votes for each, which lists they shall sign and certify, and transmit sealed to the seat of the government of the United States, directed to the President of the Senate;—The President of the Senate shall, in presence of the Senate and House of Representatives, open all the certificates and the votes shall then be counted;—The person having the greatest number of votes for President, shall be the President, if such number be a majority of the whole number of Electors appointed; and if no person have such majority, then from the persons having the highest numbers not exceeding three on the list of those voted for as President, the House of Representatives shall choose immediately, by ballot, the President. But in choosing the President, the votes shall be taken by states, the representation from each state having one vote; a quorum for this purpose shall consist of a member or members from two thirds of the states, and a majority of all the states shall be necessary to a choice. And if the House of Representatives shall not choose a President whenever the right of choice shall devolve upon them, before the fourth day of March next following, then the Vice-President shall act as President, as in the case of the death or other constitutional disability of the President. The person having the greatest number of votes as Vice-President, shall be the Vice-President, if such number be a majority of the whole number of Electors appointed, and if no person have a majority, then from the two highest numbers on the list, the Senate shall choose the Vice-President; a quorum for the purpose shall consist of two thirds of the whole number of Senators, and a majority of the whole number shall be necessary to a choice. But no person constitutionally ineligible to the office of President shall be eligible to that of Vice-President of the United States.

Article XIII

[December 18, 1865]

Section 1. Neither slavery nor involuntary servitude, except as a punishment for crime whereof the party shall have been duly convicted, shall exist within the United States, or any place subject to their jurisdiction.

Section 2. Congress shall have power to enforce this article by appropriate legislation.

ARTICLE XIV

[July 21, 1868]

Section 1. All persons born or naturalized in the United States, and subject to the jurisdiction thereof, are citizens of the United States and of the State wherein they reside. No State shall make or enforce any law which shall abridge the privileges or immunities of citizens of the United States; nor shall any State deprive any person of life, liberty, or property, without due process of law; nor deny to any person within its jurisdiction the equal protection of the laws.

Section 2. Representatives shall be apportioned among the several States according to their respective numbers, counting the whole number of persons in each State, excluding Indians not taxed. But when the right to vote at any election for the choice of electors for President and Vice President of the United States, Representatives in Congress, the Executive and Judicial officers of a State, or the members of the Legislature thereof, is denied to any of the male inhabitants of such State, being twenty-one years of age, and citizens of the United States, or in any way abridged, except for participation in rebellion, or other crime, the basis of representation therein shall be reduced in the proportion which the number of such male citizens shall bear to the whole number of male citizens twenty-one years of age in such State.

Section 3. No person shall be a Senator or Representative in Congress, or elector of President and Vice President, or hold any office, civil or military, under the United States, or under any State, who, having previously taken an oath, as a member of Congress, or as an officer of the United States, or as a member of any State legislature, or as an executive or judicial officer of any State, to support the Constitution of the United States, shall have engaged in insurrection or rebellion against the same, or given aid or comfort to the enemies thereof. But Congress may by a vote of two thirds of each House, remove such disability.

Section 4.   The validity of the public debt of the United States, authorized by law, including debts incurred for payment of pensions and bounties for services in suppressing insurrection or rebellion, shall not be questioned. But neither the United States nor any State shall assume or pay any debt or obligation incurred in aid of insurrection or rebellion against the United States, or any claim for the loss or emancipation of any slave; but all such debts, obligations and claims shall be held illegal and void.

Section 5.   The Congress shall have power to enforce, by appropriate legislation, the provisions of this article.

ARTICLE XV

[*March 30, 1870*]

Section 1.   The right of citizens of the United States to vote shall not be denied or abridged by the United States or by any State on account of race, color, or previous condition of servitude.

Section 2.   The Congress shall have power to enforce this article by appropriate legislation.

ARTICLE XVI

[*February 25, 1913*]

The Congress shall have the power to lay and collect taxes on incomes, from whatever source derived, without apportionment among the several States, and without regard to any census or enumeration.

ARTICLE XVII

[*May 31, 1913*]

Section 1.   The Senate of the United States shall be composed of two Senators from each State, elected by the people thereof, for six years; and each Senator shall have one vote. The electors in each State shall have the qualifications requisite for electors of the most numerous branch of the State Legislatures.

Section 2. When vacancies happen in the representation of any State in the Senate, the executive authority of such State shall issue writs of election to fill such vacancies; Provided, That the Legislature of any State may empower the executive thereof to make temporary appointment until the people fill the vacancies by election as the Legislature may direct.

Section 3. This amendment shall not be so construed as to affect the election or term of any Senator chosen before it becomes valid as part of the Constitution.

ARTICLE XVIII

[January 29, 1919]

Section 1. After one year from the ratification of this article, the manufacture, sale, or transportation of intoxicating liquors within, the importation thereof into, or the exportation thereof from the United States and all territory subject to the jurisdiction thereof, for beverage purposes, is hereby prohibited.

Section 2. The Congress and the several States shall have concurrent power to enforce this article by appropriate legislation.

Section 3. This article shall be inoperative unless it shall have been ratified as an amendment to the Constitution by the legislatures of the several States, as provided in the Constitution, within seven years from the date of the submission hereof to the States by the Congress.

ARTICLE XIX

[August 26, 1920]

Section 1. The rights of citizens of the United States to vote, shall not be denied or abridged by the United States or by any State on account of sex.

Section 2.   Congress shall have power to enforce this article by appropriate legislation.

ARTICLE XX

[*February 6, 1933*]

Section 1.   The terms of the President and Vice President shall end at noon on the twentieth day of January, and the terms of Senators and Representatives at noon on the third day of January, of the years in which such terms would have ended if this article had not been ratified; and the terms of their successors shall then begin.

Section 2.   The Congress shall assemble at least once in every year, and such meeting shall begin at noon on the third day of January, unless they shall by law appoint a different day.

Section 3.   If, at the time fixed for the beginning of the term of the President, the President elect shall have died, the Vice President elect shall become President. If a President shall not have been chosen before the time fixed for the beginning of his term, or if the President elect shall have failed to qualify, then the Vice President elect shall act as President until a President shall have qualified; and the Congress may by law provide for the case wherein neither a President elect nor a Vice President elect shall have qualified, declaring who shall then act as President, or the manner in which one who is to act shall be selected, and such person shall act accordingly until a President or Vice President shall have qualified.

Section 4.   The Congress may by law provide for the case of the death of any of the persons from whom the House of Representatives may choose a President whenever the right of choice shall have devolved upon them, and for the case of the death of any of the persons from whom the Senate may choose a Vice President whenever the right of choice shall have devolved upon them.

Section 5.   Sections 1 and 2 shall take effect on the fifteenth day of October following the ratification of this article.

Section 6. This article shall be inoperative unless it shall have been ratified as an amendment to the Constitution by the legislatures of three-fourths of the several States within seven years from the date of its submission.

ARTICLE XXI

[*December 5, 1933*]

Section 1. The eighteenth article of amendment to the Constitution of the United States is hereby repealed.

Section 2. The transportation or importation into any State, Territory, or possession of the United States for delivery or use therein of intoxicating liquors, in violation of the laws thereof, is hereby prohibited.

Section 3. This article shall be inoperative unless it shall have been ratified as an amendment to the Constitution by conventions in the several States, as provided in the Constitution, within seven years from the date of the submission hereof to the States by the Congress.

ARTICLE XXII

[*March 1, 1951*]

Section 1. No person shall be elected to the office of the President more than twice, and no person who has held the office of President, or acted as President, for more than two years of a term to which some other person was elected President shall be elected to the office of the President more than once. But this Article shall not apply to any person holding the office of President when this Article was proposed by the Congress, and shall not prevent any person who may be holding the office of President, or acting as President, during the term within which this Article becomes operative from holding the office of President or acting as President during the remainder of such term.

Section 2.   This Article shall be inoperative unless it shall have been ratified as an amendment to the Constitution by the Legislatures of three-fourths of the several States within seven years from the date of its submission to the States by the Congress.

ARTICLE XXIII

[*March 29, 1961*]

Section 1.   The District consituting the seat of Government of the United States shall appoint in such manner as the Congress may direct:

A number of electors of President and Vice President equal to the whole number of Senators and Representatives in Congress to which the District would be entitled if it were a State, but in no event more than the least populous State; they shall be in addition to those appointed by the States, but they shall be considered, for the purposes of the election of President and Vice President, to be electors appointed by a State; and they shall meet in the District and perform such duties as provided by the twelfth article of amendment.

Section 2.   The Congress shall have power to enforce this article by appropriate legislation.

ARTICLE XXIV

[*January 23, 1964*]

Section 1.   The right of citizens of the United States to vote in any primary or other election for President or Vice President, for electors for President or Vice President, or for Senator or Representative in Congress, shall not be denied or abridged by the United States or any State by reason of failure to pay any poll tax or other tax.

Section 2.   The Congress shall have power to enforce this article by appropriate legislation.

Article XXV

[February 10, 1967]

Section 1.   In case of the removal of the President from office or of his death or resignation, the Vice President shall become President.

Section 2.   Whenever there is a vacancy in the office of the Vice President, the President shall nominate a Vice President who shall take office upon confirmation by a majority vote of both Houses of Congress.

Section 3.   Whenever the President transmits to the President pro tempore of the Senate and the Speaker of the House of Representatives his written declaration that he is unable to discharge the powers and duties of his office, and until he transmits to them a written declaration to the contrary, such powers and duties shall be discharged by the Vice President as Acting President.

Section 4.   Whenever the Vice President and a majority of either the principal officers of the executive departments or of such other body as Congress may by law provide, transmit to the President pro tempore of the Senate and the Speaker of the House of Representatives their written declaration that the President is unable to discharge the powers and duties of his office, the Vice President shall immediately assume the powers and duties of the office as Acting President.

Thereafter, when the President transmits to the President pro tempore of the Senate and the Speaker of the House of Representatives his written declaration that no inability exists, he shall resume the powers and duties of his office unless the Vice President and a majority of either the principal officers of the executive department or of such other body as Congress may by law provide, transmit within four days to the President pro tempore of the Senate and the Speaker of the House of Representatives their written declaration that the President is unable to discharge the powers and duties of his office. Thereupon Congress shall decide the issue, assembling within forty-eight hours for that purpose if not in session. If the Congress, within twenty-one days after receipt of the latter written declaration, or, if Congress is not in session, within twenty-one days after Congress is required to assembly, determines by two-thirds vote of both Houses that the President is unable to discharge the powers and duties of his office, the Vice President shall continue to discharge the same as Acting President; otherwise, the President shall resume the powers and duties of his office.

ARTICLE XXVI

[July 1, 1971]

Section 1. The right of citizens of the United States, who are eighteen years of age or older, to vote shall not be denied or abridged by the United States or by any State on account of age.

Section 2. The Congress shall have the power to enforce this article by appropriate legislation.

APPENDIX I

BIOGRAPHICAL REGISTER OF DELEGATES
WHO ATTENDED THE FEDERAL CONVENTION[1]

Since the federal Constitution like all events in history is the product of interplay between personality and many other factors, the quality of its authors deserves attention. A total of fifty-five men attended the Convention, whereas nineteen others selected by legislatures, often in conjunction with governors, declined appointment. Among these were Richard Henry Lee, Thomas Nelson, and Patrick Henry. Prominent absentees were Jefferson and John Adams, on diplomatic missions in Europe, and Samuel Adams.

Although neither demigods nor supermen these Framers possessed an ample fund of the bullion from which constitutions are minted. Their average age was forty-three, with several of the most prominent in their thirties. Vigorously mature, age did not palsy nor youth inflame. Their educational level was high; of thirty-one college graduates Princeton claimed nine, Yale and William and Mary five each, Harvard and King's College (Columbia) three each. A variety of callings was represented, with lawyers, thirty in number, dominating. Also present were thirteen commercial or business men, ten planters, several former high ranking army officers, and three physicians. Members of several Protestant denominations took seats along with two Roman Catholics, and Deists, although presumably no avowed atheists, joined the group.[2]

In the stimulating Revolutionary epoch these participants had hammered out on the anvil of daily experience a hard blade of knowledge concerning men and events. Three recalled attending the Stamp Act Congress, seven the First

[1] These portraits draw on a variety of materials, including Allen Johnson and Dumas Malone, eds., *Dictionary of American Biography*, 22 vols., New York, 1928-1944, and the character sketches of his colleagues by William Pierce, found in Farrand, *Records*, III, 87-97.

[2] Irving Dilliard, *Building the Constitution* (St. Louis, 1937), p. 14.

Continental Congress, eight signed the Declaration of Independence and a similar number helped frame state constitutions; seven had been governors, twenty-one performed military service, and thirty-nine had sat in the Continental Congress. Sobered in this crucible of independence, they were not, as Edmund Burke found their counterparts in the French National Assembly two years later, abstract theorists, country attorneys, obscure curates or warm and inexperienced enthusiasts. Thus, presumably, "the wild *gas*, the fixed air" would not break loose in Philadelphia as at Versailles.[3] At least not often. Moreover the age was propitious: it challenged these men, who rose splendidly to their opportunity; and it appreciated leadership. Perhaps other periods in American history have contained comparable talent without demanding or receiving from it as much. And lesser lights—for there were nonentities in the State House—have not always so wisely recognized and accepted merit.

BIOGRAPHICAL REGISTER OF DELEGATES

ABRAHAM BALDWIN (1754-1807) of Georgia was a lawyer by profession. Born in Connecticut and a graduate of Yale, Baldwin quickly established himself in his adopted state after removing there in 1784. Undoubtedly a "compleat classical education" and brief ministerial career (as chaplain in the Revolutionary army) gave him that respect for learning which flowered in his work and plans for a complete educational system in his adopted state and made him "more than anyone else the Father of the University of Georgia." He gained early recognition in Georgia politics, and experience in the House of Assembly and the Confederation Congress. The ablest of Georgia's delegation, he originally opposed equal representation in the Senate. Convinced that without this the small states meant to withdraw, his "accommodating turn of mind" enabled him to facilitate a tie vote which led to equality in the second branch. Under the new government he served in the House of Representatives and the United States Senate.

RICHARD BASSETT (1745-1815) of

3 Edmund Burke, *Reflections on the Revolution in France*, ed., T. H. D. Mahoney ("The Library of Liberal Arts," No. 46, New York, 1955), pp. 59, 18, 9, and *passim*.

Delaware was a "Gentlemanly Man" of common sense and considerable wealth. Born in Maryland, he removed to Delaware at an early age. The Revolution made great demands on him. He served as captain of horse troop, member of the council of safety, in the state constitutional convention, in both branches of the legislature, and as delegate to the Annapolis Convention. A modest man, Bassett spoke little in the Convention. At home he took a leading part in ratification. A lifelong friend of Bishop Asbury and a prominent Methodist, Bassett was a "religious enthusiast," perhaps the only one in Philadelphia. Subsequently he was active politically, serving as United States Senator, chief justice of the court of common pleas, and governor of Delaware.

GUNNING BEDFORD, JR. (1747-1812) of Delaware was a lawyer whose client at the Convention was the small states. He was born in Philadelphia and graduated from Princeton in 1771. Admitted to the bar, he settled in Delaware, where he was active as a legislator, attorney general, and delegate to the Annapolis Convention. Tall, heavy, and a fluent speaker, Bedford took little apparent part in the Philadelphia deliberations after mid-July, when his case was won. Previously, at a crucial point, his impetuous nature led him to extremely intemperate remarks. He served in the Delaware Convention which ratified the Constitution.

JOHN BLAIR (1732-1800) of Virginia possessed excellent credentials. A lawyer, he combined a good education with wide experience. Having studied law at the Middle Temple in London, he served later as a burgess and in the Virginia constitutional convention was on the committee which drafted a bill of rights and plan of government. High judicial offices occupied him for almost a decade before he went to Philadelphia. Although he favored a strong central government, Blair was not an orator and played a modest role in the debates. One of three Virginians who signed the Constitution, he supported it at the Richmond ratification convention and served as an associate justice of the United States Supreme Court.

WILLIAM BLOUNT (1749-1800) of North Carolina at the outbreak of the Revolution entered public service, in which he continued in some fashion for the remainder of his life. He brought with him to Philadelphia experience gained in both houses of the North Carolina legislature and in several sessions of the Continental Congress. No speaker, Blount took no part in the debates and signed the instrument not to register assent but to attest the fact that the document was the unanimous act of the states represented. He voted for ratification at home. A speculator in Western lands, he was ambitious and often unscrupulous.

DAVID BREARLY (1745-1790) of New Jersey, a lawyer and jurist "very much in the esteem of the people," was early an outspoken Revolutionary. After brief duty as lieutenant colonel of militia he moved to a political and legal career. He was a member of the New Jersey constitutional convention and chief justice of the state Supreme Court before going to Philadelphia. "Of good, rather than of brilliant parts," this small-state representative worked closely with his colleague Paterson. He presided over the state ratification convention.

JACOB BROOM (1752-1810) of Delaware is one of the least well known of the Framers. He became a surveyor at an early age, after which he dealt in real estate and established financial and industrial enterprises. During the Revolution Broom was "not a blatant patriot," and his lengthy political experience was primarily local: he served a total of ten terms as a burgess of Wilmington (where he was also active in civic affairs), and several terms in the state legislature. After attendance at Annapolis he went to Philadelphia, where he "maintained his usual

quiet, meditative, judicial demeanor." He was devotedly religious, a product of evangelical Swedish orthodoxy.

PIERCE BUTLER (1744-1822) of South Carolina was born in Ireland. He held a major's commission in H. M. 29th Regiment and served in America before settling in the lower South at the age of twenty-seven. Although a wealthy planter, he often championed the back-country democracy in his active career as a state legislator. He took an active part in the Convention, where he defended the interests of property, and especially of slave owners. At home he supported the new frame of government and subsequently served in the United States Senate.

DANIEL CARROLL (1730-1796) of Maryland, a man of fortune and influence who was educated in Flanders, after service on the state council and in the senate became a delegate to the Continental Congress in 1781. There he signed the Articles of Confederation, so long delayed by political questions arising out of disposition of Western land. Carroll was one of two Roman Catholics in the federal Convention. Moderately active, he trenchantly defended the interests of the smaller states but supported strongly centralized government. At home he favored ratification and later became a

United States Representative. GEORGE CLYMER (1739-1813) of Pennsylvania, a successful merchant in America's largest city, was early an active supporter of the Revolution. Besides membership on the Pennsylvania council of safety, he often represented his state in the Continental Congress, where he signed the Declaration of Independence. A shy man, he spoke but little and to the point and received committee assignments in the Convention.

WILLIAM RICHARDSON DAVIE (1756-1820) of North Carolina was born in England and came to South Carolina as a youth. At Princeton, from which he graduated in 1776, he received "a good classical education." After military service he became a successful lawyer in North Carolina, where he was instrumental in founding the state university. Davie played an influential role in state politics, serving in the legislature before 1787 and as governor in 1798, although he refused to accept democracy uncritically. He favored a strong central government and took an active if minor part in Convention debates. Lest all be lost he swung his delegation to support the "great compromise." He did not remain to sign the document which he approved and for whose ratification he fought in North Carolina.

JONATHAN DAYTON (1760-1824) of New Jersey, over three months short of twenty-seven, became the youngest delegate when his father declined appointment in Jonathan's favor. After graduating from Princeton in 1776 and doing military duty, he took up the law and served in the state assembly. In Philadelphia the "little-known" Dayton tested his wings in oratorical flights supporting the small-state bloc. Pierce, who discerned a damaging impetuosity, also found an honest rectitude which made the youth valuable and gained him esteem. Dayton later served several terms in the House of Representatives, of which he was Speaker, and also in the United States Senate. His political career ended abruptly and under a cloud.

JOHN DICKINSON (1732-1808) represented Delaware, but he already possessed a solid reputation earned largely in Pennsylvania. After studying at the Middle Temple, he became an outstanding lawyer in the Quaker province. This profession he abandoned before the Revolution, as his taste ran more to politics and history. A conservative patriot, he won fame with his *Farmer's Letters* and unpopularity with his failure to further adoption of the Declaration of Independence. Representative and spokesman of a small state and of conservative interests, he attended closely to the work of the Convention, and not without effect. If Pierce found him a speaker who "with an affected air of wisdom . . . labors to produce a trifle, . . ." he nevertheless ranked him as "one of the most important characters in the United States." With his pen Dickinson strongly urged adoption of the new instrument in Delaware.

OLIVER ELLSWORTH (1745-1807) of Connecticut, a lawyer and judge of the Supreme Court of Errors, brought to Philadelphia the virtues associated with colonial New England. Simple in manner, conservative, and with a high sense of duty, he was "a Gentleman of clear, deep, and copious understanding." He possessed an excellent education, having graduated from Princeton, to which he transferred from Yale. Although he turned to law after studying theology, he remained a religious man. He became a successful attorney before undertaking judicial duties, and furthered the Revolutionary cause while gaining legislative experience in the Connecticut General Assembly and from 1777-1783 in the Continental Congress. He took a decisive role in constitution-making. Nor was he averse to building a strong central government once the interests of Connecticut and other small states were adequately secured. Not present to sign, Ellsworth approved the Constitution and actively supported it in Connecticut. Under the new government he was a United States Senator and chief justice of the United States Supreme Court.

WILLIAM FEW (1748-1828) of Georgia possessed talent, although he was neither outgoing by nature nor a ready and fluent speaker. Living on the frontier in North Carolina and Georgia as a youth, he largely educated himself. Selflessly supporting the Revolutionary cause, he served as lieutenant colonel of militia, on the state executive council, repeatedly in the General Assembly, and in the Continental Congress. From the Philadelphia deliberations, in which his role was minor, he took a month off for duties in Congress. Along with Baldwin he was the only other signer of six Georgia appointees, of whom four attended the Convention. He was a United States Senator and federal judge before removing from Georgia to New York City.

THOMAS FITZSIMONS (1741-1811) of Pennsylvania came as a youth from Ireland to Philadelphia, where he became a successful merchant. Active in supporting the colonial cause against George III, he served as a militia officer and in various other capacities, including several terms in the state legislature and in the Continental Congress. In Philadelphia

Fitzsimons, a property holder who sought a strong central government, remained largely silent. A Roman Catholic, he served in the first three Congresses, where he favored Hamiltonian policies.

BENJAMIN FRANKLIN (1706-1790) of Pennsylvania, over eighty-one and the oldest delegate, had gained world renown in a variety of careers. For over thirty years prior to the Convention public service increasingly occupied him. In different political capacities—at the Albany Congress, as colonial agent in England, in the Continental Congress, where he served on the committee which drafted the Declaration of Independence, as plenipotentiary to France and treaty negotiator with Great Britain, and as President of Pennsylvania—he came to know the leading issues and men of his day. Besides a wealth of knowledge and experience he brought to the deliberations a viewpoint thoroughly American as well as intimate acquaintance with the Old World. Through previous efforts he stamped his impress on the Constitution before 1787. And at Philadelphia, despite the rejection of his major ideas, his prestige won him a hearing, which he used to facilitate accommodation and secure adoption of a Constitution which he himself thought imperfect.

ELBRIDGE GERRY (1744-1814) of Massachusetts graduated from Harvard in 1762 before returning to Marblehead and the family mercantile business. On the eve of the Revolution election to the General Court, where he became a disciple of Samuel Adams, thrust him into the political cauldron. He burned with zeal for the republicanism of '76, which he served both in Massachusetts and the Continental Congress, where he signed both the Declaration of Independence and the Articles of Confederation. His principles apparently vindicated, Gerry, who had large sums invested in government securities and real estate, retired in 1786. He refused to attend the Annapolis Convention because of its inherent limitations. Shattered by Shays' Rebellion, however, he went to Philadelphia to secure strong central government. He was one of the most active participants in debate. But inflexible commitment to theoretical republicanism impaired his usefulness. He suspected democracy but feared power, and his colleagues found him a "Grumbletonian" who objected to what he did not propose. He refused to sign, was subsequently a member of Congress, on the XYZ mission to France, often governor of Massachusetts and Vice President under Madison.

NICHOLAS GILMAN (1755-1814) of New Hampshire arrived late.

Pierce found "nothing brilliant or striking in his character," and the French chargé d'affaires reported that he was not much loved by his colleagues. His experience included military service, local politics and membership in the Continental Congress. Although from a small state his outlook was that of a wealthy man who urged strong government. He later represented New Hampshire both as a Congressman and Senator, switching from Federalist to Jeffersonian-Republican views.

NATHANIEL GORHAM (1738-1796) of Massachusetts, a leading businessman of the Bay State, was apprenticed to a merchant at an early age. Despite a skimpy education, from the outset of the Revolution he employed his talents and good sense in an active and varied career. Besides long service in both chambers of the state legislature (he was thrice Speaker of the House), he was on the board of war, a member of the constitutional convention of 1779-1780, and judge of the Court of Common Pleas. Several times a delegate to the Continental Congress, he presided over that body in 1786. Arriving in Philadelphia "high in reputation, and much in the esteem of his Country-men," he became presiding officer of the Committee of the Whole. A plain speaker and competent debater, he actively supported strong government. "Can it be supposed," he remarked during debate, "that this vast Country . . . will 150 years hence remain one nation?" He was a member of the ratifying convention in Massachusetts.

ALEXANDER HAMILTON (1755?-1804) of New York deserves high rank as a builder of the American constitutional system. Arriving in New York as a young emigrant from the Leeward Islands, the Revolution soon interrupted his studies at grammar school and King's College. He threw himself into the American cause, where service as an aide to General Washington afforded him an unusually broad view of the problems of the struggling colonies. He early formed a vision of the fruits to be garnered by nourishing the bickering and disunited colonies into a commercially harmonious and politically united whole. In the Continental Congress, at Annapolis, and in the New York legislature he strove zealously to implement his goal. Although often underestimated, his role in the Convention at age thirty-two was not of the first rank. His colleagues nullified him and his attendance was irregular. He pleaded for a highly centralized unitary government, which has been viewed as helpful in toning the government high. His willingness to compromise and accept an imperfect instrument facilitated adoption of the document. Yet his most important work came after the Convention, in *The Federalist* papers and at Poughkeepsie, where he snatched ratification out of the hands of the opposition majority, and in breathing life into the government under the Constitution while in Washington's Cabinet.

WILLIAM HOUSTON (1755-1833?) of Georgia matriculated at the Inner Temple on July 1, 1776, but soon returned home to further American independence. Houston, a lawyer who apparently won the confidence of many contemporaries, was the son of a prominent Georgian and brother of the state governor. He was twice a member of the Continental Congress and a representative of Georgia to settle a boundary dispute with South Carolina. Pierce, who noted attractive personal qualities and a good character, was unimpressed with Houston's talents. He thought his Georgia colleague possessed scant legal and political knowledge and was no speaker. This obscure figure spoke only a few times in the Convention and did not sign the Constitution.

WILLIAM CHURCHILL HOUSTON (*c.* 1746-1788) of New Jersey played an unimportant part at Philadelphia. After graduating from Princeton in 1768 he became a professor of mathematics and natural philosophy there, resigning in 1783. Mean-while, after a stint as captain of foot militia, he had become a lawyer and politician. He undertook several legislative and official duties in New Jersey and the Continental Congress and served as a delegate to the Annapolis Convention before going to the Convention, where his views paralleled those embodied in the New Jersey plan. He did not sign the Constitution.

JARED INGERSOLL (1749-1822) of Pennsylvania, a transplanted son of New England who after graduation from Yale in 1766 studied law at the Middle Temple, was a prominent Philadelphia lawyer. Active in local and state politics, he represented his state in the Continental Congress and by 1785 was active in the movement to revise or supplant the Articles of Confederation. He was able, well educated, experienced, widely read, and a good speaker, but he was modest, and he participated little.

DANIEL OF ST. THOMAS JENIFER (1723-1790) of Maryland actively aided in the break from Britain despite long having been a defender of the proprietary interest. After service on the governor's council just before the Revolution, he became a leader in the council of safety and the Maryland senate. He attended the Continental Congress in the years from 1778 to 1782. Jenifer possessed ample wealth and good humor and was popular with his colleagues. Nationalistic in outlook, he favored closer union. "He sits silent, . . . and seems to be conscious that he is no politician," wrote Pierce, not knowing that the complicated tangle of Maryland's interests in the federal Convention often compelled Jenifer's muteness.

WILLIAM SAMUEL JOHNSON (1727-1819) of Connecticut, "much celebrated for his legal knowledge," graduated from Yale in 1744 and after taking a master's degree at Harvard began a legal career. His merits won him high office in Connecticut, where he served in both houses of the legislature, on the council, as judge of Superior Court and as colonial agent in London. A conservative patriot who moved reluctantly toward independence, he briefly came under suspicion during the Revolution. But after membership in the Confederation Congress he went to Philadelphia. A small-state man, his importance arises from his part in bringing about the compromise on representation and as chairman of the Committee on Style. He worked for ratification and became a United States Senator. An Episcopalian, he was the first president of Columbia College.

RUFUS KING (1755-1827) of Massachusetts received rank "among the Luminaries of the present Age" from his colleague Pierce. A Harvard graduate in 1777, King obtained some military experience during the Revolution and political knowledge in the General Court of Massachusetts and the Continental Congress, in each of which he served three years. In Philadelphia at thirty-two, King possessed ability, vigor, pronounced views and a reputation. Despite previous opposition to radical alteration of the Articles, he became one of the most effective spokesmen for strong national government. A good parliamentarian, he was an eloquent orator. He later became United States Minister to Great Britain and Senator from New York.

JOHN LANGDON (1741-1819) of New Hampshire acquired a sizable fortune by the time of the Revolution, and took an active part in furthering independence. He became Speaker in the lower New Hampshire chamber, a militia officer, and president (governor) of his state. In the Continental Congress he concerned himself largely with supply problems. In Philadelphia he contributed modestly to achievement of a more vigorous government. Subsequently he was a member of the New Hampshire ratification convention, again governor, and later a United States Senator.

JOHN LANSING, JR. (1754-1829?) of New York, an Albany attorney, served six sessions in the

New York legislature in the 1780's, twice as a member of Congress, and as mayor of Albany before going to Philadelphia. He departed from there on July 10, ostensibly because the Convention was exceeding its authority, actually because he discerned the outline of a government capable of ending New York's commercial exactions. At Poughkeepsie he opposed ratification. After a judicial career he resumed law practice. He disappeared mysteriously from New York City on the evening of December 12, 1829.

WILLIAM LIVINGSTON (1723-1790) of New Jersey was born in Albany. After graduating from Yale in 1741 and study at the Middle Temple he began to practice law in New York. There he supported popular and Presbyterian causes, briefly holding the upper hand against entrenched Anglican factions. Longing for peaceful retirement Livingston removed on the eve of the Revolution to New Jersey, where he became active and prominent. His service as a militia commander and in the First and Second Continental Congresses was overshadowed by his occupancy of the gubernatorial chair of his state for the first fourteen years of its independence. He worked for revision of the Articles as the old Congress grew more feeble. In the federal Convention he supported the

New Jersey Plan. Pierce found him widely educated and of first-rate talent, but not a strong thinker. He took little active part in debate, served on important committees, and aided in securing speedy and unanimous ratification in New Jersey.

JAMES MADISON (1750-1836) of Virginia remained briefly in Princeton for advanced study after graduating from the College of New Jersey in 1771. With the Revolution he plunged into Virginia politics, serving on the committee which framed a constitution and declaration of rights, in the first assembly, and on the governor's council. After membership in the Continental Congress from 1780 to 1783, he commenced the study of law and re-entered the Virginia House of Delegates. Unable to effect political improvement in the Congress under the Articles, he strove for commercial union to facilitate this end, which led to Annapolis and the federal Convention. To prepare for the latter he studied the history of confederacies. In writing "Vices of the Political System of the United States" and letters outlining a plan of constitution, he announced views which the Virginia Plan substantially embodied. Able, informed, devotedly nationalistic, his influence in the Convention was excelled by none. Yet it is doubtful if he is the "Father of the Constitution," since that document omitted important features he stressed. Madison's notes afford the best record of the debates. He fought for adoption in Virginia, shared authorship of *The Federalist* papers, took a leading role in the House of Representatives in achieving a Bill of Rights, and became the fourth President of the United States.

ALEXANDER MARTIN (1740-1807) of North Carolina merited no special notice in Philadelphia. A graduate of Princeton in 1756, his career as a militia officer ended with acquittal of a charge of cowardice. He became a success in politics: he was in the provincial congress, in both houses of the state legislature, three times governor, and in the Continental Congress. In Philadelphia he was too nationalistic for many North Carolinians and yet less "high-mounted" than his state colleagues. Leaving early he did not sign. He later abandoned moderate Federalism for moderate Republicanism, serving again as governor and as United States Senator.

LUTHER MARTIN (1748-1826) of Maryland was a lawyer who graduated from Princeton in 1766. He taught school briefly, supported the Revolution, and became the first attorney general of Maryland in 1778, a post in which he remained for twenty-seven years before resigning. He held the office again from 1818 to 1822, and was a leader of the American bar. He was in the Continental Congress before going to Philadelphia where, in his devious course, he supported both small-state principles (Western lands were involved) and supreme national power. As a speaker this "reprobate genius" of capacious memory and prodigious information had poor delivery, and such verbosity that delegates winced when he arose. He left Philadelphia to avoid signing, and waged a bitter polemic against the document in Maryland.

GEORGE MASON (1725-1792) of Virginia was active and influential in framing the Constitution, which he refused to sign, leaving Philadelphia "in an exceeding ill humor indeed." A planter in the Northern Neck, Mason read much law and assimilated the views of the Enlightenment, whose principles and outlook it was his life mission to apply in America. He furthered this goal by working in all dimensions of state government in Virginia, but never more brilliantly than as author of the Virginia Declaration of Rights and a major part of the state constitution. He refused to attend the Annapolis Convention. Having found the Articles inadequate, he insisted on stronger government resting on a broad popular base. Mason, whom Pierce found able and convincing in debate, spoke frequently. His vision was of classical republicanism. In the end he offered several reasons for rejecting the basic charter (but did not mention a temper frayed by four months of close application). Some of his objections were removed by the Bill of Rights.

JAMES McCLURG (1746-1823) of Virginia, a physician who took his medical degree at Edinburgh and then studied at Paris and London, received his appointment when Patrick Henry ("I smelt a Rat") declined. Active as a Revolutionary surgeon with the Virginia militia, he had had no political experience. His friend Madison, who thought Mc Clurg talented but modest, rescued the neophyte from one or two ventures on the stormy seas of constitution-making. Although the Virginia physician favored the Constitution, early departure prevented him from signing.

JAMES McHENRY (1753-1816) of Maryland was born in County Antrim, Ireland, received a classical education in Dublin, studied medicine with Benjamin Rush in Philadelphia and became a physician. After inheriting a large estate, he rushed off at the outbreak of the Revolution for volunteer military service, moved from the medical staff to a post as General Washington's secre-

tary, abandoned medicine, and later became a politician. After membership in the Maryland Senate and the Continental Congress, he went to the Constitutional Convention. There he took little part, being absent after four days' attendance in late May. Pierce found him "of specious talents." Subsequently he appeared in Maryland politics and as Secretary of War.

JOHN FRANCIS MERCER (1759-1821) of Maryland crowded much into the twenty-eight years before his late appearance in Philadelphia, where he opposed the centralizing tendencies and departed within two weeks. He did not sign and worked against ratification in Maryland, to which he had only shortly before removed from his native Virginia. Educated at William and Mary, he had performed military duty and briefly practiced law before entering politics. He had served often in the lower Virginia chamber, and in the Continental Congress before going to Philadelphia. Under the new Constitution he was a member of the lower Maryland house and the national Congress, and governor of his adopted state.

THOMAS MIFFLIN (1744-1800) of Pennsylvania, born to a wealthy Quaker merchant family, spent a year in Europe after graduating from the College of Philadelphia before returning to a mercantile career. But politics enticed him. An ardent patriot, he was in the forefront of the radical Whigs in the First Continental Congress. Before reappearing in state politics Congress launched him on a military career, whereupon he became a major general and got involved in acrimony and intrigue. In Philadelphia Mifflin was in constant attendance but remained almost totally silent. Subsequently he was chairman of the state ratification convention and thrice governor during the 1790's. The rising tide of Jeffersonianism found him sympathetic.

GOUVERNEUR MORRIS (1752-1816) of Pennsylvania, a transplanted New Yorker, was one of the most forceful and influential delegates. Upon graduation from King's College in 1768 he became a lawyer and following family tradition entered public service. An aristocrat and conservative, he nevertheless actively supported independence. He helped draft the New York state constitution and after defeat for re-election to the Continental Congress removed to Pennsylvania. There he abandoned law for business and became assistant to Robert Morris, Congressional Superintendent of Finance. A delegate at thirty-five, he was strongly nationalistic and favored high-toned government. Although skeptical of democracy, his belief in the political depravity of man permitted him few illusions concerning aristocracy. He realized that Americans possessed the political training which he thought requisite to constitutional government. Undaunted and brilliant in debate, possessing wit and charm, Morris captured attention and led it on unaccustomed ideological forays. Yet he weakened his own influence; Pierce found him "fickle and inconstant, never pursuing one train of thinking—nor even regular." He gave the Constitution its final literary style. Later, as Minister to France, he witnessed the French effort at constitution-making.

ROBERT MORRIS (1734-1806) of Pennsylvania came to America from England as a youth and established himself as one of the leading merchants in the colonies before the Revolution, in which he labored mightily. The council of safety and other political posts engaged him in Pennsylvania. At the Continental Congress in July he voted against the Declaration of Independence as premature but affixed his name to it in August. He also signed the Articles of Confederation. He did much supply business—at a profit—for the Congress, and was the able financier of the Revolution from 1781 to 1783. He brought to Philadelphia great prestige and knowledge of American conditions. Favoring a union of states with more power at the center and possessing a reputation as a speaker who "bears down all before him," he nevertheless sat almost silent through the Convention. He refused the treasury post in the new government, but served as Senator from Pennsylvania.

WILLIAM PATERSON (1745-1806) of New Jersey, who presented the small-state plan, was a formidable antagonist of the large states. Born in County Antrim, Ireland, Paterson came to America at an early age and was graduated from Princeton—where he later took a master's degree—in 1763. A lawyer, he had sound accomplishments to his credit before arriving in Philadelphia. Besides duty as an officer with the Minute Men, he had been in the provincial congress, in the state constitutional convention, attorney general, and in the legislative council of his state. Even so, Paterson possessed more ability than reputation. Then thirty-four, he understood the political art, debated effectively and had a good sense of timing. A man "whose powers break in upon you, and create wonder and astonishment," he helped insure the importance of the states in the constitutional system before accepting a powerful federal government. No evidence records his attendance after July 23, when his goal was secure,

but he signed the document and favored ratification in New Jersey. He was governor and chancellor of his state before becoming an associate justice of the Supreme Court, where he manifested a nationalistic outlook.

WILLIAM PIERCE (c. 1740-1789) of Georgia was a soldier in the Revolution and in the Continental Congress before establishing his chief claim to fame in the Constitutional Convention. He favored but did not sign the new instrument, being absent from Philadelphia after July 1 because of business difficulties. Nor did Pierce, who entered debate only three times, contribute greatly to the work of the Framers. His Convention notes add little to what is known from other more valuable sources. But his character sketches of colleagues in "the wisest Council in the World" afford valuable insight into the qualities and conduct of those who drafted the American Constitution.

CHARLES PINCKNEY (1757-1824) of South Carolina was a Charleston lawyer who served in the lower house of the state legislature and in the Continental Congress, where he strove not only to strengthen the existing government but also to secure a convention to amend the Articles. Almost thirty years old, Pinckney misrepresented his Convention age as twenty-four to establish a claim as the youngest delegate. He participated actively in the debates, submitting at the outset a plan which did not, contrary to his later claim, adumbrate the completed Constitution. Returning home, the wealthy, handsome, and able Carolinian resumed active public service. Frequently governor, he was in the state constitutional convention of 1790, the General Assembly, the United States Senate, and became Minister to Spain.

CHARLES COTESWORTH PINCKNEY (1746-1825) of South Carolina, a second cousin of Charles, received his education at Christ Church College, Oxford, where he heard the law lectures of Sir William Blackstone, and studied law at the Middle Temple. After brief legal experience in England he pursued scientific studies on the continent. Returning home, he gained admission to the bar and was a successful attorney when the Revolution began. Civil duties in the provincial assembly and congress, as attorney general, on the Council of Safety and in both houses of the state legislature, preceded his winning high rank and reputation as a military officer. He was moderately active in Philadelphia, favoring invigorated government, but jealous of the peculiar interests of his slaveholding, free-trading state. After supporting the Constitution in the ratifying convention, he shared in making a new state constitution in 1790. He declined several high offices, went as Minister to France in 1796-97, and was the Federalist candidate for Vice President in 1800 and for president in 1804 and 1808.

EDMUND RANDOLPH (1753-1813) of Virginia appeared in Philadelphia distinguished for his talents and highly renowned. Of a prominent family, he met many outstanding men in his youth before entering the College of William and Mary and becoming a lawyer. Then he added luster to his name while furthering American independence, serving as aide to General Washington, as the youngest member of the Virginia Convention which adopted a constitution, as attorney general, in the Continental Congress, and as governor. He also attended the Annapolis Convention. Then thirty-four, he presented the Virginia Plan and actively participated in the debates. His work on the Committee of Detail was influential in shaping the Constitution. But his ability fell short of his reputation. When eight ratifications made the question for Virginia one of facilitating or preventing union, Randolph, who had refused to sign, threw his prestige behind adoption. Subsequently he became United States Attorney General and Secretary of State.

GEORGE READ (1733-1798) of Delaware, a lawyer and moderate Whig, moved slowly toward the break with Great Britain, signing and supporting the Declaration of Independence after initially voting against it. He helped write a constitution for Delaware, was politically significant there, went to Annapolis, and favored a convention to revise the Articles. To gain greater leverage in the Convention he obtained the restriction placed in the Delaware credentials. In Philadelphia, where Pierce found his oratorical efforts "fatiguing and tiresome," he argued for abolition of all state boundaries as a means of advancing small-state welfare. He signed the Constitution and was instrumental in making Delaware the first state to ratify. Subsequently he was in the United States Senate and chief justice of Delaware.

JOHN RUTLEDGE (1739-1800) of South Carolina, termed "the most gifted and devoted leader of the ruling group of the eighteenth century in South Carolina," was prodigiously active in public service. Called to the English bar after study at the Middle Temple, he soon returned to launch his American career amidst the Revolution. He helped write a new constitution for South Carolina in 1776, became president of the General Assembly, stiffened his state's resistance to Red Coats, and served in the legislature. He gained wider renown in the Stamp Act Congress, and in the First and Second Continental Congresses. His knowledge of British constitutional law proved valuable in the debate with Whitehall. As a delegate he spoke for property interests, particularly the slave-owning rice, indigo, and cotton planters of Carolina, and distrusted democracy. The Constitution showed his influence. Later he became a justice of the South Carolina and United States Supreme Courts.

ROGER SHERMAN (1721-1793) of Connecticut rose from a humble station in life to a position of great influence. Born poor, he "resolved to conquer poverty, wrapped himself in his own manliness," farmed, surveyed and cobbled shoes until, through law and trade, he gained property, from which he vaulted into politics and statesmanship. Industrious, he served long in New Haven and Connecticut administrative, legislative, and judicial posts. He acquired widespread influence and unsurpassed experience by prolonged service in the Continental Congress. In Philadelphia he was initially disposed to improve the Articles, but soon abandoned his long support for strengthening the old government in favor of more fundamental reconstruction. But he demanded that state rights be secured before consenting to exalt central powers. Although awkward, odd-shaped and even "grotesque and laughable," Sherman was "as cunning as the Devil," clearheaded, and "extremely artful" in accomplishing his objects. His "compromise" on representation found its way into the Constitution. He later served in both houses of Congress. A Puritan of a type then largely extinct, Sherman was the only one who signed the Articles of Association (1774), the Declaration of Independence, the Articles of Confederation, and the Constitution.

RICHARD DOBBS SPAIGHT (1758-1802) of North Carolina possessed at twenty-nine a record of some six years service in the House of Commons, of which he had been Speaker, and of two years in the Continental Congress. A democrat in political conviction, he favored a stronger government. He lacked aptitude for debate, and although he attended faithfully, his influence in the Convention was negligible. He signed the Constitution and worked for its adoption in North Carolina. Subsequently he served three terms as governor of his state and was in Congress.

CALEB STRONG (1745-1819) of Massachusetts, a lawyer who graduated with distinction from Harvard in 1764, won prominence in his state and the respect of his colleagues by public service. He was county attorney for twenty-four years. During the Revolution he served on the Northampton committee of safety. In the General Court, as a member of the constitutional convention of 1779-80, and as a state senator he widened his horizons. A dedicated Calvinist, he balanced support of closer union with advocacy of the local democracy he knew well. He approved the Constitution but did not sign, since family illness called him home in late August. He helped to secure ratification in the Massachusetts convention and was later a United States senator and often governor of the Bay State.

GEORGE WASHINGTON (1732-1799) of Virginia reluctantly left Mt. Vernon for Philadelphia, where he greatly impressed his stamp on the Federal Convention. His sense of responsibility for public welfare and his vision of a united people came early in his adult life, and experience—as a militia commander, burgess, in the First and Second Continental Congresses, as commanding officer of the Continental Army, and Virginia planter—ripened these convictions. During the Revolution he demonstrated his respect for the rule of law and the process of self-government: he used sparingly dictatorial powers given him by a feeble and panicky Congress and rebuffed intrigues designed to gain him a throne. Both as military chief and hard-pressed planter he saw the need for a central government with adequate power, and his efforts at repairing defects of the old authority plus the shadow of Shays' Rebellion led him again to the national stage. An impartial and responsible Convention president, his immense prestige reassured the waiting country and guaranteed a hearing for the result. As President of the United States he breathed vigor into the nation whose organic law he helped shape.

HUGH WILLIAMSON (1735-1819) of North Carolina lived a curiously interesting life. The French chargé d'affaires reported him "bizarre to excess." Upon graduation from the College of Philadelphia in 1757, he studied theology and preached until doctrinal controversies drove him to science. After holding a professorship of mathematics he acquired a medical degree in Utrecht and practiced in Philadelphia, where he became a member of the American Philosophical Society and a keen student of astronomy. Abandoning medicine, he undertook a mercantile career in North Carolina, where he became surgeon general to state troops during the war, and launched his political career. From membership in the House of Commons he went to the Continental Congress, where several sessions convinced him a more vigorous national government was needed. A capable debater but poor speaker, he announced his views often and on a variety of issues. "It is difficult to know his character well," wrote the perplexed French observer of him; "it is even possible that he does not have any; . . . ." In North Carolina Williamson labored for ratification and later went to the House of Representatives. Subsequently he removed to New York City and pursued a literary and scientific career.

JAMES WILSON (1742-1798) of Pennsylvania was a Scot who attended the University of St. Andrews before emigrating and becoming a lawyer. To experience gained in the exacting school of Pennsylvania politics and as a representative of his state in the Continental Congress he wedded knowledge gained from close study of law, government, and history. "All the political institutions of the World he knows in detail," said Pierce, "and can trace the causes and effects of every revolution from the earliest stages of the Graecian commonwealth down to the present time." At forty-five, strong in his powers, Wilson insisted upon a supreme central government based upon the people, thus clearly anticipating nationalism and democracy. More clearly than anyone else he defended the federal principle with the concept of dual sovereignty. Not an outstanding speaker, he was a skilled and resolute debater. He fought for adoption of the federal document in Pennsylvania, and modeled that state's constitution of 1790 upon it. His hope of founding a distinctly American jurisprudence never materialized. Long a bold land speculator, his grandiose plans for colonizing immigrants overextended him, his debtors hounded him on his seat on the United States Supreme Court, and he died a broken and tragic figure.

GEORGE WYTHE (1726-1806) of Virginia, renowned for legal knowledge, left the Convention early (June 4) for other duties. After participating in Virginia politics and in the Continental Congress (he signed the Declaration of Independence), Wythe gave himself increasingly to serious study of the law, in which character he remains best known. He helped to revise the laws of Virginia following independence, served on the high court of chancery and became the first professor of law in

America (at the College of William and Mary in 1779). In a judicial decision in 1782 he clearly stated that a court could restrain a legislative body which violated the constitution. Wythe was widely read, an able speaker and excellent writer, but Pierce found him "no great politician," since his view of man was overly sanguine. His departure prevented him from signing, but he approved the Constitution and in Virginia offered the resolution for ratification.

ROBERT YATES (1738-1801) of New York studied law under his fellow-delegate William Livingston, after which he fervently supported American independence, both in Albany and New York state offices. Later he went on the state supreme court and became ex officio a member of the Council of Revision. In the Convention he took notes which are next in importance to Madison's. But he departed early in July, charging that delegates were exceeding their powers and that state sovereignty would be lost under a national government. He continued his opposition in published letters and at the Poughkeepsie convention, but accepted the ratified document. He later ran for governor with Federalist support.

APPENDIX II

POPULATION ESTIMATES*

To illuminate the clash of interests especially in the early weeks of the debate, information on the demographical data available to members is given here, based on that of two delegates. Speaking in behalf of the Constitution in 1788 in South Carolina, and interested in explaining the three-fifths ratio, C. C. Pinckney referred to "the numbers in the different states, according to the most accurate accounts we could obtain" and cited the statistics he had used at Philadelphia. David Brearly left among his papers population estimates which he used at Philadelphia, and a computation of the distribution of delegates based on an earlier congressional recommendation for tax quotas.[1] As a basis of comparison relevant data from the first federal census of 1790 are also offered.[2]

	PINCKNEY		BREARLY		
	Total	*Colored*	*White*		*Colored*
N. H.	102,000		82,000 to	102,000	
Mass.	360,000		352,000		
R. I.	58,000		58,000		
Conn.	202,000		202,000		
N. Y.	233,000		238,000		
N. J.	138,000		138,000 to	145,000	
Penn.	360,000		341,000		
Dela.	37,000		37,000		
Md.	218,000 [3]	80,000	174,000		80,000
Va.	420,000	280,000	300,000		300,000
N. C.	200,000	60,000	181,000		
S. C.	150,000	80,000	93,000		
Ga.	90,000	20,000	27,000		
	2,568,000	520,000	2,223,000 to 2,250,000		

* Note: Footnotes to Appendix II appear on page 409.

REPRESENTATION BASED ON CONGRESSIONAL RECOMMENDATION OF SEPTEMBER 27, 1785

State	Quota of Tax	Delegates	
Virginia	$ 512,974	16	
Massachusetts	448,854	14	} 42¾
Pennsylvania	410,378	12¾	
Maryland	283,034	8¾	
Connecticut	264,182	8	
New York	256,486	8	} 42½
North Carolina	218,012	6¾	
South Carolina	192,366	6	
New Jersey	166,716	5	
New Hampshire	105,416	3¼	
Rhode Island	64,636	2	
Delaware	44,886	1¼	
Georgia	32,060	1	
	$3,000,000	90 [4]	

CONCLUSIONS

Based on Pinckney's Data

Order of States by Population	Population of Top Three	
1. Virginia	Virginia	420,000
2. Massachusetts	Massachusetts	360,000
3. Pennsylvania	Pennsylvania	360,000
4. New York		1,140,000
5. Maryland		
6. Connecticut	Population of Next Six [5]	
7. North Carolina	New York	233,000
8. South Carolina	Maryland	218,000
9. New Jersey	Connecticut	202,000
10. New Hampshire	North Carolina	200,000
11. Georgia	South Carolina	150,000
12. Rhode Island	New Jersey	138,000
13. Delaware		1,141,000

Population of Northern States, Including Delaware   1,490,000

Population of Southern States   1,078,000   (including three-fifths of 520,000 Negroes)

FEDERAL CENSUS OF 1790

State	Free (White)	Free (Other)	Slave	Total
N. H.	141,097	630	158	141,885
Mass.	373,324	5,463	None	378,787
R. I.	64,470	3,407	948	68,825
Conn.	232,374	2,808	2,764	237,946
N. Y.	314,142	4,654	21,324	340,120
N. J.	169,954	2,762	11,423	184,139
Penn.	424,099	6,537	3,737	434,373
Dela.	46,310	3,899	8,887	59,096
Md.	208,649	8,043	103,036	319,728
Va.	442,117	12,866	292,627	747,610
N. C.	288,204	4,975	100,572	393,751
S. C.	140,178	1,801	107,094	249,073
Ga.	52,886	398	29,264	82,548
				3,637,881

Footnotes to Appendix II.

1 [Farrand, *Records*, III, 253; I, 573-74; Ford, ed., *Journals of the Continental Congress*, XXIX, 767.]

2 [Department of Commerce and Labor, U.S. Bureau of the Census, *Heads of Families at the First Census of the United States Taken in the Year 1790: Virginia* (Washington, 1908), p. 8.]

3 [Subsequent figures in this column included three-fifths of those in the adjoining (Colored) column: i.e., five blacks count as three whites with respect to representation. Thus the *total* population by Pinckney's estimate was 2,776,000, which is obtained by adding to the former total *two*-fifths (208,000), or the remainder already not included.]

4 [Each state was to receive representation in proportion to its tax quota, and thus the number of delegates slightly exceeds the maximum number (ninety) of proposed delegates.]

5 [As is clearly evident, the population of the six states next in order of size after Virginia, Massachusetts, and Pennsylvania was needed to counterbalance those three.]

INDEX